Frameworks, Methodologies, and Tools for Developing Rich Internet Applications

Giner Alor–Hernández
Instituto Tecnológico de Orizaba, Mexico

Viviana Yarel Rosales–Morales
Instituto Tecnológico de Orizaba, Mexico

Luis Omar Colombo–Mendoza
Instituto Tecnológico de Orizaba, Mexico

A volume in the Advances in Web Technologies and Engineering (AWTE) Book Series

Managing Director:	Lindsay Johnston
Acquisitions Editor:	Kayla Wolfe
Production Editor:	Christina Henning
Development Editor:	Haley Kang
Typesetter:	Michael Brehm
Cover Design:	Jason Mull

Published in the United States of America by
Information Science Reference (an imprint of IGI Global)
701 E. Chocolate Avenue
Hershey PA, USA 17033
Tel: 717-533-8845
Fax: 717-533-8661
E-mail: cust@igi-global.com
Web site: http://www.igi-global.com

Library of Congress Cataloging-in-Publication Data

Library of Congress Cataloging-in-Publication Data

Alor-Hernandez, Giner, 1977-
  Frameworks, methodologies, and tools for developing rich Internet applications / by Giner Alor-Hernandez, Viviana Yarel Rosales-Morales, and Luis Omar Colombo-Mendoza.
      pages cm
  Includes bibliographical references and index.
    ISBN 978-1-4666-6437-1 (hardcover) -- ISBN 978-1-4666-6438-8 (ebook) -- ISBN 978-1-4666-6440-1 (print & perpetual access) 1. Internet programming. 2. Web applications. 3. Web site development. 4. JavaScript (Computer program language) 5. Application software--Development. 6. Software frameworks. I. Rosales-Morales, Viviana Yarel, 1986- II. Colombo-Mendoza,
Luis Omar, 1987- III. Title.
  QA76.625.A44 2015
  006.7--dc23
                                        2014026479

This book is published in the IGI Global book series Advances in Web Technologies and Engineering (AWTE) (ISSN: Pending; eISSN: pending)

British Cataloguing in Publication Data
A Cataloguing in Publication record for this book is available from the British Library.

Advances in Web Technologies and Engineering (AWTE) Book Series

Ghazi I. Alkhatib
Princess Sumaya University for Technology, Jordan
David C. Rine
George Mason University, USA

ISSN: Pending
EISSN: Pending

MISSION

The **Advances in Web Technologies and Engineering (AWTE) Book Series** aims to provide a platform for research in the area of Information Technology (IT) concepts, tools, methodologies, and ethnography, in the contexts of global communication systems and Web engineered applications. Organizations are continuously overwhelmed by a variety of new information technologies, many are Web based. These new technologies are capitalizing on the widespread use of network and communication technologies for seamless integration of various issues in information and knowledge sharing within and among organizations. This emphasis on integrated approaches is unique to this book series and dictates cross platform and multidisciplinary strategy to research and practice.

The **Advances in Web Technologies and Engineering (AWTE) Book Series** seeks to create a stage where comprehensive publications are distributed for the objective of bettering and expanding the field of web systems, knowledge capture, and communication technologies. The series will provide researchers and practitioners with solutions for improving how technology is utilized for the purpose of a growing awareness of the importance of web applications and engineering.

COVERAGE

- Knowledge Structure, Classification, and Search Algorithms or Engines
- Quality Of Service and Service Level Agreement Issues Among Integrated Systems
- Integrated User Profile, Provisioning, and Context-Based Processing
- Radio Frequency Identification (RFID) Research and Applications in Web Engineered Systems
- Data and Knowledge Capture and Quality Issues
- IT Readiness and Technology Transfer Studies
- Case Studies Validating Web-Based IT Solutions
- Virtual Teams and Virtual Enterprises: Communication, Policies, Operation, Creativity, and Innovation
- Data Analytics for Business and Government Organizations
- Human Factors and Cultural Impact of IT-Based Systems

IGI Global is currently accepting manuscripts for publication within this series. To submit a proposal for a volume in this series, please contact our Acquisition Editors at Acquisitions@igi-global.com or visit: http://www.igi-global.com/publish/.

Titles in this Series

For a list of additional titles in this series, please visit: www.igi-global.com

Handbook of Research on Demand-Driven Web Services Theory, Technologies, and Applications
Zhaohao Sun (University of Ballarat, Australia & Hebei Normal University, China) and John Yearwood (Federation University, Australia)
Information Science Reference • copyright 2014 • 474pp • H/C (ISBN: 9781466658844) • US $325.00 (our price)

Evaluating Websites and Web Services Interdisciplinary Perspectives on User Satisfaction
Denis Yannacopoulos (Technological Educational Institute of Piraeus, Greece) Panagiotis Manolitzas (Technical University of Crete, Greece) Nikolaos Matsatsinis (Technical University of Crete, Greece) and Evangelos Grigoroudis (Technical University of Crete, Greece)
Information Science Reference • copyright 2014 • 354pp • H/C (ISBN: 9781466651296) • US $215.00 (our price)

Solutions for Sustaining Scalability in Internet Growth
Mohamed Boucadair (France Telecom-Orange Labs, France) and David Binet (France Telecom, France)
Information Science Reference • copyright 2014 • 288pp • H/C (ISBN: 9781466643055) • US $190.00 (our price)

Adaptive Web Services for Modular and Reusable Software Development Tactics and Solutions
Guadalupe Ortiz (University of Cádiz, Spain) and Javier Cubo (University of Málaga, Spain)
Information Science Reference • copyright 2013 • 415pp • H/C (ISBN: 9781466620896) • US $195.00 (our price)

Public Service, Governance and Web 2.0 Technologies Future Trends in Social Media
Ed Downey (State University of New York, College at Brockport, USA) and Matthew A. Jones (Portland State University, USA)
Information Science Reference • copyright 2012 • 369pp • H/C (ISBN: 9781466600713) • US $190.00 (our price)

Performance and Dependability in Service Computing Concepts, Techniques and Research Directions
Valeria Cardellini (Universita di Roma, Italy) Emiliano Casalicchio (Universita di Roma, Italy) Kalinka Regina Lucas Jaquie Castelo Branco (Universidade de São Paulo, Brazil) Júlio Cezar Estrella (Universidade de São Paulo, Brazil) and Francisco José Monaco (Universidade de São Paulo, Brazil)
Information Science Reference • copyright 2012 • 477pp • H/C (ISBN: 9781609607944) • US $195.00 (our price)

E-Activity and Intelligent Web Construction Effects of Social Design
Tokuro Matsuo (Yamagata University, Japan) and Takayuki Fujimoto (Toyo University, Japan)
Information Science Reference • copyright 2011 • 284pp • H/C (ISBN: 9781615208715) • US $180.00 (our price)

DISSEMINATOR OF KNOWLEDGE

www.igi-global.com

701 E. Chocolate Ave., Hershey, PA 17033
Order online at www.igi-global.com or call 717-533-8845 x100
To place a standing order for titles released in this series, contact: cust@igi-global.com
Mon-Fri 8:00 am - 5:00 pm (est) or fax 24 hours a day 717-533-8661

Table of Contents

Chapter 15

Preface

WEB DEVELOPMENT EVOLUTION: FROM STATIC WEB PAGES TO RICH INTERNET APPLICATIONS

The Web has become one of the most important platforms for quickly and effectively transmitting information to people. In 1990, the Web started with HTML technology, which was originally devised to represent static information through a Web browser. The data flow was in a unidirectional way, from server-side to client-side. However, there was no personalization; most Websites did not authenticate users because there was no need.

Over time, Web applications took advantage for business purposes, showing dynamic content to users by enhancing client-side information technologies with JavaScript and bringing components like Applets and ActiveX, or plugins such as Adobe™ Flash™. On the server-side, there were information technologies that provided dynamism to the Web content. One of the first technologies for this purpose was CGI, which in 1993 represented a standard interface for passing dynamic content from server-side to client-side. Three years later, Java Applet emerged besides consolidated technologies such as PHP and Microsoft™ ASP. At that time, Web applications used the .Net as a platform for business, rendering dynamic content to users based on back-end business logic and database content. Developers enhanced the Internet's capabilities to meet the demands of business applications by including scripts—JavaScript and VBScript—and components, such as Applet and ActiveX™, to the client (user) computer. While this user experience was to some extent enhanced, the fundamental "document-driven" synchronous approach of traditional Internet applications remained the same. As user experience requirements grew in complexity, this approach proved to be a handicap for complex business applications. Though there had been significant progress in server-side implementations, the means of rendering information to the end-user remained the same. As a result, the need to incorporate the rich, interactive, and responsive features of desktop applications was increasingly felt.

At that time, there was also a necessity of incorporating the main features of desktop applications: responsiveness and interactivity. A deterrent to fulfill this necessity was the difficulty of handling multi-transaction business workflows. The one-way nature of traditional Internet applications represented continuous Web page refreshing, making it difficult to represent large amounts of complex data and denying rich user experiences.

The last phase in this Web development evolution is RIA (Rich Internet Application) starting with technologies such as Adobe™ Flex, JavaFX™, or Ajax. Ajax incorporates standards-based presentation using XHTML and CSS, dynamic display, and interaction using the Document Object Model, data interchange, and manipulation using XML and XSLT, as well as asynchronous data retrieval using

XMLHttpRequest and JavaScript binding everything together. Adobe™ AIR™ lets developers use Flex technology to build RIAs that deploy on a wide range of devices such as smartphones, tablets, televisions, desktops, and netbooks. AIR™ applications run across operating systems, and they are easily delivered by using a single installer file. With AIR™, Flex developers can use their existing skills, tools, and code to build highly engaging and visually rich applications that combine the power of local resources and data with the reach of the Web.

WHAT THIS BOOK IS ABOUT

This book is about the last phase in the Web development evolution (i.e., RIAs). In order to cover this topic, the following elements are identified and addressed: 1) development methodologies, 2) development dimensions, 3) application frameworks, and 4) development tools. In addition, some case studies aimed at implementing these concepts are discussed in this book. Therefore, this book is intended to provide a comprehensive view of current practices on RIAs development. RIAs are a new generation of Internet applications that combine behaviors and features of Web and desktop applications such as: 1) client-server architecture, 2) data-intensive handling and business logic execution both on the client-side and the server-side, which results in advanced mechanisms of client-server communication, and 3) highly interactive multimedia content. Therefore, this kind of Web applications allows users to do interactive data explorations through attractive visual interfaces, increasing usability and performance (Martínez-Nieves, Hernández-Carrillo, & Alor-Hernández, 2010). RIAs are the future of today's enterprise Web applications: they enhance the user experience, deliver functionality of desktop applications, and provide the portability and data reach that enterprise Web applications provide. A RIA changes the way the client Web application interacts with the server, removing or minimizing frequent server transactions from the user experience. RIAs offer the best of both worlds: the rich client and the reach of the enterprise. "Rich" is a term to describe how engaging and interactive a user interface is at the presentation tier. "Reach" describes the connectivity to the other tiers of the application. RIAs promise a presentation tier that all users see in the same way regardless of the platform, coupled with the powerful data-rich environment that enterprise Web applications can deliver.

In Web development, there are three fundamental factors to be considered: 1) Web development methodologies, 2) Web frameworks, and 3) toolkits. Web development methodologies can be categorized into two groups: 1) Software Development Methodologies for Traditional Web Applications and 2) Software Development Methodologies for RIAs. The methodologies of the first group pose some problems accommodating Web-specific aspects in terms of their methods and implementation; however, they were the pioneer for the development of new methodologies or extensions of existing methodologies. Some of these methodologies are WSDM, SOHDM, OOHDM, and UWE. The methodologies of the second group were developed by taking into account existing methodologies in order to satisfy the needs and features of RIAs development. Some examples are RUX Method, OOH4RIA, OOHDM Extension, and UWE-R.

In the case of Web frameworks, the options for developing RIAs can be grouped into three categories: 1) JavaScript-based frameworks, 2) non-JavaScript-based frameworks, and 3) multi-device frameworks. The JavaScript-based frameworks are open source containing a set of pre-written JavaScript code, which help facilitating the development of the JavaScript-based applications. This allows the development of applications by using the same code written in these JavaScript frameworks instead of writing the same line of code each time individually, which becomes more difficult and time consuming. Some examples of these JavaScript-based frameworks are Dojo, jQuery, Prototype, and Sencha ExtJS. The non-JavaScript-based frameworks are based on proprietary programming languages, and these frameworks are typically used under paid licenses. Some examples are Adobe Flex, JavaFX, Silverlight, and OpenLaszlo, to mention but a few. Multi-device frameworks cover two kinds of applications for mobile devices: 1) native applications that are applications written for a specific device's hardware and operating system, 2) Web-based applications, and 3) hybrid applications, which are applications built using Web technologies and wrapped in device-specific native application containers. These frameworks have the ability to support multiple mobile platforms such as iOS™ and Android™ at the same time. Some examples of these multi-device frameworks are PhoneGap, iUi, ipFaces, and Sencha Touch.

In the case of Toolkits, there are different Integrated Development Environments (IDEs) for RIAs development. According to its architecture, these IDEs can be classified into the following two major groups: 1) standalone applications and 2) plug-in applications. Some examples of standalone applications for RIAs development are Adobe Flash Builder, NetBeans, and Microsoft Visual Studio, among others. As plug-in applications are SapphireSteel Amethyst plugin for Visual Studio™, E(fx)clipse plugin for Eclipse™, and Eclipse4SL plugin for Eclipse™.

Figure 1 presents a general perspective about the aforementioned factors.

In this book, a novel view of RIAs development is proposed; it considers some issues relevant not only to rich UI design purposes but to software quality purposes. Thereby, the topics related to RIAs development that are covered in this book are multimedia support, AOP (Aspect-Oriented Programming) support, the use of design patterns, and the use of UI patterns, as depicted in Figure 1.

Figure 1. A general perspective about the RIA development stack

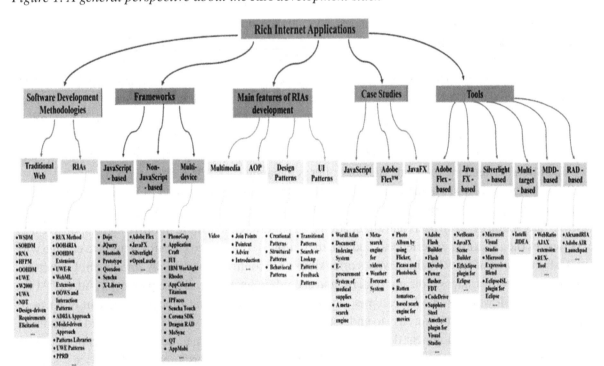

Multimedia content is crucial for RIAs. It provides richest content to Web applications by presenting information more dynamically and entertainingly. As examples of multimedia contents are videos and image galleries. The use of image galleries enhances the ability to customize views on the fly and provides real-time visual representations of a selected item. The possibility to represent graphics, audio, and video is considered an inherent ability of RIAs (Rich Internet Applications). In fact, along with UI transformations, visual continuity and temporal are factors affecting one of the distinguishing features of RIAs: the enhanced UI.

AOP allows adding new features to Web applications without changing the original source code. For instance, when a legacy application requires of an authentication method, it is possible to develop a separate method using AOP and without changing the original structure of the application. This is especially relevant for adapting legacy Web 1.0 application UIs to RIA UIs as a common practice in the development of RIAs. Some of the software quality factors that can be achieved in the development of RIAs by using AOP are: 1) Maintainability, 2) Extensibility, and 3) Reusability. Maintainability is very important for RIAs development, since it enables one to make changes as effectively and efficiently as possible. Moreover, the AOP provides a high level for maintainability. Extensibility is another crucial aspect in the RIAs development, because the new functionality sometimes needs to be added to an application that is in operation, and it is necessary to ensure that the application does not fail. Finally, Reusability is important not only in software development but also in the AOP. In fact, Reusability encapsulates the functionality required to be able to reuse it on subsequent occasions. This reduces development time and improves productivity. In the cases of both RIAs and software development, the development time is very expensive.

Design patterns are important in software development, as well as in the development of both traditional Web applications and RIAs. One of the main uses of the design patterns is for reusability purposes (i.e., for simplifying the work) and, thus, offering a solution that had been previously tested and which was successfully applied to a problem that manifests repeatedly. In fact, RIA technologies are based on the software reusability principle in the sense that UIs are built starting from reusable widgets or UI controls organized in component hierarchies. This is more evident in the case of the non-JavaScript-based RIA frameworks because of the declarative UI definition model based on UI markup languages such as MXML, FXML, and XAML. A well-known Design Pattern on Web applications development is MVC (Model-View-Controller). The MVC pattern separates the domain modeling, the presentation, and the actions into three classes and based on the user input: 1) Model, 2) View, and 3) Controller. MVC pattern is a fundamental Design Pattern for the separation of user interface logic from business logic. Fortunately, the emergence of Web applications has helped resolve some of the ambiguity, since the separation between the view and the controller is apparent.

RIAs design involves two main stages: 1) application structure design and 2) UIs design. This book focuses on the second stage of RIAs design. Rich UIs design typically involves the use of UI patterns to ease the interaction between users and applications. UI patterns enable more intuitive and responsive user experiences (i.e., rich user experiences). Indeed, they allow developers to encourage users to engage with applications. Most of the RIA frameworks offer simple UI controls that natively implement UI patterns (e.g., progress bar [progress indicator pattern] and accordion [expand/collapse pattern] in Adobe™ Flex or JavaFX™). However, some UI patterns require more developmental time and effort in order to be implemented. Therefore, it is not easy to understand the differences between UI controls and UI patterns.

Nowadays, RIAs development demands design principles of Web and desktop applications, which are implemented by the so-called interaction design patterns. Furthermore, mobile devices, such as smartphones and tablet computers, have also been involved in RIAs development due to the ubiquitous requirements of Web 2.0 applications (Finkelstein, Savigni, Kimmerstorfer, & Pröll, 2002). In this sense, RIAs are known as multi-device RIAs. This term covers RIAs that run as cross-browser Web applications, cross-platform desktop applications, and mobile applications. A Web browser-based RIA is a Web 2.0 application that integrates desktop-like features. A desktop-based RIA is a kind of application that is able to run off-Web browsers. A mobile RIA is a native mobile application with an improved UI.

The new trends in the development of RIAs can be identified by analyzing the steps on the Web evolution, from Web 2.0 to Web 4.0, passing through cloud computing as a trend on the Web 2.0 evolution. Cloud computing could be the best example of where the RIAs development is going both in commercial and academic fields. A new kind of RIA known as semantic RIA has recently emerged in the context of Web 3.0. Semantic RIAs try to solve the issues related to interoperability between systems by using ontologies and linked data principles. In the case of Web 4.0, the necessity of a ubiquitous Web has led to the emergence of context-aware Web applications by taking advantage of RIA technologies in order to offer rich user experiences.

Figure 2 depicts the conceptual map that illustrates the structure of this book.

Figure 2. Conceptual map of the general structure of the book

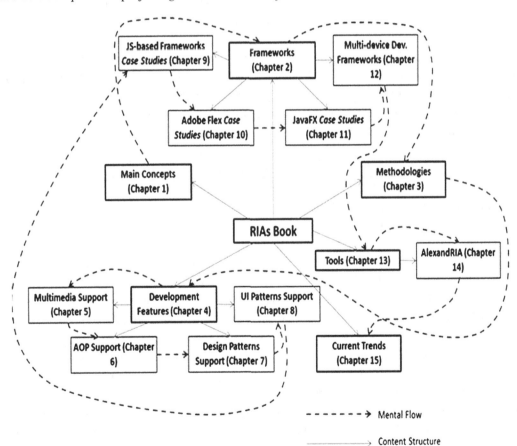

Hence, this book is structured as follows:

Chapter 1, titled "Basic Concepts on RIAs," presents an overview of RIA features, and it explains the most important concepts for RIAs development, as well as their benefits and importance in several domains. In this chapter, a standard architecture for RIAs is described. This architecture has three well-defined layers: 1) the client-side that renders the rich user interface, 2) a controller layer where the business logic is executed, and 3) a data transactions manager. Important domains of Web development are presented, and in each one of them, the importance of RIAs is explained emphasizing particular features of each domain. Finally, experiences and successful stories of using RIAs in B2C e-commerce domain are presented. Some of these successful cases mentioned are Kodak EasyShare, MINI USA, FootJoy™, The Broadmoor Hotel™ and BlueGreen Vacation Rentals™, Verizon Wireless™, Yankee Candle Company, and Charles Schwab.

Chapter 2, titled "Frameworks for RIAs Development," describes the most popular options for RIAs development. For practical purposes, these options are classified into two categories: 1) JavaScript-based frameworks and 2) non-JavaScript-based frameworks; even though there are other classifications reported in the literature, this classification is used in this chapter and throughout the book. In fact, this classification allows for a quick understanding of the technologies for RIAs development by abstracting technical details about intended software architectures.

Chapter 3, titled "Software Development Methodologies for Traditional Web Applications and RIAs," presents a review of the state-of-the-art on methodologies for RIAs development. For this purpose, methodologies for traditional Web applications development are firstly presented, since, in some cases, methodologies for RIAs development are either extensions of existing Web (and hypermedia) methodologies or new UI design methods used on top of already existing Web methodologies. New approaches covering the RIAs features without relying on legacy Web models are also discussed in this chapter.

Chapter 4, titled "Important Factors on RIAs Development," discusses some software quality metrics such as usability, scalability, and reusability of RIAs development. The chapter describes the importance of using multimedia content and UI (User Interface) patterns not only for improving the appearance of RIAs but also for delivering rich user experiences. Likewise, this chapter depicts the importance of leveraging AOP (Aspect-Oriented Programming) capabilities and implementing design patterns to ease the RIAs maintenance and enable RIAs reusability.

Chapter 5, titled "Multimedia Support for Native/Embedded Video Playback on Frameworks for RIAs Development," discusses the capabilities of RIA frameworks in the context of multimedia content support. For this purpose, several alternatives for implementing video playback functionality are presented by using both JavaScript-based RIA frameworks to and non-JavaScript-based RIA frameworks. Examples of JavaScript-based RIA frameworks having multimedia content support are Dojo, jQuery, Prototype, and Mootools. Examples of non-JavaScript-based RIA frameworks are Adobe Flex™, JavaFX™, Silverlight™, and OpenLaszlo. For each case study the mandatory files are mentioned. The chapter also shows a screenshot where video player is displayed and code snippets that were used are presented. Finally, a comparative analysis of video playback support for each framework is presented in terms of video container formats and encoding types.

Chapter 6, titled "Aspect-Oriented Programming (AOP) Support on RIAs Development," emphasizes the importance of employing Aspect-Oriented Programming (AOP) on software development, especially in software engineering. Some advantages in the development of RIAs by using AOP are Maintainability, Extensibility, and Reusability. This chapter presents a review of several success stories of AOP implementation in real world development projects and discusses the lessons learned in these projects.

The works analyzed in the state-of-the-art are classified by Web development, Usability Engineering, and other related perspectives. Finally, the chapter also addresses AOP support between JavaScript-based RIA frameworks and non-JavaScript-based RIA frameworks providing either native or third-party AOP facilities. Some code snippets depicting the use of these facilities for implementing AOP concepts are also presented.

Chapter 7, titled "Design Patterns Support for RIAs Development," presents a review of Design Patterns proposed by GOF classification is presented. GOF classifies Design Patterns in Creational Patterns, Structural Patterns, and Behavioral Patterns. Some implementation examples of GoF Design Patterns are presented by using both JavaScript-based frameworks and non-JavaScript-based frameworks for RIAs development. Additionally, the chapter also presents a comparative analysis that summarizes the review of the capabilities of the RIA frameworks in the context of GoF Design Patterns support between JavaScript-based RIA frameworks and non-JavaScript-based RIA frameworks. Finally, this chapter also mentions how to solve different programming problems by using Design Patterns.

Chapter 8, titled "UI Patterns Support on RIAs Development," a review of UI patterns supported by using non-JavaScript-based frameworks and JavaScript-based frameworks for RIAs development is presented. For this purpose, the UI Patterns are classified in Transitional Patterns, Lookup Patterns, and Feedback Patterns. Additionally, this chapter presents a series of applications samples depicting the use of not only UI controls but also non-visual functions or classes (as applicable) for implementing the supported UI patterns. These applications are intended to clarify the differences and similarities between UI controls and UI patterns. Finally, the chapter presents a comparative analysis that summarizes the review of the capabilities of the RIA frameworks in the context of rich UI design.

Chapter 9, "Case Studies Using JavaScript-Based Frameworks," discusses the development of four different SOAP Web services-based thin-client applications using jQuery, Prototype, Dojo, and JSP. The chapter, indeed, addresses the development of a world atlas application, a document indexing a search system, an e-procurement system for the healthcare domain, and a meta-search engine for eBay and Amazon products. These case studies, as well as case studies presented in subsequent chapters, exemplify the use of some UI patterns for accomplishing rich design principles such as stay on the page and use transitions. Similarly, reviews of some similar real world implementations publicly available on the Internet are provided for each case study presented in this chapter. Finally, the chapter presents a review of the support for invoking SOAP-based Web services using Java. This is intended to be a preamble for the case studies and the use and application of SOAP-based Web services.

Chapter 10, titled "Case Studies Using Adobe Flex™," presents two case studies about the development of REST (Representational State Transfer) Web services-based RIAs using Adobe Flex™ along with HTML and JavaScript. The chapter addresses the development of a meta-search engine for YouTube and Vimeo videos, as well as the development of a forecast weather system based on Yahoo! Weather. In addition, the chapter also offers a review of the support for consuming RESTful Web services in Adobe™ Flex™ as a preamble to these case studies.

Chapter 11, titled "Case Studies Using JavaFX™," presents four case studies on the development of JavaFX™-based RIAs built on top of popular social networking Websites. The chapter addresses the development of three photo album applications based on Flickr™, Picasa™, and Photobucket™ Websites, respectively. In addition, the development of a search engine for movies based on Rotten Tomatoes™ Website is finally presented. For each case study, the chapter provides a review of some similar real world implementations publicly available on the Internet.

Chapter 12, "Multi-Device RIAs Development," introduces the concept of multi-device RIA to describe a kind of RIA that can run on a variety of devices starting from the same code base. This includes not only cross-browser Web applications but also out-of-browser applications, namely cross-platform desktop and mobile applications. Thereafter, the chapter presents an overview of multi-device development frameworks. The supported platforms and the main capabilities are described for each framework mentioned. Furthermore, this section includes both a brief description of the most popular mobile operating systems for mobile devices and a comparison table for summarizing the main features of the multiplatform development frameworks.

Chapter 13, titled "An Overview of RIAs Development Tools," provides a review of RIAs development tools, including both official and third-party tools. For this purpose, the two major approaches for RIAs development already identified in the literature were considered: 1) framework-based development approaches and 2) MDD approaches. However, this classification was extended by introducing a third category: RAD approaches. Thereby, the chapter reviews not only IDEs for RIA frameworks-based developments but also addresses other support tools for RAD such as code generation tools. Likewise, based on their architecture, IDEs for RIAs development are reviewed and classified into the following two major groups: 1) standalone applications and 2) plugin applications. Some development tools presented are Adobe™ Flash Builder™, NetBeans IDE™, Microsoft™ Visual Studio™, WebRatio™, RUX-Tool™, and AlexandRIA.

Chapter 14, titled "AlexandRIA: A Visual Tool for Generating Multi-Device RIAs," explains the use of AlexandRIA for developing cloud services-based RIAs by implementing UI patterns. Unlike other RIA development tools described in Chapter 13, AlexandRIA is entirely focused on the fully automatic source and native code generation of RIAs, and it entirely addresses multi-device RIAs development. In this chapter, the use of the UI design process behind AlexandRIA is also demonstrated by means of a sample development scenario addressing the development of a cloud services APIs-based cross-platform mobile RIA. This scenario is further revisited in a case study that addresses the automatic generation of an equivalent application using AlexandRIA. In addition, this section of the book provides a review of both the UI patterns and the cloud services APIs supported by AlexandRIA as a preamble to the case study.

Chapter 15, titled "New Trends on RIAs Development," presents the new trends on RIAs development by considering the steps on the Web evolution, from Web 2.0 to Web 4.0, passing through cloud-based RIAs development and mashups-rich UIs development as two easily visible trends related to Web 2.0. Semantic RIAs, RMAs (Rich Mobile Applications), context-aware RIAs, and ubiquitous Web applications are some of the academic proposals related to Web 3.0 and Web 4.0 that are discussed in this chapter. Similarly, some commercial efforts from companies such as IBM™, TopQuadrant™ Inc., and Salesforce.com Inc. are also discussed in this chapter.

TARGET AUDIENCE

This book is targeted at professional developers and students wishing to improve their knowledge of Web engineering and of the way it can be applied to the RIAs development. Some of the concepts covered (methodologies, frameworks, tools) will assume a basic level of prior knowledge and understanding. If the reader requires any further reading related to these topics, the authors provide a list of suggested titles at the end of each chapter. If the reader wishes to learn how to develop RIAs, as well as about all the features of this kind of application, this is undoubtedly the book for them.

CREDITS

Whilst some of the topics covered in this book were implemented based on the authors' personal experiences, many of them have been previously identified and explained by other people. This work is an effort of the combined experience from the authors and other researchers, whose studies are fully covered in the references sections.

Giner Alor-Hernández
Instituto Tecnológico de Orizaba, Mexico

Viviana Yarel Rosales-Morales
Instituto Tecnológico de Orizaba, Mexico

Luis Omar Colombo-Mendoza
Instituto Tecnológico de Orizaba, Mexico

REFERENCES

Finkelstein, A. C. W., Savigni, A., Kimmerstorfer, E., & Pröll, B. (2002). Ubiquitous web application development - A framework for understanding. In *Proceedings of 6th Systemics, Cybernetics, and Informatics Conference* (pp. 431–438). Academic Press.

Martínez-Nieves, L. A., Hernández-Carrillo, V. M., & Alor-Hernández, G. (2010). An ADV-UWE based phases process for rich internet applications development. In *Proceedings of IEEE Electronics, Robotics and Automotive Mechanics Conference*, (pp. 45 –50). IEEE.

Acknowledgment

Authors are always be grateful for the talented technical reviewers who help review and improve their books. The knowledge and enthusiasm they brought to this project was simply amazing.

Thus, authors would like to thank: Ulises Juárez-Martínez, PhD, for his support, especially in Chapters 4 and 6, in the AOP subject; Desdemona Almazan-Morales, BSc, and Luis A. Barroso, PhD, from the Instituto Tecnólogico de Estudios Superiores de Monterrey Campus Central de Veracruz for their support in the English review process in some sections of the book; Gabriela Cabrera-Zepeda, MSc, Chief of the Division of Research and Postgraduate Studies of the Instituto Tecnológico de Orizaba for her help and support in this project; Maria Fernanda Villafuerte-Bianchi, BA, for her support in the proofreading process; and all our colleagues and friends from the Instituto Tecnológico de Orizaba for all their support.

Giner Alor-Hernández
Instituto Tecnológico de Orizaba, Mexico

Viviana Yarel Rosales-Morales
Instituto Tecnológico de Orizaba, Mexico

Luis Omar Colombo-Mendoza
Instituto Tecnológico de Orizaba, Mexico

Chapter 1
Basic Concepts on RIAs

ABSTRACT

Chapter 1 presents an overview of RIA features, and it explains the most important concepts for RIAs development, as well as their benefits and importance in several domains. In this chapter, a standard architecture for RIAs is described. This architecture has three well-defined layers: 1) the client-side that renders the rich user interface, 2) a controller layer where the business logic is executed, and 3) a data transactions manager. Important domains of Web development are presented, and in each one of them, the importance of RIAs is explained emphasizing particular features of each domain. Finally, experiences and successful stories of using RIAs in B2C e-commerce domain are presented.

1. INTRODUCTION

The Web or WWW (World Wide Web) is an information distribution system comprised of interlinked hypertext or hypermedia accessed by using the Internet. To access these media, a Web browser is required. The user is able to view different websites, which are composed of web pages that can contain text, images, videos or multimedia content. The user can browse the web pages that make up the website, through hyperlinks which cause a great amount of traffic between the client and the server as every time the user clicks on one of the hyperlinks. So, the whole page is loaded when the user requires some data or some interaction, this task implies to make another request from the server which causes the data can be slowly displayed. This slowness is increased as the amount of data requested is increased. The

Web was created in 1989 by the Englishman Tim Berners-Lee and the Belgian Robert Cailliau, while they were working at CERN (CERN means European Organization for Nuclear Research) in Geneva, Switzerland and it was published in 1992. Since then, Berners-Lee has played an active role in guiding the development of Web standards and over the last few years he has focused his vision on the Semantic Web.

In recent years, the term Web 2.0 has emerged. This term is associated with Web applications that make them easier to share information, interoperability, user-centered design and the collaboration with the World Wide Web. Some examples of Web 2.0 applications are Web communities, Web services, social networks, web sites that host videos, wikis, blogs, mashups and folksonomies, to mention but a few. The term is strongly associated with Tim O'Reilly, due to this

DOI: 10.4018/978-1-4666-6437-1.ch001

term was coined at the conference about Web 2.0 from O´Reilly Media in 2004 (O'Reilly, 2004). Although the term suggests a new version of the World Wide Web, it does not refer to an update process of technical specifications over the Web, but rather it refers more to cumulative changes in the way in which the Web is used by designers and final users.

Among the characteristics of web applications, there are some advantages over desktop applications. Some of these advantages are: 1) it is not necessary to carry out installations and updates on every computer where the application is running, these can now be carried out on the server-side and 2) they can run on different operating systems, which are well-known as platform-independent, cross-platform or multi-platform. However, there are also some disadvantages for these types of applications: 1) there is no immediate response to the acts, actions or events carried out by the user on graphical interfaces and 2) it is not possible to drag and drop documents, texts, images or any multimedia content.

RIAs (Rich Internet Applications) become a necessary way of increasing the advantages and avoiding the disadvantages of traditional Web applications. RIAs are similar to Web applications but they also share the majority of the characteristics of desktop applications. These applications use a standardized Web browser to be run and via add-ons and through a virtual machine the additional characteristics are added. RIAs are applications that combine the advantages of both Web applications and traditional applications, and they seek to improve the user experience. Rich Internet Applications combine features and functionality of desktop applications, but they are delivered over the Web.

Commonly when the user clicks on a hyperlink, there is a constant refreshing of Web pages on traditional Web applications. This situation produces a high amount of traffic between the client and the server, resulting in the same web page being refreshed with a minimal change. By using RIAs, this process does not require a refresh process on each Web page, but the whole application is loaded from the beginning and it only produces a communication with the server when external data are required such as communication with databases or with some external files. RIAs have a particular way to handle and process information which is another difference. Today traditional desktop applications exclusively rely on client-side processing. When a task is initiated, the local system's resources are leveraged to process the request. In contrast, a Web application exclusively relies on the server-side technology to process a request. With the use of RIAs, the load is shared by both client-side and server-side technology. RIAs represent the next transition in the evolution of Web applications; they promise the richness, interactivity and usability lacking in many of today's web applications.

2. BASIC CONCEPTS

RIAs constitute a new paradigm on Web development, which are currently being released with great success in the world of IT (Information Technology) and business. The best way of understanding what RIAs are, is by placing them within the context of other related technologies such as ASP (Active Server Pages) or JSP (Java Server Pages). In order to have a better understanding about the concept, it is necessary to think about technological solutions in terms of two characteristics: reach and richness. "Richness is the ability of incorporating intuitive interactivity and user interfaces on the client-side, and reach is the ability of the application to be available to any user" (Namscimbene, 2005). In 2004, a Macromedia study[1] compared a traditional Web application built with JSP technology with an identical application built with Macromedia Flex. The study revealed that both server requests and CPU usage were dramatically decreased in a Flex-based Application. The Flex-based applications used .8%

average server CPU utilization under heavy load with minimal peaks of 50% while the JSP-based interface under the same load used 21.2% server CPU utilization with peaks up to 100%.

RIAs work in an asynchronous fashion which enables them to be more dynamic than traditional Web applications. Therefore, they reduce the difference between Web-based applications and desktop applications. Some advantages that RIAs represent when are compared with traditional Web applications are presented below:

- **Immediate Access:** At any moment, the user does not lose control of the web page that he is visiting due to the access times are very short.
- **Graphical Interface Features:** The RIAs technologies enable functions such as the drag & drop from one part of the screen to another.
- **Responsiveness and Interactivity:** RIA carries out the data processing on the client-side. This situation results in a reduced network traffic and faster response as the application leverages the client CPU (Central Processing Unit). Also, when a button or a URL (Uniform Resource Locator) is clicked, the corresponding section of the web page is only asynchronously reloaded, and not the whole page. This action provides continuous visual reference to users, so they are not distracted by interface changes.
- **Real-Time Communication:** It enables users to collaborate and share information on the Internet through real-time communication channels like instant messenger, video on demand, audio/video conference, among others.
- **Ease of Maintenance:** For example, by modifying and/or deleting items without needing of refreshing the current web page, either to improve performance or to fix bugs (Veit, 2008).

"RIAs are a type of application that offers various advantages over traditional Web applications. RIAs function as a combination of the advantages of both Web applications and traditional applications" (Viveros García & García Godoy, 2009). RIAs have arisen from the needs of both Web applications, as well as desktop applications, achieving a combination of the advantages of both of them: i.e. a RIA is an intermediate between traditional Web applications (thin-client) and desktop applications (fat-client) (Rivero et al., 2007).

Nowadays, there are several concepts and definitions about RIAs. The RIA term was firstly used in March 2002 by Macromedia. RIA was defined as a new model for developing Web Applications that separates data server services from the rich user interface, which is presented through a plugin that is executed at runtime on a Web browser.

Some concepts only compare RIAs to desktop applications in a general way ignoring important features like server-side processing and asynchronous data loading. For instance, Wikipedia (Wikipedia, 2011) defines RIA as follow: *"A rich internet application is a web application that has many of the characteristics of desktop applications, typically delivered either by way of a site-specific browser, via a browser plug-in, independent sandboxes, or virtual machines..."*.

This concept has changed due RIAs are not only implemented on Web browsers, thanks to the emergence of new Web development platforms; they perfectly run on desktop and mobile devices. The following extract highlights offline and online functionality, local data storage and client-side processing capabilities as emphasized by Linaje (Linaje et. al., 2008): *"Some of the novel features of RIAs affect the UI (User Interface) and the interaction paradigm; others extend to architectural issues, such as, the client-server communication and the distribution of the data and business logic. They support online and offline usage, sophisticated UIs, data storage and processing capabilities directly at the client side, powerful interaction tools leading to better usability and personalization, lower bandwith consumption and better separation between presentation and content".*

Brambilla (Brambilla et. al., 2008) defines RIA as: *"Web applications that exploit the power of Web clients for increasing the responsiveness and usability of the web UI, by offering functionalities similar to the ones of desktop applications. RIAs follow the client/server paradigm, but opposite to traditional web applications, RIAs are able to transfer the processing of UI, business logic and data management to the client, possibly using asynchronous communications".* This concept refers to the capability of returning processing to client-side and taking advantage of the constant improvements of the hardware configurations.

Likewise, Bozzon (Bozzon et. al., 2006) discusses the role that the client-server architecture takes and its asynchronous workflow, defining a RIA as follow: *"They are a variant of Web-based systems providing sophisticated interfaces for representing complex processes and data, minimizing client-server data transferring and moving the interaction and presentation layers from the server to the client. Typically, a RIA is loaded by the client along with some initial data; then, it manages data rendering and event processing, communicating with the server when the user requires further information or must submit data".*

As conclusion, the following concept can be inferred emphasizing the main differences among traditional Web applications: *"RIAs are applications typically executed by any RIA-capable device that renders a Rich User Interface and they use data that can be processed both by the server-side and the client-side."*

By RIA-capable device, any electronic device that executes JavaScript-based and third-party technologies (JavaFX, Silverlight and Adobe Flex, to mention a few) for RIA development is considered. One of the main principles of RIAs development is the asynchronous data loading which means that they are able to obtain chunks of data without refreshing the entire Web site. The concept of richness, involved in the RIA definition, is due to its ability of improving the traditional Web Application features in five basic aspects:

1. The application uses the client-side memory in which the data is locally manipulated and stored. Once the entire task is done, it is sent back to the server-side.

2. The RIAs use the client's processing capability. It enables both the server-side and the client.side to carry out complex operations, resulting in a different navigation structure in comparison with traditional Web applications.

3. RIAs allow both synchronous and asynchronous communications. The data distribution between client and server expands the produced event features, since they are originated, detected, advised and processed in different ways.

4. The presentation and complex interaction given to the user are augmented. RIAs show themselves as single Web page avoiding unnecessary loading and allowing data to be displayed in progressive way or when it is needed.

5. RIAs combine the flexibility of Web user interfaces with the processing power of desktop applications.

In synthesis, RIAs are systems that allocate most of the load processing of the user graphic interface to the client-side while the predominant part of control processing and data management remains on server-side. From this perspective, a standard architecture for RIA development is represented in Figure 1. In Figure 1, three layers for a typical RIA development are defined: 1) the client-side rendering the rich user interface, 2) a controller layer which executes business logic, 3) a data transactions manager.

In Figure 1, the architecture has three main properties:

Figure 1. A standard architecture for RIAs

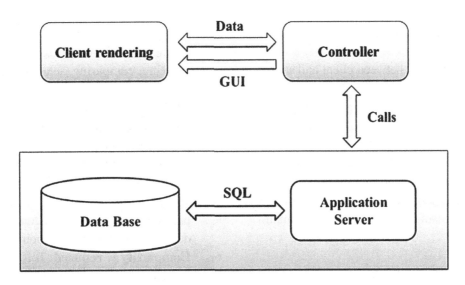

1. **Data Management:** In traditional Web applications, data resides on the server-side. In a RIA, application data can be distributed between server-side and client-side. Therefore, a RIA can use the client's persistent and volatile content. Data can be manipulated on the client-side, and finally sends them to the server-side once the operation has been completed.

2. **Both-Sides Controllers:** In traditional Web applications, there is only one controller at the server-side that orchestrates the computation of the Web page. At each user interaction, the whole Web page is computed and reloaded. At the client-side, a second controller is introduced in a RIA, which is responsible of computing and refreshing a section of a Web page. Data processing can be executed both at client-side and server-side. RIAs have a different navigation structure from Web 1.0 applications, due to the augmented processing capability of the client. In RIAs, both the client-side and the server-side can carry out complex operations.

3. **Client/Server-Side Communication:** In RIAs, mechanisms to minimize data transfers

are introduced which move interaction and presentation layers from the server-side to client-side. Conversely to Web applications, RIAs use both synchronous and asynchronous communications. Pull and push communication capabilities are available. Data distribution and functionality across client and server broadens the features of the produced events as they can be originated, detected, notified, and processed in a variety of ways.

These properties represent the core of RIAs, since all RIA implement at least one of them.

3. MAIN CROSS-DOMAINS BENEFITS OF RIAS

RIAs solve problems of traditional Web applications. The main problems in traditional Web application occur when the navigation is necessary in order to:

- Represent workflows.
- Browse structured information.

- Implement complex user interfaces.

These aspects can cause:

- Increased traffic between client and server.
- An increased workload on the server-side.
- A decreased client response time (Rivero et al., 2007).

RIAs are accessed from the Internet. RIAs solve the accessibility and mobility problems of desktop applications. In next section, the impact and importance of RIAs on different domains are discussed.

3.1. The Importance of RIAs in E-Commerce

ITs are frequently changing because there are new user needs. It is important to take into account the emergent ITs because they offer several benefits to the people involved such as more powerful development, fast execution and integration among applications. E-commerce is one of the main usages of the Internet where its application has been increased with the development of Web applications. RIAs provide more benefits to business entities, shoppers and developers in e-commerce domain. The main benefits for business entities in e-commerce are listed below:

1. **Products are showed anywhere and anytime:** Through RIAs, the business entities can show their products to their customer regardless where they are and when they access. The customer can buy without having to be into a store.
2. **The shopping process is easy:** RIAs build interactive, intuitive, animated and easy applications. Therefore, they allow users to explore products in an easier and faster approach.
3. **A better shopping experience is achieved:** The shopping experience allows customer to visit and buy more frequently. This situation is achieved by providing interactions between the user and the application. For example, it allows searching, retrieving, showing, comparing, selecting and buying products in the same Web page.
4. **The product demand is increased:** When the detailed information of products is presented through rich user interfaces, the user's interest for purchasing is increased.
5. **More information of products is exposed:** The procurement process of the available products is described to customers in a more detailed way for using at their own benefit.
6. **Complexity is reduced:** It is necessary to represent product information in a simple way and to guide the customer in selecting his products. When the user watches a single Web page, the user does not need to select all products' features and send information to build a new Web page. RIAs allow selecting all features and updating products into a same Web page.
7. **Fewer returns:** When the customer knows all about a product, the customer does not have any doubt of buying the product. It allows customer satisfaction and reduces the indices of purchase returns.
8. **Less investment in development:** There are a lot of open source Web frameworks for designing, creating and building RIAs. Therefore, the business entities can use e-commerce to show their products or services with less investment.
9. **Video integration:** Video integration offers new ways to display products information. For example, through video, guidance or instructions about application, services or products can be provided. It also makes more attractive the Web application.
10. **The shopping time is reduced:** Because shopping time is less, the customer does not leave the application, increasing the products sold.

The main benefits for shoppers in e-commerce are listed below:

1. **Products can be customized:** These applications allow easily customizing products such as sneakers, clothing, bags to mention but a few. It offers new ways for shopping because the RIAs allow selecting features of products and at the same time they are always configured in a single Web page.
2. **The user shopping experience is better:** With a single Web page, the user shopping experience is fast, continuous, and interesting because the Web page refresh is not required. Therefore, customers perceive a Web site that provides a better response time.
3. **More product information is provided:** RIAs provide several components such as video, image and effects that show all product information needed to know the product or service in less time. This makes the shopping process easier.
4. **Fast response to the user's needs:** When the user needs a product or service, the user only needs to visit the application. The user does not need to leave his home or his office.

The main benefits for developers in e-commerce are listed below:

1. **The RIAs promote the use of SOA (Service Oriented Architecture):** With both RIA and SOA, rich application development is easier and faster. The integration of both technologies allows increasing the shared information through scalable applications.
2. **There are several design tool, IDE (Integrated Development Environment) and open source frameworks:** These tools allow the RIA development in an easier way since they provide a set of components, events; effects and libraries where developers only needs to configure them.

3. **RIAs have an advanced user capability and interactive user interfaces for building custom rich interfaces to customers:** It also provides an easier way for integrating both designer and developer tasks.

The e-commerce systems are very important for business entities because they attract potential customers, and they expose the products anywhere and anytime. These benefits show how RIAs can bring improvement to e-commerce domain thanks to a new generation of internet applications providing interactive, intuitive and dynamic ways to explore the products and services information.

3.2. The Importance of RIAs in E-Learning

Over the last few years, great efforts have been made to offer e learning systems, however the high percentage of failure in e-learning courses has been attributed to the poor design of the online experience which does not motivate the students to achieve a better learning process since they only offers repetitive, boring tasks and some other frustrations.

In order to improve these systems, the learning software should also contain multimedia elements such as simulations, explorations, drag and drop exercises, among others. E-learning systems should be active and they should offer a teaching-learning process in a dynamic and interactive way.

Nowadays, the developers of e-learning systems can use RIAs technologies in order to combine a variety of multimedia contens and external applications for building enriched content and improving the experience of learning online.

RIAs technologies are characterized by enabling a higher quality and improving the experience of online interaction. RIAs offer some benefits on e-learning domain which are listed below:

1. The student can access information and courses from any location. This helps to maximize the reach of the audience.
2. RIAs can run without modifications, over the Internet from multiple platforms. With this advantage, the student can receive information from wherever he is and without needing previous software installations.
3. Attractive user interfaces can be provided, with a high level of interactivity. Ease of use and the capacity of attracting the student's attention are essential in the success of e-learning systems. By building courses more attractive to the student, retention is achieved and with this the courses are successfully completed by the student.
4. Audio, video, images and texts can be used in order to improve the contents of e-learning applications; it improves the student's experience. RIAs provide many facilities to include any type of multimedia content which is of great help and it is beneficial to students.
5. RIAs are compatible with mobile workflow, enabling users to work both online and offline. RIAs offer advantages over traditional Web applications because they can be used for the design of courses or contents for e-learning systems.

RIAs offer better features than traditional Web applications by providing the feature of including multimedia content and the user interfaces design with a greater of interactivity level. Therefore, the designer of these learning experiences can significantly improve the motivation and the experiences of the user, which in this case is the student.

3.3. The Importance of RIAs in E-Entertainment

Today, e-Entertainment is very popular, attributing to a huge number of commercial game titles, while only in US having an annual turnover far exceeding the American Box Office. Additionally, there is a wide spread total of specialized game consoles, with a total number being larger than the amount of home personal computers.

By using RIAs, it is possible to design interactive interfaces including video games for the Web or to develop Web applications for watching movies on the Internet without having to leave the home.

RIAs offer some benefits on e-entertainment domain which are listed below:

1. The user can access video games online, without needing to buy consoles or accessories.
2. It is possible to add a high level of interactivity with user interfaces to make the use of applications and content more attractive. These user interfaces can help to the administrators to control the content, enabling actions such as drag and drop, and the ability to practically paginate the contents thus avoiding the refreshing of web pages.
3. It is possible to add video players or multimedia content with personal controls. This offers a greater control as much for the administrator as for the consumer.

RIAs combine avant-garde technology with innovative business practices to provide cost-effective business solutions for small and medium businesses, large corporations and governmental organizations.

As it can be seen in this section, RIAs can be implemented in diverse domains. RIAs can be implemented in e-government or in e-health; whenever the application requires it. There are also some successful case studies on RIA development; in the following sections some of these are described.

4. SUCCESSFUL STORIES ON RIAS DEVELOPMENT

Experiences and Successful Stories of Using RIAs in B2C E-Commerce Domain

Many years ago, Web pages were based in HTML-based technology. These HTML-based Web pages contained text, images, and form elements like text boxes, lists, combo boxes and hyperlinks. When a user clicked a hyperlink the Web browser loaded another Web page where all the content had to be replaced by a new HTML-based document and the previous content was disappeared. If the user returned to reload the previous content, the information often was lost. This interaction did not allow rich user experience.

Unlike Web applications designed with traditional HTML, a RIA enrich the user experience by combining the strengths of desktop and Web applications increasing and improving the options and capabilities of them. Among the new experiences that RIAs give to a user are:

1. Provide a rich user interface similar to the "look and feel" present in desktop applications.
2. Applications developed with these technologies use user interface controls with higher performances and functionalities. Examples of them are horizontal or vertical menus, navigation tree menus, tabbed panels, videos, and controls for capturing data, among others.
3. Users interact with the application to get an immediate response to this, it is not necessary to redraw the Web page when new data are loaded.
4. The applications enable users to perform common operations that were only available on desktop applications and they were not possible to perform in traditional HTML-based Web pages: drag&drop, resize, among others.
5. There is not need for complex setup process to access Web sites or applications (in some cases only requires a plug-in).
6. RIAs receive immediate response. It is not necessary waiting for a connection to and from the server-side to get a result.

An important improvement offered by RIAs is the development of interactive Web sites. Now, customers have the chance to see online the products and even they change and customize them according to their needs. A RIA well-designed site offers to consumers a complete shopping experience: the customer is visually guided step by step through the process, since selecting the products catalog until the payment. Some success stories where RIAs have been applied in order to improve the productivity are described below.

Kodak EasyShare (www. kodakgallery.com)

It is a subsidiary of Eastman Kodak Company™ that offers online services for handling of digital images to millions of customers around the world. Some services are storing, displaying, sharing photos and ordering prints. The company developed a Web-based platform to handle millions of digital photographs, digital-quality printed albums, photo sharing among users. Furthermore, the company needed to be capable of expanding the functionality to add new products in the future and not limited only to the manipulation of images, plus offer the user a great experience when using a fully interactive platform. To carry out the above, Kodak EasyShare launched Photo Books in 2004 that allowed to users to create their own photo books by a striking interface where they could drag and drop images on the pages of a book, change the page, change the background, among other options. In Photo Books, users could also view the content without loss of time and avoiding reloading the entire Web page to update only the book page.

Among the benefits gained by using Photo Books include:

- Innovation of providing the photo album service to its customers.
- Increasing sales by offering the option of printing the album created by the customer or individual photos.
- Attracting a greater number of customers by providing compatibility between the Kodak EasyShare software for PC and on-line version.
- Providing more products over the Internet.
- Developing a platform capable of being expanded in terms of functionality

MINI USA (www.miniusa.com)

MINI USA is a division of BMW™ North America. MINI USA is responsible of producing MINI cars in the U.S. market; the goal of developing a RIA was to promote the brand with a unique brand of car customization. With the implementation of a RIA, users had a new experience of the Web site management. The main feature was the customization of Web pages allowing users to manufacture his own MINI car through a simple process that adds nonlinear elements either inside or outside the car; the navigation ensured that all options of exchange were available in a part of the Web page. Users could see the exact car that they were getting and could understand the price implications of their configuration choices at each step of the purchasing process.

With this new development, it allowed people to customize their own personal MINI through a simple, non-linear five-step process that included the ability to add aftersales MINI Motoring Accessories such as custom roof graphics and wheels. The navigation assured that everything aws viewable on one web page. This rules-based

architecture assured that it only allowed the ability of configuring a vehicle that could actually be purchased, and it allowed MINI to easily maintain the rules, as the vehicle specifications change from model year to model year. When users finished the configuration process of a car, they could give it a name, save it, calculate payments for it and easily send their configuration to a MINI dealer or a friend. MINI encouraged them to configure and save as many customized MINIs as they like. The customization feature offered the following benefits:

- An increasing in registered customers.
- The majority of registered clients configured a MINI.
- Customers were attracted by the way they could customize a MINI car to their needs.
- Customization was done in an easy way; all information was always available on screen.
- The information was directly sent to a MINI dealer, giving greater confidence to the customer.

FootJoy™ (www.footjoy.com)

As one of the major brands in the Acushnet Company™, FootJoy is a main manufacturer and distributor of golf shoe and golf glove products in the world. They are estimated to own 55%-60% of each of those markets. Other products include socks, outerwear and accessories. The company distinguished itself in two ways: by the quality of its products and service, and by its reputation for innovation in golf shoe and glove technology. They believe they have a very good feel for the consumer, his or her needs and how to serve them. They faced several challenges:

- Improve the usability of the site. They wanted to provide a two-way interactive experience with a look and feel better representing the brand. They wanted the ability to support the customer and better spotlight or merchandize information such as new products, news, among others.

- Enable the customer to develop a relationship with the company by mirroring on the website the kind of expertise and guidance the customer would get in person in a FootJoy store. Specifically, they wanted to develop the Product Finder based on product knowledge captured from FootJoy experts, to allow visitors to quickly identify themselves and their needs, and to map these needs to an appropriate product.
- Put a strategic technology foundation in place, including content management, and ties into their legacy product system, that would serve as a base for future website development.
- Bring organization to the catalog content to allow them to update on-line catalogs more rapidly by themselves, without involving expensive and over-booked technical resources.
- Create a participatory site fostering community, by soliciting user feedback through on-line polls, and by providing information about products, golf courses, tips, expert interviews and weather reports.

In order to retain their substantial market share, FootJoy developed a RIA called Product Finder in order to present a series of questions that guide the visitor through a product selection process, similar to how an expert might engage the customer in the store. Content such as pictures of golf shoes or gloves and brief textual product descriptions are pulled from the content management system. In early September 2003, FootJoy launched myjoys. com, a RIA to revolutionize the way Golf Shoes were purchased online. Through this application, customers could access an elegant shoe creation interface that allowed them to see exactly what their shoe will look like as they design and change it (MyJoys offered the user 2 base and 14 saddle

colors option as well as the chance to personalize the shoe with up to 3 letters and/or numbers). Leather stocks were checked in real-time, via Flash Remoting, notifying the customer if their leather selection is unavailable and emailing them when it was back in stock. The application included a fully integrated shopping cart and check-out process, including encryption (via Verisgn SSL), anti-fraud credit card checking and real-time address checking and tax calculation to ensure an accurate and secure check-out experience. The "My FootJoy" area allowed users to save custom shoes to their wish list and track their orders. Customized shoe orders were directly sent to China where the shoes were manufactured and shipped to the customer within 3 weeks.

FootJoy exceeded the usage expectations by over 200%. At an average of $150 per shoe order, this unexpected increase had a substantial increase on revenue for FootJoy, and it observed a substantial increase the ROI on the MyJoys application.

The Broadmoor Hotel™ and BlueGreen Vacation Rentals™ (www.broadmoor. com, www.bluegreenrentals.com)

The online travel reservations have become a fairly common occurrence. But it is often frustrating. Frequently, users traverse through several web pages of search and result screens, selecting hotels, dates and room types, then by only checking availability to discover that there is not room at the inn, or the unaffordable room rate is not revealed until the very end, forcing the user to repeat the process again. At the same time, the Web is the cheapest sales channel for hotels. By using a travel agent can cost a hotel 15%-30% of the revenue in commissions, and many large hotels and chains must pay to use a global distribution system (GDS) to electronically distribute their inventory. If the hotels can move more reservations to the Web, they can save substantial money. But the main issue is that they need to be assured that they are not going to move people to the Web only to have them unable to complete a reservation. If a better experience leads to more completed reservations and thus increased revenues, then a Web site that provides a better experience becomes an imperative for the hotels.

Webvertising, a firm in Houston Texas, markets a suite of products and services for hotels, including OneScreen, an innovative, easy-to-use, single screen interface for on-line reservations. Over 800 independent hotels, hotel companies and destination marketing organizations now use Webvertising's solutions to manage room inventory and electronic distribution over the Web. OneScreen allowed over 200 hotels, like the Broadmoor, a Mobil 5-star luxury hotel, and time-share organizations, like Bluegreen Vacation Rentals, offer a better reservation experience to travelers to an increased number of reservations and room nights booked. Today most hotels use a traditional multi-step, multi-page reservation approach for online reservations. The challenge for the Broadmoor was to fundamentally change the user's reservation experience such that the simplicity, clarity and ease of use of the experience led to a more satisfied customer and increased bookings. The key factor was reducing the number of steps involved in making the registration process.

The impact of the OneScreen RIA on the hotels was stunning. Webvertising's hotel customers reported online reservations in general increasing 46% over the previous year, due to the natural growth in the use of the Web to make reservations. However, hotels that moved from an HTML-based interface to the OneScreen interface observed an additional increase of 89% in reservations. Furthermore while the average conversion rate (from visitor to buyer) for hotels using the HTML-only interface was 2.3%, it was almost double that with the OneScreen interfaces. In one instance, the Greenbrier Hotel observed a dramatic 8-fold increase in conversions from 2.7% for their HTML-based interface to 22% when they used OneScreen. For most hotels, even a 1%

increase could be worth hundreds of thousands of dollars a year.

Verizon Wireless™ (www. verizonwireless.com)

Verizon Wireless is the largest operator of mobile telephony in the U.S. with 80 million active customers. In order to publicize its products and services to a wider audience, Verizon developed an online store which offered ringtones, ringback tones and more. The main objective of the shop was to support millions of subscribers and high transaction volumes, also providing a lightweight application for customers to easily download MP3 files. The platform was developed by using Adobe Flash providing to customers a flexible experience offering several benefits for both the company and the customers:

- Increase online incomings related to ringtones and ringbacks tones to be available whenever on the store.
- Provides access to an extensive library of MP3 files to registered customers.
- The platform is scalable to provide more products.

Yankee Candle Company

The Yankee Candle Company is another strong example of how a RIA-based configurator impacted a company. It is a designer, manufacturer, retailer and wholesaler of premium, scented candles in the U.S. They directly sell through their stores, catalogs and on-line Web site, as well as through partners. They had strong growth plans, and wanted to create a better e-commerce environment than their current website offered. They faced the challenge of increasing buyer confidence to improve sales of custom candles on-line. Customers buy custom candles for very important events such as weddings or corporate events, and they typically buy them in bulk. The problem was that buyers had difficultly visualizing what the custom candle would look like once they had made all the selections. The initial version of the Web site's custom candle section used HTML-based pages and required that users check boxes to select the candle color and fill out a form with the text for the candle label message. Once the color was selected, they could never see what this configuration actually looked like before being asked to buy the candle in bulk and on faith. It was no wonder because people would abandon their shopping cart or call customer service for reassurance that the candle would look like what they imagined.

Yankee Candle felt that this section of the website was ineffective. This was corroborated by data indicating that the average purchase was smaller on-line than through other channels. This was also an indication that they were doing an inadequate job of up selling and cross selling on-line.

Technically the problem was that using HTML-based technology they could not represent what the final product would look like.

The Yankee Candle chose to develop a Flash-based user interface for the custom candle configurator for several reasons. First, it allowed them to dynamically render a picture of the candle, based on the user's selections. It also allowed them to create a better Web customer experience that would behave consistently across platforms, a benefit of the broad reach and cross-platform support. Second, they could develop the application more quickly and thus less expensively than with alternative technologies. This was due in part to the development tools, which provided out-of-the-box user interface components such as drop down menu boxes, and because they were able to integrate the presentation layer into their existing backend system, which consisted of an Oracle product database and BroadVision eCommerce system.

While the majority of the site was HTML-based technology, the custom candle configurator is a single screen Flash-based interface that utilizes

their existing e-commerce infrastructure. It obtained data and imagery from the product database and ecommerce system. As users selected the label and fragrance and enter the label's text message, they immediately observed a realistic picture of the custom candle as it did appear when complete. Users were encouraged to select optional finishing touches such as wrapping the candle in fabric or adding a ribbon or a flower, creating the opportunity for Yankee Candle to upsell the customer. The user could construct "what-if" scenarios at any point to see what it did look like and what it did cost for both the basic candle as well as the additional options.

The end result was that this real-time visualization of their custom candle gave consumers a higher level of confidence, and they bought more candles. Yankee Candle observed a 25% increase in both product revenue and average order size, exceeding their expectations. In addition, they had a 70% drop off in calls to their call center for the custom candle line, and they received multiple customer testimonials with positive feedback on the website. There was an additional surprising result: their own call center representatives started going to the website and using the configurator when fielding customer calls.

Charles Schwab

Charles Schwab's marketing planning calendar provides an excellent example of an application for cross-departmental data visualization. The Charles Schwab Corporation is a provider of securities brokerage and related financial services, including retail, telephone and Internet-based brokerage operations. Schwab's marketing department needed to centralize the planning, tracking and analysis of all marketing initiatives and make the information visible and accessible to both executives and marketing project coordinators. They needed to build a highly complex enterprise reporting application. They were faced with many challenges. They needed to:

- Address multiple types of users with different information needs and visualization requirements
- Present deep, multi-dimensional data sets (e.g., how much money was spent on which projects over what time) in an intuitive, logical and visual way
- Provide sophisticated yet easy-to-use reporting tools usable by both executives and project planners
- Deliver responsive and interactive tools that allowed the user to be in control

They chose to develop a custom data visualization solution to be able to dynamically communicate to different constituents. The sophistication of the data visualization required a wholly new approach and exceeded what was realistic using HTML-based technology or any out-of-the-box or web-based calendaring tools. They wanted, for example, a drilldown Gantt chart in which they could see the spending details of a particular project. It was not possible to do that in HTML-based technology. To meet two different and distinct user needs they developed two views: timeline and analysis.

The timeline view presented information in the form of a dynamic Gantt-style calendar and it was targeted at project coordinators. By using this view, project managers could quickly and easily visualize the overall time-based status of multiple projects. Drill down capabilities allowed the project manager to click to see individual project details within a program, such as budget data, or to manipulate projects, such as plan advertising for a different media channel. The tool gave them a framework to visualize and manipulate the detailed marketing planning information.

The analysis view presented an aggregated holistic view that allowed Schwab marketing executives to answer bigger questions, like "How am I spending money in the first quarter?" With this dynamic visual tool, Schwab executives could rapidly analyze marketing expenses across initia-

tives and time, and realize a more efficient use of the marketing budget. They could change the selected characteristics to pose different questions and get a different view on the data. By using this tool, they could slice and dice and then visualize the information in useful ways that were not possible before.

These use experiences presented in different domains give samples of the range and kind of business benefits afforded by using RIAs. RIAs transformed the applications configuration, especially when they required enhanced visualization. RIAs allowed to buyers purchase products off a single screen and see the product that it was the result of their selections improving the user experience.

5. CONCLUSION

In this chapter, a general overview of Web applications and how they emerged has been provided in order to place the reader in the context of the RIAs development. Also the most relevant information about RIAs was discussed. The case studies presented give a sample of the range and kind of business benefits afforded by Rich Internet Applications. These case studies show how RIAs have the ability to handle various kinds of complexities and enable wholly new kinds of Web applications. While some results were visibly more dramatic or compelling, taken as a whole they begun to have an alternative picture of how Web applications can be, and how they can in many instances, fundamentally change a company's business or the nature of the game with their competitors.

In e-business applications, RIAs allowed hotels to dramatically increase their reservations, revenues and room nights booked by simplifying the workflow complexity of making a reservation. RIAs transformed configuration applications, especially when they required enhanced visualization. For both MINI USA and The Yankee Candle

Company, the ability of a Rich Internet Application to let buyers purchase products off a single screen and see the product that was the result of their selections transformed the user experience. Finally, Schwab demonstrated that RIAs could have a strong impact on internal corporate applications, by facilitating data visualization and reporting across different groups of users.

REFERENCES

Bozzon, A., Comai, S., Fraternali, P., & Carugui, G. T. (2006). Capturing RIA concepts in a web modeling language. In *Proceedings of the 15th international Conference on World Wide Web WWW 06*, (pp. 907-908). ACM. Retrieved from http://discovery.ucl.ac.uk/1320284/

Brambilla, M., Preciado, J. C., Linaje, M., & Sanchez Figueroa, F. (2008). Business Process-based Conceptual Design of Rich Internet Applications. In *Proceedings of Eighth International Conference on Web Engineering*, (pp. 155-156). IEEE. Retrieved from http://ieeexplore.ieee.org/lpdocs/epic03/wrapper.htm?arnumber=4577879

Linaje, M., Preciado, J.C., Morales-Chaparro, R., & Sanchez-Figueroa, F. (2008). On the Implementation of Multiplatform RIA User Interface Components. In *Proceedings of ICWE 2008 Workshops, 7th Int. Workshop on Web-Oriented Software Technologies*, (pp. 44-49). ICWE. Retrieved from http://icwe2008.webengineering.org/Program/Workshops/ISBN978-80-227-2899-7/icwe2008ws-CD/individual-files/02icwe2008ws-iwwost08-linaje.pdf

Namscimbene, C. (2005). *Adobe & Macromedia Sales Engineer en el distribuidor ALAB S.A.* Retrieved 6 July 2011 from http://www.canal-ar.com.ar/noticias/noticiamuestra.asp?Id=2639

O'Reilly, T. (2005). What is Web 2.0. Design Patterns and Bussiness Models for the Next Generation of Software. *Design, 65*(65), 17-37. Retrieved from http://papers.ssrn.com/sol3/papers.cfm?abstract_id=1008839

Rivero, J. M., & Buzzo, M. H. (2007). *Definición de Rich Internet Applications a través de Modelos de Dominio Específico*. Retrieved from: http://revista.info.unlp.edu.ar/tesinas/tesis51.pdf

Veit, F. (2008). *Introducción a Tecnologías Enriquecidas para Internet*. (Unpublished thesis). Facultad de Ingeniería, Universidad ORT Uruguay, Uruguay.

Viveros García, M. C., & García Godoy, D. (2009). *Elaboración de una guía para el desarrollo de aplicaciones en extjs. (Unpublished thesis)*. Instituto Tecnológico de Orizaba.

Wikipedia. (2011). *Rich Internet Application*. Retrieved 02 Feb 2011, from http://en.wikipedia.org/wiki/Rich_Internet_application

ADDITIONAL READING

Fraternali, P., Rossi, G., & Sánchez-Figueroa, S. (2010). Rich Internet Applications. *IEEE Internet Computing, 14*(3), 9-12. Citeseer. Retrieved from http://ieeexplore.ieee.org/lpdocs/epic03/wrapper.htm?arnumber=5481362

Shahrooz Feizabadi. (n.d.). *History of the World Wide Web*. Retrieved from http://ei.cs.vt.edu/book/chap1/htx_hist.html

uclm.es. (n.d.). *A CERN invention you are familiar with: The World Wide Web*. Retrieved from http://www.uclm.es/profesorado/ricardo/CursoHTML/Presentacion/CERN/web.html

w3.org. (n.d.a). *A Little History of the World Wide Web, from 1945 to 1995*. Retrieved from http://www.w3.org/History.html

w3.org. (n.d.b). *Some early ideas of HTML.* Retrieved from http://www.w3.org/MarkUp/historical

w3.org. (n.d.c). *The World Wide Web - past, present and future.* Retrieved from http://www.w3.org/People/Berners-Lee/1996/ppf.html

KEY TERMS AND DEFINITIONS

Business to Customer (B2C): Some strategies of commercial enterprises to get directly to the customer or end user.

E-Commerce: The marketing of products or services through electronic media and especially via Internet.

E-Entertainment: The way of providing entertainment through electronic media and especially via Internet.

E-Learning: The way the impartation of knowledge and education through electronic media and especially via Internet.

Rich Internet Applications: Applications that are deployed over the Web, this type of applications combines features and functionality of Web applications and desktop applications.

Web 2.0: Web applications that allow for easier-to-share information, interoperability, user-centered design, and collaboration with the World Wide Web.

World Wide Web (WWW): An information distribution system comprised of interlinked hypertext or hypermedia accessed by using the Internet.

ENDNOTES

[1]   "Flex Performance Brief: A Comparison of Flex and JavaServer Pages Applications", Macromedia white paper, May 2004.

Chapter 2
Frameworks for RIAs Development

ABSTRACT

Chapter 2 describes the most popular options for RIAs development. For practical purposes, these options are classified into two categories: 1) JavaScript-based frameworks and 2) non-JavaScript-based frameworks; even though there are other classifications reported in the literature, this classification is used in this chapter and throughout the book. In fact, this classification allows for a quick understanding of the technologies for RIAs development by abstracting technical details about intended software architectures. In the case of JavaScript-based framework, some frameworks were selected and analyzed such as Dojo, jQuery, Mootools, and Prototype. In the case of non-JavaScript-based frameworks, frameworks selected and analyzed were Adobe Flex™, JavaFX™, Silverlight™, and OpenLaszlo™. For each framework, the architecture, functionality, and properties are described.

1. INTRODUCTION

There are many options for developing RIAs (Rich Internet Application). RIA frameworks have become popular in recent years. "A framework is a defined support structure in which another software project is organized and developed. Commonly, a RIA includes support for programs, libraries, and an interpreted language in order to help develop different components of a project" (Viveros García & García Godoy, 2009).

According to their license type, RIA frameworks can be classified into open source frameworks – such as jQuery – and commercial frameworks – such as Adobe Flex™. The most popular

options for RIAs development are described in this chapter in order to help developers and designers in the decision making process about the RIA technology to be used considering which best suits the features of the project to be carried out. This chapter discusses the different technologies for RIAs development.

2. FRAMEWORKS FOR RIAS DEVELOPMENT

In recent years, several classifications for RIAs have been proposed. These classifications address different aspects of RIAs, such as functional-

DOI: 10.4018/978-1-4666-6437-1.ch002

ity, target runtime environment and, other more complex issues, such as the software development technology (Toffetti, Comai, Preciado, & Linaje, 2011). Some of these classifications of RIAs are presented below.

Four main aspects of the application development are considered basing on the user's experience:

- **Rich Presentation:** RIAs offer client-side event-handling and widgets similar to desktop-based UIs. This permits partial page updates, support interaction with visual data representations, and multimedia content (e.g., audio, video).
- **Client Data Storage:** It is possible to store data on the client-side with different levels of persistence (in a temporal way while the application is running).
- **Client (and Distributed) Business Logic:** It is possible to carry out complex operations directly on the client-side, such as data navigation/filtering/sorting with multiple criteria, domain-specific operations, and local validation of data. It is also possible to distribute the Business Logic between the client and the server-side, (e.g., to validate some form fields on the client and others on the server-side).
- **Client-Server Communication:** RIAs support synchronous communication between client and server-side to distribute domain objects, data, computation, and provide server-push (e.g., in collaborative/ monitoring applications) (Toffetti et al., 2011).

Depending on each of the application's *functionalities*, the features above can be combined to obtain standalone applications, collaborative applications, or simply more appealing UIs (UI stands for User Interface) for existing Web applications. In terms of growing number of features and development complexity, a RIA's may typically

falls into one of the following types of application (that they can be possibly combined to obtain complex RIAs):

- **Traditional Web applications with RIA-makeover:** Where simple isolated RIA capabilities (usually for partial page updates) are added to a traditional Web application (e.g., Facebook™).
- **Rich UIs:** Web applications with widget-based UIs, where the client-side logic is an extension layer over the browser, superseding core browser responsibilities, such as handling events and managing states and the rich user interfaces components work in a coordinate way (e.g., Gmail™).
- **Standalone RIAs:** Web applications capable of running both inside and/or outside the browser in a connected and/or disconnected fashion (e.g., SlideRocket™).
- **Distributed RIAs:** Where the application data and logic are (sometimes dynamically) distributed across client and server-side. Moreover, on-line collaboration is supported and client-server communication is used to fill the gap between objects and events living across the application components (e.g., Google Docs™) (Toffetti et al., 2011).

Currently, RIAs capabilities can be implemented in a number of different client-side technologies. These technologies can be broadly classified into three categories according to the *runtime environment*:

- **JavaScript-Based:** The client-side business logic is implemented using the JavaScript scripting language (the approach is also known as "AJAX", which stands for Asynchronous JavaScript and XML). Moreover, UIs are based on a combination of HTML (HyperText Markup Language) and CSS (Cascading Style Sheets). The

Figure 1. Classification schema for RIAs development

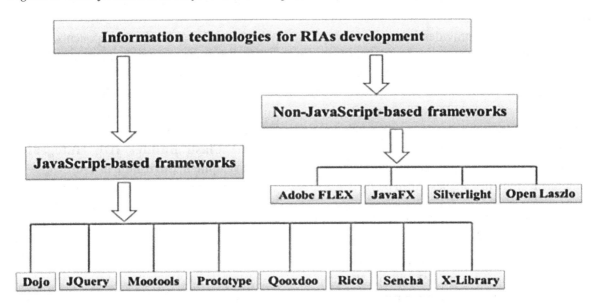

main advantage of this approach is that it relies on both built-in browser JavaScript support and W3C (World Wide Web Consortium) standards.

- **Plug-in-Based:** Advanced rendering and event processing are granted by browser's plug-ins interpreting specific scripting languages, XML (Extensible Markup Language), or media files (e.g., Adobe Flex™, JavaFX™, Silverlight™).
- **Runtime Environments:** Applications are downloaded from the Web but they are executed outside the browser using a desktop runtime environment (e.g., Java Web Start, Adobe AIR™). These solutions offer client-side capabilities and off-line usage with full access to the underlying operating system. Many RIA technologies can be used to develop applications for these runtimes (e.g., development technologies can be used for Adobe AIR™, Javascript-based and/or Flash-based) (Toffetti et al., 2011).

In order to address the multiple options for developing RIAs, this chapter presents a classification schema of RIAs. This classification was made according to the development technology. Figure 1 shows this classification schema, which is simpler than other proposals. More specifically, the shcema consists of two categories: the first groups JavaScript-based frameworks and the second groups non-JavaScript-based frameworks.

2.1. Non-JavaScript-Based Frameworks

The first set for developing RIAs is non-JavaScript-based frameworks. Merely the most popular and therefore most used frameworks on the market were considered.

2.1.1. Adobe Flex™

Flex is an open source framework for developing mobile applications for Apple iOS™, Android™ and BlackBerry™ Tablet OS. It is also used for traditional Web and desktop applications that are deployed in the major Web browsers and operating systems using the same code-base (Adobe, 2011).

Moreover, Flex provides a programming language and a programming model based on standards supported by common design patterns (Adobe, 2011).

Finally, along with the Flash Player and Adobe AIR runtime environments, Flex also belongs to the so-called Adobe Flash Platform, and it comprises different components/modules. These components/modules are described below:

1. **MXML and ActionScript Languages:** MXML is a declarative XML-based language that permits describing the distribution, appearance and behavior of the application's user interface. ActionScript 3.0 is an ECMAScript-based object-oriented language which anables to define the application's business logic. The MXML (Macromedia eXtensible Markup Language) and ActionScript source code are compiled together into a single SWF file, which comprises the Flex-based application.

2. **The Flex Framework SDK Components:** The Flex SDK (Software Development Kit) is a set of user interface components, such as lists, buttons, and graphics, among others. It includes the Adobe Flex™ framework (component class library) and the Flex compiler. Flex compiler enables to freely develop and deploy Flex-based applications.

3. **The Flash Builder IDE (Integrated Development Environment):** An Eclipse™-based IDE for Adobe Flex™-based application development. Flash Builder™ provides support for building Adobe Flex™-based and ActionScript-based applications for Android™, BlackBerry™ Tablet OS and Apple™ iOS™.

4. **The Runtime Environment for Web Browser, Adobe Flash Player™:** Adobe Flash Player™ is a multiplatform runtime environment for Web browsers-based applications. It permits deploying Adobe Flex™-based applications in a Web browser using a plugin (McCune & Subramaniam, 2008).

Figure 2. Main Adobe Flex™ components

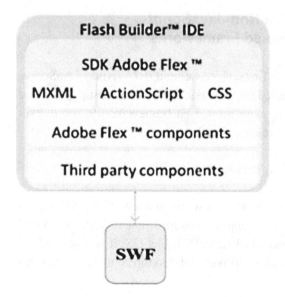

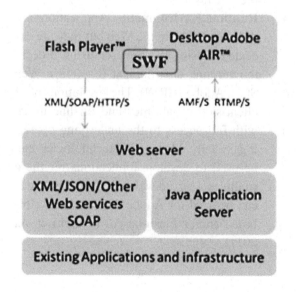

Figure 2 depicts the interaction among the components/modules involved in Adobe Flex™.

Adobe Flex™ provides a standards-based middle tier presentation server specifically designed for construction of server-based RIAs. Adobe developed Flex with the aim of improving the user's experience in creating rich dynamic Internet applications and to help developers accomplish more with fewer resources.

The advantages of using Adobe Flex™-based technology are listed below.

- The Web browser-based applications run within a controlled environment, the Adobe Flash player™ plugin. Therefore, it is not necessary to consider the Web browser features. According to Adobe, Adobe Flash Player™ is currently installed on over one billion of desktop computers across Web browsers and operating systems (Flash Player, 2012),.
- Adobe Flex™ is a mature technology.
- IDE support comes not only from Adobe with FlashBuilder but also from Jetbrains with IntelliJ IDE.
- Adobe Flex™, especially since the release of Adobe AIR™, represents a powerful option for RIAs development (Smeets, Boness, & Bankras, 2008).

Table 1. Adobe Flex™ properties

Developers	Adobe™
Features	**Deployment platforms.** **Adobe Flash Player™:** Windows™, Mac OS™, Linux™, Solaris™, Android™ and BlackBerry Tablet OS™ +*0 **Adobe AIR™:** Windows™, Mac OS™, Android™ and Apple iOS™
	Development platforms Windows™, Mac OS™, Ubuntu™ and Fedora™ (Adobe Flex™ SDK 4.6)
Version	Current release 4.6
License	Proprietary (Free Adobe Flex™ SDK) and Mozilla™ Public License (MPL) 1.1 (Open Source Adobe Flex™ SDK)

The most important Adobe Flex™ properties are presented in Table 1.

Some success stories of using Adobe Flex™ on the development of well-known Web sites are described in Table 2.

The Adobe AIR™ runtime environment enables developers to use HTML, JavaScript™, Adobe Flash™, and ActionScript™ in order to build Web applications that run as stand-alone client applications without the Web browser constraints. In fact, it is a consistent and flexible runtime environment that allows deploying Adobe Flex™-based applications as desktop and native mobile applications. (Adobe AIR™, 2011).

Table 2. Success stories of Adobe Flex™

Website	Description
Honda™, www.buildyourhonda.eu	This website allows users to customize their motorcycles, while they can visualize the results. This application was built using the Adobe Creative Suite™, Adobe Flash Player™, Adobe Flex™, Adobe Flash Builder™, and Adobe Photoshop™.
Standard Chartered Bank™, standardchartered.com	In order to enable rich user experiences through an interactive and visually attractive website, the banking firm Standard Chartered Bank™ developed the user interface of its website using Adobe Flex™.
New York Times™, timesreader.nytimes.com / webapp / TimesReader.do	The dynamic digital reader of the New York Times™, called Times Reader 2.0, was developed using Adobe Flex™ and Adobe AIR™.
Philips Lighting™, www.lighting.philips.com	This RIA enables users to dynamically manage and manipulate large amounts of real-time information (e.g., sales figures, costs models, order histories) trough an interface developed with Adobe Flex™.

2.1.2. JavaFX™

JavaFX™ is an application platform for developing and deploying RIAs that runs on a variety of devices. It is fully integrated with the JRE (Java Runtime Environment), and it leverages the performance and ubiquity of the Java-based platform. JavaFX-based applications run on any desktop and Web browser running the JRE, they can easily integrate them to JME (Java Platform Micro Edition). JavaFX™ allows opening possibilities of applications development for mobile phones, TVs and other devices. Noteworthy that only the pre-2.0 versions have mobile devices-support.

The JavaFX™ platform includes the following components:

- **The FXML Language:** A scriptable, XML-based, markup language for building Java object graphs.
- **The JavaFX SDK:** Which includes:
  - The runtime environment of JavaFX™ Desktop (Desktop JavaFX™ Runtime).
  - APIs (APIs stands for Application Programming Interfaces) for JavaFX™.
  - The JavaFX™ compiler.
- **The NetBeans™ IDE for JavaFX™:** JavaFX™ technologies are integrated with the NetBeans™ IDE, a mature and powerful development environment, which allows developing, previewing, and debugging JavaFX™ applications more easily.
- **Java FX™ Scene Builder:** JavaFX™ Scene Builder is a commercial free software tool for visually designing JavaFX™ application GUIs (Graphical User Interface) in FXML. It is a component of the JavaFX™ platform which was initially developed by Sun microsystems™ and it is actually maintained by Oracle™ Corporation.

Table 3. JavaFX™ properties

Developers	Oracle™ Corporation	
Features	**Deployment platforms** Any operating system using JVM (Java Virtual Machine)	
	Development platforms Any operating system (JDK 1.7)	
Version	Current release 2.2	
License	BCL (Binary Code License)	

The most important JavaFX™ properties are presented in Table 3.

The advantages of using JavaFX™-based technology are listed below:

- Java™ programmers use standard Java™-based libraries in JavaFX™ applications.
- The JavaFX™ platform includes developer tools: the NetBeans™ IDE for JavaFX™ and the JavaFX™ plugin for NetBeans™, both as freeware. It also provides design tools: the JavaFX™ plugin for Adobe Photoshop™ and Adobe Illustrator™, as freeware (Oracle Corporation, 2011).

The disadvantages of using a JavaFX™-based technology are listed below:

- It is stacked on top of the JRE. The JRE is available on every major platform (and many minor ones). However, it is not ubiquitously installed. The same is true of Adobe Flex™/AIR™ and Silverlight™, of course, but Flash is a lighter-weight solution than the whole JRE+JavaFX™ and the latter is basically a default on the target platform anyway (Smeets et al., 2008).
- JavaFX™ is an immature technology in a field that has several more mature competitors such as Adobe Flex™/AIR™ and Silverlight™.

Table 4. Success stories of JavaFX™

Website	Description
Ubivent™, http://www.ubivent.com/en/start	Ubivent™ is a Europe's virtual event specialist offering a virtual event platform. The platform allows online communication between thousands of participants, providing a real event feeling. This platform is built on JSE (JSE stands for Java Standard Edition) 7 taking advantage of the Java Web Start technology.
Celer Technologies™, http://celer-tech.com/products/framework/	Celer Technologies™ is a global financial software company with knowledge on the financial technology sector. It offers an end-to-end financial trading framework featuring rich GUIs developed in JavaFX™ v. 2.2.
DooApp™, http://www.dooapp.com/index.php/fr/produits	DooApp™ is a software company headquartered in France. It specializes on the development of tools addressing the needs of green building professionals. It also offers a platform called Infiltrea™ for measuring airtightness. Infiltrea™ is built on JSE 6 making extensive use of JavaFX™.

Table 4 describes some success stories of using JavaFX™ on the development of well-known out-of-browser RIAs.

2.1.3. Silverlight™

Silverlight is a powerful development tool for creating engaging and interactive user experiences for Web and mobile applications. Silverlight™ is a free plug-in powered by the .NET framework and compatible with multiple browsers, devices and operating systems. It brings a new level of interactivity wherever the Web works (Microsoft, 2011a). Silverlight™ introduces support for running Silverlight™ applications with desktop features in the browser, video quality and performance improvements, and features that improve developer productivity. Microsoft Silverlight™ platform consists of two main frameworks, and an installation and updating component. These features are described in Table 5.

For further details, the elements of the .NET framework for Microsoft Silverlight™ are described in Table 6.

The advantages of using Microsoft Silverlight are listed below:

- It allows accessing to the .NET framework programming model in order to develop Silverlight™-based applications using dy-

Table 5. Microsoft Silverlight™ Features

Feature	Description
Basic Presentation Framework	Components and services related to the design of user interfaces and user interaction. This includes data provided by the user, user interface controls, multimedia playback, digital rights management, data links, and presentation features such as vector graphics, text, animations and images. It includes XAML (eXtensible Application Markup Language) language for the design of user interfaces.
.NET Framework for Silverlight™	The .NET framework contains components and libraries that provide data integration facilities, extensible Windows™ controls, networking, distribution (RSS / Atom) facilities, XML serialization, and garbage collection facilities. Moreover, it includes the LINQ (Language-Integrated Query) query language, the CLR (Common Language Runtime) and DLR (Dynamic Language Runtime) runtime environments.
Installation and Upgrade Component	Control installation and upgrade that simplifies the installation process of applying for new users. Subsequently, it provides low-impact automatic updates (Microsoft™, 2011a).

Table 6. .NET framework components for Microsoft Silverlight™

Element	Description
Data	It supports features of LINQ and LINQ for XML (XLinq) query languages, which facilitate the process of integrating data from disparate sources. It also supports the use of classes for XML-based serialization and data management.
Base Class Libraries (BCL)	The .NET framework provides a set of base class libraries which provide functions and features that can be used with any .NET framework-supported programming language, such as Visual Basic, C#, Visual C++, among others. The base class library contains standard programming features such as collections, XML parsing, data type definitions, I/O facilities (for reading and writing to files), reflection and globalization, to mention but a few. Furthermore, it contains some non-standard features, such as the LINQ query language, the ADO.NET class library (for database interactions), drawing capabilities, as well as forms and Web support.
Windows Communication Foundation (WCF)	Windows Communication Foundation provides a unified programming model for rapidly building service-oriented applications that communicate across the Web and the enterprise. It provides features to simplify the access to remote data and services. It includes support for cross-domain HTTP (Hypertext Transfer Protocol) requests, RSS (Really Simple Syndication) / Atom content syndication and JSON (JavaScript Object Notation), POX (Plain Old XML) and SOAP (Simple Object Access Protocol) formats.
Windows Presentation Foundation (WPF)	It provides a rich set of controls, such as a button, a calendar, check box, data grid, date picker, hyperlink button, list box, radio button, and ascroll viewer, among others.
Dynamic Language Runtime (DLR)	It supports dynamic compilation and execution of scripting languages, such as JavaScript and IronPython for scheduling applications based on Silverlight™. DLR also includes a model of compatibility with other languages to be used with Microsoft Silverlight™ (Microsoft, 2011b).

namic languages, such as IronPython and IronRuby, or compiled languages like C # and Visual Basic™ (Microsoft™, 2011b).

• Microsoft ™ Corporation provides two different IDEs: Microsoft Expression Studio™ for designers and Microsoft Visual Studio™ for developers; the latter is provided as freeware.

The disadvantages of using Microsoft Silverlight™ are listed below:

• Microsoft Silverlight™ does not have support for the Linux operating system; nevertheless, there is an open source implementation called Moonlight (version 2.0) for Linux™ and other operating systems based on Unix/X11 (Moonlight, 2011).
• The Microsoft Silverlight™ plugin has a lower market penetration for Flash Player™, and even lower than the JRE. However, Microsoft has distributed a plugin for Silverlight™ with the latest ver-

Table 7. Silverlight™ properties

Developers	Microsoft™ Corporation
Features	**Deployment platforms** Windows™, Mac OS™ and Windows Phone™
	Development platforms Windows™ and Mac OS™ (Silverlight™ SDK 5)
Version	Current release 5
License	Proprietary

sion of its operating system, Windows™ 7. According to the British Computer Society, Windows 7 is now installed on over 20% of personal computers connected to the Internet (b*cs, 2011*).

The most important Silverlight™ properties are presented in Table 7.

Table 8 presents some success stories of well-known websites developed using Silverlight™.

Table 8. Success stories of Silverlight™

Website	Description
Siemens™, siemensplmcampus.com	The website features a virtual exhibition of the Siemens™ PLM Software campus. Siemens™ PLM Software is a software development company specialized in Product Lifecycle Management. Users can know how the business works by interacting with the virtual buildings provided.
Mazda™, mazda.co.uk / car-configurator	This website shows a Mazda™ brand car customizer. It incorporates high-resolution images and external features, such as 360-degree views and zoomed interior views (Silverlight™ showcase, 2011).
Digital Mixup™, mixupdigital.com	Mixup™ is an online digital music and video store. The website aims to provide a rich user experience for seeking, purchasing, and downloading songs and albums.

2.1.4. OpenLaszlo™

OpenLaszlo™ is an open source platform for developing and delivering Web applications with usable user interfaces. The OpenLaszlo™ platform enables developers to develop applications with typical rich user interface capabilities of desktop client software taking advantage of the no-download Web deployment model. These applications run on all leading Web browsers on all leading desktop operating systems using XML-based code. OpenLaszlo™ is a product developed by Laszlo Systems and it was published under the Common Public License (CPL) (Smeets et al., 2008).

OpenLaszlo™ uses a proprietary programming language called LZX to define application user interfaces. LZX is an XML-based markup language that embeds JavaScript-based business logic (Smeets et al., 2008).

OpenLaszlo supports LZX code compilation into executable binaries for DHTML (DHTML stands for Dynamic HyperText Markup Language) and Flash execution environments (Laszlo Systems, Inc, 2013c).

The OpenLaszlo™ SDK consists of: 1) a built-in Java compiler, 2) a JavaScript-based library runtime, and 3) a Java-based servlet that provides additional services to running applications (Laszlo Systems, Inc, 2013c). These components are described in Table 9.

OpenLaszlo™ uses existing technological infrastructure and standards as shown in Figure 3. Two application deployment models are thouroughly described below:

- Mediated by the OpenLaszlo Server: the OpenLaszlo™ server is always running. It compiles the source code as needed, and it sends the resulting file (SWF or JavaScript) to the client in order to execute the ap-

Table 9. OpenLaszlo™ platform components

Component	Description
OpenLaszlo™ Compiler	It compiles LZX files into executable binaries for specific environments. OpenLaszlo™ currently covers Flash (SWF format) versions 8.9 and 10, as well as DHTML.
OpenLaszlo™ Servlet	It intercepts application requests for traditional media types and for SOAP and XML-RPC Web services.
Laszlo™ Foundation Class (LFC)	It is a runtime library that includes user interface components rich, data binding facilities, and network services, among other features (Laszlo Systems, Inc, 2013a).

Figure 3. Deployment model for OpenLaszlo™ platform

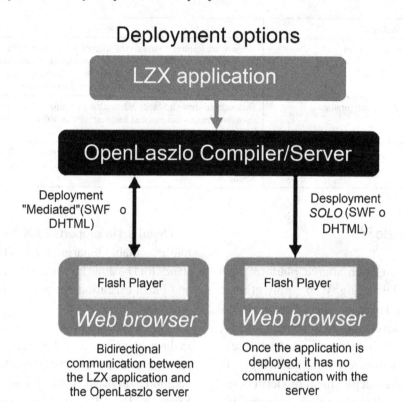

plication either using the Flash Player™ plugin or directly in a Web browser. The OpenLaszlo™ server intercepts application requests through the use of a variety of protocols.

- SOLO (stands for Standalone OpenLaszlo Output): the LZX source code is pre-compiled into either a stand-alone SWF file that can be placed within an HTTP Web server, or into a JavaScript-based file. Therefore, OpenLaszlo™-based applications can directly communicate with other servers using the SOLO deployment model. (Laszlo Systems, Inc, 2013a).

The advantages of using OpenLaszlo™ are listed below:

Table 10. OpenLaszlo™ properties

Developers	Laszlo Systems™
Features	**Deployment platforms** Any operating system
	Development platforms Any operating system
Version	Current release 4.9.0
License	Common Public License

- OpenLaszlo™ is an open source platform.
- The OpenLaszlo™ architecture enables different deployment models depending on the applications requirements (Theserverlabs, 2011).

Table 11. Success stories of OpenLaszlo™

Website	Description
Walmart™, walmart.com	The Walmart™ multinational used this open source technology to redesign its website, adding rich functionality (Laszlo Systems, Inc, 2013b).
Gliffy™, gliffy.com	It is a Web-based and free CASE (Computer Aided Software Engineering) tool offered as an alternative to commercial CASE tools, such as Microsoft Visio™. This application was entirely developed using OpenLaszlo™. This provides rich capabilities such as drag and drop (Laszlo Systems, Inc, 2013b).
Fnac™, fnac.com	Fnac™ is an international company headquartered in France, and it is specialized in electronics and entertainment software sales. Fnac™ is an online shopping cart developed in OpenLaszlo™ allows users to easily compare deals and options before making a buy decision (Laszlo Systems, Inc, 2013b).

The main disadvantage of using OpenLaszlo™ is that the OpenLaszlo™-based applications performance can be affected when SOLO deployment model is used (Laszlo Systems, Inc, 2013a). The most important OpenLaszlo properties are presented in Table 10.

Table 11 describes several success stories of well-known websites developed using OpenLaszlo™.

2.2. JavaScript-Based Frameworks

JavaScript is an object-oriented scripting language used for defining Web browser-based applications client-side. JavaScript enables Web developers to programmatically create objects on a Web page. It provides a platform for manipulating these objects on-the-fly. Since the introduction of the Asynchronous JavaScript and XML technology (AJAX), JavaScript has evolved to become far more useful. It currently brings a whole new level of interactivity to Web-based programming. In fact, prior to Ajax, any server-side processing or database access required the entire page to be refreshed or a new page to be rendered by the Web browser.

Ajax stands for Asynchronous JavaScript and XML, although the reference to XML is no longer valid as Ajax requests can return responses in other several formats, such as JSON. Ajax enables JavaScript to asynchronously submit an HTTP request to the Web server, and render the response without refreshing or rendering a new page. Furthemore, the developer can use the DOM (Document Object Model) to modify part of the Web page in order to display the changes or data returned as part of the HTTP response.

A JavaScript-based framework or library is a set of utilities and functions that make it much easier to produce cross-browser compatible JavaScript code. Each library can be extensively tested across different versions of existing Web browsers in order to ensure that a JavaScript-based RIA is similarly executed across different platforms (RibosoMatic, 2013).

According to the authors' point of view, the eight most popular JavaScript-based frameworks for RIAs development are presented below.

2.2.1. Dojo

Dojo is a framework that contains APIs and widgets (controls) to facilitate Web applications development using AJAX-based technology. Dojo contains an intelligent packaging system, UI effects, function libraries to drag and drop widgets APIs, event abstraction, storage APIs on the client, and interaction with AJAX-based APIs. Dojo also solves common usability issues, such as navigation and browser detection, URL withstands changes in the address bar (bookmarking), and the ability to lay down when AJAX / JavaScript is not supported on the client-side (RibosoMatic, 2013). Dojo is much more than a framework. Its creators

Table 12. Dojo properties

Developers	Alex Russell, 2004; David Schontzler, and Dylan Schiemann. It is equally important to mention support provided by the Dojo Foundation.
Sponsors	IBM™, Google™, AOL™ and Nexaweb™.
Features	Dojo supplements are prepackaged components consisting of JavaScript, HTML, and CSS assets, which can be used to develop RIAs. • Menus, tabs, and tooltips • Sortable tables, dynamic graphics, and 2D vector drawing • Animation effects and the possibility of creating personalized animations • Support for drag and drop • Forms and validation routines for parameters • Calendar, time and clock selector • Online rich text editor • Core components (dijit) accessible from earlier versions and screen reader
	Browser support Internet Explorer™ 6-9 Mozilla Firefox™ 3.6+ Safari™ 5+ Opera™ 10.5-12 Chrome™ 13+
Version	Stable release 1.8, October 10, 2012
License	Berkeley Software Distribution (BSD) y Academic Free License (AFL)

refer to it as the JavaScript toolset ("toolkit") that allows professionals to develop Web applications easily and quickly. Furthermore, Dojo has a free-software license type (Eguíluz Pérez, 2008). Dojo saves time and offers a powerful performance and scale in its development process. (Dojotoolkit, 2014). The most important Dojo properties are presented in Table 12.

By using Dojo, developers can build web pages more usable. This might manifest itself in a variety of ways. The web page should be faster. It should be better looking. It should be easier to operate by the user. It should help the user properly enter the required information, and the web page should be easier to navigate. Dojo provides enhancements in usability such as HTML form elements that provide additional functionality. These enhancements should make the current form elements behave in more useful ways. Performance can be improved either by making things run faster or by making things appear to run faster. The ideal way to make a process appear faster is to have the process run while the user is doing something else

rather than just having him wait for the process to complete. Ajax provides the ideal mechanism to support this technique. Dojo in conjunction with Ajax allow to a web page to asynchronously make data requests of the server while the user is continuing to work. The web page appears to the user to be faster and more responsive. Data validation can be improved by bringing the validation of data closer to the entry of data. Dojo supports the ability to send small validation requests to the server without requiring an entire form to be submitted. (Harmon, 2008).

2.2.2. jQuery

jQuery is a concise JavaScript library that simplifies HTML document traversing, event handling, animation, and Ajax interactions for rapid Web development. In fact, the jQuery compressed version is only 20 KB. Moreover, jQuery and Prototype share many ideas; they also have function names in common. However, their internals have some drastic differences. JQuery simplifies JavaScript

Table 13. jQuery properties

Developers	John Resig, 2006.
Sponsors	Microsoft™ and Nokia™ companies announced that this library would be included in their platforms. Microsoft™ would add it in the Visual Studio™ version 3 IDE, enabling ASP.NET and ASP.NET MVC-based development. On tbe other hand, Nokia would integrate the library within the Web Run-Time platform.
Features	• Selecting DOM elements • Interactivity and DOM tree changes, including support for CSS 1-3 and basic XPath plugin • Events • Handling the CSS style sheet • Effects and animations • Custom Animations • AJAX • Supports extensions • Various Utilities as browser information, operating with objects and vector functions for common routines, etc. (jQuery, 2012)
	Browser support Internet Explorer™ 6+ Mozilla Firefox™ 2.0+ Safari™ 3+ Opera™ 10.6+ Chrome™ 8+
Version	Stable release 1.8.3, November 13, 2012
License	General Public License (GPL) y Massachusetts Institute of Technology License (MIT)

programming - including AJAX calls and DOM manipulation -, while the jQuery documentation is very complete and includes many examples (Eguíluz Pérez, 2008). The most important jQuery properties are presented in Table 13.

jQuery has been considered as the best option for the web development community. This has been reflejected in the developmet of well-known major websites such as MSNBC, and well-regarded open source projects including SourceForge, Trac, and Drupal.

In comparison with other toolkits that are focused on JavaScript techniques jQuery aims to change the way that web developers think about creating rich functionality in their web pages. Rather than spending time juggling the complexities of advanced JavaScript, designers can leverage their existing knowledge of Cascading Style Sheets (CSS), Extensible Hypertext Markup Language (XHTML), and good old straightforward JavaScript to manipulate web page elements

directly, making more rapid development a reality (Bibeault & Katz, 2008).

2.2.3. MooTools

MooTools is a compact and modular Object-Oriented JavaScript framework designed for intermediate and advanced JavaScript developers. It permits writing powerful, flexible, and cross-browser code with itswell-documented and coherent API (Mootools, 2012). MooTools is released under the Open Source MIT software license, which provides de oportunity to use it and modify it in every circumstance. The most important MooTools properties are presented in Table 14.

Some frameworks are focused on re-creating a somewhat traditional inheritance model and MooTools is focused on this and highly encourages code reuse and develop modular designs. JavaScript has a prototypal inheritance model, and

Table 14. Mootools properties

Developers	The MooTools Dev Team
Sponsors	Unknown
Features	MooTools includes many components. A remarkable one is the download application available on MooTools website that allows users to download only the parts of the library that they plan to use, including dependencies. Users can also choose to download the compression level of the file. Some of the component categories of … are outlined below: • **Core:** it is a collection of support functions that makes use of the other components. • **Class:** it is the base library for MooTools object instantiation • **Natives:** it is a collection of improvements to native JavaScript object by adding I functionality, compatibility, and new methods that simplify the code. • **Element:** it has many improvements and compatibility to the HTML object. • **Effects:** Advanced API to encourage Elements • **Remote:** it provides an interface for XHR requests, and tools for JSON Cookie. • **Window:** it provides an interface, valid for any browser, for customer information, such as window size.
	Browser support Internet Explorer™ 6+ Mozilla Firefox™ 2+ Safari™ 3+ Opera™ 9+ Chrome™ 4+
Version	Stable release 1.4.1 October 6, 2011
License	MIT

MooTools creates a structure to take advantage of this model in a way that is more familiar to Java developers (Newton, 2008).

2.2.4. Prototype

Prototype takes the complexity out of client-side Web programming. It was built to solve real-world problems. It also adds useful extensions to the Web browser-scripting environment and provides Ajax and DOM APIs. Prototype is a JavaScript-based framework that aims to ease development of dynamic Web applications. It offers a familiar class-style object-oriented framework, extensive Ajax support, higher-order programming constructs, and easy DOM manipulation. It was created by Sam Stephenson in February 2005 as part of the foundation for Ajax support in Ruby on Rails. Prototype is implemented as a single JavaScript file, usually named prototype.js. Prototype is also distributed as part of larger projects, such as Ruby on Rails, script.aculo.us and Rico. Nowadays, it is

Table 15. Prototype properties

Developers	Sam Stephenson and Prototype Core Team
Sponsors	Unknown
Features	Prototype enables to deal with Ajax calls in a very easy, fun, and especially safe way (cross-browser). In addition to simple requests, this module also deals smartly with JavaScript code returned from a server and provides helper classes for polling. Ajax functionality is contained in the global Ajax object. The transport for Ajax requests is XmlHttpRequest, with browser differences safely abstracted from the user. Actual requests are made by creating instances of the Ajax. Request object.
	Browser support Internet Explorer™ 6+ Mozilla Firefox™ 1.5+ Safari™ 2.0.4+ Opera™ 9+ Chrome™ 2+
Version	Stable release 1.7.1 June 5, 2012
License	MIT

used by 3.9% of all websites, which makes it one of the most popular JavaScript libraries (Prototypejs, 2014). The most important Prototype properties are presented in Table 15.

It might seem odd to state that a JavaScript library can extend the language in which it was written, but that is exactly what Prototype does. JavaScript provides a mechanism known as prototype-based inheritance (from which this library derived its name). In fact, several scripting languages provide features for extending the base objects of the language. Ruby does it, and many of the extensions provided by Prototype are borrowed from Ruby. Once could describe Prototype's goal as making JavaScript feel more like Ruby (Crane, Bibeault & Locke, 2007).

2.2.5. Qooxdoo

Qooxdoo is a JavaScript library that offers many facilities for developing advanced JavaScript-based interfaces, including a debug console, event management, and source control, among others. It is supported by the most current versions of popular Web browsers, and it is released under a GNU Lesser General Public License (LGPL) free

Table 16. Qooxdoo properties

Developers	qx community
Sponsors	Unknown
Features	• It allows developers to abstract HTML, CSS, and DOM-based applications. • Object Oriented Programming • Cross-browser • AJAX • Native desktop look and feel
	Browser support Internet Explorer™ 6+ Mozilla Firefox™ 2+ Safari™ 3.0+ Opera™ 9+ Chrome™ 2+
Version	Stable release 1.0.1 January 27, 2010
License	LGPL and Eclipse Public License (EPL)

software license (RibosoMatic, 2013). Qooxdoo is a comprehensive and innovative framework for RIAs development. Furthermore, Qooxdoo is an object-oriented and JavaScript-based programming language for developing cross-browser applications where any expertise in HTML, CSS, or DOM is not required. It includes a set of development tools, a platform-independent GUI toolkit and an advanced client-server communication (Qooxdoo, 2014). The most important Qooxdoo properties are presented in Table 16.

Qooxdoo is a universal JavaScript framework with a coherent set of individual components and a powerful toolchain. It is open source under liberal licenses, and supported by one of the world's leading web hosts, 1&1(Qooxdoo, 2014).

2.2.6. Rico

Rico is a functions library for creating Javascript-based RIAs. It is object-oriented, which makes it easy to refactor Web application user interfaces to rich user interfaces (Openrico, 2014). Rico provides responsive animations for smooth effects and transitions that can communicate user interface changes more interactively than traditional Web applications. Furthermore, this JavaScript library provides a very simple interface in order to register Ajax request handlers as well as HTML elements or JavaScript objects as Ajax response objects. From this perspective, multiple elements and/or objects may be updated as the result of one Ajax request (RibosoMatic, 2013). Rico is based on Prototype, and it includes networking facilities, complex user interface controls - such as calendars and trees -, drag and drop functionality, and user interface effects. Moreover, Rico is released freely and as an open-source under the Apache 2.0 software license for either personal or commercial use. The most important Rico properties are presented in Table 17.

Table 17. Rico properties

Developers	Richard Cowin and OpenRico.org
Sponsors	Open Rico.org and Sabre Airline Solutions
Features	**Components** Rico 2.0 extends the component set from the previous versions. For instance, The live grid component has been expanded to include filtering, column resizing, and several more features. The core of Rico 2.0 has been designed to enable custom components to be more easily built. **Animation Effects** Rico 2.0 provides responsive animation for smooth effects and transitions that can communicate user interface changes more interactively than traditional Web applications. Unlike most effects, Rico 2.0 animation can be interrupted, paused, resumed, or have other effects applied to it in order to enable quick responsive interaction, which otherwise, the user would not have time to wait for. **Behaviors** Rico can be used to create components that behave similarly to those found in Adobe Flex™ and OpenLaszlo™. **Styling** Rico provides several cinematic effects, as well as some simple visual style effects in a very simple interface.
	Browser support Internet Explorer™ 5.5+ Mozilla Firefox™ 1.5+ Safari™ 2.0.3+ Opera™ 9+ Chrome™ 2+ The Drag and Drop is not supported on Safari™.
Version	Stable release 3.0.9 June 4, 2012
License	Apache 2.0

Table 18. Sencha ExtJS properties

Developers	Jack Slocum, Brian Moeskau, Aaron Conran and Rich Waters, created as Ext JS
Sponsors	On June 15, 2010 it was announced that Ext JS, jQTouch and Raphaël would be merged in order to give rise to a new organization called Sencha. Ext JS is still available separately at the new website along with Sencha, Sencha Touch, Ext GWT, Ext Designer, Animator and Sencha Ext Core.
Features	There is a set of components (widgets) to be included within a Web application. Some of these components are listed below: • Tables and text areas • Fields for dates • Numeric fields • Combos • Radiobuttons and checkboxes • HTML Editor • Data elements (with read-only modes, sortable data, columns that can be blocked and dragged, among other features) • Data Tree • Tabs • Toolbar • Windows-style menus • Panels divisible into sections • Sliders • Graphics Several of these components are able to communicate with the server-side using AJAX. Sencha ExtJS also contains features that allow adding interactivity to HTML-based web pages, some examples are: • Dialogs • QuickTips show validation messages and information on individual fields.
	Browser support Internet Explorer™ 6+ Mozilla Firefox™ 3.6+ Safari™ 4+ Opera™ 11+ Chrome™ 10+
Version	Stable release 4 April 4, 2011
License	GNU GPL version 3, comercial

2.2.7. Sencha ExtJS

It is another popular JavaScript-based framework. It began as an addition to the Yahoo!™ YUI™ library. In addition to its common utilities, Sencha ExtJS includes a number of ready-to-use user interface components. Sencha is released under either as free software under the General Public License (GNU GPL) or as commercial software aimed at providing technical support (Eguíluz Pérez, 2008). Sencha is a lightweight cross-browser JavaScript library that promotes high performance and allows developers to develop dynamic Web pages and rich user interfaces (Sencha, 2011). It was formerly called Ext JS before it was acquired by Sencha™ Inc. Therefore, it is still possible to find Ext JS reference on the Web, as well as information that can cause misinterpretation mistaking a framework which is actually still the same. The most important Sencha ExtJS properties are presented in Table 18.

Sencha Ext JS is one of the industry's most powerful desktop application development platforms with unparalleled cross-browser compatibility, advanced MVC architecture, plugin-free charting, and modern UI widgets (Sencha, 2014).

2.2.8. X-Library

It is a collection of loosely-bound, cross-browser, Javascript functions and objects. (RibosoMatic,

Table 19. X-Library properties

Developers	Michael Foster and Cross-Browser
Sponsors	cross-browser.com
Features	The many X Demos demonstrate how to use **X** in a variety of Javascript applications - from simple to complex. Javascript-based unobtrusive codes can be found in some features, such as menus, event-handling demos, form enhancements, debugging tools, dynamic layouts, and much more. There are several animation demos illustrating several different animation techniques. ***X Documentation*** The X Viewer provides comprehensive documentation for all **X** functions and objects - source, syntax, arguments, dependencies, links to demos, and more. X does not implement its own object or event models. **X Tools** **XAG** is a library file aggregator. XAG scans application files and creates a custom **X** library file, which contains only those **X** variables, functions, and objects (X symbols) used in an application. **XPP** is a simple text preprocessor. It supports conditional output and text replacement. These features enable to perform obfuscation and conditional compilation. **Browser support** Internet Explorer™ 7-9 Mozilla Firefox™ 3.5+ Safari™ 4.0+ Opera™ 10.6+ Chrome™ 4+
Version	Stable release 4.23 May 14, 2011
License	GNU LGPL

2013).It contains core DOM/Style functions, unobtrusive enhancements, utility functions, and objects such as menus and tab panels. It also contains some some experimental stuff. X-Library has been extensively tested on a wide range of operating systems and browsers. X-Library is distributed as free software under the GNU Lesser General Public License (LGPL) software license, even for commercial projects. However, there are some limitations and requirements (Cross-browser, 2014). Table 19 presents the most important X-Library properties.

3. CONCLUSION

It important to notice that the purpose of this section was not to determine which of the frameworks presented is better or worse. Instead, the goal of this chapter was to outline the main characteristics of each framework. This will help developers make the right decision about the RIA framework that best suits the features of the project they will carry out including budget, calendar as well as functional and non-functional requirements.

Therefore, since new functionalities are constantly added to the frameworks herepresentedit is recommended that developpers constantly check and update the frameworks to obtain the new versions.

Moreover, some of the JavaScript-based frameworks are able to work together and they complement each other; however, this is not possible with other frameworks and it is almost impossible to consider in the case of non-JavaScript-based frameworks.

Regarding these non-JavaScript-based frameworks, it is imperative to consider the type of application to be developed, i.e., the application architecture, because these frameworks are targeted at different functionalities, from standalone applications to traditional Web applications with RIA-makeover. Furthermore, the intended runtime environment must also be considered, since these frameworks commonly require Web browser plug-ins or a desktop runtime environment depending on the application type. Finally, in the specific case of Web-browser based RIAs development, the framework capabilities and limitations related to both the database storage distribution and the business logic distribution are key issues.

REFERENCES

Adobe AIR. (2011). *Adobe AIR*. Retrieved January 30, 2011, from http://www.adobe.com/products/air/

Adobe. (2011). *Flex overview*. Retrieved January 29, 2011, from http://www.adobe.com/products/flex/overview

BCS. *(2011). Windows 7 market share excedes 20% mark*. Retrieved February 6, 2011, from http://www.bcs.org/content/conWebDoc/38577

Bibeault, B., & Katz, Y. (2008). jQuery in Action. Greenwich, CT: Manning Publications Co.

Crane, D., Bibeault, B., & Locke, T. (2007). *Prototype and Scriptaculous in Action*. Greenwich, CT: Manning Publications Co.

Cross-Browser. (2014). *X-library*. Retrieved January, 2014, from http://www.cross-browser.com/

Dojotoolkit. (2014). *Dojotoolkit*. Retrieved February, 2014, from http://www.dojotoolkit.org/

Eguíluz Pérez. J. (2008). *Introducción a AJAX*. Librosweb. Retrieved February, 2014, from http://librosweb.es/ajax/

Flash Player. (2012). *Statistics*. Retrieved December 18, 2012, from http://www.adobe.com/mx/products/flashruntimes/statistics.html

Harmon, J. E. (2008). *Dojo: Using the Dojo JavaScript Library to Build Ajax Applications*. Addison Wesley Professional.

JQUERY. (2012). *Documentation*. Retrieved September, 2012, from http://docs.jquery.com/

Laszlo Systems, Inc. (2013a). *Architecture*. Retrieved January 29, 2013, from: http://www.openlaszlo.org/architecture

Laszlo Systems, Inc. (2013b). *OpenLaszlo Architecture*. Retrieved February 6, 2011, from: http://www.openlaszlo.org/lps4.9/docs/developers/architecture.html

Laszlo Systems, Inc. (2013c). *OpenLaszlo Showcase*. Retrieved February 6, 2011, from: http://www.openlaszlo.org/showcase

McCune, D., & Subramaniam, D. (2008). Getting to Know Flex. In *Adobe Flex 3.0 for Dummies* (pp. 9–16). Indianapolis, IN: Wiley Publishing, Inc.

Microsoft. (2011a). *Arquitectura de Silverlight*. Retrieved January 30, 2011, from: http://msdn.microsoft.com/es-es/library/bb404713(v=VS.95).aspx

Microsoft. (2011b). *Información general sobre Silverlight*. Retrieved January 30, 2011, from: http://msdn.microsoft.com/es-es/library/bb404700(v=VS.95).aspx

Moonlight. (2011). *Moonlight*. Retrieved January 30, 2011, from: http://www.mono-project.com/Moonlight

Mootools. (2012). *Mootools*. Retrieved August, 2012, from: http://mootools.net/

Newton, A. (2008). *MooTools Essentials: The Official MooTools Reference for JavaScript and Ajax Development*. Berkely, CA: Apress.

Openrico. (2014). *Openrico*. Retrieved August, 2014, from: http://openrico.org/

Oracle Corporation. (2011). *Develop Expressive Content with the JavaFX Platform*. Retrieved January 29, 2011, from: http://javafx.com/about/overview/index.jsp

Prototypejs. (2014). *Prototypejs*. Retrieved January, 2014, from: http://www.prototypejs.org/

Qooxdoo. (2014). *Qooxdoo*. Retrieved April, 2014, from: http://qooxdoo.org/

RibosoMatic. (2013). *Listado de librerías, frameworks y herramientas para AJAX, DHTML y JavaScript*. Retrieved August, 2013, from: http://www.ribosomatic.com/articulos/top-librerias-ajax-dhtml-y-javascript/

Sencha. (2014). *Sencha ExtJS*. Retrieved April, 2014, from: http://www.sencha.com/products/extjs/

Smeets, B., Boness, U., & Bankras, R. (2008). Introducing Rich Internet Applications (RIAs). In *Beginning Google Web Toolkit: From Novice to Professional* (pp. 1–19). New York: Apress.

Theserverlabs. (2011). *Rich Internet Applications, Frameworks evaluation*. Retrieved February 6, 2011, from: http://www.theserverlabs.com/brochures/RIA_Frameworks-TSL-evaluation.pdf

Toffetti, G., Comai, S., Preciado, J. C., & Linaje, M. (2011). State-of-the Art and trends in the Systematic Development of Rich Internet Applications. *Journal of Web Engineering*, *10*(1), 70–86.

Viveros García, M. C., & García Godoy, D. (2009). *Elaboración de una guía para el desarrollo de aplicaciones en extjs. (Unpublished thesis)*. Instituto Tecnológico de Orizaba.

ADDITIONAL READING

Adobe. (2012). *Flex, What is Flex?* Retrieved September, 2012, from http://www.adobe.com/es/products/flex.html

Microsoft. (2012). *Silverlight 5*. Retrieved September, 2012, from http://www.microsoft.com/silverlight/

Oracle Corporation. (2012). *JavaFX*. Retrieved September, 2012, from http://www.oracle.com/technetwork/java/javafx/overview/index.html

KEY TERMS AND DEFINITIONS

Framework: A software-defined structure on which other software project is designed and developed.

HyperText Markup Language (HTML): Markup language for developing Web pages. It is a standard that serves as a reference for the development of Web pages in different versions, it defines a basic structure and a code (HTML code).

JavaScript-Based Frameworks: Frameworks which were developed in the JavaScript-based programming language such as *Dojo*, *Prototype*, and *Mootools*.

Non-JavaScript-Based Frameworks: Frameworks which were developed in its own programming language such as *AbobeFlex*™, *JavaFX*, and *Silverlight*™.

RIA Framework: These are frameworks for Rich Internet Applications development.

Standalone RIAs: They are RIAs that can be deployed inside or outside of a Web browser and can be executed on/offline.

Traditional Web Applications: These are software applications which are displayed in a Web browser, and in which each user interaction with the application means fully recharge the application to display the updated information.

Chapter 3
Software Development Methodologies for Traditional Web Applications and RIAs

ABSTRACT

Chapter 3 presents a review of the state-of-the-art on methodologies for RIAs development. For this purpose, methodologies for traditional Web applications development are firstly presented, since, in some cases, methodologies for RIAs development are either extensions of existing Web (and hypermedia) methodologies or new UI design methods used on top of already existing Web methodologies. New approaches covering the RIAs features without relying on legacy Web models are also discussed. Some examples of Web development are UWE (UML-Based Web Engineering), which became UWE-R (UWE for RIAs), and WebML Extension, which is an extension of WebML (Web Modeling Language). These methodologies had to be modified in order to add new features to support the needs of RIAs development. Some other methodologies for RIAs development are RUX Method, OOH4RIA, OOHDM Extension, and PPRD.

1. INTRODUCTION

Software Engineering is the study and application of engineering to the design, development, and maintenance of software. The main issues of Software Engineering are design patterns, architectural styles, and software development methodologies. Hence, the importance of studying the different software development methodologies proposed in the literature for traditional Web applications and RIAs. According to the Oxford dictionary a methodology is *"a system of methods used in a*

special area of study or activity" and in this case it is about software development.

In the one hand, there are software development methodologies for traditional software development such as RUP (Rational Unified Process), Scrum and XP (eXtreme Programming). In the other hand, there are also software development methodologies for Web development such as UWE (UML-based web engineering), WebML (Web Modeling Language) and OOHDM (Object-Oriented Hypermedia Design Method), among others. However, the aforementioned software de-

DOI: 10.4018/978-1-4666-6437-1.ch003

velopment methodologies for Web development do not consider the RIAs (Rich Internet Applications) features, i.e. they do not cover the development aspects of this application kind as they are only used on traditional Web applications, omitting aspects of RIAs. Preciado et al. (Preciado et al., 2005) discussed about the quantity and type of software. development methodologies and tools that have been proposed for the design and development of Web applications. However, traditional Web applications continue to be insufficient to support the interaction and presentation of the features demanded by the user. Recently, RIAs provided a solution to these problems as they provide new levels of interactivity and presentation. The use of RIAs is exponentially growing; however there is a serious problem: lack of complete software development methodologies for this type of application. Preciado et al. (Preciado et al., 2005) described the main characteristics needed to model RIAs and an assessment process was proposed in order to obtain a suitable methodology to be able for achieving this goal. This process was used to evaluate how suitable some of the existing methodologies are and to demonstrate that each one has very few RIA characteristics. From this perspective, a new methodology is necessary or an extension of an existing one. Preciado et al. (Preciado et al., 2005) determined that none of the methodologies in these areas were suitable for modeling RIAs. RIAs offer new multimedia and interactivity features. Preciado et al. (Preciado et al., 2005) discussed that multimedia as much as hypermedia constitutes fields that are required to help in the identification of new software development methodologies for RIAs. RIAs have been of great importance on web development over the last few years. For this reason, diverse studies have proposed new development methodologies and/or extensions of existing methodologies for RIAs development.

In this chapter, a set of application development methodologies is presented. These methodologies are divided into two main groups, the first group is a set of methodologies used for traditional Web applications, and at the second group the methodologies for RIAs development are presented. In this second group is easy to identify that most methodologies are extensions of methodologies used in traditional Web applications to which had to make adjustments for supporting features of RIAs.

2. SOFTWARE DEVELOPMENT METHODOLOGIES FOR TRADITIONAL WEB APPLICATIONS

Firstly, the traditional methodologies for Web development are presented since they were the pioneers for the creation of new methodologies or extensions of existing methodologies to meet the needs for RIA development. Escalona and Koch (Escalona & Koch, 2004) carried out a review of methodologies for Web development, an improved extension of this review is presented below.

2.1. WSDM: Web Site Design Method

WSDM is a user-centered approach for the development of Web sites that models the application based on the information requirements of the users' groups (Detroyer & Leune, 1998). The development process is divided into four phases. WSDM phases are presented in Figure 1 and they are described below:

- *User modeling*, where users are classified and grouped in order to study system requirements according to each user group,
- *Conceptual design*, where a UML class diagram is designed to represent the static model of the system and a navigational model is designed to represent the possibilities of navigation,
- *Implementation design*, where models of the conceptual design are easily translated into an abstract language to be understood by the computer, and

Figure 1. Overview of the WSDM phases

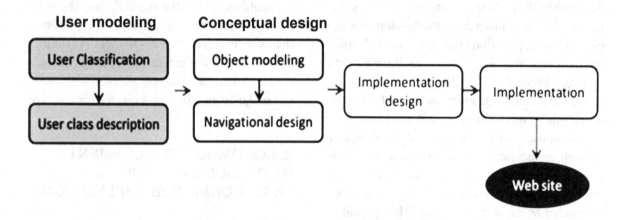

- *Implementation,* where the implementation design result is written in a specific computer programming language.

The most important phase is user modeling. It aims on the identification of the different users' roles by performing the following two tasks:

- *Users' classification* is the identification of the potentials users/visitors of the website and their classification according to their interests and navigation preferences. WSDM proposes to analyze the organization environment where the application will be used, and it focuses the attention on the stakeholders of the business processes supported by the application. In WSDM, the relationships between stakeholders and business process activities performed are graphically represented by conceptual maps of roles and activities.
- *Users' group description* is the detailed description of the users' groups identified in the previous task. The information requirements, functional requirements and security requirements for each user's group are described with the help of a data dictionary.

The remaining phases in the WSDM process are based on the users' classification of this first phase.

2.2. SOHDM: Scenario-Based Object-Oriented Hypermedia Design Methodology

The SOHDM approach was the first approach emphasizing the importance of a process that allows capturing and defining the applications requirements to the analysts (Lee et al., 1998). SOHDM has similarities with OOHDM (Schwabe & Rossi, 1998), but it proposes a requirement specification based on scenarios. The SOHDM architecture is presented in Figure 2.

The following six tasks are performed during the SOHDM life cycle; for practical purposes, only the first one is relevant:

1. *Analysis,* where requirements are described by using scenarios;
2. *Object model realization,* where a UML class diagram is built in order to present the static structure of the system;
3. *View design,* which expresses how the system will be presented to the user;

Figure 2. Overview of the SOHDM architecture

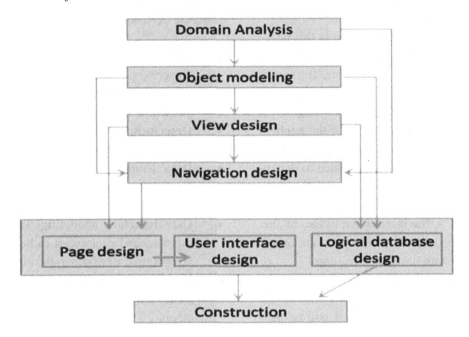

4. *Navigational design*, where a navigational class model is developed in order to express the possibilities of navigation in the system;

5. *Realization of the implementation*, where web pages, the interface and the database are developed; and, finally,

6. *Construction of the system*, where the system is built.

The requirements definition starts on designing a context diagram, similar to the DFD (Data Flow Diagrams) defined by Yourdon (Yourdon, 1989). To build this context diagram, the analyst has to identify the external entities that communicate with the application, and the events that trigger the communication between these entities and the application. The set of events is specified as a table showing the entities that participate in an event. SOHDM proposes associating a scenario with each event. Scenarios are graphically represented by using a proprietary notation called SAC (Scenario Activity Chart). A scenario describes the interaction process between the user and the application, when an event triggers an activity. It specifies the activity flow, objects involved and transactions performed.

SOHDM proposes a process to get the conceptual model of the application out of these scenarios. The proposed conceptual model is represented by a UML class diagram. The next step in the SOHDM development process is the regrouping of these classes with the objective of obtaining a navigational class diagram.

2.3. RNA: Relationship-Navegational Analysis

RNA is a methodology that offers a sequence of steps for developing Web applications mainly focusing on analysis (Bieber et al., 1998). The RNA phases are:

• **Phase 1 – Environment Analysis:** The objective is to analyze the audience's characteristics. Stakeholders of the application are identified and classified in different groups according to their roles (similar to the user modeling phase of WSDM presented in Figure 1).

- **Phase 2 – Element Analysis:** In this phase all elements of interest to the application are identified, e.g. documents, forms, information, mock-ups, among others.
- **Phase 3 – Meta-Knowledge Analysis:** It achieves to build a schema of the application. RNA proposes to identify objectives, processes and operations related to the application, and to describe the relationships among those elements.
- **Phase 4 – Navigation Analysis:** In this phase, the schema of the previous one is enlarged with navigation features.
- **Phase 5 – Implementation Analysis:** Consists of the identification of how the models described in phase 4 will be produced in a computable language (Bieber et al., 1998).

RNA only provides some guidelines of the actions to be performed in each phase. Neither modeling concepts nor a notation is proposed, but the RNA approach is one of the methodologies focused on the importance of requirements specification in the development process of Web applications. It emphasizes the need of the separation between the analysis of conceptual requirements and the analysis of navigational requirements.

2.4. HFPM: Hypermedia Flexible Process Modeling

The HFPM presented by Olsina (Olsina, 1998) is a wide engineering-based approach, which includes analysis-oriented *descriptive* and *prescriptive* process modeling strategies. It includes technical, management, cognitive and participatory tasks. Therefore, HFPM provides guidelines for the planning and managing of a Web project covering the whole life cycle of a software project. It consists of thirteen phases where each phase HFPM defines a set of tasks. For practical purposes, Requirements

Model is the most relevant phase whose related tasks are defined as follows:

- **Problem Description:** HFPM does not prescribe a concrete technique to perform the problem description, e.g. natural language can be used.
- **Description of Functional Requirements:** It is covered by using use cases.
- **Data Modeling for the Identified Use Cases:** It proposes the design of a UML class diagram.
- **User Interface Modeling:** It implements sketches and prototypes to be used in the presentation of drafts to the customer.
- **Non-Functional Requirements Description:** such as security, performance, among others.

HFPM proposes on the one hand a detailed process to handle requirements. On the other hand, it does not prescribe specific techniques, which can be freely chosen by analysts and developers.

2.5. OOHDM: Object Oriented Hypermedia Design Model

OOHDM is a widely accepted method for Web applications development (Schwabe & Rossi, 1998), whose first versions were focused on the design phase and they did not include requirements engineering. The OOHDM phases are presented in Figure 3.

The processes in OOHDM are divided in four phases producing the following results:

1. The *conceptual model*, represented as a class model, is built in order to show the static aspect of the system.
2. The *navigational model* consists of a navigation class diagram and a navigation structure diagram. The first one represents the static possibilities of navigation in the system. The second one extends the navigation class

Figure 3. Overview of the OOHDM phases

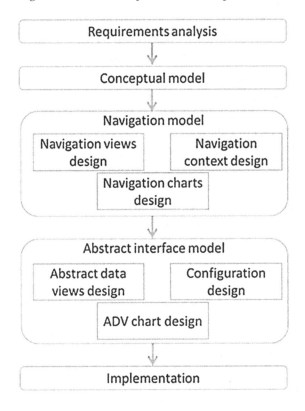

diagram by including access structures and navigation contexts.

3. The *abstract interface model* was developed by using a special technique named ADVs (Abstract Data Views) (Schwabe & Rossi, 1998).

4. The *implementation* consists in the implemented code and it is based on the previous models.

The capture and definition of requirements were introduced later in OOHDM by Vilain, Schwabe and Sieckenius (Vilain et al., 2000) who proposed the use of UIDs (User Interaction Diagrams). UIDs are based on the well-known technique of use cases. Use cases are used to capture the requirements but are considered in OOHDM as ambiguous and insufficient for the definition of the requirements of Web applications, use cases are mainly related to the interaction be-

tween the user and the system. Therefore, for the specification of the requirements, this approach suggests the refinement of use cases for building UIDs, which are used to graphically model the interaction between users and system without considering specific aspects of the interface. The process to get an UID from a use case is described very carefully in the approach.

2.6. UWE: UML-Based Web Engineering

UWE is a methodological approach for the development of Web applications based on the Unified Process (Jacobson et al., 1999) and (Booch et al., 1999). It is mainly based on the most relevant concepts provided by other methods, but a UML notation is defined (UML profile), that defines a systematic and semi-automatic design process (Hennicker & Koch, 2000).

UWE covers the whole life cycle of Web applications and focuses on adaptive applications. It includes a specific requirements engineering phase where requirements elicitation, specification and validation are handled as separate activities of the process. The final result of the capture phase of requierements in UWE is a use case model completed with documentation describing the users of the application, the adaptation rules, the interfaces and the details of the use case relevant for the use case implementation. The latter can be textually described or modeled by UML activity diagrams.

UWE classifies requirements into two groups: functional and non-functional. Functional requirements in UWE are:

- Content requirements.
- Structure requirements.
- Presentation requirements.
- Adaptation requirements.
- User model requirements.

Moreover, UWE proposes interviews, questionnaires and checklists as appropriated techniques for the requirements capture, and use cases, scenarios and glossaries for the requirements specification. To validate them, UWE proposes walk-through, audits and prototypes (Koch & Wirsing, 2001).

2.7. W2000

W2000 (Baresi et al., 2001) is an approach that also extends UML notation to model multimedia elements. These multimedia elements are inherited from HDM (Hypermedia Design Model) (Garzotto et al., 1993). The development process of W2000 is divided into three phases: requirements analysis,

hypermedia design and functional design. For practical purposes, the first one is described below.

The requirements analysis in W2000 is divided into two sub-activities: functional requirements analysis and navigational requirements analysis. The requirements elicitation starts with an analysis of the different user roles, i.e. the actors which will interact with the application. Every identified actor has his own navigation and functional requirements model. The latter model is represented by a UML use case model. The navigational requirements are modeled in another use case diagram representing the navigation possibilities of the actors. The graphic notation is defined as a UML extension. The W2000 model is presented in Figure 4.

Figure 4. W2000 model

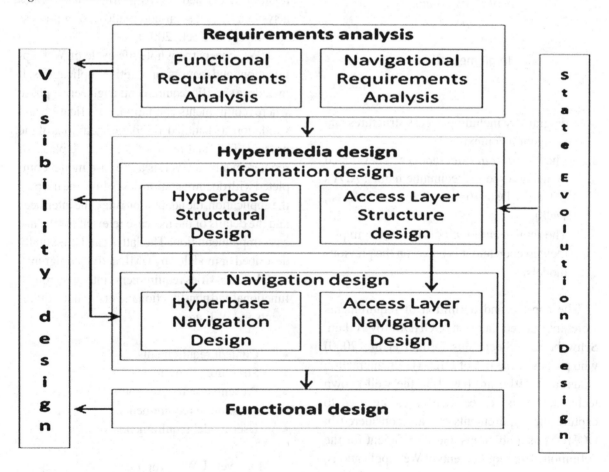

2.8. WebML: Web Modeling Language

The WebML is a high-level specification language for hypermedia applications. WebML follows the style of both, Entity-Relationship and UML offering a proprietary notation and a graphical representation by using the UML syntax. This notation is complemented with a set of activities to be performed for the development of Web applications, such as requirements specification, data design and hypertext design (Ceri et al., 2002).

The methodology is focused on requirements collection and requirements specification. It proposes the use of techniques, such as interviewing and analysis of documentation, but retrains from the use of prescriptive checklists for requirements capture. Requirements collection starts with user identification and personalization needs. In addition data requirements and functional as well non-functional requirements are gathered. The navigation or specific hypertext structuring requirements are not separately treated. Requirements specification (called requirements analysis) consists in a classical use case specification supplemented with a semi-structured textual description. The use of activity diagrams is proposed by this method to express the workflow of complex use cases. A template-based description and mockups (sketches) are suggested for the specification of the site view and the style guidelines. Finally, acceptance tests are mainly proposed to check non-functional requirements.

2.9. NDT: Navigational Development Techniques

NDT is a technique to specify and analyze the navigation aspects in Web applications. NDT is focused on the elicitation and specification techniques selected by NDT for the capture and definition of requirements. The requirements analysis workflow in NDT starts capturing requirements and studying the environment applying interviews,

brainstorming and JAD (Joint Application Development) techniques. In a second step, the system objectives are captured and described. Based on these objectives, the system requirements are identified; NDT classifies them into (Escalona et al., 2002):

- Storage information requirements.
- Actor requirements.
- Functional requirements.
- Interaction requirements.
- Non-functional requirements.

Interaction requirements are represented by phrases and visualization prototypes. Phrases show how the information of the system is retrieved and are represented by a special language named BNL (Bounded Natural Language) (Brisaboa et al., 2002). Visualization prototypes are used to represent the system navigation, data visualization and user's interaction.

The whole process to elicit and specify objectives and requirements proposed by NDT is mainly based on templates or patterns. In addition, it uses other requirements definition techniques like use cases and glossaries. The NDT approach proposes a different template for each kind of requirement, so requirements and objectives are described in a structured way. Some fields in the templates only accept specific values allowing a systematic process. The requirements specification workflow finishes with the revision of the requirements catalogue and the development of a trazability matrix which allows knowing whether the specification covers all the possible requirements.

In the context of the NDT project a case tool, called NDT-Tool, was developed. This tool supports the filling of the templates and automatic extraction of the design results out of the templates.

The NDT development process is a process that could be described as bottom-up. The NDT process is focused on a detailed engineering phase of requirements-driven objectives, which includes both the capture, as the definition and verification of requirements.

The process begins by defining the objectives. Based on these objectives, a process is described in order to capture and define different system requirements. These objetives are classified and treated depending on the type to which they belong. NDT divides requirements:

- **Storage Requirements:** Define what information, will be manage the system and how they relate to each other. NDT can also define natures of new data which will be used in the system.
- **Requirements of Stakeholders:** Define the roles that can interact in system and the relationships that may occur between them.
- **Functional Requirements:** Allow defining the system functionality.
- **Requirements of Interaction:** Define how information is displayed, how they can navigate the system and recovery criteria that are offered.
- **Non-Functional Requirements:** Include other system requirements (Escalona et al., 2002).

2.10. Design-Driven Requirements Elicitation

The Design-driven Requirements Elicitation is a part of the design-driven process proposed by Lowe and Eklund (Lowe & Eklund, 2002) in order to develop Web applications. It consists in capturing, defining and validating requirements during the design process, i.e. the design activities should be carried out in such a way that the requirements could be handled and managed at the same time. The process is based on prototyping in order to explore possible solutions and problems to be solved. Users and customers define the requirements based on the study of these prototypes. It is an iterative process, which consists in reducing

customers and clients' doubts. The cycle has three phases: evaluation, specification and construction.

This design-driven process was defined based on an exhaustive analysis of "best practices" in the development of Web commercial application. It treats all the requirements in the same manner. The requirements are: content, interface protocol, navigational structure, look and feel, data internal representation, versions, change control, security, content management, control access, efficiency, user monitoring, functionality support, system adaptation, user identification, among others.

3. SOFTWARE DEVELOPMENT METHODOLOGIES FOR RIAS

In the literature, some works have been reported in order to propose software development methodologies for RIAs. From this perspective, Busch and Koch (Busch & Koch, 2009) carried out a literature review of methodologies for RIA development. An extended version of this literature review is presented and discussed in order to establish software development methodologies for RIAs.

3.1. RUX Method

Preciado et al. (Preciado et al., 2007) discussed the difficulty of implementing a methodology of Engineering Software in RIA development. RIAs are obtaining great acceptance thanks to the facilities they provide to develop Web applications with multimedia, high levels of interactivity, collaborative work, and/or homogeneous presentation requirements at the client-side. Preciado et al. (Preciado et al., 2007) proposed an integrated Web Engineering approach based on WebML and the RUX-Model conceptual models for supporting a high-level design of these applications and their automatic code generation. The RUX method combines modeling of the presentational aspects of RIAs with an existing method for designing Web applications. UWE is complemented with the RUX method for the UI design. The approach consists of the transformation of UWE presentation model to a RUX abstract interface model (AIM), which is afterwards enriched with typical RIA user interface actions. In this approach, RIA features are introduced into models at a lower level of abstraction than in the current approach. The authors planned extend their research in two ways; the first one is by combining RUXModel with other models apart from WebML and the second one is to extend WebML and/or RUXModel to cover the entirety of the basic concepts of the different models identified on RIAs.

Preciado et al. (Preciado et al., 2008) proposed an approach based on RIA development through the combination of UWE, a method to model data and business logic, with RUX-Method for the modeling of the User Interfaces of the RIAs. The authors presented an approach based on the model for RIA development by combining UWE and RUX-Method. UWE is more suitable for model features i.e. data and business logic for Web applications and RUX-Method was applied to the design of the user interfaces of RIAs. This approach provides a simple way to enrich Web 1.0 applications that resembles Web 2.0. The approach considers the static and dynamic navigation in business processes. The future work includes an improvement of this approach through the inclusion of specific operations of RIAs, such as completing the data entry in text fields on the client-side, which it is still not possible with Web 1.0. The authors planned to extend the elements of the model for RUX-Method, for example presenting the client with the delivery of requests to the background server or to perform an operation and extend the UWE model elements to represent the corresponding data to server operations. Also, an expansion of the UWE description techniques is considered in order to include the requirements of RIA characteristics, such as animation, asynchronous communication between the client and the server. The general schema of RUX Method is shown in Figure 5.

Brambilla et al. (Brambilla et al., 2008) presented the methodology and the combination of conceptual models to cover the design and development of Web applications with the support of rich

Figure 5. Overview on the RUX method

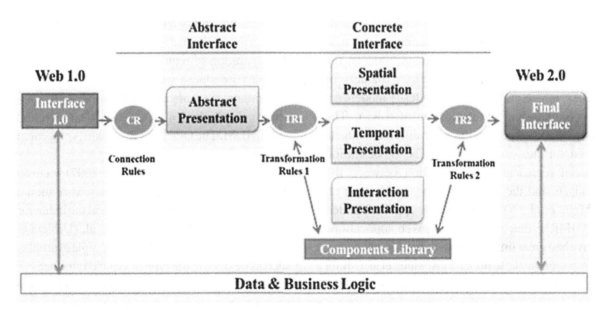

interfaces. To specify the design of high-level user tasks, the research used model business processes, which become data and the navigation model of a Web application, and a presentation model was applied to obtain a RIA. It used a standard modeling language to describe business workflows that are translated into WebML, a specification of a Web application implemented in accordance with the paradigm of a single typical page of RIAs. Finally, the characteristics of RUX-Method are integrated, refining the design of the rich interface. A methodology and a set of conceptual models to cover the design and development of RIAs were provided to achieve a high level in the design of the view that business process models use. A BPMN (Business Process Modeling Notation) language was translated into a WebML language to therefore integrate the characteristics of RUX-Method and this demonstrated how to refine rich interfaces. The combination of the proposed models enabled a fine design and a rich interaction. Due to the generality of this approach, the design of business based processes was applied to other hypertext browsing models and other presentation models. It is only necessary to specify the new assignments.

3.2. OOH4RIA

OOH4RIA extends the OOH method (Object-Oriented Hypermedia) introducing many new model elements for two additional models: the presentation and the orchestration models of RIAs, which complement the OO-H models for the domain and the navigation of a RIA. The presentation model captures the different widgets used for the user interface. The orchestration model represents the interaction between the widgets and the rest of the system. Meliá et al. (Meliá et al., 2008) used a new approach called OOH4RIA due to the fact that Web applications have had great limitations on their user interfaces. To overcome these limitations, Meliá et al. (Meliá et al., 2008) proposed richer and more efficient

graphics that are similar to those of desktop applications. However RIAs are complex and their development requires design and implementation. Moreover, RIAs development is a great challenge of the Web engineering as it requires modification and the introduction of new aspects. OOH4RIA uses a development process based on the model and that extends the OOH methodology. The OOH development process is described in Figure 6.

This introduces new structures and behavior models to constitute a complete RIA and to apply transformations that reduce the effort and accelerate the Web development. This approach was implemented in the GWT (Google Web Toolkit) framework. The approach generates Java-based code for the server-side application and, HTML and JavaScript for the client-side code. The OOHRIA models to OO-H models are similarly specified by using UML syntax by means of MOF (Meta-Object Facility) meta-models.

3.3. Object Oriented Hypermedia Design Method (OOHDM) Extension

Urbieta et al. (Urbieta et al., 2007) presented a new approach in the design of interfaces for RIAs. The approach used the ADV design model which enables to express a high level of abstraction from the structure and behavior of the User Interface. Furthermore, the use of advanced techniques for the separation of requirements enables to create complex interfaces with a simple composition. The authors presented the foundations of this approach, the fundamental steps and the integration of OOHDM. The OOHDM extension is presented in Figure 7.

Urbieta et al. (Urbieta et al., 2007) focused on OOHDM and on the ADV framework model designed to specify the structure and the behavior of RIA user interfaces. Urbieta et al. (Urbieta et al., 2007) demonstrated this with simple examples such as designing the type of typical interfaces of RIAs by using *ADVcharts*. The authors did this to

Figure 6. OOH4RIA development process

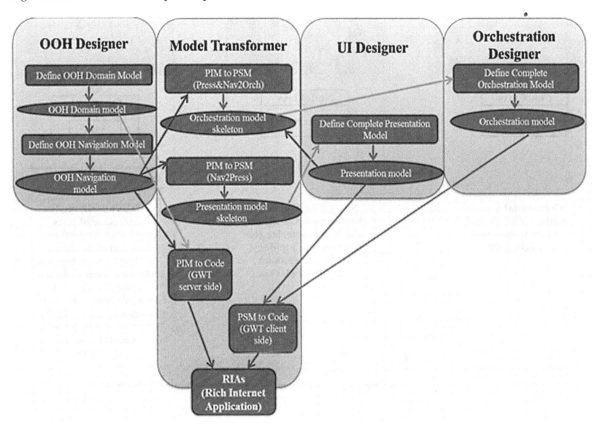

achieve the goal that their objects are shown or are hidden in the interface, i.e. how the information expands or contracts on the screen.

3.4. UWE-R

UWE-R (Machado et al., 2009) is a light-weighted extension of UWE for RIAs, covering navigation, process and presentation aspects. Hence, new modeling elements are defined that inherit structure and behavior from UWE elements. In contrast to many studies, UWE-R uses stereotypes for many of the extensions instead of meta-attributes. UWE-R is shown in Figure 8.

3.5. WebML Extension

With regard to extensions of existing methods, Bozzon et al. proposed in (Bozzon et al., 2006) the modeling of distributed data and events in data-intensive RIAs focusing on client or server side actions. WebML distinguishes between data distributed on client-side and server-site as well as persistent and temporary objects. In particular, WebML was extended by enriching data specifications with two dimensions: (1) data location and (2) data duration. WebML extension´s process is described in Figure 9.

Location can be either server-side or client-side; duration can be persistent or temporary. WebML introduces new modeling elements for the modeling of hypertext for the computation on the client-side. The authors showed how the

Figure 7. OOHDM extension, design framework for RIA

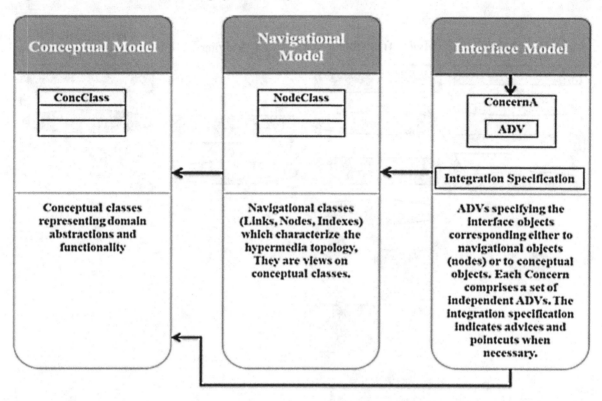

Figure 8. UWE-R navigation's extensions

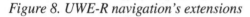

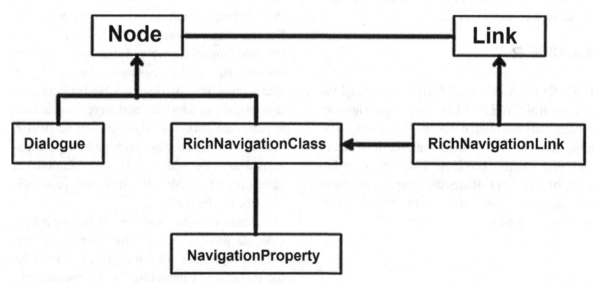

Figure 9. WebML Extension. The WebML process

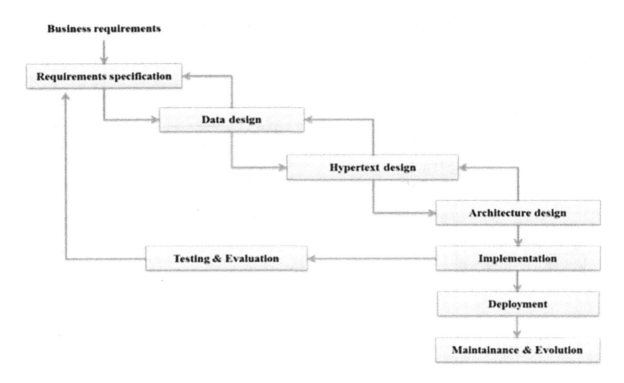

events can be explicitly described and together with the other concepts of a Web ML, with the aim of specifying the collaborative aspect of RIAs.

3.6. Object Oriented Web Solution (OOWS) and Interaction Patterns

In order to define the interaction model, the interaction pattern concept is used to describe a solution for a common user-system interaction. These interactions patterns are presented as guidelines for producing the RIA interface code based on a set of transformation rules. OOWS´s interaction model is presented in Figure 10.

Such interaction pattern models the structural aspects of the pattern; the behavioral aspects are only textually described. No details are given on the transformation rules in (Valverde & Pastor, 2008). OOWS method proposes to create an interaction model to address RIA features (Valverde & Pastor, 2008).

3.7. ADRIA Approach

Dolog and Stage (Dolog & Stage, 2007) also proposed a new method called ADRIA (A Method for Abstract Design of Rich Internet Applications), which employs interaction spaces, tasks models and state machines. This method is focused on the design of events triggered by user interactions. ADRIA' activities are described in Figure 11.

The main disadvantage of this new method is the reengineering of legacy Web applications which requires modeling from scratch.

3.8. Model-Driven Approach Proposed by Martinez-Ruiz et al.

Martinez-Ruiz et al. (Martinez-Ruiz et al., 2006) explained the problem of the development of graphical user interfaces on RIAs development and the social environment in which can be implemented, i.e., the education of the user, the social

Figure 10. OOWS: Interaction model

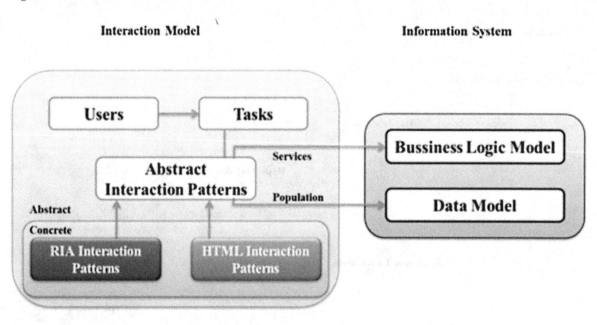

Figure 11. Activities in ADRIA

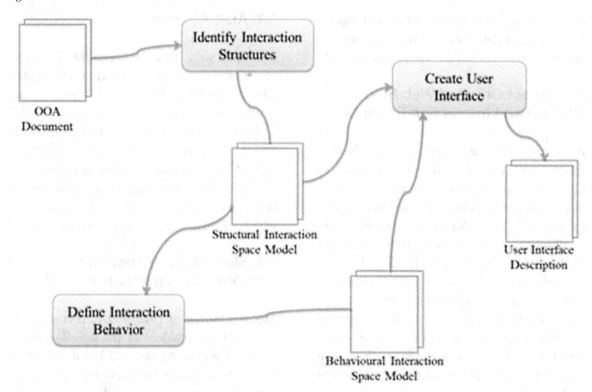

background, the knowledge that this person has, to mention but a few. Therefore it is necessary to conduct an analysis of these requirements and to propose a solution to solve these problems. The designed interfaces have to be platform-independent and vendor-independent. Therefore, the authors proposed a method for designing these types of user interfaces. The proposal was a design based on the model and it applies a series of XSLT (Extensible Stylesheet Language Transformations) model transformations to transform an abstract interface model into a final user interface that is coded on a specific platform. UsiXML was used to model all the levels. A method for designing Graphical RIAUIs is presented in Figure 12.

Different technologies based on this model were proposed. Furthermore, this approach atomizes the translation of user interfaces defined in UsiXML into documents with XAML XSL. These are transformations that are carried out in a preliminary evaluation. The authors are compiling a repository of all the components defined in XAML in order to complete the translation of XSLT in a Java-based implementation prototype called RIAZML but this is in an early stage of development.

3.9. Pattern Libraries

The pattern library is based on the work from the internal pattern library with a number of new patterns created to express the rich interaction of Ajax style applications (Scott, 2009). The anatomy of a RIA pattern is shown in Figure 13.

Patterns described in the book of Mahemoff (Mahemoff, 2006) are just a concise way to rep-

Figure 12. Method for designing graphical RIAUIs

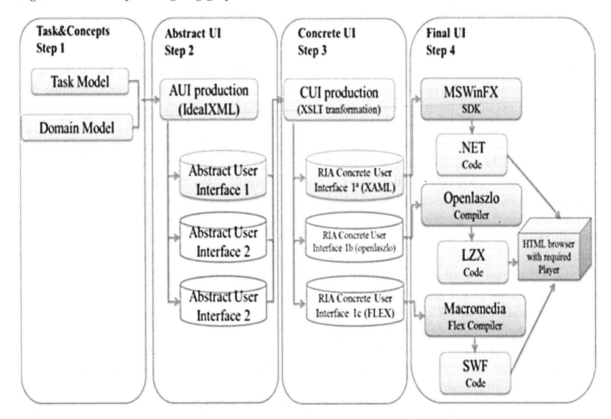

Figure 13. Anatomy of a RIA pattern

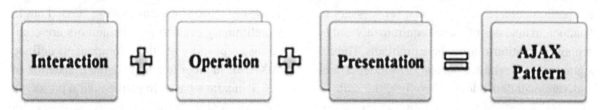

resent the knowledge embodied in Ajax-based applications. The point is to discover best practices by investigating how developers have successfully traded off conflicting design principles. Ajax is all about usability, so the patterns are particularly focused on delivering usability in the face of constraints, most notably: user capabilities and expectations, bandwidth limits, the stateless nature of HTTP, the complexity of JavaScript.

3.10. UWE Patterns

Desing Patterns have been proved for efficient RIA programming (Mahemoff, 2006). UWE propose to apply desing patterns at a higher abstraction level, i.e. modeling, to achieve the objectives of minimizing the design efforts and maximizing the expressiveness of the models used on RIAs development. The attention is focused on the use of state machines for the representation of the patterns – a widely used modeling technique. UWE patterns are used to describe the behavior of the RIA features; in contrast to the interaction patterns introduced in (Valverde & Pastor, 2008) that only model the structure of the pattern. The models of the RIA patterns can be integrated in almost all existing software development methodologies. In this sense, it is a general approach for all UML methods. The use of these RIA patterns only requires the definition of extension points in the methodology, and afterwards the specification of how to integrate them in a language such as UWE, which makes them easily reusable (Preciado et al., 2008).

3.11. PPRD: Phases Process for RIAs Design and Development

Alor-Hernandez et al. (Alor-Hernandez et al., 2012) proposed a Phases Process RIAs Development called PPRD. PPRD is a development process to build RIAs that it allows only focusing in main activities to transform user requirements into a software product through six phases which are shown below.

1. **Requirements Identification:** This phase involves gathering requirements and it is expressed by the user to obtain a document with a set of user requirements.
2. **Requirements Analysis:** The objective of this phase is finding and representing the real requirements a through UML use case diagrams and UML activities diagrams to the people involved in the development such as users, customers and developers.
3. **Application Architecture Definition:** It is important to define the platform on which the application will run in order to obtain a set of information technologies through which the development will be done.
4. **Conceptual Model:** This phase identifies the objects involved among users and the application objects that jointly execute various features. In order to obtain the conceptual model is necessary to analyze the result of the last phases to generate UML class diagrams that represent the objects, their properties and attributes, as well as associations among classes.

5. **Navigation Model:** Navigational model is represented by UML class diagrams showing the nodes and existing links in the navigation structure. A node represents a view, a component or element of presentation; the association represents a link between nodes, to display or to process information.

6. **Presentation Model:** This phase is intended to express, through the use of ADVs, interfaces that allow interaction between the user and application. When this phase has finished, a set of ADVs is obtained. An ADV indicates the necessary objects in an interface, its states, behaviors and interactions with other objects (Rossi et al., 2008). The particularity of this phase lies in the way of designing an ADV.

The order of presentation of the previous phases indicate the optimal order of the activities to be performed in the initial design and development of RIAs, but as an incremental and iterative development process, it is possible to return to any stage at any given time. PPRD process is described in Figure 14.

An extension to the PPRD called PPMRD for source code generation of multi-device RIAs is proposed in (Colombo-Mendoza et al., 2011). As a salient contribution, the proposal covers multi-device applications in comparison with other approaches where they are focused on software modeling allowing the code generation in a semi-automatically way. PPMRD extension process is described in Figure 15.

The phases of PPMRD are described below.

Figure 14. Integration of the implementation phases in PPRD for source code generation of multi-device RIAs

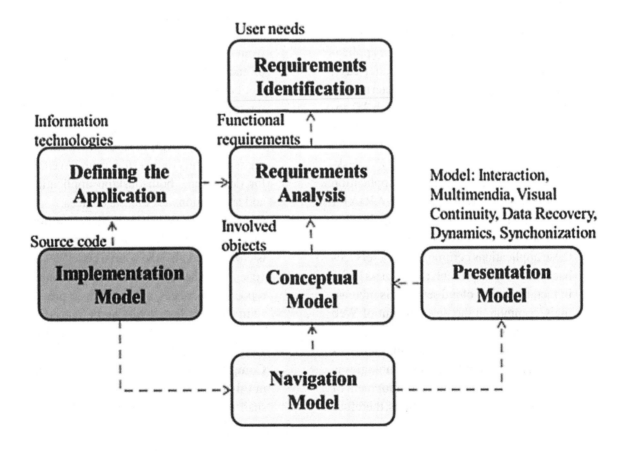

Figure 15. a) Integration of PPMRD in PPRD b) Phases of PPMRD

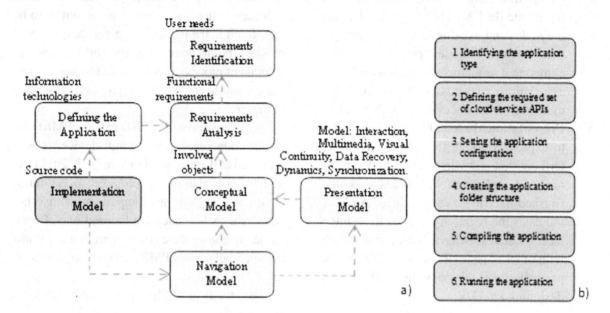

1. **Identifying the application type:** In this phase, the required type of multi-device RIA is determined. Here, one of the following kinds of RIAs is selected: Web browser-based application, desktop application or application for mobile devices. In the latter case, also the target platform must be determined. A Web browser-based RIA is a Web 2.0 application that integrates desktop-like features and it can be simply based on HTML and JavaScript or on a RIA technology. A desktop RIA is a traditional desktop application with an improved (enriched) GUI. A RIA for mobile devices is a native mobile application with an improved GUI. The architecture of these applications commonly has a services back-end which represents the business logic; in fact, the use of cloud services is increasingly common in the development of Web 2.0 applications.

2. **Defining the required set of cloud services APIs:** The demand for RIA technologies is driven by the increase in the development of cloud services-based applications; therefore cloud services APIs required to develop a RIA are identified in this phase. It is possible to include 2 or more cloud services APIs in the same RIA. Functions obtained from cloud services APIs are independent of each other. In this sense, each function can be displayed as a widget. Widgets are interactive elements that are created and controlled through scripting.

3. **Setting the application configuration:** This phase demands more effort from developer for developing both desktop applications and applications for mobile devices.

4. **Creating the application folder structure:** In this phase, the application folder structure is created and also the source code files are generated. The use of a software components repository is necessary in order to provide source code files which can be reused according to the application type identified and the cloud APIs required.

5. **Compiling the application:** If applicable, in this phase the application's source code shall be compiled into an executable code.

For example, for compiling MXML files, the Adobe™ Flex SDK application compiler must be used in order to obtain the corresponding SWF files. This compiler is invoked using the mxmlc command-line tool. The compilation syntax must contain the name of the main MXML file and optionally can contain a space-separated list of parameters, like the library-path parameter which indicates the path of the required SWC files. As result of the application compilation, the executable code files such as SWF files are generated. SWF files run in a different way depending on the type of application.

6. **Running the application:** In this phase, the native code is generated and finally the application is deployed on the target device. To deploy Web-browser based applications, application wrappers must be created if compiled files are SWF files, for example. An application wrapper is a simple HTML or a server-side Web page that embeds SWF files. Once the wrapper was created, it is possible to display the Web browser-based application on any Web browser that integrates the required plugin like the Adobe Flash Player™ plugin. To deploy both desktop applications and applications for mobile devices, an installation file must be created. Installation files for mobile devices are commonly signed using digital signing certificates either self-signed certificates or certificates issued by Certification Authorities (CAs).

4. CONCLUSION

There are many different software development methodologies for RIA development, and given the need of developing a methodology that would cover all the needs of this type of application, many researchers have worked on this topic, resulting in a large number of proposals, some of which have been very successful. Like with the

software development methodologies, there is also a need to create CASE tools that permit the easy development of RIAs, i.e., the development of software development methodologies are the first steps leading to the development of CASE tools. These are very useful in software development as they help to reduce both time and financial costs and they facilitate software development. CASE tools are aided in the development process, for example in semi-automatic code generation, in UML editors, or in version controls just to name a few. Even though there is still much to be achieved on RIAs development, some researchers are presenting very interesting proposals to develop this type of application.

REFERENCES

Alor-Hernandez, G., Hernandez-Carrillo, V. M., Ambros-Antemate, J. F., & Martinez-Nieves, L. A. (2012). Improving the Shopping Experience in B2C E-Commerce Systems using Rich Internet Applications. In K. Rezaul (Ed.), Strategic and Pragmatic E-Business: Implications for Future Business Practices (pp. 72–99). Academic Press. doi:10.4018/978-1-4666-1619-6.ch004

Baresi, L., Garzotto, F., & Paolini, P. (2001). Extending UML for Modeling Web Applications. In *Proceedings of the 34th Annual Hawaii International Conference on System Sciences*. IEEE Comput. Soc. Retrieved from http://ieeexplore.ieee.org/lpdocs/epic03/wrapper.htm?arnumber=926350

Bieber, M., Galnares, R., & Lu, Q. (1998). Web Engineering and Flexible Hypermedia. In P. Brusilovksy & P. De Bra (Eds.), *Proceedings of the 2nd Workshop on Adaptive Hypertext and Hypermedia Hypertext 98*. Retrieved from http://wwwis.win.tue.nl/ah98/Bieber.html

Booch, G., Rumbaugh, J., & Jacobson, I. (1999). *The Unified Modeling Language User Guide*. Addison-Wesley.

Bozzon, A., Comai, S., Fraternali, P., & Carughi, G. (2006). Conceptual modeling and code generation for rich internet applications. In *Proceedings of the 6th International Conference on Web Engineering*. ACM. Retrieved from http://discovery. ucl.ac.uk/1334175/

Brambilla, M., Preciado, J. C., Linaje, M., & Sanchez-Figueroa, F. (2008). Business Process-Based Conceptual Design of Rich Internet Applications. In *Proceedings of 2008 Eighth International Conference on Web Engineering* (pp. 155-161). IEEE. Retrieved from http://ieeexplore.ieee.org/lpdocs/epic03/wrapper.htm?arnumber=4577879

Brisaboa, N. R., Penabad, M. R., Places, A. S., & Rodriguez, F. J. (2002). A documental database query language. *Advances in Databases, 2405,* 242–245.

Busch, M., & Koch, M. (2009). *State of the art. Rich Internet Applications* (Technical Report 0902). Academic Press.

Ceri, S., Fraternali, P., Bongio, A., Brambilla, M., Comai, S., & Matera, M. (2002). *Designing Data-Intensive Web Applications. Database*. Morgan Kaufmann Publishers Inc. Retrieved from http://www.amazon.com/dp/1558608435

Colombo-Mendoza, L. O., Alor-Hernandez, G., & Rodríguez-González, A. (2011). *An Extension to PPRD for Source Code Generation of Multi-device RIAs*. Paper presented at the International Conference on Computers and Advanced Technology in Education. New York, NY.

Detroyer, O., & Leune, C. (1998). WSDM: A user centered design method for Web sites. *Computer Networks and ISDN Systems, 30*(1-7), 85-94. Retrieved from http://linkinghub.elsevier.com/retrieve/pii/S0169755298000427

Dolog, P., & Stage, J. (2007). Designing Interaction Spaces for Rich Internet Applications with UML. *Techniques, 4607,* 358-363. Retrieved from http://www.springerlink.com/index/10.1007/978-3-540-73597-7

Escalona, M., & Koch, N. (2004). Requirements Engineering for Web Applications – A Comparative Study. *Journal of Web Engineering, 2*(3), 193-212. Citeseer. Retrieved from http://citeseerx.ist.psu.edu/viewdoc/download?doi=10.1.1.153.5974&rep=rep1&type=pdf

Escalona, M. J., Torres, J., & Mejías, M. (2002). Requirements Capture Workflow in Global Information Systems. In *Proceedings of OOIS*. Springer-Verlag. doi:10.1007/3-540-46102-7_31

Garzotto, F., Paolini, P., & Schwabe, D. (1993). HDM - A model-based approach to hypermedia applications design. *ACM Transactions on Information Systems, 11*(1), 1–23. doi:10.1145/151480.151483

Hennicker, R., & Koch, N. (2000). A UML-based methodology for hypermedia design. In *Proceedings of the 3rd international conference on The unified modeling language advancing the standard* (Vol. 1939, pp. 410-424). Springer-Verlag. Retrieved from http://portal.acm.org/citation.cfm?id=1765218&dl=GUIDE&coll=GUIDE

Jacobson, I., Booch, G., & Rumbaugh, J. (1999). *The Unified Software Development Process*. Addison-Wesley.

Koch, N., & Wirsing, M. (2001). Software engineering for adaptive hypermedia applications. *Ph Thesis FAST Reihe Softwaretechnik, 12*. Retrieved from http://citeseerx.ist.psu.edu/viewdoc/download?doi=10.1.1.24.4017&rep=rep1&type=pdf

Lee, H., Lee, C., & Yoo, C. (1998). A scenario-based object-oriented methodology for developing hypermedia information systems. In *Proceedings of the Thirty First Hawaii International Conference on System Sciences,* (pp. 47-56). IEEE Comput. Soc. Retrieved from http://ieeexplore.ieee.org/lpdocs/epic03/wrapper.htm?arnumber=651682

Lowe, D., & Eklund, J. (2002). *Client Needs and the Design Process in Web Projects.* Paper presented at the Web Engineering Track of the WWW2002 Conference. New York, NY.

Machado, L., Filho, O., & Ribeiro, J. (2009). UWE-R: An extension to a web engineering methodology for rich internet applications. *WSEAS Transactions on Information Science and Applications, 6*(4), 9.

Mahemoff, M. (2006). *Ajax Design Patterns.* O'Reilly.

Martinez-ruiz, F., Artcaga, J., Vanderdonckt, J., Gonzalez-calleros, J., & Mendoza, R. (2006). A first draft of a Model-driven Method for Designing Graphical User Interfaces of Rich Internet Applications. In *Proceedings of 2006 Fourth Latin American Web Congress,* (pp. 32-38). IEEE. Retrieved from http://ieeexplore.ieee.org/lpdocs/epic03/wrapper.htm?arnumber=4022089

Meliá, S., Gómez, J., Pérez, S., & Díaz, O. (2008). A Model-Driven Development for GWT-Based Rich Internet Applications with OOH4RIA. In *Proceedings of 2008 Eighth International Conference on Web Engineering,* (pp. 13-23). IEEE. Retrieved from http://ieeexplore.ieee.org/lpdocs/epic03/wrapper.htm?arnumber=4577865

Olsina, L. (1998). *Building a Web-based Information System applying the Hypermedia Flexible Process Modeling Strategy.* Paper presented at the 1st International Workshop on Hypermedia Development, Hypertext'98. Pittsburgh, PA.

Preciado, J. C., Linaje, M., Comai, S., & Sanchez-Figueroa, F. (2007). Designing Rich Internet Applications with Web Engineering Methodologies. In *Proceedings of 2007 9th IEEE International Workshop on Web Site Evolution,* (pp. 23-30). IEEE. Retrieved from http://ieeexplore.ieee.org/lpdocs/epic03/wrapper.htm?arnumber=4380240

Preciado, J. C., Linaje, M., Morales-Chaparro, R., Sanchez-Figueroa, F., Zhang, G., Kroiß, C., & Koch, N. (2008). Designing Rich Internet Applications Combining UWE and RUX-Method. In *Proceedings of 2008 Eighth International Conference on Web Engineering,* (pp. 148-154). IEEE. Retrieved from http://ieeexplore.ieee.org/lpdocs/epic03/wrapper.htm?arnumber=4577878

Preciado, J. C., Linaje, M., Sanchez, F., & Comai, S. (2005). Necessity of methodologies to model Rich Internet Applications. In *Proceedings of Seventh IEEE International Symposium on Web Site Evolution,* (pp. 7-13). IEEE. Retrieved from http://ieeexplore.ieee.org/lpdocs/epic03/wrapper.htm?arnumber=1517975

Rossi, G., Urbieta, M., Ginzburg, J., Distante, D., & Garrido, A. (2008). Refactoring to Rich Internet Applications. A Model-Driven Approach. In *Proceedings of 2008 Eighth International Conference on Web Engineering,* (pp. 1-12). IEEE. Retrieved from http://ieeexplore.ieee.org/lpdocs/epic03/wrapper.htm?arnumber=4577864

Schwabe, D., & Rossi, G. (1998). Developing Hypermedia Applications using OOHDM. *Methodology, 98,* 1-20. Retrieved from http://citeseerx.ist.psu.edu/viewdoc/summary?doi=10.1.1.40.4780

Scott, B. (2009). *RIA Patterns. Best Practices for Common Patterns of Rich Interaction.* Retrieved from http://www.uxmatters.com/mt/archives/2007/03/

Urbieta, M., Rossi, G., Ginzburg, J., & Schwabe, D. (2007). Designing the Interface of Rich Internet Applications. In *Proceedings of 2007 Latin American Web Conference LAWEB 2007*, (pp. 144-153). IEEE. Retrieved from http://ieeexplore.ieee.org/lpdocs/epic03/wrapper.htm?arnumber=4383169

Valverde, F., & Pastor, O. (2008). Applying Interaction Patterns: Towards a Model-Driven Approach for Rich Internet Applications Development Francisco Valverde, Oscar Pastor. In *Proceedings of IWWOST* (pp. 13-18). Retrieved from http://icwe2008.webengineering.org/program/workshops/isbn978-80-227-2899-7/icwe2008ws-cd/individual-files/02icwe2008ws-iwwost02-valverde.pdf

Vilain, P., Schwabe, D., & Souza, C. S. D. (2000). A Diagrammatic Tool for Representing User Interaction in UML. *Lecture*, 133-147. Retrieved from http://citeseerx.ist.psu.edu/viewdoc/summary?doi=10.1.1.32.4062

Yourdon, E. (1989). *Modern Structured Analysis*. Prentice-Hall.

ADDITIONAL READING

Homeria Open Solutions. (n.d.a). *RUX-T*ool. Retrieved from http://www.homeria.com/#!/page16.do?kcond367.att3=33&kcond25.att3=33

Homeria Open Solutions. (n.d.b). *Homeria Open Solutions S.L.* Retrieved from http://www.homeria.com/

Homeria Open Solutions. (n.d.c). *WebRatio*. Retrieved from http://www.homeria.com/#!/page16.do?kcond367.att3=32&kcond25.att3=32

WebRatio. (n.d.). *WebRatio*. Retrieved from http://www.webratio.com/portal/content/es/home;jsessionid=3FC6937BF069B713FC8400F3EB6C7FC0

KEY TERMS AND DEFINITIONS

Methodology: A set of methods to be used for a particular purpose to conduct a study or activity.

Software Development Methodologies: Methodologies that are used to structure, plan, and control the process of software development.

Software Development Methodologies for RIAs: Methodologies that are used in the RIAs development such as *RUX Method*, *OOH4RIA*, and *UWE-R*.

Software Development Methodologies for Traditional Web Applications: Methodologies that are used in the traditional Web applications development such as *UWE*, *WebML*, and *OOHDM*.

Software Engineering: The study and application of engineering to the design, development, and maintenance of software.

Traditional Methodologies: Methodologies that are used in the traditional software development such as *RUP*, *Scrum*, and *XP*.

Traditional Web Applications: These are software applications which are displayed in a Web browser, and in which each user interaction with the application means fully recharge the application to display the updated information.

Chapter 4
Important Factors on RIAs Development

ABSTRACT

Chapter 4 discusses some software quality metrics such as usability, scalability, and reusability of RIAs development. The chapter describes the importance of using multimedia content and UI (User Interface) patterns not only for improving the appearance of RIAs but also for delivering rich user experiences. Likewise, this chapter depicts the importance of leveraging AOP (Aspect-Oriented Programming) capabilities and implementing design patterns to ease the RIAs maintenance and enable RIAs reusability. In this chapter, four concepts about Web development and RIAs development were selected. These concepts are Multimedia Support, AOP Support, Design Patterns Support, and UI Pattern Support and are described in detail in this chapter.

1. INTRODUCTION

Clearly, the use of RIAs (Rich Internet Application) provides several advantages. Users' experience in the use of applications is improved since RIAs applications are very easy to use. Moreover, Rich Internet Applications also offer ameliorations in terms of connectivity, instant display of the applications, and access speed. However, one of the most remarkable characteristics of RIAs is the fact that installation is not required. RIAs merely require refreshing the browser so that applications are automatically updated to new versions. In comparison with the use of executable programs, this characteristic greatly diminishes the risk in computers of being infected by viruses. Finally,

RIAs also cater for a better capacity of response, since users are able to interact with the information without reloading the website. Currently, several companies – such as Flickr™ or Gmail™ –are focusing on RIAs development.

There exist four highly important aspects of RIAS. These aspects are:

- **Scalability:** Scalability is a complex concept to define in the field of computer systems. It basically refers to a system's ability to grow and be adapted to changes. Nowadays, it is important to consider the scalability of systems. This would permit to forsee and be prepared for any eventual change in any system. The use of AOP

DOI: 10.4018/978-1-4666-6437-1.ch004

(Aspect-Oriented Programming) provides remarkable benefits in terms of scalability, since AOP is a type of programming which facilitates the introduction of new functionalities and modifications into already-developed systems.

- **Usability:** In terms of computing, usability refers to the ease with which people are able to interact with software systems; it involves concepts of HCI (Human-Computer Interaction). In order to achieve usability, the systems designed must facilitate the exchange of information between machines and people. One way of promoting this kind of information exchange is through efficient and easy-to-use User Interfaces (UIs). These types of interfaces are developed using User Interfaces Patterns (UI-Patterns) that favor friendly UIs and, therefore, improve the usability of both software systems and RIAs.

- **Support for Different Types of Contents:** The content of a RIA refers to information that is directly provided to the user and contains the message to be transmitted. Therefore, support for different kind of contents is of great importance in RIAs development. Contents can range from text, images, videos, or animations, among others. Multimedia contents are so important today that several websites exclusively dedicate to the transmission of this kind of content. For instance, Youtube™ focuses on video transmission, while Flickr™ is a website for image hosting, sharing, and posting. Although multimedia content may be varied, videos remain the most popular since they can include images, text, audio, and animations, which are also other forms of multimedia content.

- **Reusability:** As it name suggests, the concept refers to the ability to reutilize one part of a software system in order to use it differently within the same system, or build a new system. A quite straightforward way to implement reusability in RIAs is through the use of design patterns. In fact, some design patterns rely on reusability by default. For instance, Façade is a pattern whereby information can be differently presented merely by switching the interfaces and reusing functionalities. This is particularly useful in graphic design.

These four aspects are remarkably important for RIA's development. They provide RIAs a better appearance and offer new functionalities, such as a more efficient capacity of response and interactivity.

The present chapter describes each of the four concepts abovementioned; both their importance and usage are explained.

2. MULTIMEDIA SUPPORT ON RIAS

Integration of multimedia content is currently a key issue in the development of traditional Web applications, and consequently in Rich Internet Applications development. Multimedia refers to the "diffusion of information in more than one way, including the use of text, audio, graphics, animated graphics, and video" (Freedman, 1999). According to this definition, multimedia involves different types of information; however, videos are the most used type of content since it can include other types of information such as images, audio, and text.

Etymologically, the word *multimedia* means "multiple media," and in terms of of information technology, it refers to the existence of "multiple intermediaries between the source and the destination of the information, that is, that various means are used to store, transmit, display or receive information". In other words, multimedia refers to any combination of text, audio, and images. From this perspective, a television or a newspaper would be considered a multimedia device. However, in the

Figure 1. Image gallery example

case of RIAs, the appropriate term for multimedia is digital multimedia, which can be defined as "the digital integration of text, graphics, images, video, animation, audio and any other means into a computer system". The common support for this type of media is the electronic type, where a computer system is responsible of generating the presentation of the information in a correct

Multimedia content is very important for RIAs. It provides richest content to Web applications by presenting information in a more dynamic and entertaining way. Some examples pf multimedia contents are videos and image galleries, to mention a few. The use of image galleries enhances the ability to customize views on the fly, and it provides real-time visual representations of a selected item. An image gallery on a website is a collection of images or photos uploaded to a website and available for website visitors to view. This term originally emerged from the term "gallery" which first referred to a narrow passageway on a ship joining rooms similar to corridors. In an image gallery, this passageway is provided by using buttons, lists, and comboBoxes, among others; although the most popular are the buttons. The Forward and Back buttons in a gallery manually allow the passageway of the images. Also, other functionalities such as start, stop, close or hide can be provided by using buttons. In some cases, it is possible to enlarge the image by using a lightbox component. This component helps

not to lose the focus of application's main page. Therefore, when users desire to access the image gallery, the lightbox component is deployed. On the other hand, when users desire to quit the image gallery, the lightbox component is closed and users are returned to the page on which they were previously. An example of this kind of gallery is presented in Figure 1.

The image file format support in a photo/image gallery is an important aspect to be considered. Some of the most popular image file formats are described in Table 1

Video playback is another very important and oustanding multimedia content in RIAs development. It is imperative to mention that video formats involve two different technology concepts: containers (sometimes called wrappers) and codecs (short for coder/decoder). Codecs are used inside a container and for this reason video formats can be mistaken. The container describes the file structure: where the various pieces are stored, the way they are interleaved, and which codecs are used by which pieces. It may specify an audio codec as well as video. It is used to package the video and its components (audio/metadata) and is identified (usually) by a file extension such as .AVI, .MP4 or .MOV, among some others. A codec (short for "coder/decoder") is a way of encoding audio or video into a stream of bytes. It is the method used to encode the video. It can also be

Table 1. Compressed Image file formats (Miano, 1999)

Format	Description
BMP (BMP means Bitmap file format)	Windows BMP is the native image format in Microsof™t Windows™ operating systems. It supports images with 1, 4, 8, 16, 24, and 32 bits per pixel; although BMP files using 16 and 32 bits per pixel are rare. BMP also supports simple run-length compression for 4 and 8 bits per pixel.
JPEG (JPEG stands for Joint Photographic Experts Group)	JPEG has become the most commonly used format for storing photographic images. The power of the JPEG format is that, for photographic images, it provides the greatest compression of any bitmap format in common use. A photograph that takes 1 MB to store in a Windows BMP file can usually be compressed down to 50 KB with JPEG. Although JPEG is computationally intensive, its outstanding compression generally outweighs the processing required.
GIF (GIF stands for Graphics Interchange Format)	The main features of GIF are: • Up to 256 colors using 1 to 8 bits per pixel • Multiple images per file Due to its better compression and greater color depth, JPEG has generally replaced GIF for photographic images. Yet, GIF is used for other applications; but legal entanglements have certainly condemned it to obsolescence. A GIF file consists of a fixed area at the start of the file followed by a variable number of blocks and ending with an image trailer.
PNG (PNG stands for Portable Network Graphics)	The PNG format uses a lossless compression process and supports: • Up to 48 bits per pixel in color images • 1-, 2-, 4-, 8-, and 16-bit sample precision • Alpha channel for full control of transparency • Sophisticated color matching Due to the use of the legal issues surrounding the use of GIF, PNG is now used instead of GIF in those applications where GIF is not a suitable alternative.

Table 2. Most Common Containers for Video (Buchanan, 2013)

Format	Description
AVI (AVI stands for Audio Video Interleave)	A Windows standard multimedia container
MPEG-4 Part 14 (known as .mp4)	It is the standardized container for MPEG---4.
FLV (FLV stands for Flash Video)	It refers to the format used to deliver MPEG video through Flash Player.
MOV	Apple's QuickTime container format
VOB (VOB means DVD Video Object)	It is DVD's standard container.
ASF (ASF stands for Advanced Systems Format)	A Microsoft format designed for WMV and WMA.

said that the container is the file itself, while the codec is the content.

It is worth mentioning that the video file format (codecs and containers) support in a Web component is an important aspect to be considered. Some of the most popular containers are described in Table 2.

Some of the most popular codecs are described in Table 3.

Videos are the most used type of content in RIAs development, since it can cover other types of information such as images, audio, and text. For this reason, it is noteworthy to mention the

Table 3. Most Common Codecs for Video (Buchanan, 2013)

Format	Description
MPEG (MPEG stands for Moving Pictures Expert Group)	Three video formats, MPEG 1, 2, and 4. • *MPEG-1*: Old, supported by everything (at least up to 352x240), and reasonably efficient. • *MPEG-2*: A version of MPEG---1, with better compression. 720x480. It is Used in HDTV (High-definition television), DVD, and SVCD (Super Video Compact Disc). • *MPEG-4*: A family of codecs, some of which are open source, others Microsoft™ proprietary.
H.264	Most commonly used codecs for videos uploaded to the web. It is part of the MPEG---4 codec.
MJPEG (MPEG stands for Motion JPEG)	This codec consists of a stream of JPEG images. It is common in video files from digital cameras and it is a reasonable format for editing videos. However, it does not compress well, which is why it is not suitable for Web distribution.
DV (DV stands for Digital Video)	It is usually used for video grabbed via firewire off a video camera. It is fixed at 720x480 @ 29.97FPS, or 720x576 @ 25 FPS. It is not very highly compressed.
WMV (WMV stands for Windows Media Video)	A collection of Microsoft proprietary video codecs. Since version 7, WMV has used a special version of MPEG4.
RM (RM stands for Real Media)	A closed codec developed by Real Networks for streaming video and audio
DivX	In early versions, essentially an ASF (incomplete early MPEG---4) codec inside an AVI container; DivX 4 and later are a fuller MPEG---4 codec…no resolution limit.
Quicktime™ 6	Apple's implementation of an MPEG4 codec.

video file formats that exist, as well as the way they can be used on Web applications.

Videos are used in well-known video playback websites. One of the most important websites for video playback is YouTube™. YouTube™ is a website where users can upload and share videos, and its popularity has considerably grown during the last years. It is known by a lot of people around the world. The YouTube™'s success is based on three factors: 1) it is free, 2) it is easy to handle, and 3) it is social. With these three premises, YouTube™ has become the most visited website for video playback around the world. Vimeo™ is another website that clearly exemplifies the success of sharing multimedia content over the Web. It is an online community that permits sharing videos worldwide. From this perspective, Vimeo™ is very similar to You-Tube™; however, unlike YouTube™, Vimeo™ provides option for downloading videos to the user's computer. One disadvantage of Vimeo™ is that some videos can be merely played using the most recent version of the QuickTime™ video player. Furthermore, Vimeo™ does not permit the use of the RSS syndication format for retrieving new video entries. Another website for video playback is VideoEgg™. VideoEgg™ is a video publishing system which translates any media file into a single format of compression and playback. The main advantage of VideoEgg™ is that it makes all formats compatible. Therefore, users do not need to download various video players to watch the videos, or worry about the various file formats in which these videos were recorded. Yashi™ and VSocial™ are two examples of new websites to host videos. These websites accept more compression formats than other websites for video playback.

Another website for video playback is Netf-lix™. It is a video platform that offers a completely legal exchange in streaming movies and TV shows for a monthly subscription fee. Nowadays, NetFlix has around 15 million subscribers offline and online in U.S. and Canada. To understand the size of NetFlix™, statistics of Internet traffic in U.S. in 2011 indicated that around 21% of download traffic (from the suppliers to the final customer) was consumed by NetFlix™ protocols. Only the

HTTP protocol in U.S. was able to overcome the download traffic of Netflix™. In 2012 Netflix™ video streaming was the single largest source of peak downstream Internet traffic in the U.S., according to a new report by Sandvine. The streaming video service now accounts for 29.7% of peak downstream traffic, up from 21 percent in 2011 (Sandvine, 2012).

The aforementioned websites clearly depict the importance of multimedia content in Web applications, particularly on Rich Internet Applications. Nowadays, not only the websites dedicated to video playback use video players on their Web pages, but also many developers integrate video players or multimedia content into their applications with the purpose of attracting users and making these Web applications more interactive.

3. ASPECT-ORIENTED PROGRAMMING (AOP) SUPPORT ON RIAS

Object-Oriented Programming (OOP) proved to be a well-established and modern technology to model real domain problems. Some problems demand difficult design decisions as their nature do not fit well the OOP approach. The programming technique of Aspect-Oriented Programming supports the problem nature of cross-cutting concerns as an extension to OOP. The AOP describes a development methodology for separating cross-cutting concerns during software development (Kiczales, Lamping, Mendhekar, Maeda, Lopes, Loingtier & Irwin, 1997). In contrast to Object-oriented programming, where the common functionality is pushed up in the hierarchy tree, AOP separately defines such aspects and uses an AOP environment to manage the correct composition to a single executable program (Elrad, Filman & Bader, 2001).

Diverse works have been proposed to give support to this paradigm in combination with other features of software engineering. Some of the most important works are mentioned below.

In (Heo & Choi, 2006) Aspect-Oriented Programming has been introduced as the method to improve the assembling process in software product line. The method that assembles core asset and variabilities was described by grammar elements such as Join point, pointcut, and advice without code-change. In other work (Kwanwoo, Botterweck & Thiel, 2009), authors mentioned that Aspect-Oriented Programming provides effective means for modularizing feature implementation. Furthermore, current AOP tools were discussed in order to provide a mechanism for switching aspect modules on and off to configure a product. The conclusion was this becomes infeasible in the context of large-scale product lines with thousands of variations. In (Tahir & Ahmad, 2010) the authors analyzed that the AOP is a promising technology that is used today to add cross-cutting concerns to software applications. AOP can be used to transparently instrument the code at compile-time. This research suggests AOP as a new technique that can be used for collecting software maintainability dynamic metrics data. Therefore, an AOP-based framework for collecting dynamic metrics has been designed and implemented, and finally, it has been evaluated. The evaluation results showed that the framework is a reasonable approach for collecting a maintainability dynamic metrics. In (Zhou, Ji, Zhao & Liu, 2010) authors proposed an AOP approach to ensure that the interactions among components are strictly conformed to the sated API usage policies of the components. Also, by using AOP can separate the constraints violation checking code from the normal functional code via the so called aspects, thus improving the software quality by separation of concern. Experiments showed that using AspectJ as the AOP implementation technique, the performance is comparable to the non-embedded code. In other work (Chen, Lin & Cheng, 2012) the authors described COCA (COCA stands for Computation Offload to Clouds using AOP). COCA is a programming framework that allows smart phones applications developers to easily offload part of the computation to servers in the cloud. COCA works at the source level. By harnessing the power of AOP, COCA inserts appropriate offloading code into the source code of the target application based on the result of static and dynamic profiling. As a proof of concept, the authors integrated COCA into the Android development environment and fully automate the new build process, making application programming and software maintenance easier. With COCA, mobile applications can now automatically offload part of the computation to the cloud, achieving better performance and longer battery life.

The AOP has been few used in Web engineering; however, in recent years, a few frameworks have been extended in several ways in order to provide the necessary support to implement this new paradigm. The AOP is a "method of implementation in which programs are organized into components, features, and specifications of quantification to permit the realization of the system" (Juárez Martínez, 2008).

The AOP allows the implementation of certain concepts relevant to the performance of a system. The methodology of the AOP for the development of aspect-oriented systems is performed similarly to other methodologies (Czarnecki, 1999) (Laddad, 2003). The principal purpose is to satisfy system requirements or, more generally, concerns. A concern is something of interest to those involved in a software project, considering more than a requirement, some piece of code or some concept (Clarke & Baniassad, 2005) (Jacobson & Ng, 2005). To better understand the main functionality of AOP, this programming paradigm is explained in terms of performance. From this perspective, when a program source code is modified in order to enable certain functionality, a high risk of failure arises. In the worst of the cases, the program will stop working. Applying the AOP ensures that the source code remains intact and does not lose its core functionality. Therefore, new functionality is added, while the functionality that is already working is not changed.

In synthesis, the AOP allows to add new functionalities to applications. In the case of RIAs, AOP allows adding new features to Web applications without changing the original source code. For instance, when a legacy application requires of an authentication method, it is possible to develop a separate method using AOP and without changing the original structure of the application. Another example of the use of AOP is when an application requires additional modules, such as reports generation and information to be displayed in a graphical way. In this case, let us suppose that the legacy application does not include these modules. For this reason, the modules need to be separately developed and then some AOP techniques can be introduced in order to incorporate these capabilities.

Usability is most often defined as the ease of use and acceptability of a system for a particular class of users carrying out specific tasks in a specific environment. Whereas ease of use affects the end users' performance and satisfaction, acceptability affects whether the product is used or not. One of the basic lessons in HCI is that usability must be considered before prototyping take place. The earlier critical design flaws are detected, the more likely they can be corrected. Thus, User Interface design should more properly be called User Interface development, analogous to software development, since design usually focuses on the synthesis stages, and user interface components include metaphors, mental models, navigation, interaction, appearance, and usability (Holzinger, 2005). Still, the process of usability engineering and its iterative approach is often costly and time consuming. Hence, using automation to decrease time and costs of usability evaluations directly impacts on the economic success of products. The process of usability evaluation can described by the following activities: (1) Capture: collecting usability data, (2) Analysis: interpreting usability data; and (3) Critique: suggesting solutions. Using

AOP the "capture" phase is directly influenced as the effort to collect information can be drastically reduced, while the quality of usability data can be increased and easily customized (Ivory & Hearst, 2001).

Authorization, Caching, Communication, Configuration Management, Exceptions Management, State Management, and Validation represent some other examples of how the AOP is useful for RIAs development in order to introduce new capabilities to RIAs and Web applications.

AOP extends the traditional Object Oriented Programming model to improve code reuse across different object hierarchies. The basic concept in AOP is a concern, which is a common behavior typically scattered across methods, classes, object hierarchies, or even entire object models (jboss, 2013). AOP provides a solution for abstracting crosscutting code that spans object hierarchies without functional relevance to the code it spans. Instead of embedding cross-cutting code in classes, AOP allows to abstract the crosscutting code into a separate module (known as an aspect) and then apply the code dynamically where it is needed. A dynamic application of the crosscutting code is achieved by defining specific places (known as pointcuts) in the object model where crosscutting code should be applied. At runtime or compile time – depending of an AOP framework – crosscutting code is injected at the specified pointcuts. Essentially, AOP permits introducing new functionality into objects without the objects' needing any knowledge on that introduction (Ekabua, 2012).

AOP introduces some concepts. These concepts are presented below (Laddad, 2003):

3.1. Crosscutting

The implementation of the weaving rules by the compiler is called crosscutting. The weaving rules cut across multiple modules in a systematic way in order to modularize the crosscutting concerns. There exist two types of crosscutting defined as static and dynamic crosscutting.

1. **Dynamic Crosscutting:** Dynamic crosscutting is the weaving of new behavior into the execution of a program. Dynamic crosscutting augments or even replaces the core program execution flow in a way that crosscutting modules modifies the system's behavior.

2. **Static Crosscutting:** Static crosscutting is the weaving of modifications into the static structure—the classes, interfaces, and aspects—of the system. Static crosscutting by itself does not modify the execution behavior of the system. The most common function of static crosscutting is to support the implementation of dynamic crosscutting. For instance, add new data and methods to classes and interfaces can be carried out in order to define class-specific states and behaviors that can be used in dynamic crosscutting actions. Another use of static crosscutting is to declare compile-time warnings and errors across multiple modules.

3.1.1. Dynamic Crosscutting Elements

The elements involved in the dynamic Crosscutting are three: join points, pointcuts, and advices.

1. **Join Point:** A *join point* is an identifiable point in the execution of a program. It could be a call to a method or an assignment to a member of an object.

2. **Pointcut:** A *pointcut* is a program construct that selects join points and collects context at those points. For example, a pointcut can select a join point that is a call to a method. It could also capture the method's context, such as the target object on which the method was called and the method's arguments.

3. **Advice:** *Advice* is the code to be executed at a join point that has been previously selected by a pointcut. Advice can execute before, after, or around the join point. Around advice can modify the execution of the code that is

at the join point; it can replace it, or it can even bypass it. Using an advice a message can be logged before executing the code at certain join points that are spread across several modules.

3.1.2. Static Crosscutting Elements

The elements of static crosscutting are introductions and compile- time declarations.

1. **Introduction:** The *introduction* is a static crosscutting instruction that introduces changes to the classes, interfaces, and aspects of the system. It makes static changes to the modules that do not directly affect their behavior. For example, a method or field to a class can be added.
2. **Compile-Time Declarations:** The *compile-time declaration* is a static crosscutting instruction that allows adding compile-time warnings and errors upon detecting certain usage patterns.

The aforementioned concepts are depicted in Figure 2.

Figure 2 is a graphic representation of what happens with the application code. It depicts where the crosscuttings are located and how the join points are identified. It also identifies what modules are introduced, which are reusable and which can be used in more than one place in the same application.

To an extent, it is easy to implement new fucntionalities or correct errors in applications using AOP. Figure 2 represents an application in which reusable modules can be identified. These modules posses a specific/certain functionality and can be integrated into a part of the application by merely introducing it through a Join Point and a Crosscutting.

4. DESIGN PATTERNS SUPPORT ON RIAS

Design Patterns are widely used in software development, as well as in Web applications development. In this case, a design pattern facilitates the solution to recurring problems, applying effective solutions that were tested before.

A design pattern systematically names, motivates, and explains a general design that addresses a recurring problem in the design of object-oriented systems. It describes the problem, the solution, in

Figure 2. AOP Representation

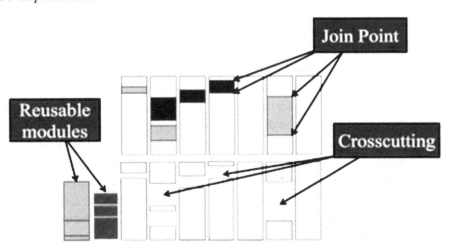

the moment of applying the solution and its consequences. The solution is a general agreement of the objects and classes that solve the problem. The solution is customized to solve the problem in a particular context (Gamma, Helm, Johnson & Vlissides, 1994).

Each pattern describes a problem that occurs over and over again in our environment, and then describes the core of the solution to that problem, so that you can use this solution a million times more, without having to do it the same way twice (Alexander, Ishikawa & Silverstein, 1977).

A well-known design pattern on Web applications development is the MVC (MVC Model-View-Controller). The MVC pattern separates the domain modeling, the presentation and the actions based on the user input into three classes: 1) Model manages the behavior and data of the application domain, responding to both requests for information about its state (usually from the view) and instructions to change state (usually from the controller), 2) View manages the display of information, 3) Controller interprets the mouse and keyboard inputs from the user, informing the model and/or the view to change as it is appropriate. It is important to notice that both View and Controller depend on Model. However, Model depends on neither View nor Controller. This separation allows Model to be built and tested independently from the visual presentation. The separation between View and Controller is secondary in many rich-client applications, and, in fact, many User Interface frameworks implement the roles as one object. In Web applications, on the other hand, the separation between View (the browser) and Controller (the server-side components handling the HTTP request) is very well defined.

Model-View-Controller is a fundamental design pattern for the separation of user interface logic from business logic. Unfortunately, the popularity of the pattern has resulted in a number of faulty descriptions. Particularly, the term

"controller" has been used to stand for different things in different contexts. Fortunately, the advent of Web applications has helped resolve some of the ambiguities, since the separation between the view and the controller is so apparent.

The use of design patterns in software development in remarkably important. There exist several classifications of design patterns made by different authors; however, all of them agree in the importance of design patterns for the improvement of the structure of the code that is being written.

Design patterns can be used in order to solve different issues and they propose different objectives. Some of these objectives are:

- Provide catalogs of reusable elements in software development by taking into account that reusability is a higly important aspect in the development of both software and RIAs.
- Avoid reiteration when finding solutions to already-known problems which have been previously solved.
- Standardize the method for designing software systems.
- Facilitating learning of new generations of software designers by pre-existing knowledge.

Similarly, design patterns do not attempt to:

- Impose some given desing alternatives above others.
- Eliminate inherent creativity in the design process of a software system.

It is not mandatory to use design patterns in the design of software systems. Nevertheless, this is a highly recommended option in cases where the problem has not been solved yet, or when the present problem is similar to another which has already been solved by using design patterns.

In Software engineering, the design patterns were classified by the GoF[1] into three types:

Table 4. Classification of Design Patterns proposed by GoF

Creational Patterns	Structural Patterns	Behavioral Patterns
Abstract Factory	Adapter	Chain of Responsibility
Builder	Bridge	Command
Factory Method	Composite	Interpreter
Prototype	Decorator	Iterator
Singleton	Facade	Memento
	Flyweight	Observer
	Proxy	State
		Strategy
		Template Method
		Visitor
		Mediator

1) Creational patterns, 2) Structural patterns, 3) Behavioral patterns. The Table 4 provides a high-level description of the twenty-three design patterns described by the GoF.

Design patterns are important in software development, as well as in the development of both Web applications and RIAs. Design patterns are applied in many ways in and in different aspects of RIAs. A very clear example is the visualization of information. For instance, let us assume that that there is some information that needs to be displayed on a RIA. Originally, this information is shown on a tabular way; however, it is required to show the same information differently. This is a constant problem problem for which it is possible to use a common solution. The best solution is to apply design patterns to the same information through different interfaces. In this particular case, the Facade pattern can be used, and thus a number of different interfaces without changing the programming logic can be applied. This makes possible to display some kind of information, such as a pie chart or a bar chart, among others. In this case, the behavior patterns are also an essential part of RIAs, since these patterns focus on the events, and RIAs are event-driven applications.

As it was previously mentioned, design patterns are critical in RIAs development. One of the main uses of the design patterns is to simplify the work and, thus, offer a solution that had been previously tested and whichwas successfully applied to a problem that manifests repeatedly In RIAs development, various elements and components are in common use. For instance, lighboxes and progress bars, among other GUI (GUI stands for Graphic User Interface) components are used for solving problems in the same way that arise every time. Therefore, if the design patterns are implemented as functional solutions allow reducing both time and development costs, they also simplify the developer's work.

5. USER INTERFACE DESIGN PATTERN (UI PATTERN) SUPPORT ON RIAS

There is a need for better understanding and improving the method for designing RIAs. The appearance of Web applications is almost as important as their functionalities. RIAs are a particular case since one of their main features is the improved user experience. In this case, problems of user interface design are common and repeatable in RIAs development, which is why interface design patterns have been established.

The Interface Design Patterns are recurring solutions to solve common design problems. Design patterns are standard reference points of the experience of the designer of the user interface (Scott & Neil, 2009).

About User Interface Design Patterns, several works have been proposed on different topics, some of the most important are mentioned below.

First, an analysis to identify UI design patterns in mobile devices - more specifically interaction patterns - was presented by (Raj & Komaragiri, 2009). This analysis demonstrated that a prototyping tool is useful in solving the constraints of usability and consistency, as well as in reducing the time taken to develop a mobile application. Moreover, a structured collection of user interface design patterns for mobile applications was presented (Nilsson, 2009). The paper described the use of these patterns to solve six identified problems in mobile application development. The collection of user interface design patterns has different levels of abstraction and shows how patterns may be used to present problems and solutions at different levels of detail. Similarly, another work (Richard, Robert, Malo & Migneault, 2011) explained that failing to use UI design patterns when developing a system interface entails an important loss of productivity and quality. The authors identified 30 UI patterns that were made available in a library and compared them in four modes of presentation: pattern thumbnails, application types, decision trees and alphabetical mode. Another proposal (Korozi, Leonidis, Margetis & Stephanidis, 2009) presented a new design framework called MAID that helps designers easily create user interfaces. Tho this design framework, a widgents library was supplemented. This library could be used in different application panels or for entirely different applications. The MAID tool development process could be decomposed in the following four phases: 1) UI Definition, 2) Application Data Integration, 3) UI Adaptation and 4) Deployment. Another approach (Seffah, Forbrig & Javahery, 2004) highlighted the problems in developing User Interfaces for multiple devices, such as computers, laptops or mobile telephones. Authors presented about a research on the Multiple User Interface (MUI) and the most important problems surrounding MUI development models. Finally, a set of HCI patterns was presented and the types of cross-platforms recommended for each pattern were discussed. In (Javahery, Sinnig, Seffah, Forbrig & Radhakrishnan, 2007) a pattern-based UI design process consisting of a set of input variables was proposed. These variables encapsulate

user requirements and context information. The output process is a set of patterns, which can be combined in a conceptual design or used as a user interface prototype.

In (Tidwell, 2011), the author categorized a set of patterns according to different facets of UI design. The categories include Content Organization, Navigation, Page Layout, and Actions/Commands. These kinds of patterns have been used to develop more effective UI for desktop applications, websites, web applications and mobile devices. Similarly, another research work (Seffah & Taleb, 2012) discussed how they way patterns could be used as a central artifact in the process of deriving a design from user experiences and requirements. The research presented a review of the evolution of pattern usages in UI design. Finally, the authors presented a study on pattern-based design where they discussed how user experiences could be incorporated into the pattern selection process through the use of user variables, pattern attributes, and associated relationships.

Finally, in (Scott & Neil, 2009) the Interface Design Patterns were basically divided into three categories: 1) Transitional Patterns, 2) Search or Lookup patterns, and 3) Feedback Patterns. This classification will be used since the authors' point of view is the most complete and easy to understand. These Interface Design Patterns are described in the next subsections.

5.1. Transitional Patterns

These types of patterns are used to change the aspect of a user interface. They are special effects that occur during a certain period of time and which, principal aim is to capture the user's attention. Each transitional pattern is described below:

- **Brighten and Dim:** This pattern is used to focus the user's attention on a particular component, either a dialog box or a lightbox component, among others. This pattern can be seen, for example, when a dialog in a lightbox-like element is opened, and then the focus is transferred to the dialog, dimming the rest of the screen.

- **Expand/Collapse:** This pattern is used when there is a great amount of information to show and there is also a possibility of showing the information partially. This means that the information can be divided and displayed in parts. The most used user interface component for implementing this pattern is the accordion. A common use for the accordion is a website menu where the options are expanded when the cursor is pressed and are contracted to free up space when the cursor is moved away.

- **Animation:** This pattern is used to provide the user an attractive view of the application. The user interface components used to exemplify this pattern are the slides, the drag & drop component, and animations with images. For instance the use of drag and drop is highly useful when the application has several components in a specific order and at one point the order can be changed. In this case, the user merely has to take the item and drag it to the new position in the same window. This provides easy user interactionwith the application. There are many uses for animations; in fact, animation is one of the most common and practical user interface components of RIAs. It is important to notice that this behavior was previously available only for desktop applications. .

- **Spotlight:** This pattern is used to indicate that something in the user interface has changed. This indication happens either by changing the spotlight of place or simply highlighting or underlining the changed element. As an example, the Hotmail™ home page highlights the email address field when the user is writing on this field; then, when the user changes the spotlight

to the password field this is the field that now appears highlighted.

5.2. Search or Lookup Patterns

These types of user interface design patterns were developed to provide assistance in the execution of searches. The main objective of Lookup Patterns is to facilitate to the search for information for users since the patterns react to data entry in real time:

- **AutoComplete:** It is a pattern designed to ease the user experience; it provides suggestions, as well as the possibility to auto complete the text that tp be written, for exampleinto a text box or a combo box. The best-known autocomplete example is the Google™ search engine. Once the search entry is being written, the suggestions related are displayed; then, when one of the suggestions is selected, the words in the text box are completed.

- **Live Suggest:** This pattern is very similar to the AutoComplete pattern. The difference relies on the fact that Live Suggest patterns provide real-time suggestions for creating searches. The aforementioned example about Google™ also serves to exemplify this pattern; however, there are many other search engines that use Live Suggest such as the YouTube™ website and the Yahoo!™ search engine.

- **Live Search:** This pattern is very similar to the previous two. Nevertheless, it provides greater advantages by displaying real-time results once a search entry is being written. Moreover, this pattern is considered an evolution of the AutoComplete and Live Suggest patterns. In fact, it has been implemented in most of the websites that have used the other two aforementioned patterns. For instance, the Google™ search engine uses this pattern.

- **Refining Search:** This type of pattenrs is another variation of the AutoComplete and Live Suggest patterns. The difference is that Refining Search patterns provide filters to refine searches. This offers the most adequate results in the shortest time possible. The Amazon™ website has a search engine based on this user interface pattern. In addition to completing and suggesting an entry for creating a search, Amazon™'s search engine provides a list to filter what is required to search.

5.3. Feedback Patterns

These patterns allow acting in real time, and they are useful to keep the user informed of what is happening in a Web application:

- **Live Preview:** This pattern was designed for preventing errors. It is used to inform the user how the application will interpret the data entered. For example, when a Google™ account is created, the user's name is requested, also the example of the data format required is shown in the text box below.
- **Progressive Disclosure:** This pattern was designed to show information to the user only when necessary, and this avoids overloading the user interface of the application. In order to create a Google™ account, the Google™ accounts website displays a message in red letters when an invalid user name is entered. This is a clear example of the progressive disclosure user interface pattern.
- **Progress Indicator:** This pattern was designed to indicate the progress of a complex task within an application. The most common user interface component implementing this pattern is the progress bar. It is used when the user should be informed about the progress of the requested action.

For instance, the Facebook™ website uses this pattern in order to show a progress bar which informs the user that a task is in progress while the interface content is being loaded.
- **Periodic Refresh:** This pattern is used to show new content in an application. The content is updated starting from user interactions or interactions with third-party applications, such as news channels. An example of this pattern is the Twitter™'s website timeline, which requires constant user interaction to keep itself update.

The usage of the user interface patterns outlined depends on the usability requirements. In this case, for each usability criterion, the need and impact should be adjusted on the user interface, since the patterns should be useful to the user and not harm its interaction with the application.

6. CONCLUSION

This chapter discusses four of the most important aspects to consider for RIAs development based on the other four key features for RIA's development and which were mentioned in the introduction of this book. From the author's perspective, the four aspects presented in this chapter can help improve the appearance of RIAs and offer new capabilities, such as responsiveness and interactivity. Multimedia support provides richer content to Web applications by presenting information more dynamically and attractively. Moreover, AOP allows incorporating new functionalities and scalability to Web applications in a non-invasive way. Design patterns offer possibilities of reusing well-known solutions to recurring problems. Finally, User Interface Design Patterns offer solutions to well-identified design problems on user interfaces and facilitate usability in software systems.

Nowadays, both the client and the software developer seek efficient, rapid, and agile developments. However, in this case it is also crucial to consider the final user of the software/application. Although the functioning of the software system is indeed very important, developers must not put aside the appearece of the system. Therefore, it can be stated that both functionality and appearance should go together in the development of software systems.

Also, programming languages themselves have today been implementing Design Patterns within their codes in order to support good programming practices. This is highly important for two reasons. First, desing patterns help the developer make not only functional but also efficient codes, and second, they provide elements to promote reusability in the systems. Another remarkable aspect is the AOP, which has been gently introducing itself in the development of software systems, and which is of great help in scalability and maintainance.

Several studies concerning UI Patterns have been carried out in order to define and classify them. For this reason, the need for developing ready-to-use interfaces for final users has arised, as well as the need for improving these users' interaction with the systems. Similarly, multimedia contents help improve and make more appealing the appeareance of the interfaces. The main objective of this is to ameliorate the content of the software systems, particularly of RIAs.

As a final conclusion it can be stated that the aspects exposed all along this chapter will enable programmers to develop efficient, well-structured, and better-looking applications. Moreover, all the elements mentioned in the chapter were presented so they can be implemented in RIAs, which results in a great advantage with respect to the use of traditional Web applications.

REFERENCES

Alexander, C., Ishikawa, S., & Silverstein, M. (1977). *A Pattern Language: Towns, Buildings, Construction*. Oxford University Press.

Buchanan, M. (2013). *A Guide to Understanding Video Containers & Codecs*. Retrieved January, 2013, from http://library.rice.edu/services/dmc/guides/video/VideoFormatsGuide.pdf

Chen, H. Y., Lin, Y. H., & Cheng, C. M. (2012). COCA: Computation Offload to Clouds Using AOP. In *Proceedings of the 12th IEEE/ACM International Symposium on Cluster, Cloud and Grid Computing (CCGrid 2012)* (pp. 466-473). Washington, DC: IEEE Computer Society. doi:10.1109/CCGrid.2012.98

Clarke, S., & Baniassad, E. (2005). *Aspect-Oriented Analysis and Design - The Theme Approach*. Addison-Wesley Professional.

Czarnecki, K. (1999). *Generative Programming: Principles and Techniques of Software Engineering Based on Automated Configuration and Fragment-Based Component Models*. (PhD thesis). German: Technische Universitat Ilmenau.

Ekabua, O. (2012). Using Aspect Oriented Techniques to Build-in Software Quality. *International Journal of Computer Science Issues*, 9(4), 250–255.

Elrad, T., Filman, R. E., & Bader, A. (2001). Aspect oriented programming: Introduction. *Communications of the ACM*, 44(10), 28–32. doi:10.1145/383845.383853

Freedman, A. (1999). *Diccionario bilingüe de computación*. Mc Graw Hill.

Gamma, E., Helm, R., Johnson, R., & Vlissides, J. (1994). *Design Patterns: Elements of reusable Object-Oriented Software*. Boston, MA: Addison-Wesley Longman Publishing Co., Inc.

Heo, S. H., & Choi, E. M. (2006). Representation of Variability in Software Product Line Using Aspect-Oriented Programming. In *Proceedings of the Fourth International Conference on Software Engineering Research, Management and Applications (SERA '06)* (pp. 66-73). Washington, DC: IEEE Computer Society.

Holzinger, A. (2005). Usability engineering methods for software developers. *Communications of the ACM*, *48*(1), 71–74. doi:10.1145/1039539.1039541

Ivory, M. Y., & Hearst, M. A. (2001). The state of the art in automating usability evaluation of user interfaces. *ACM Computing Surveys*, *33*(4), 470–516. doi:10.1145/503112.503114

Jacobson, I., & Ng, P. W. (2005). *Aspect-Oriented Software Development with Use Cases*. Addison Wesley Professional.

Javahery, H., Sinnig, D., Seffah, A., Forbrig, P., & Radhakrishnan, T. (2007). Pattern-based UI design: adding rigor with user and context variables. In *Proceedings of the 5th international conference on Task models and diagrams for users interface design (TAMODIA'06)* (pp. 97-108). Berlin: Springer-Verlag. doi:10.1007/978-3-540-70816-2_8

Jboss. (2013). *Aspect Oriented Programming (AOP) Support*. Retrieved January, 2013, from http://docs.jboss.org/jbossas/jboss4guide/r2/html/aop.chapt.html

Juárez Martínez, U. (2008). *Énfasis: Programación Orientada a Aspectos de Grano Fino*. (PhD thesis). Centro de Investigación y de Estudios Avanzados del Instituto Politécnico Nacional.

Kiczales, G., Lamping, J., Mendhekar, A., Maeda, C., Lopes, C., Loingtier, J. M., & Irwin, J. (1997). Aspect-oriented programming. In M. Aksit, & S. Matsuoka (Eds.), *Ecoop'97: Object-Oriented Programming* (pp. 220–242). Berlin: Springer-Verlag.

Korozi, M., Leonidis, S., Margetis, G., & Stephanidis, C. (2009). MAID: a Multi-platform Accessible Interface Design Framework. In *Proceedings of the 5th International Conference on Universal Access in Human-Computer Interaction. Part III: Applications and Services (UAHCI '09)* (pp. 725-734). Berlin: Springer-Verlag. doi:10.1007/978-3-642-02713-0_77

Kwanwoo, L., Botterweck, G., & Thiel, S. (2009). Feature-Modeling and Aspect-Oriented Programming: Integration and Automation. In *Proceedings of the 2009 10th ACIS International Conference on Software Engineering, Artificial Intelligences, Networking and Parallel/Distributed Computing (SNPD '09)* (pp. 186-191). Washington, DC: IEEE Computer Society.

Laddad, R. (2003). *AspectJ in Action: Practical Aspect-Oriented Programming*. Greenwich, CT: Manning Publications Co.

Miano, J. (1999). *Compressed Image File Formats: Jpeg, Png, Gif, Xbm, Bmp*. New York, NY: ACM Press/Addison-Wesley Publ. Co.

Nilsson, E. G. (2009). Design patterns for user interface for mobile applications. *Advances in Engineering Software*, *40*(12), 1318–1328. doi:10.1016/j.advengsoft.2009.01.017

Raj, A., & Komaragiri, V. (2009). RUCID: Rapid Usable Consistent Interaction Design Patterns-Based Mobile Phone UI Design Library. In *Proceedings of the 13th International Conference on Human-Computer Interaction. Part I: New Trends* (pp. 677-686). Berlin: Springer-Verlag. doi:10.1007/978-3-642-02574-7_76

Richard, J., Robert, J.-M., Malo, S., & Migneault, J. (2011). Giving UI Developers the Power of UI Design Patterns. In *Proceedings of the 2011 international conference on Human interface and the management of information - Volume Part I (HI'11)* (pp. 40-47). Berlin: Springer-Verlag. doi:10.1007/978-3-642-21793-7_5

Sandvine. (2012). *Global Internet Phenomena Report: 2H 2012*. Retrieved January, 2013, from www.sandvine.com/news/global_broadband_trends.asp

Scott, B., & Neil, T. (2009). *Designing Web Interfaces: Principles and Patterns for Rich Interactions* (1st ed.). O'Reilly Media, Inc.

Seffah, A., Forbrig, P., & Javahery, H. (2004). Multi-devices "Multiple" user interfaces: Development models and research opportunities. *Journal of Systems and Software, 73*(2), 287–300. doi:10.1016/j.jss.2003.09.017

Seffah, A., & Taleb, M. (2012). Tracing the evolution of HCI patterns as an interaction design tool. *Innovations in Systems and Software Engineering, 8*(2), 93–109. doi:10.1007/s11334-011-0178-8

Tahir, A., & Ahmad, R. (2010). An AOP-Based Approach for Collecting Software Maintainability Dynamic Metrics. In *Proceedings of the 2010 Second International Conference on Computer Research and Development (ICCRD '10)* (pp.168-172). Washington, DC: IEEE Computer Society. doi:10.1109/ICCRD.2010.26

Tidwell, J. (2011). *Designing Interfaces* (2nd ed.). Sebastopol, CA: O'Reilly Media, Inc.

Zhou, J., Ji, Y., Zhao, D., & Liu, J. (2010). Using AOP to ensure component interactions in component-based software. In *Computer and Automation Engineering (ICCAE), 2010 the 2nd International Conference on* (Vol. 3, pp. 518-523). Singapore: IEEE Computer Society.

ADDITIONAL READING

Flickr. (2012). Retrieved November, 2012, from www.flickr.com

Gmail. (2012). Retrieved November, 2012, from mail.google.com

Netflix. (2012). Retrieved November, 2012, from www.netflix.com/

Vimeo (2012). Retrieved November, 2012, from www.vimeo.com

YouTube. (2012). Retrieved November, 2012, from www.youtube.com

KEY TERMS AND DEFINITIONS

Aspect-Oriented Programming: It is a new programming paradigm that describes a development methodology for separating crosscutting concerns during the software development.

Design Patterns: It is a proven solution a common and recurring problem, this solution is designed for a particular context.

Multimedia: It is the representation of information through different means of distributions such as audio, text and images, but mainly video.

Reusability: It is the ability to develop a new software system reusing components or code fragments, from other or others software systems.

Rich Internet Applications: Rich Internet Applications are applications that are deployed over the Web, this type of applications combines features and functionality of Web applications and desktop applications.

Scalability: A characteristic of a system, model or function that describes its capability to cope and perform under an increased or expanding workload.

Usability: It is the ease with which people can use something in particular, and in this case a software system.

User Interface Design Pattern: UI design patterns are solutions to common user interface problems.

ENDNOTES

[1]   GoF stands for Gang of Four that are the authors of the book, *"Design Patterns: Elements of Reusable Object-Oriented Software"*. This important book describes various development techniques and pitfalls in addition to providing twenty-three object-oriented programming design patterns. The four authors were Erich Gamma, Richard Helm, Ralph Johnson and John Vlissides.

Chapter 5
Multimedia Support for Native/Embedded Video Playback on Frameworks for RIAs Development

ABSTRACT

Chapter 5 discusses the capabilities of RIA frameworks in the context of multimedia content support. For this purpose, several alternatives for implementing video playback functionality are presented by using both JavaScript-based RIA frameworks to and non-JavaScript-based RIA frameworks. Examples of JavaScript-based RIA frameworks having multimedia content support are Dojo, jQuery, Prototype, and Mootools. Examples of non-JavaScript-based RIA frameworks are Adobe Flex™, JavaFX™, Silverlight™, and OpenLaszlo. For each case study the mandatory files are mentioned. The chapter also shows a screenshot where video player is displayed and code snippets that were used are presented. Finally, a comparative analysis of video playback support for each framework is presented in terms of video container formats and encoding types.

1. INTRODUCTION

The possibility to represent graphics, audio and video is considered an inherent ability of RIAs (Rich Internet Applications). In fact, along with GUI (Graphic User Interface) transformations, visual continuity and temporal behavior, it is a factor affecting one of the distinguishing features of RIAs: the enhanced GUI (Preciado et al., 2005). Hence the importance of evaluating and knowing

what frameworks for RIAs development natively support these features.

The present chapter primarily focuses on reviewing the support for video playback on both JavaScript-based and non-JavaScript-based frameworks, because the support for the other types of media, i.e., audio and graphics, is a pre-requisite to support video playback.

As is explained in this chapter, most of the non-JavaScript-based frameworks for RIAs development provide support for all the media types

DOI: 10.4018/978-1-4666-6437-1.ch005

in a unified way and in terms of GUI controls. However;, non-JavaScript-based RIA frameworks provide support for media content in three different ways: 1) by using embedded standard (default) media players, 2) by using own GUI controls and 3) by using <audio> and <video> HTML5-based tags.

From this perspective, this chapter is intended to review the first two aforementioned approaches under the concept that JavaScript-based RIA frameworks do not commonly have video playback support as part of its core. Instead, they provide mechanisms for extending that core (by means of plug-ins or add-ons), so that there be different third-party implementations for video playback support. Therefore, we have considered the third-party plug-ins outlined in (Rosales-Morales et al., 2011).

2. MULTIMEDIA SUPPORT INTO JAVASCRIPT-BASED FRAMEWORKS

Various files formats are used for video playback. Each one of these formats provides certain features. Both the formats and their features are described below:

- **FLV (Flash Video)** is a container file format used to deliver video over the Internet using Adobe Flash Player™ versions 6-10. Flash Video content may also be embedded within SWF (Shockwave Flash) files. There are two different video file formats known as Flash Video: FLV and F4V. The audio and video data within FLV files are encoded in the same way as they are within SWF files. The format has quickly established itself as the format of choice for embedded video on the web. YouTube™, Hulu™, Google Video™, Yahoo Video™, Metacafe™, Reuters™, and many other news providers are examples of websites using Flash video format.

- **MPEG (Moving Picture Experts Group)** is a working group of experts formed by ISO (International Organization for Standarization) and IEC (International Electrotechnical Commission) to set standards for audio and video compression and transmission. MPEG algorithms compress data to form small bits that can be easily transmitted and then decompressed. MPEG achieves its high compression rate by storing only the changes from one frame to another, instead of storing each entire frame. The video information is then encoded using a technique called Discrete Cosine Transform (DCT).

- **RMVB (Real Media Variable Bitrate)** is a variable bitrate extension of the RealMedia™ multimedia compression format developed by RealNetworks™. As opposed to the more common RealMedia™ container – which holds streaming media encoded at a constant bit rate – RMVB file extension, compared with DVDRIP, is typically used for multimedia content locally stored.

- **WMV (Windows Media Video)** is a subset of Microsoft™'s Advanced Systems Format (ASF) container format. WMV files can be played by video players such as MPlayer or Windows™ Media Player™, the latter being only available for Microsoft™ Windows™ and Macintosh™ (Mac™) systems. WMV is a closed source, propriety codec that cannot be manipulated.

In the following sections, the support for video playback for RIAs development is discussed.

2.1. Video Playback Support Using Dojo

Dojo supports video playback by means of the DojoX package. Beyond that, DojoX is a module

Figure 1. Video playback using Dojo

for the development of extensions to the Dojo toolkit; it is a repository for more stable and mature extensions and it also acts as an incubator for experimental code, a testbed for additions to the main toolkit. Also, the DojoX package provides native controls to manipulate videos as part of its "av" module. DojoX uses the Adobe Flash Player™ plug-in to play FLV videos and it also requires a Web server.

In order to show this support, a PHP-based Web application which uses XAMPP was developed. XAMPP is a solution stack package mainly consisting of Apache HTTP Server, MySQL database management system (DBMS) and PHP-based and Perl-based interpreters. The implementation of this sample application is depicted in Figure 1, where a screenshot of the full video player is presented. This video player implements the Play and Pause controls.

A snippet of the Dojo-based source code is depicted in Figure 2. The figure presents important aspects of the video player provided by Dojo. The controls for volume, play time, and bar progress of the video player are implemented in this code fragment. The description of the video to be played is described in line 11 of the code fragment.

The HTML-based source code for implementing a video player for the FLV videos is depicted

in Figure 3, which includes the playback controls provided by the Dojox widget class.

Table 1 summarizes the features of the DojoX classes related to multimedia support.

2.2. Video Playback Support Using jQuery

jQuery supports embedded video playback of diverse video container formats, such as MPEG-4, FLV, and AVI (Audio Video Interleave), to mention but a few. It also supports both local and remote video files, as well as live and recorded media. This is achieved by means of different jQuery plug-ins, i.e., extensions to the jQuery's prototype object.

In the context of JavaScript-based RIAs development, the embedded video playback support is commonly incorporated by using pop-up dialog boxes. In jQuery, it is addressed by the jQuery ThickBox plugin. This is explained in Table 2.

Furthermore, by using the jQuery framework plugin, the jQuery Multimedia Portfolio can be used in order to play FLV video files. The plugin displays diverse kinds of media content by means of a gallery. Figure 4 depicts the use of the jQuery Multimedia Portfolio plugin to embed a local FLV video file into a jQuery-based RIA. In addition,

Figure 2. Snippet of Dojo-based source code used for implementing video playback

```
1    dojo.require("dojox.av.FLVideo");
2    dojo.require("dojo.parser");
3    var prgDim, volDim, progressNode, volumeNode, sliderNode, volsliderNode, durNode, timeNode;
4    dojo.addOnLoad(function() {
5          progressNode = dojo.byId("progress");
6          volumeNode = dojo.byId("volume");
7          sliderNode = dojo.byId("slider");
8          volsliderNode = dojo.byId("volslider");
9          durNode = dojo.byId("dur");
10         timeNode = dojo.byId("time");
11         w = new dojox.av.FLVideo({initialVolume:.1, mediaUrl: "video/VideoArdillaMarlin2.flv",
12   autoPlay:true, isDebug:false}, "vid");
13         toggle = function() {
14               if(w.isPlaying) { w.pause(); }
15               else{ w.play(); }
16         }    …
```

Figure 3. Snippet of HTML-based source code used for implementing video playback in Dojo

```
1    <table id="player">
2        <tr>
3            <td><h1>Framework: Dojo</h1></td><td></td>
4        </tr>
5        <tr>
6            <td colspan="2" style="height:100%;"><div id="vid" style="height:100%;"></div></td>
7        </tr>
8        <tr>
9            <td style="text-align:left;"><input id="time" type="text" /></td>
10           <td style="text-align:right;"><input id="dur" type="text" /></td>
11       </tr>
12       <tr>
13           <td colspan="2"><div id="progress"><div id="slider"></div></div></td>
14       </tr>
15       <tr>
16           <td><button onclick="toggle();">Play/Pause</button>
17               <button onclick="w.play('video/VideoArdillaMarlin2.flv');">Play</button></td>
18           <td style="text-align:right;"><div id="volume"><div id="volslider"></div></div></td>
19       </tr>
20   </table>
21   …
```

Table 1. Summary of DojoX classes related to media support (dojox.av module)

Class/Component	Description	Approach	Container Formats Supported
FLVideo (dojox.av)	It is a full-featured class that provides the ability to play FLV videos within the Dojo environment. It provides the typical play (), pause(), seek() and volume() playback functions[1]. It offers two defining methods: a declarative (markup-based) approach and a programmatic approach.	Native	FLV and MP4 with H.264 video compression.
widget (dojox.av)	It provides base player control widgets for building a media player, including a play button, a volume button, a progress slider, a status container, and the player container[2].	-	-

Table 2. Summary of JavaScript files related to jQuery-based video playback support

Script/Component	Description	Approach	Container Formats Supported
jquery-multimedia-portfolio. js	It is a carousel that automatically detects the file extension of each media added to it and applies an adapted media player. It supports images, audio, and video[3].	Embedded	FLV with H.264 video compression.
Slider	In its basic form, it is a horizontal slider with a single handle, which can be moved by using the mouse or the arrow keys.	-	-
thickbox.js	It is a dialog widget written on top of the jQuery library. It is intended to show images, inline content, iframe content, or content served through AJAX in a hybrid modal[4].	Embedded	None (possible via the <iframe> tag)

Figure 4. Video playback using jQuery

Figure 5. Snippet of the jQuery-based source code used for implementing video playback

```
1    ...
2    <script type="text/javascript" src="js/jquery.js"></script>
3    <script type="text/javascript" src="js/jquery.dimensions.js"></script>
4    <script type="text/javascript" src="js/ui.mouse.js"></script>
5    <script type="text/javascript" src="js/ui.slider.js"></script>
6    <script type="text/javascript" src="js/jquery.multimedia-portfolio.js"></script>
7    <script type="text/javascript">$(document).ready(function(){$("ul.multimedia-
8    portfolio").multimedia_portfolio({width: 800});});</script>
     ...
```

Figure 6. Snippet of the HTML-based source code used for implementing video playback in jQuery

```
1    …
2    <div class="page">
3        <h1>Framework: jQuery in a gallery</h1>
4        <center>
5            <ul class="multimedia-portfolio">
6                <li>
7                    <a href="VideoArdillaMarlin2.flv"><img src="thumbnails/yt.jpg" width="800px"
8    height="1000px" title="Video" /></a>
9
10               </li>
11           </ul>
12       </center>
13   </div>
14   …
```

Figures 5 and 6 present snippets of the corresponding source code. These snippets involve the use of several files, such as:

- jquery.js
- jquery.dimensions.js
- ui.mouse.js
- ui.slider.js
- jquery-multimedia-portfolio.js

Because the video playback is implemented as part of a media gallery, it is possible to add more videos or images. Figure 4 illustrates a gallery implemented using jQuery Multimedia Portfolio. The figure shows a video inside the gallery as well as the progress bar for the video playback. With this component, it is possible to 1) add more videos or images into the gallery and 2) navigate among the different contents._

Figure 5 depicts the code fragment which includes all the necessary files for the implementation of the gallery, as well as a function to install jQuery Multimedia Portfolio.

Figure 6 depicts the HTML-based fragment code for the implementation of the gallery. The ongoing integration of the video into the gallery can be observed in line 7.

Table 1 summarizes the features of the jQuery classes related to multimedia support.

2.3. Video Playback Support Using Mootools

MooTools does not provide video playback support as part of its core. Therefore, third-party extensions must be used to achieve this purpose. In fact, there is an official repository for MooTools plug-ins hosted at http://mootools.net/forge/. These plugins support local and remote recorded video based on QuickTime File Format (QTFF), SWF, and Ogg video container formats, among others.

In this sense, a popular plug-in called Videobox can be used in order to embed diverse kinds of video file formats into MooTools-based RIAs as it is outlined in Table 3. It is important to remark that the MooTools Videobox plug-in uses the SWFObject JavaScript library in order to embed Adobe Flash™-based media content.

Figure 7 depicts the use of the MooTools Videobox plug-in for implementing playback support for YouTube™ videos (SWF video files). In addition, snippets of the corresponding source code are presented in Figures 8 and 9. These snippets involve the use of several files such as:

- mootools.js
- swfobject.js
- videobox.js
- videobox.css

Table 3. Summary of JavaScript files related to MooTools-based video playback support

Script/Component	Description	Approach	Container Formats Supported
videobox.js	It provides a means to show videos by using overlays; it is in a lightbox for videos. The videobox.js file is an add-on to the Motools library[5].	Embedded	SWF (YouTube, Metacafe and Google videos), QuickTime File Format (QTFF): MOV file format, ASF: WMV file format and FLV: FLV file format.
swfobject.js	It is a JavaScript library used to embed Adobe Flash™ content into a Web page. It offers two embed methods: a markup-based approach and a method relying on JavaScript[6].	Embedded	SWF

Figure 7. Video playback using Mootools

Figure 8. Snippet of the MooTools-based source code used for implementing video playback

```
1    …
2    <div>
3          <a href="http://www.youtube.com/v/MrXfbyj26Vk?version=3&amp;hl=es_MX" rel="vidbox"
4    id="flvvideo" title="Mootools y Videobox" >Video</a>
5    </div>
6    …
```

Figure 9. Snippet of the HTML-based source code used for implementing video playback in MooTools

```
1    …
2    <script type="text/javascript" src="js/mootools.js"></script>
3    <script type="text/javascript" src="js/swfobject.js"></script>
4    <script type="text/javascript" src="js/videobox.js"></script>
5    <link rel="stylesheet" href="css/videobox.css" type="text/css" media="screen" />
6    …
```

Table 4. Summary of JavaScript files related to Prototype-based video playback support

Script/Component	Description	Approach	Container Formats Supported
lightwindow.js	It is a modal window for many media types, including images, videos, Adobe Flash™ content, and PDF files. It is also a modal windos for other types of content, such as inline content and external pages. It is built on top of the Prototype framework[7].	Embedded	AVI, SWF (custom Adobe Flash™ content), QuickTime File Format (QTFF) and ASF, MPEG-2, among other container formats. Virtually any file format (via configuration).
scriptaculous.js	It is a collection of JavaScript GUI libraries. It provides a visual effects engine, a drag-and-drop library, as well as a set of GUI controls, among other elements. It is an add-on to the Prototype framework[8].	-	-

Figure 7 illustrates video playback using Mootools. The picture contains a video hosted in the well-known video website YouTube™. The element used for video playback is a Viedeobox element, which permits the activation or deactivation tasks of the video playback. There is a link with the directions needed for the activation and a button to close the component for the deactivation.

Figure 8 depicts a code fragment including the link of the video hosted on YouTube™ as well as the link that activates the VideoBox component.

Figure 9 illustrates the code fragment containing the inclusion of the necessary files in order to implement the video player.

In Table 3 summarizes the features of the Mootools classes related to multimedia support, particularly the VideoBox plugin.

2.4. Video Playback Support Using Prototype

Prototype supports embedded video playback of all major video container formats, such as AVI, FLV, and ASF, among others, although this is not part of Prototype's basic functionality, but of third-party plug-ins. The Prototype media plug-ins publicly available over Internet like – such as those available at http://www.prototype-plugins. com/ – provide support for local and remote recorded video.

Similarly, another example of plug-ins for Prototype is Light Window. Light Window is a fully featured and well-documented media plug-in built on top of Prototype. It allows for virtually emebedding any media format into Prototype-based RIAs. This is explained in Table 4.

Figure 10. Video playback using Prototype and Script.aculo.us

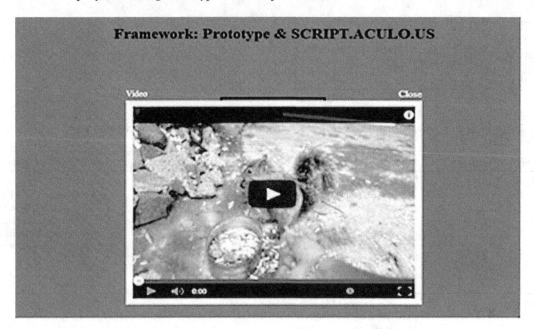

Figure 11. Snippet of the source code using Prototype for video playback

```
1    ...
2    <a class="lightwindow"
3    params="lightwindow_width=425,lightwindow_height=344,lightwindow_loading_animation=true"
4            title="Video" href="http://www.youtube.com/v/MrXfbyj26Vk?version=3&amp;hl=es_MX">
5            <img src="img/youtube.png" />
6    </a>
7    ...
```

The use of the Prototype LightWindow plug-in for implementing playback support for YouTube videos (SWF files) is depicted in Figure 10. In addition, a snippet of the corresponding source code is presented in Figure 11. This implementation involves the use of several files such as:

- prototype.js
- scriptaculous.js
- lightwindow.js
- lightwindow.css

The Script.aculo.us JavaScript library is typically used to provide visual effects to Prototype-based RIAs. It is thus a dependency of the Prototype LightWindow plug-in.

Figure 10 illustrates a video player implemented by using Prototype; the video appears within a window. In addition to the close buttom, this window contains certain other configurable parameters, such as the size of the window, among others.

Figure 11 represents a code fragment. The link of the video that is being played and the configurable parameters of the window in which the video is embedded can be found in line 4.

2.5. Video Playback Support Using Qooxdoo

Qooxdoo only has the ability to embed remote video into containers. In fact, Qooxdoo does not

Figure 12. Video playback using Qooxdoo

Framework: Qooxdoo

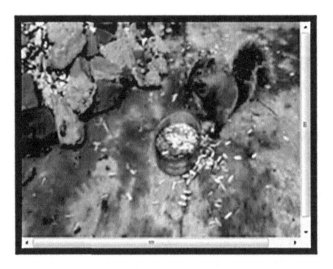

Figure 13. Snippet of the HTML-based source code used for implementing video playback in Qooxdoo

```
1   …
2   <div id="b1"
3   style="position:absolute;background:red;top:100px;left:400px;overflow:scroll;width:365px;heigh
    t:365px">
4       <embed src="http://www.youtube.com/v/MrXfbyj26Vk?version=3&amp;hl=es MX" width="350"
5   height="350">
6       </embed>
7   </div>
8   …
```

have its own video player component; hence, the video playback is achieved by means of a Qooxdoo utility or helper class. In fact, the helper.js file is the only requirement for incorporating video playback support into Qooxdoo-based RIAs.

The use of the Qooxdoo JavaScript framework for implementing playback support for YouTube™ videos (SWF files) is depicted in Figure 12. In addition, a snippet of the corresponding source code is presented in Figure 13.

Figure 12 illustrates the video player implemented with Qooxdoo; both, the video and the scrolls can be observed in the image. The component in which the video was embedded is configurable. This means that features of width, height, and whether the component should sup-

port scrolls can be indicated. If the video is of bigger size than the component, it will then appear incomplete.

In Figure 13, the link of the video that is being played is found in line 14. Similarly, the component configuration used to implement the player can be found in the same line.

2.6. Video Playback Support Using Rico

Rico is able to embed remote recorded video into JavaScript-based RIAs by using a native panel container. In this case,, the rico.js file is the only requirement, sicne the file is in charge of creating the main Rico object. Additional JavaScript files

Figure 14. Video playback using Rico

can be required depending on the functions to be implemented, because Rico is built on top of the Prototype framework and also includes support for jQuery, MooTools, Dojo, and Sencha Ext JS frameworks.

Figure 14 illustrates a video player implemented by using the Rico framework. It is important to mention that the video player here was developed under a tabs component. For the purpose of this research, only one tab was implemented; however, additional tabs can be implemented in cases where more videos or functionalities are required.

Figure 15 depicts a code fragment of the video player on Rico. Both the link of the video that is being played and the component configuration appear in line 10.

2.7. Video Playback Support Using Sencha ExtJS

Sencha Ext JS requires an extension for video playback. There is an official repository for third-party extensions for Sencha products which is

called Sencha market and it is available at https://market.sencha.com/. The range of video container formats supported by these extensions includes: MPEG-4, QuickTime File Format (QTFF), and RealMedia video container formats.

In this case, a popular Sencha Ext JS media extension called Ext.ux.YoutubePlayer allows for embedding videos hosted on the YouTube™ website along with common playback controls into JavaScript-based RIAs using native Ext JS GUI controls. According to the above, the format supported by this extension is only SWF, as it is explained in Table 5.

The use of the Sencha Ext JS YoutubePlayer plug-in is depicted in Figure 16. Additionally, a snippet of the corresponding source code is depicted in Figure 17.

Figure 16 shows the video player implemented in Sencha Ext JS. This video player contains the basic controls for playback, such as play, stop, forwarding, and volume, among others.

Figure 17 shows a code fragment in which the main characteristics of the video player are

Figure 15. Snippet of the HTML-based source code used for implementing for video playback in Rico

```
1    …
2    <div id="tabsExample">
3        <div>
4            <div class="panelheader">
5                Video
6            </div>
7        </div>
8        <div class="panelContentContainer">
9            <div class="panelContent">
10               <embed src="http://www.youtube.com/v/MrXfbyj26Vk?version=3&amp;hl=es_MX"
11   width="480" height="360">
12               </embed>
13           </div>
14       </div>
15   </div>…
```

Table 5. Summary of JavaScript files related to Sencha Ext JS-based video playback support

Class/Component	Description	Approach	Container Formats Supported
Ext.ux.YouTubePlayer	It is a component utilizing the YouTube chromeless player API.	Embedded	SWF (YouTube videos)
Ext.ux.YouTubePlayer.Control	It provides a functionality for loading YouTube videos, as well as for the typical playback controls - such as playing and pausing videos, muting and unmuting videos, and setting the volume, among others[9].	Native	-

Figure 16. Video playback using Sencha Ext JS

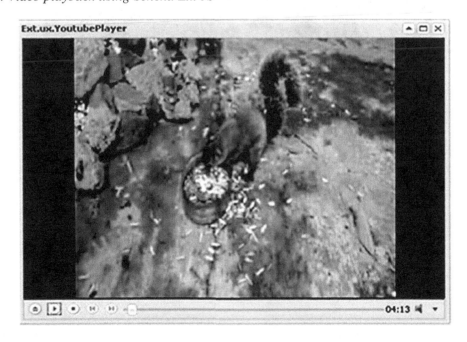

Figure 17. Snippet of the Ext JS-based source code used for implementing video playback

```
1    …
2    Ext.onReady(function(){
3        var playerPanel = new Ext.ux.YoutubePlayer({
4            developerKey: DEVELOPER_KEY,
5            playerId   : 'myplayer',
6            border: false,
7            ratioMode: 'strict',
8            hideMode: 'visibility',
9            bgColor: "#000000",
10           bodyStyle: 'background-color:#000000;'
11       });
12       playerPanel.on('ready', function(panel, player) {
13           panel.cueVideoById('Us-TVg40ExM', 0);
14       }, playerPanel);
15   var w = new Ext.Window({
16       title  : 'Ext.ux.YoutubePlayer',
17       layout: 'fit',
18       maximizable: true,
19       animCollapse: false,
20   …
```

Figure 18. Video playback using X-Library

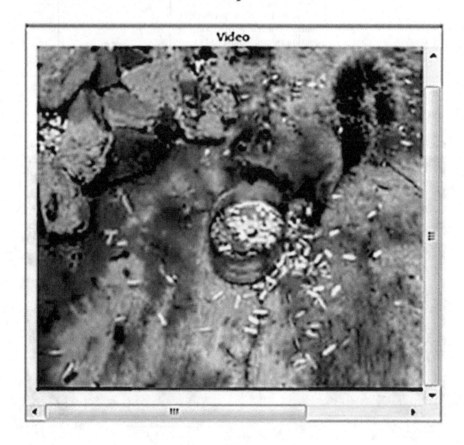

implemented. Examples of such characteristics are color and other functionalities of the player.

2.8. Video Playback Support Using X-Library

Like Rico, X-Library supports embedded video playback as part of its core. In detail, it permits embedding remote recorded video into JavaScript-based RIAs by using typical containers, such as tab panels and accordions, since it does not have native video playback controls.

Moreover, the use of the X-Library framework for implementing playback support for YouTube™ videos (SWF files) is depicted in Figure 18. In addition, a snippet of the corresponding source code is presented in Figure 19. This implementation involves the use of the files listed below which are described in Table 6.

- offline.js
- v3.css
- tpg_def.css
- x.js
- xtabpanelgroup.js

Figure 18 presents the video player implemented in the X-Library. In this case the video is embedded into any component which will support it.

Figure 19 shows a code fragment corresponding to the implementation of the video player through the use of X-Library.

In Table 6 summarizes the features of the X-Library classes related to multimedia support.

2.9. Comparison

Table 7 summarizes an overview of the video playback capabilities provided by the JavaScript-based RIA frameworks analyzed in this chapter. As it can be inferred from this analysis, most of the frameworks do not have native controls related to media playback. In fact, they only allow for video embedding (video player Web browser plug-ins) within native containers. Furthermore, it is important to notice that most of the frameworks providing customized video playback support require third-party extensions.

3. MULTIMEDIA SUPPORT INTO NON-JAVASCRIPT-BASED FRAMEWORKS

The RIA technology must offer a rich set of media APIs or tags (in the specific case of markup languages, such as HTML5) that exploit client-side graphics, hardware acceleration capabilities, and ensure consistently deployment across diverse platforms in order to deliver high-performance

Figure 19. Snippet of the source code using X-Library for video playback

```
1    ...
2    <div>
3        <div id='tpg1' class='tabPanelGroup'>
4            <div class='tabGroup'>
5                <a href='#tpg11' class='tabDefault'>Video</a>
6                <span class='linkDelim'> | </span>
7            </div>
8            <div id='tpg11' class='tabPanel'>
9                <embed src="http://www.youtube.com/v/MrXfbyj26Vk?version=3&amp;hl=es_MX"
10   width="480" height="360">
11               </embed>
12           </div>
13       </div>
14   </div>
15   ...
```

Table 6. Summary of JavaScript files related to X-Library-based video playback support

Script/Component	Description	Approach	Container Formats Supported
x.js	It represents the X-Library entry point. In fact, it defines the main X-Library object.	-	-
xtabpanelgroup.js	It provides a downgradable tab panel container, i.e., a tab panel that is downgraded when JavaScript is disabled.	Embedded	Unknown

Table 7. Summary of video playback capabilities among the JavaScript-based RIA frameworks analyzed in this chapter

Framework	Video files formats supported and mandatory files	Component in which the video is displayed
Mootools	It supports video and audio in a remote way. It supports popular video file formats such as AVI, WMV and SWF. Mandatory files: mootool.js, swfobject.js, videobox.js, videobox.css	It plays the video in a component called VideoBox.
Prototype	It supports video and audio in a remote way. The video file formats supported are AVI, FLV, among others. Mandatory Files: prototype.js, scriptaculous.js, lightwindow.js, lightwindow.css	The video is played embedded in a container component that provides the framework using functions of the Scriptaculous framewok
JQuery	It supports video playback in FLV file format and also remote video playback in the most used formats, such as MPEG and AVI, among others. Mandatory Files: thickbox-compressed.js, jquery.dimensions.js, ui.mouse.js, ui.slider.js, jquery.multimedia-portfolio.js, thickbox.css, multimedia-portfolio.css, jquery.js	In the first case, it uses a gallery for video playback and in the second case it uses a container component.
Dojo	It only supports FLV video files format Mandatory Files: DojoX	For video playback, it uses a DojoX video player requiring Flash.
Qooxdoo	It supports video and audio in a remote way. The video files supported are AVI, FLV to name a few. Mandatory Files: helper.js.	The video is played in a container component.
Rico	It supports video and audio in a remote way. The video files supported are AVI and FLV, among others. Mandatory Files: rico.js	The video is played in an embedded way in a container component.
Sencha Ext JS	It supports video and audio in a remote way coming from the YouTube website. The video files supported are FLV, AVI, MPEG, and WMV, among others. It uses a ExtJS plugin called Ext.ux.YoutubePlayer	The video is played in the video player provided by the plugin.
X-Library	It supports video and audio in a remote way. The video files supported are AVI, FLV, to mention a few. Mandatory Files: offline.js, v3.css, tpg_def.css, x.js, xtabpanelgroup.js.	The video is played in a container component.

portable RIAs. This criterion is assessed with respect to the variety of media file formats that are natively supported by the RIA technology for video playback only.

3.1. Video Playback Support Using Adobe Flex™

The Adobe Flex™ Spark skinning and components architecture consists of four main parts: a layout engine, an effects (animation) engine, a graphics library, and a components library. As part of the Spark components library, some GUI controls and classes related to media processing are provided as it is summarized in Table 8. In addition, other relevant ActionScript classes related to network management on working with remote video are summarized in Table 9 (Subramaniam, 2010).

As it can be inferred from the summarized analysis above, in the context of developing Adobe Flex™-based applications, some multimedia functionalities can be achieved by means of ActionScript™ classes from the Flash platform, particularly from the Flash media framework which includes classes such as Sound, Camera, and Microphone, besides the Video class.

As it can be inferred from the analysis presented above, the use of the Video class in conjunction with the NetStream and NetConnection classes may result in advanced media applications, such as video sharing applications for user communities where live video recorded by a user is sent to a server and then it is broadcasted from the server to other users.

Furthermore, it is important to notice that the Video class is not a GUI control like VideoDisplay and VideoPlayer controls; nevertheless, it is a display object that represents the visual space in which the video runs in the GUI and it can be manipulated like any display object by using

Table 8. Summary of ActionScript™ classes related to media support

Class	Description	Package	File Formats Supported (Video)	Supported Delivery Technologies	Type of Media Supported
VideoPlayer	It is a skinnable video player which has a fully-featured GUI in order to control video playback[10].	spark. components	FLV and MPEG-4-based containers such as F4V and MP4 ("Understanding video formats," n.d.).	Local, progressively downloaded, streaming (over RTMP (Real Time Messaging Protocol) protocol) and dynamic streaming media (over RTMP and HTTP protocols).	Live or recorded media.
VideoDisplay	It is the chromeless version of the VideoPlayer control, which does not support skinning[11].	spark. components mx.components			
StreamingVideoSource	It represents a streaming video source. The VideoPlayer control can take a StreamingVideoSource instance as its source property[12].	spark. components. mediaClasses			
Video	It permits displaying videos in Flash-based applications without embedding the videos in the SWF files[13].	flash.media			

Table 9. Summary of ActionScript™ classes related to network management

Class	Description	Package	Server Compatibility
NetStream	In the context of video files loading by means of the Video class, it represents the source of the video content. It opens a one-way streaming channel over a NetConnection object[14].	flash.net	-
NetConnection	In the context of video files loading by means of the Video class, it represents the connection to the video file. It creates a two-way connection between a client and a server[15].		Flash Media Server (RTMP protocol) or an application server running Flash Remoting MX or the Adobe Cirrus service[16] (RTMFP protocol).

Figure 20. Adobe Flex VideoPlayer™ control

positioning, transformations, filters and other capabilities.

Figure 20 depicts the usage of the Adobe Flex VideoPlayer™ control in the development of a Web browser-based RIA embedding a video player. This sample application plays the MP4 (H.264) video available at http://clips.vorwaerts-gmbh.de/VfE_html5.mp4. The Adobe Flex VideoPlayer™

control defines a skin part for each player area; therefore, it defines a videoDisplay skin part and a playerControls skin part. The playerControls part has in turn a play/pause button, a scrub bar (timeline), a current time display, a duration display, a volume bar, and a fullscreen button.

A snippet of the corresponding source code is presented in Figure 21. This snippet only excludes

Figure 21. Snippet of the Adobe Flex™-based source code

```
1   <s:VGroup width="100%" height="100%" horizontalAlign="center" verticalAlign="middle">
2       <s:VideoPlayer source="http://clips.vorwaerts-gmbh.de/VfE_html5.mp4"/>
3   </s:VGroup>
```

the definition of the application container, which is the first element in a MXML application.

3.2. Video Playback Support Using JavaFX™

The JavaFX™ media framework provides well-tested media functionality across all platforms where JavaFX™ is supported. Some of the functions supported by the JavaFX™ media stack include the following elements: FLV container, MP3 audio, MPEG-4 container, HTTP and FILE protocol support, progressive download, seeking,

buffer progress, and playback functions. All this is summarized in Table 10 (Castillo, n.d.).

Unlike the Adobe Flex VideoPlayer™ control, the JavaFX MediaPlayer™ control does not have built-in player controls, it merely provides the typical player functions, such as play(), pause() and stop(). Additionaly, JavaFX MediaPlayer™ has properties such as, mute and volume, which apply to all media types (audio and video). Furthermore, the media concept in JavaFX™ is based on all the classes contained within the javafx.scene. media package. Thus, these classes must be used in combination to create media players, either audio or video players.

Table 10. Summary of JavaFX™ classes related to media support

Class	Description	Package	Container Formats Supported (Video)	Supported Delivery Technologies	Type of Media Supported
Media	It represents a media resource that contains information, such as the source URI as well as the metadata contained in the media source[17].	javafx.scene. media	FLV and MPEG-4-based containers with H.264/AVC video compression ("Package javafx.scene. media," n.d.).	Local, progressive download and media streaming over HTTP protocol.	Live or recorded media.
MediaPlayer	It provides the controls for playing media. It does not contain any visual element; thefore, it must be used with the MediaView class[18].				
MediaView	It represents a JavaFX™ Node that provides a view of media being played by a MediaPlayer instance. It supports animation and effects[19].				

Figure 22. JavaFX™-based video player (desktop RIA)

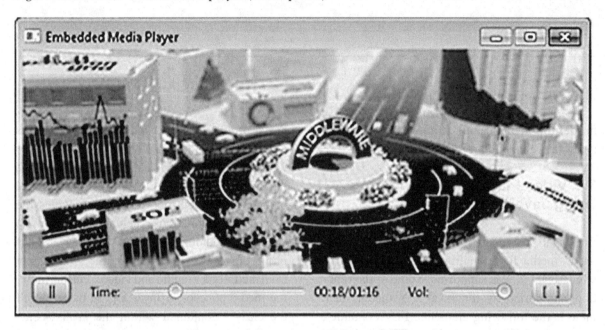

Figure 22 depicts the enhanced version of the sample video player available at http://docs. oracle.com/javafx/2/media/playercontrol.htm. This version adds the fullscreen functionality by means of the JavaFX™ ToggleButton control, a type of button with the ability to be selected. In detail, the fullscreen functionality is achieved by simply calling the Stage setFullScreen() function over the primary stage of the application, which causes the stage attempts to enter fullscreen mode using an undecorated window. As can be inferred, the JavaFX™ Stage class is the top-level container of any JavaFX™ application.

Furthermore, it is important to remark that this video player integrates a time display. This time display is implemented by using a JavaFX™ Label control and the JavaFX™ Duration class, a class that defines a duration of time and it provides utility methods like, for example, methods that return the number of milliseconds, seconds, minutes and hours in a specified period of time. The time display shows the ratio of the video playback time with respect to the duration of the video that is being loaded. Therefore, it is properly settled by

using the MediaPlayer getCurrentTime() method and the Media getDuration() method. It is worth mentioning that the getDuration() method returns an "UNKNOWN" value if the media opened does not have a known duration, such as live streaming.

In fact, this enhanced video player is a JavaFX™ custom control integrating playback functions similar to the built-in functions of the Adobe Flex VideoPlayer™ control. Figure 23 depicts a snippet of the source code defining part of the custom playback controls implemented for this sample application.

3.3. Video Playback Support Using Silverlight™

The Silverlight™ platform as a whole consists of two major parts: the Core Presentation Framework and the .NET Framework for Silverlight™. The whole media functionality provided by Silverlight™ is integrated into the former component and it features playback and management of diverse types of audio and video file formats such as WMV and MP3.

Figure 23. Snippet of the JavaFX™-based source code

```
1   Media media = new Media(MEDIA_URI);
2   MediaPlayer mediaPlayer = new MediaPlayer(media);
3   MediaView mediaView = new MediaView(mediaPlayer);
4   VBox mvPane = new VBox();
5   mvPane.setAlignment(Pos.CENTER);
6   mvPane.getChildren().add(mediaView);
7   HBox mediaBar = new HBox();
8   mediaBar.setAlignment(Pos.CENTER);
9   final Button playButton  = new Button(">");
10  mediaBar.getChildren().add(playButton);
11  Label timeLabel = new Label("Time: ");
12  mediaBar.getChildren().add(timeLabel);
13  Slider timeSlider = new Slider();
14  timeSlider.setMinWidth(50);
15  mediaBar.getChildren().add(timeSlider);
16  …
```

Table 11. Summary of Silverlight™ classes related to media support

Class	Description	Package	Container Formats Supported (Video)	Supported Delivery Technologies	Type of Media Supported
MediaElement	It represents an object containing audio, video or both. In this case, it is a rectangular area that can display video or play audio on its surface[20].	System.Windows.Controls	ASF with WMV and VC-1 video compression, MP4 with H.264 video compression as well as 3GP and 3G2 with H.264 and H.263 video compression ("Supported Media Formats, Protocols, and Log Fields," n.d.).	Local, progressive download, and media streaming (Windows Media Streaming Media over HTTP protocol).	Live or recorded

Table 11 summarizes the features of the Silverlight™ classes related to media support ("Silverlight Architecture," n.d.).

Similar to the JavaFX MediaPlayer™ control, the Silverlight™ MediaElement control does not integrate built-in player controls and it exposes similar playback functions instead. Therefore, these playback functions must be associated to GUI event handlers over GUI controls (typically buttons and sliders) manually added by the developer. However, unlike JavaFX™, Silverlight™ abstracts all the media functions and properties in only one class. This can result in time and effort saving in the development of media-intensive applications.

Figure 24 depicts the Silverlight™-based version of the video player developed in previous section of this chapter (Video playback support using JavaFX™). The fullscreen functionality is also added by means of a toggle button (a Silverlight™ ToggleButton control). Nevertheless, in this case, the fullscreen functionality is based on the Silverlight™ Content class, which exposes APIs that relate to the Silverlight™ content area, i.e., the area that is declared by the width and height properties in the application initialization. In detail, the IsFullScreen property of the Content instance hosting the application is settled to true when the user selects the toggle button. This makes the Silverlight™ plug-in display as a fullscreen plug-in.

Furthermore, the time display area of the video player is implemented by using the Silverlight™ Label control as it is depicted in the source code snippet presented below. In addition, the .NET Framework DispatcherTimer class is used. This class represents a timer integrated into the queue

Figure 24. Silverlight™-based video player (Web browser-based RIA)

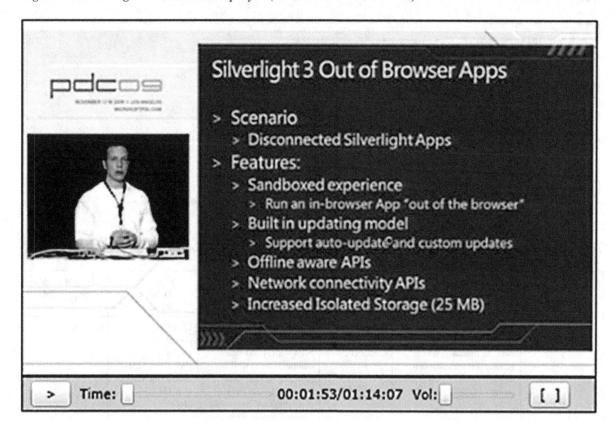

of work items for a thread. The timer interval is settled to 1000 milliseconds (one second), so that the video playback time is updated to the value returned by the Position property of the MediaElement control each time the timer interval has elapsed (every second). On the other hand, the video duration is obtained by means of the MediaElement NaturalDuration.TimeSpan property, which is able to obtain the duration of the media file currently opened. It is worth mentioning that the NaturalDuration property returns an "Automatic" value when the media opened does not have a known duration, such as live streaming. It is important to notice that the source code snippet depicted in Figure 25 merely includes part of the definition of the custom playback controls.

3.4. Video Playback Support Using OpenLaszlo™

OpenLazlo™ applications can be deployed either as proxied by the OpenLaszlo™ server or as standalone applications ("SOLO" deployment mode). Therefore, media loaded at runtime by OpenLaszlo™ applications can either be proxied through the OpenLaszlo™ server or be directly loaded. In any case, they can have either of two runtime targets: Adobe Flash Player™ or AJAX, i.e., they can be compiled to SWF files.

According to the above, video in OpenLaszlo™ is handled by the underlying platform runtime, the Adobe Flash Player™; in fact, the OpenLaszlo™ video APIs described in this chapter work only in OpenLaszlo™ applications compiled for the Flash

Figure 25. Snippet of the Silverlight™-based source code

```
1   <StackPanel       x:Name="LayoutRoot"       Background="White"       HorizontalAlignment="Center"
    VerticalAlignment="Center" Margin="0,0,0,0">
2      <Border Width="500" Height="300" BorderThickness="1" BorderBrush="Black">
3         <MediaElement DownloadProgressChanged="downloadProgressHandler" x:Name="video"
4   Width="500" Height="300" Source="http://ecn.channel9.msdn.com/o9/pdc09/wmv/CL20.wmv"
    HorizontalAlignment="Left" DataContextChanged="video_DataContextChanged"/>
5      </Border>
6      <Border Width="500" Height="30" BorderThickness="1" BorderBrush="Black" >
7         <StackPanel Width="500" Height="30" Background="#FFCCCCCC"
8   HorizontalAlignment="Center" VerticalAlignment="Center" Orientation="Horizontal">
9            <Button       x:Name="playButton"       Width="35"       Height="22"       Content="&gt;"
10  Margin="8,0,0,0"/>
            <sdk:Label Name="timeLabel" Height="24" Content="Time:" Margin="8,0,0,0"/>
11           <Slider Name="timeSlider" Width="140" Maximum="1"/>
12           ...
13        </StackPanel>
14     </Border>
15  </StackPanel>
```

runtime target. In detail, OpenLaszlo™ video APIs give developers access to the full functionality of media players, such as the Adobe Flash™ Media Server and the Red5 Media Server, which is an open source implementation of the Adobe Flash™ Media Server supporting the RTMP protocol ("Media Support," n.d.).

The set of classes described in Table 12 contains two kinds of elements: 1) basic classes acting as extensions that wrap Adobe Flash Player™ APIs and 2) higher level GUI components entirely written in LZX (OpenLaszlo™'s markup language). In this case, similar video playback capabilities can be achieved by using either the VideoView class in conjunction with standard GUI controls – such as buttons and sliders aimed at controlling playback functions – or the VideoPlayer component, which has built-in playback controls, like the Adobe Flex VideoPlayer™ component.

Figure 26 depicts the usage of the OpenLazlo™ VideoPlayer component in the development of a RIA embedding a native video player. This sample application plays the FLV (VP6) video also used by the JavaFX™-based video player (see section 5.3.2 of this chapter). The video is available at http://download.oracle.com/otndocs/products/javafx/oow2010-2.flv.

It is important to notice that this sample application uses the default look and feel of the GUI components involved. As it is depicted in Figure 26, the OpenLaszlo VideoPlayer™ component does not integrate the fullscreen functionality, which is the contrary in the case of the Adobe Flex VideoPlayer™ component.

In addition, the source code implemented for this sample application which consists only of three lines of source code is depicted in Figure 27.

3.5. Comparison

On the understanding that a media type is the combination of a container format and one or more encoding types, Table 13 summarizes a comparison of the support for media types among the non-JavaScript-based RIA frameworks analyzed in this chapter. This comparative analysis considers the container formats outlined at the beginning of this chapter. Fromr this perspective, due to its popularity, some MP4-based container formats (F4V and 3GP) are included in addition to the MP4 container format itself.

Finally, it is important to notice that a media type involves not only video compression formats but also audio compression formats. However,

Table 12. Summary of OpenLaszlo™ classes related to media support

Class	Description	Package	Container Formats Supported (Video)	Supported Delivery Technologies	Type of Media Supported
VideoView	It is a visual object used to show video from a video server. It is an extension of the View class, which is the most basic visual element, and it is optimized for video streaming[21].	lps. components. extensions.av	FLV with VP6 and Sorenson Spark video compression.	Local, progressive download and media streaming (Flash Media Server or Red5 Media Server over HTTP and RTMP protocols).	Live or recorded
MediaStream	It opens a connection in order to receive streaming media. It permits controlling the stream created by the VideoView class, i.e., it is used in conjunction with a VideoView instance[22].				
VideoPlayer	It is a higher level component providing essential GUI controls for handling audio and video (playback controls)[23].	lps. components. av			

Figure 26. OpenLaszlo™-based video player

Figure 27. OpenLazlo™-based source code

```
1   <canvas width="100%" height="80%">
2       <videoplayer       width="540"       height="241"       align="center"       valign="middle"
3   url="http://download.oracle.com/otndocs/products/javafx/oow2010-2.flv"/>
    </canvas>
```

Table 13. Summary of support for media types among non-JavaScript-based frameworks for RIAs development

Video Container Formats	Framework			
	Adobe Flex™	JavaFX™	Silverlight™	OpenLaszlo™
FLV	Yes (VP6 and Sorenson Spark)	Yes (VP6)	No	Yes (VP6 and Sorenson Spark)
MP4	Yes (H.264/AVC)	Yes (H.264/AVC)	Yes (H.264/AVC)	No
F4V	Yes (H.264/AVC)	No	No	No
3GP	Yes (H.264/AVC)	No	Yes (H.264/AVC and H.263)	No
ASF	No	No	Yes (WMV and VC-1)	No

for the purposes of this chapter, Table 13 merely summarizes the second type of compression..

4. CONCLUSION

In the case of JavaScript-based RIAs frameworks, the plug-ins analyzed in this chapter are not the only options for integrating native/embedded video playback support into JavaScript-based RIAs. In fact, the range of video containers and compression formats supported by a JavaScript-based RIA framework may significantly vary depending on the plug-ins selected. Moreover, the publication of the fifth revision of the HTML standard opens up new possibilities for rich media support due to the inclusion of the <audio>, <video> and <canvas> tags. These new features are intended to facilitate the integration of multimedia and graphical content on the Web without depending on proprietary Web browser plug-ins and APIs. However, these new features are not completely supported by all Web browsers yet. Because HTML5 is a W3C candidate recommendation to date, so that this video playback support approach is not addressed in this chapter.

On the other hand, although the decoding of some audio and video compression formats relies on operating system-specific media engines, the support for video playback into non-JavaScript-based RIA frameworks is commonly conditioned by the video container and compression formats natively supported by the involved Web browser plug-ins and runtime environments. Thus, in the case of Adobe Flex™, Adobe Flash Player™, and Adobe AIR™, they provide support for the FLV and F4V container formats, which are currently considered the fact standard for online video. However, in the case of Silverlight™, the Silverlight™ plug-in provides support for the ASF container format that is related to several proprietary codecs developed by Microsoft™.

According to what has been mentioned above, the selection of a technology for developing multimedia-interactive RIAs may depend on the video file formats involved, as well as on the amount of development effort necessary to incorporate the functionalities intended. In fact, as it was explained throughout this chapter, some non-JavaScript-based frameworks do not provide built-in support for video playback. This can result in an increase in development time and effort. As a summary, not only the capabilities of the frameworks represent a determining factor in this evaluation, but also the extent to which the capabilities are exposed as developer-friendly APIs.

REFERENCES

Architecture, S. (n.d.). *MSDN*. Retrieved May 10, 2013, from http://msdn.microsoft.com/en-us/library/bb404713(v=vs.95).aspx

Castillo, C. (n.d.). 1 Introduction to JavaFX Media. *JavaFX Documentation*. Retrieved May 9, 2013, from http://docs.oracle.com/javafx/2/media/overview.htm#CJAHFAHJ

Package javafx.scene.media. (n.d.). *JavaFX 2.2*. Retrieved May 9, 2013, from http://docs.oracle.com/javafx/2/api/javafx/scene/media/package-summary.html

Preciado, J. C., Linaje, M., Sanchez, F., & Comai, S. (2005). Necessity of methodologies to model Rich Internet Applications. In *Proceedings of the Seventh IEEE International Symposium on Web Site Evolution* (pp. 7–13). Washington, DC: IEEE Computer Society. doi:10.1109/WSE.2005.10

Rosales-Morales, V. Y., Alor-Hernández, G., & Juárez-Martínez, U. (2011). An overview of multimedia support into JavaScript-based Frameworks for developing RIAs. In *Proceedings of 2011 21st International Conference on Electrical Communications and Computers (CONIELECOMP)* (pp. 66–70). doi:10.1109/CONIELECOMP.2011.5749341

Subramaniam, D. (2010, March 8). *A brief overview of the Spark architecture and component set*. Retrieved May 9, 2013, from http://www.adobe.com/devnet/flex/articles/flex4_sparkintro.html

Support, M. (n.d.). *OpenLaszlo wiki*. Retrieved May 22, 2013, from http://wiki.openlaszlo.org/MediaSupport

Supported Media Formats, P., & Fields, L. (n.d.). *MSDN*. Retrieved May 9, 2013, from http://msdn.microsoft.com/en-us/library/cc189080(v=vs.95).aspx

Understanding Video Formats. (n.d.). *Adobe Flash Platform*. Retrieved May 9, 2013, from http://help.adobe.com/en_US/as3/dev/WS5b3ccc516d4fb-f351e63e3d118a9b90204-7d46.html

ADDITIONAL READING

Basics of Video. (n.d.). *Adobe Flash™ Platform*. Retrieved May 9, 2013, from http://help.adobe.com/en_US/as3/dev/WS5b3ccc516d4fb-f351e63e3d118a9b90204-7d50.html

Designing Rich Internet Applications. (n.d.). *MSDN*. Retrieved May 10, 2013, from http://msdn.microsoft.com/en-us/library/ee658083.aspx

Spark VideoPlayer and VideoDisplay Controls. (n.d.). *Adobe Flex 4.6*. Retrieved May 9, 2013, from http://help.adobe.com/en_US/flex/using/WSc78f87379113c38b-669905c51221a3b97af-8000.html

KEY TERMS AND DEFINITIONS

Bit Rate: The number of bits that are conveyed or processed per unit of time. It is quantified by using the bits per second (bit/s or bps) unit.

Container Type: It specifies the file format used to store the encoded audio, video and other media data.

Encoding Type: It specifies how sampled audio or video data are stored and it usually implies a particular compression algorithm.

Graphic User Interface: It is a part of the system software that acts as a user interface, i.e. it provides a mechanism for the user to interact with a software, these mechanisms can be text, images and other graphics.

Media Players: These are players for multimedia content, especially video content, which can support various formats.

Progressive Download: The process of load the video data in sequence when a video is delivered from a standard Web server.

Streaming: Technique alternative to progressive download where the client computer never downloads the entire video at one time.

ENDNOTES

1   http://dojotoolkit.org/reference-guide/1.9/dojox/av/FLVideo.html#dojox-av-flvideo

2   http://dojotoolkit.org/reference-guide/1.9/dojox/av/widget.html#dojox-av-widget

3   http://www.openstudio.fr/jQuery-Multimedia-Portfolio.html?lang=fr

4   http://thickbox.net/

5   http://videobox-lb.sourceforge.net/

6   https://code.google.com/p/swfobject/

7   http://www.p51labs.com/lightwindow/

8   http://script.aculo.us/

9   https://code.google.com/p/ext-ux-youtube-player/

10   http://help.adobe.com/en_US/FlashPlatform/reference/actionscript/3/spark/components/VideoPlayer.html

11   http://help.adobe.com/en_US/FlashPlatform/reference/actionscript/3/mx/controls/VideoDisplay.html

12   http://help.adobe.com/ru_RU/FlashPlatform/reference/actionscript/3/spark/components/mediaClasses/StreamingVideoSource.html

13   http://help.adobe.com/en_US/FlashPlatform/reference/actionscript/3/flash/media/Video.html

14   http://help.adobe.com/en_US/FlashPlatform/reference/actionscript/3/flash/net/NetStream.html

15   http://help.adobe.com/en_US/FlashPlatform/reference/actionscript/3/flash/net/NetConnection.html

16   http://labs.adobe.com/technologies/cirrus/

17   http://docs.oracle.com/javafx/2/api/javafx/scene/media/Media.html

18   http://docs.oracle.com/javafx/2/api/javafx/scene/media/MediaPlayer.html

19   http://docs.oracle.com/javafx/2/api/javafx/scene/media/MediaView.html

20   http://msdn.microsoft.com/en-us/library/system.windows.controls.mediaelement(v=vs.95).aspx

21   http://www.openlaszlo.org/lps3.4/docs/reference/index.html?videoview.html

22   http://www.openlaszlo.org/lps3.4/docs/reference/index.html?mediastream.html

23   http://www.openlaszlo.org/lps4.9/docs/reference/lz.videoplayer.html

Chapter 6
Aspect–Oriented Programming (AOP) Support on RIAs Development

ABSTRACT

Chapter 6 emphasizes the importance of employing Aspect-Oriented Programming (AOP) on software development, especially in software engineering. Some advantages in the development of RIAs by using AOP are Maintainability, Extensibility, and Reusability. This chapter presents a review of several success stories of AOP implementation in real world development projects and discusses the lessons learned in these projects. The works analyzed in the state-of-the-art are classified by Web development, Usability Engineering, and other related perspectives. Finally, the chapter also addresses AOP support between JavaScript-based RIA frameworks and non-JavaScript-based RIA frameworks providing either native or third-party AOP facilities. Some code snippets depicting the use of these facilities for implementing AOP concepts are also presented.

1. INTRODUCTION

Nowadays, AOP (Aspect-Oriented Programming) is one of the concepts on computer programming primarily used in research and industry. Its use is an evolutionary way of developing software that improves upon OOP (Object-Oriented Programming), in the same way that OOP improved upon procedural programming. OOP introduced the concepts of encapsulation, inheritance, and polymorphism for creating a hierarchy of objects that model a common set of behaviors. Although OOP has become relevant, it has failed in handling common behaviors that extend across unrelated objects. This means that OOP enhances vertical relationships but not horizontal relationships. As an example, logging code is often horizontally scattered across object hierarchies, but it has nothing to do with core functions of the objects scattered across. This situation occurs with other types of code, such as security and exception handling AOP provides a solution for abstracting crosscutting code that spans object hierarchies without functional relevance to the code it spans. AOP is a tool that enables to abstract the crosscutting code into a separate module, known as an aspect, rather than

DOI: 10.4018/978-1-4666-6437-1.ch006

embedding crosscutting code in classes and then dynamically applying the code where it is needed. The application of the crosscutting code is achieved by defining specific places, known as pointcuts, in the object model where the crosscutting code should be applied (Ekabua, 2012). Depending on the intended AOP framework, crosscutting code is injected at the specified pointcuts at runtime or compile-time. Ideally, AOP introduces a very powerful concept, which allows the introduction of new functionalities into objects without the objects needing to have any knowledge of that introduction (Holmes, 2012). Defects and deterioration of software are caused by changes in source code, and a lot of these changes cannot be avoided; however, they can be minimized. In most cases, when changes are made to software, the entire program is reengineered (Fayad & Adam, 2001).

Changes are inseparable part of software evolution. Changes take place in the process of development as well as during software maintenance. Huge costs and low speed of implementation are characteristic to change implementation. Often, change implementation implies a redesign of the whole application. The necessity of improving the software adaptability is fairly evident. Changes are usually specified as alterations of the base application behavior. Sometimes, it is needed to revert a change, which would be best done if it were expressed in a pluggable way. Another benefit of change pluggability is apparent if the change has to be reapplied. However, it is impossible to have a change implemented to fit any context, but it would be sufficiently helpful if a change could be extracted and applied to another version of the same base application. Such a pluggability can be achieved by representing changes as aspects (Dolog, Vrani´c & Bielikov´a, 2001). Some changes appear as real crosscutting concerns in the sense of affecting many places in the code, which is yet another reason for expressing them as aspects. This would be especially useful in the customization of web applications.

Typically, a general Web application is adapted to a certain context by a series of changes. With the arrival of a new version of the base application, all these changes have to be applied to it. In many occasions, the difference between the new and the old application does not affect the structure of changes.

A successful application of AOP requires a structured base application. Well-structured Web applications are usually based on the MVC (Model-View-Controller) pattern with three distinguishable layers: model layer, presentation layer, and persistence layer (Bebjak, Vranic & Dolog, 2007).

AOP can be implemented in RIAs. This kind of programming is capable of providing many benefits to RIAs, such as adding new levels of security and functionality without modifying the original code application. As it was mentioned above the advantages of applying AOP development of RIAs are varied and very important. Some of the most important advantages in the development of RIAs by using AOP are mentioned below:

- **Maintainability** is very important for RIAs development, since it enables to make changes as effectively and efficiently as it is possible. Moreover, the AOP provides a high level for maintainability.
- **Extensibility** is other important aspect in the RIAs development because sometimes the new functionality needs to be added to an application that is in operation, and is necessary to ensure that the application does not fail.
- **Reusability** is an important point not only in software development but also in the AOP. In fact, Reusability encapsulates the functionality required for reuse on subsequent occasions. This reduces development time and improves productivity. In the cases of both RIAs t and software development the development time is very expensive.

In this chapter, the use of AOP on software development, particularly on software engineering, is addressed. It must be mentioned that several technologies have adopted the use of AOP; therefore, there is an extensive variety of programming languages used for the implementation of AOP. Two of these programming languages are AspectJ and CaesarJ, among others. However, the prupose of this chapter is not to detail programming languages. Instead,

The following section addresses several works on web engineering with AOP support. These works have been grouped into three topics: Web development, Usability Enginerring and other perspectives with AOP support.

2. RESEARCH WORKS ON WEB ENGINEERING WITH AOP SUPPORT

AOP is an important programming paradigm and, recently, it has been used many times by developers, including Web developers. This is why it is important to emphasize on AOP in this chapter. Diverse works have been proposed to give support to AOP in combination with others features of Web engineering. Web Engineering covers various issues, and some of the most important are Case Tools for Web development, code generation, collaborative Web development, development and deployment of Web services, and the usability of Web applications. From these issues, the most important were selected based on the objectives of AOP. Some of the most important works are mentioned below, and they were grouped into three themes, Web development, usability engineering, and other perspectives with AOP support.

2.1. Web Development with AOP Support

In (Resendiz & Aguirre, 2005) the authors described that with the appearance and adoption of new Web services standards and technologies, de-

veloping and maintaining distributed applications is becoming a complex task. Unfortunately, most of the known approaches to develop applications embrace problems about physical distribution since the early phases of design. Thus, in order to reduce the complexity in the development of Web-based applications, authors proposed an approach emphasizing on locality transparency in the application design; thus, they left the physical distribution concerns in a later phase of the development process.

In order to address this modularization concerns, AOP was adopted as a programming model that provides the means to integrate the distribution aspects in an application whenever it is needed. The AOP paradigm allowed the system designer to obtain a distributed version of the application by integrating a Web services communication and coordination infrastructure. The main contribution of this work consisted in simplifying the development process of Web-based applications. This reduced the costs of production and maintenance of the applications and, at the same time, it provided a considerable increase in applications' flexibility and dynamism.

Similarly, (Hmida, Tomaz & Monfort, 2005) explained that Web service is the fitted technical solution that provides the required loose coupling in order to achieve SOA. In previous works, the authors proposed an approach using the AOP paradigm to increase the adaptability of Web services. This approach suffers from some deficiencies as a dependency for both the programming language (Java) and the SOAP engine (AXIS). Therefore, authors proposed to increase the adaptability of Web services by using the main AOP agreed semantics - advices, pointcuts and joinpoint – in order to change the original Web service behavior. Authors proposed to use an XML language for describing pointcuts, joinpoint and to referencing advices. The invocation of advices (Web services) was accomplished by an XQuery engine to assure SOAP engine independency and advices are implemented as Web services to promote programming language independency.

(Verheecke, Vanderperren & Jonckers, 2006) presented an innovative technique based on the fact that Service-oriented architectures are designed to support loose coupling between interacting software applications. Using Web services technology, SOAs (Service-Oriented Architecture) support the creation of distributed applications in a heterogeneous environment. The ultimate SOA goal is to let developers write applications that are independent of the specific services they use - applications that select and integrate services on the fly. Currently, service developers use the Web services description language to describe their services and publish the documentation in a registry. Service clients can browse these registries to find a service that matches their need and to determine how to communicate with it. By analyzing the WSDL documentation, the client can integrate the service and invoke it through XML-based SOAP communication. The Web Services Management Layer provides adaptive middleware that used AOP dynamic to solve several crosscutting concerns in service-oriented architectures.

In addition (Xu, Tang, Tang, Xu & Xiao, 2007) explained that although there can be some value in accessing a single Web service, the greater value was derived from assembling Web services into more powerful composite Web services. Web service flows are composite Web services based on process. The authors applied AOP concepts to support the dynamic adaptation of Web service flows. They also provided the approach for describing aspect as extension to BPEL, considering how to reuse the definition of an advice that may have different types at different pointcuts. They presented an approach for verifying the correctness of the web service flows weaved with aspects before they were deployed.

Moreover in (Ponnalagu, Narendra, Krishnamurthy & Ramkumar, 2007) the authors provided a novel approach for specifying and relating non-functional properties for distributed component Web services that can be used to adapt a composite Web service. This approach used a distributed AOP technology to model an adaptive architecture for composition and execution of Web services. Existing Web service adaptation mechanisms are limited only to the process of Web service choreography in terms of Web service selection/invocation vis-a-vis pre-specifled (Service Level Agreement) SLA constraints. This system extended this idea by representing the non-functional properties of each Web service - composite and component - via AOP. Hence, the system modeled a relation function between the aspects of the composite Web service and the individual aspects of the component Web service. This enabled mid-flight adaptation of the composite Web service - in response to changes in non-functional requirements - via suitable modifications in the individual aspects of the component Web service. From the end users' viewpoint, such upfront aspect-oriented modeling of non-functional properties enables on-demand composite Web service adaptation with minimal disruption in quality of service.

(Patel & Pandey, 2009) described sensor network applications that are executed in diverse scenarios, different platforms, and in an uncontrolled environment. Both data aggregation and data handling at the middleware demand an approach to integrate functionalities of various interests from diverse network clusters. Therefore, instead of a proprietary solution for individual problems, it is desirable to have a platform that is independent from the service-oriented architecture. SOA is composed of interactive Web services called by client applications. Secured access and use of Web services is a primary requirement in these applications. From software engineering point of view, authentication and logging are the crosscutting concerns for the Web services. Instead of using a conventional object-oriented approach for handling concerns in every class or method, authors proposed to use of AOP paradigm to reduce the code overhead of the system.

In (Zhang, Meng & Liu, 2009), authors proposed that nowadays Web services are the best way to solve cross-platform, cross-language, and loosely coupled distributed systems in Web environment. However, because of some crosscutting concerns in web services – such as logging, authorization, and transaction, among others – the systems that were constructed by integrating web services have some problems caused by the code-tangling and code-scattering. In order to solve the aforementioned problems, AOP was introduced into web services. The crosscutting concerns were separated and performed individually as aspectual services and a weaver weaves them when the system runs. And after researching SOA and multi-tier architecture, a system architecture based on aspectual services and web services was proposed.

After the analysis of different works about the Web development, particularly about the adoption of AOP in both the development and deployment of Web services, it is easy to idenitfy the advantages that AOP offers to developers. In fact, some of the most common issues in this area can be solved with the use of this new programming paradigm (AOP). As it can be observed in the works presented above, issues such as how to increase resilience and reusability of Web services can be relatively resolved with ease by using AOP.

2.2. Usability Engineering by Using AOP

In (Lippert & Lopes, 2000), the authors described that AOP is intended to ease situations that involve many kinds of code tangling. The reserach reported on a study to investigate AOP's ability to ease tangling related to exception detection and handling. Authors took an existing framework written in Java ™, the JWAM framework, and partially reengineered its exception detection and handling aspects using AspectJ™, which

is an aspect-oriented programming extension to Java. The authors found that AspectJ™ supported implementations that drastically reduced the portion of the code related to exception detection and handling. In one scenario, was authors were able to reduce the code by a factor of 4. They also found that, with respect to the original implementation in plain Java, AspectJ provided better support for different configurations of exceptional behaviors, more tolerance for changes in the specifications of exceptional behaviors, better support for incremental development, better reuse, automatic enforcement of contracts in applications that use the framework, and cleaner program texts.

Likewise, in (Tarta & Moldovan, 2006) Usability is explained as one of the most important qualities of a software system. Designing for usability is a complex task and sometimes it is expensive. Automatic usability evaluation can ease the evaluation process. The authors tried to analyze where and how AOP can be used in order to develop modules to support automatic usability evaluation. A small family budget application was used to test the module designed and implemented by using AOP.

In (Ruengmee, Silva, Bajracharya, Redmiles & Lopes, 2008) it is described that in spite of the modularization benefits supported by the AOP paradigm, different usability issues have hindered its adoption. The decoupling between aspect definitions and base code, and the compile-time weaving mechanism adopted by different AOP languages, require developers to manage the consistency between base code and aspect code themselves. These mechanisms create opportunities for errors related to aspect weaving invisibility and non-local control characteristics of AOP languages. The authors described XE (Extreme Editor), an IDE that supports developers in managing these issues in the functional aspect-oriented programming domain.

In the work of (Barbosa, Honorio, Leite da Silva & Lopes, 2009), optimization of complex systems was analyzed because this demands advanced methods that are implemented in specialized software. Multiple combinations of optimization methods, objective functions, and constraints further complicate the problem of developing this software, making it hard to create, maintain, and evolve. To overcome this problem, the research presented a new development methodology based on ideas of AOP applied to optimal power flow problems. This new methodology supported a clean separation of concerns, and mantained dependencies to a minimum level. The optimization method is self-contained and completely independent from the rest of the system; for each optimization scenario, the solution binded the optimization with the concrete problem at runtime. This approach improved the ability to deal with several different objective functions and constraints. Thus, is also provided flexibility, maintainability, and usability to the development and evolution effort without degradation of the computational time. In order to evaluate it, the model was compared with the traditional OOP paradigm by using several software metrics.

Moreover in (Holzinger, Brugger & Slany, 2011) the authors explained that Usability Engineering can be seen as a crosscutting concern within the software development process. On the other hand, AOP is a technology to support separation of concerns in software engineering. Therefore, it seems reasonable to support usability engineering by applying a technology designed to handle distinct concerns in one single application. Remote usability testing has been proven to deliver good results, and AOP is the technology that can be used to streamline the process of testing various software products without mixing concerns by separating the generation of test data from program execution. The authors presented a sample application, discussed their practical experiences with this approach, and provided recommendations for further development.

Usability is one of the most important aspects of both software systems and RIAs. Also, as it can be observed, AOP is of great help for problem

solving concerning usability engineering, especially since one of the most common problems in Usability Engineering is modularization. In this case, AOP provides facilities for applying modularization easily.

2.3. Other Perspectives with AOP Support

In the work (Kulesza, Sant'Anna, Garcia, Coelho, Von Staa & Lucena, 2006) one of the main promises of AOP is to promote improved modularization of crosscutting concerns, thereby enhancing the software stability in the presence of changes. The reserach presented a quantitative study that assesses the positive and negative effects of AOP on typical maintenance activities of a Web information system. The study consisted of a systematic comparison between the object-oriented and the aspect-oriented versions of the same application in order to assess to what extent each solution provided maintainable software decompositions. This analysis was driven by fundamental modularity attributes, such as coupling, cohesion, conciseness, and separation of concerns. Authors found that the aspect-oriented design had exhibited superior stability and reusability through the changes, as it had resulted in fewer lines of code, improved separation of concerns, weaker coupling, and lower intra-component complexity.

Moreover in (Ortiz, Bordbar & Hernandez, 2008) the MDA (Model-driven architecture) was introduced to shorten the software development time, produce better quality of code, and promote the reuse of software artifacts. On the other hand, AOP was motivated by the need to create decoupled systems, which were easier to maintain. As a result, it ccould be argued that adopting AOP and MDA side-by-side will provide advantages from both sets of techniques. However, adapting a new technology often entails extra cost and effort, including cost associated with training and support for the software tool. Therefore, it is crucial to evaluate the usefulness of applying both techniques dependently. The research also presented a quantitative approach to evaluate the use of MDA and AOP in service-oriented environments.

Another work (Xu & Huang, 2009) discussed that AOP is an emerging programming paradigm. Now the concept of aspect-orientation stretches over other development phases and other domains. A great amount of research has focused on aspect-oriented Web service composition domain. However, none of them offers a formal foundation for the aspect-oriented service composition. However, in (Xu & Huang, 2009), authors proposed a Petri net-based algebra for aspect-oriented Web service composition. In this model, Web service composition was modeled as a basic composition net and aspect nets, and then a weaving mechanism was provided in order to compose the basic net and aspect nets. The formal semantics of the composition operation was expressed in terms of Petri nets. Thus, the properties of woven composite service could be verified and analyzed based on the underlying Petri net.

In addition (Li, Zhang & Wang, 2010), authors described why the AOP is good at solving the difficulty in OOP of crosscutting concerns, and loosens the system from higher standpoints. Based on the characteristics of web application system, the paper introduced the AOP idea, and designed a kind of multi-player architecture based on MVC. It also emphasized on the analysis of crosscutting concerns in web system, including authorization, exception, logging, and time handler. Additionally, using AspectJ language, authors designed implementations to solve these crosscutting concerns to distributed enterprise web-based systems based on J2EE platform. At the end, comparing with OOP, the research presented a summary of the advantaged of the AOP usage.

This section presented a set of related works on diverse topics about Web Engineering. All of them agree in the advantages of AOP implementation in order to solve diverse problems in Web development. As it could be observed, several

issues about the reusability of codes and even of complete modules can be solved with the implementation of this new programming paradigm.

Moreover, as it could be observed along the previous works analyzed, AOP has been used in several contexts of Web Engineering due to its many capabilities and benefits. It must be mentioned that developers are considering including AOP within their developments because of the popularity that it has gained through recent years. In fact, AOP has demonstrated its usefulness in different areas of software development.

3. AOP SUPPORT ON JAVASCRIPT-BASED FRAMEWORKS

There are several JavaScript-based frameworks for RIAs development such as Dojo, jQuery, Mootools, Qooxdoo, Prototype, Rico, Sencha ExtJS, X-Library, GWT, Cappuccino, SproutCore, Spry, midori and YUI Library to mention a few.

However, this chapter merely analyzes eight of these JavaScript-based frameworks: Dojo, jQuery, Mootools, Qooxdoo, Prototype, Rico, Sencha ExtJS and X-Library. These frameworks have been divided into two groups: 1) JavaScript-based frameworks with AOP support and; 2) JavaScript-based frameworks without AOP support. The following subsections thoroughly explain the scope of the AOP support provided by each one of these frameworks.

3.1. JavaScript-Based Frameworks for RIAs Development with AOP Support

It must be mentioned that AOP support on JavaScript-based frameworks is limited, and it is not possible to apply and identify each one of the AOP concepts, since not all concepts are implemented in the frameworks. The JavaScript-based frameworks with AOP support are presented below.

Table 1. Elements for AOP support in Dojo (Harmon, 2008)

AOP Elements Supported
• Join Point • Pointcut • Advice (before)

Table 2. Parameters of dojo.connect function

Object Parameter	This parameter represents an object containing the method whose execution will be treated as an event. This property contains a reference to the object.
Method Parameter	Method whose execution is treated as an event. The method name is a string.
HandlerObject Parameter	It represents an object containing the method that will act as the event handler. This property contains a reference to the object.
handlerMethod Parameter	It indicates a method that will act as the event handler. The method name is a string.

3.1.1. AOP Support in Dojo

Dojo (version 1.5) has AOP support. Dojo supports Dynamic Crosscutting, and the elements supported are presented in Table 1.

The function that provides AOP support in Dojo is:

dojo.connect (object, method, handlerobject, handlermethod)

This function adds an advice before of invoking a method. Advices represent the implementation of the Aspects; this means that they contain the code implementation of the new functionality. The advices are inserted into the Join Point, and, to do this, advices must be previously defined in Pointcuts. However, in this case, is clear to observe the Pointcut and Join Point are implicit in the method used.

Advices are useful in the development of RIAs and their main use is to modify any behavior of an application previously developed in order to provide new functionalities. An advice into the RIAs can be used in different cases, for example: 1) add authentication methods for users, 2) add methods to accept use terms, and 3) add steps in a purchase process, among others.

This function associates an event handler with the execution of a method. The parameters to this function are presented in Table 2 (Harmon, 2008).

The following example is a code fragment used to write a message on standard output (console). The message is just to exemplify, but the function could do anything else. For doing this,

the *foo* and *bar* functions are provided and are presented below:

```
1 function foo() {
2 console.log("Running foo");
3 }
4 function bar() {
5 console.log("Running bar");
6 }
```

Now, once the *foo function* is executed, *bar function* is also executed. In order to understand better the procedure, the traditional way of solving the problem is shown below. To do this, a code line in the *foo* method is added in order to execute the *bar* method.

```
1 function foo() {
2 console.log("Running foo");
3 bar();
4 }
```

Although the proposed solution works, the codification is static. To achieve this in a dynamic way, Dojo provides a solution.

By using Dojo, it is possible to consider the execution of a function as an event in which another function is associated as a control of events, *dojo.connect* function provides this association, and the example is presented below:

```
1 dojo.connect(null, "foo", null,
"bar");
```

The *Dojo.connect* function provides the functionality that the AOP specifies, such as the management of events, i.e., the *pointcut*, the *join point*, and the *advice* are implicitly established through in the *Dojo.connect* function, the advice is sent *before* the execution continues its normal way. Once the foo function is executed, the bar function is automatically executed.

It is a simple example of AOP support, but it demonstrates the functionality of the *Dojo.connect* function. The standard use of this approach enables to dynamically add the features to be applied into many types of objects. For example, if new functionalities are required in some methods, then these functionalities can be carried out after that the function was written. To do this, a new function must be added, this function must contain the new functionality that is required in the application; next the assignment of a registration method will be required for each function that needs this new functionality; thus, the AOP will be put into practice within the application and this avoid adding the new code for each function where new functionality is manually required. The AOP approach is better since it does not directly codify in the method and it is not needed to modify the functions. According to industry references, each time the code is altered, there is high probability that something stops functioning. Thus, if it is possible to avoid changing the methods, it is better (Harmon, 2008).

In the cases of RIAs, this example can be applied in several cases, e.g. to add functionality before executing a specific action. A practical example would display a warning message before doing an action or show a contract before finalizing a transaction. This would happen in order

to carry out other actions before the final one without losing focus of the main application. This situation is presented in Figure 1.

In Figure 1, *dojo.connect* function was used and added to a Web application or a RIA in order to display a warning message before an action takes place. With AOP support, this functionality can be added in cases where the legacy application was not included. In the legacy application, once the carousel image finder is oppressed, a search is performed and the information to the user is presented. However it is important to verify whether the user is an adult and if he or she is aware of the terms of use. For this, a function must be added which is called every time that the search function is invoked. Then, the new function is executed before the search function sends a message to the user. Next, the user requires pressing the OK button to continue. Once this was done, the information is displayed to the user, and with just a few changes, functionality can be added to a Web application without compromising a proper operation.

3.1.2. AOP Support in jQuery

JQuery version 1.4 is able to support Aspect-Oriented Programming through a plugin called JQuery AOP.

Moreover, JQuery AOP version 1.3 is a small JQuery plugin that adds AOP features to JavaScript and is integrated within jQuery. jQuery AOP permits adding Advice (Before, After, After Throw, After Finally, Around and Introduction) in some instances of the objects; it also enables to define crosscutting using regular expressions, it works with global functions and methods; also, it is possible to remove advices after being used, and it is very compact. The use of jQuery AOP is very simple. It is only required to include a .js file in the source code (jquery-aop, 2014).

In RIAs, the application of this AOP functionality is very practical, since it is very common to

Figure 1. A Dojo-based RIA by using AOP support

need and add a new functionality into the application. JQuery is a very useful tool since it provides several functions that can be useful many times, For instance, where new sections need to be added into the application, or new features must be included into a specific section of the application, so the function of jQuery is to decide which section or feature is the most appropriate to use.

jQuery supports Dynamic Crosscutting and Static Crosscutting. The elements supported are presented in Table 3.

In this case, an advice after a method will be exemplified. An advice into the RIAs can be used in various cases, especially after invoking

Table 3. Elements for AOP support in jQuery (jquery-aop, 2014)

AOP Elements Supported
• Join Point • Pointcut • Advice (before, after, around) • Introduction

a method. Some scenarios for using advices into RIAs are: 1) add methods to retrieve information previously entered by a user, 2) add methods to recurrently store information in a database management system, 3) add calls to a Web server to retrieve information, to mention but a few.

Add an Advice after a Method

after(Map pointcut, Function advice) returns Array<Function>

This function creates an advice after the defined pointcut. The advice will be executed after the pointcut method has successfully completed the execution, and it will receive one parameter with the result of the execution. This function returns an array of weaved aspects (Function). Parameters to this function are presented in Table 4 (jquery-aop, 2014).

The next example shows two different ways of adding an advice after a method are described:

Table 4. Parameters of after function

Map Pointcut Parameter	Definition of the pointcut to apply the advice. A pointcut is the definition of the object/s and method/s to be weaved. • Target: it is the object to be weaved. • Method: it is the name of the function to be weaved
Function Advice Parameter	Function containing the code that will be called after the execution of the pointcut. It receives one parameter with the result of the pointcut's execution. The function can choose to return this same value or provide a different one.

```
1           //example 1
2 jQuery.aop.after({target: window,
method: 'MyGlobalMethod'},
3           function(result) {
4
alert('Returned: ' + result);
5                       return result;

6           }
7);
8 //example 2
9 jQuery.aop.after({target: String,
method: 'indexOf'},
10          function(index) {
11                  alert('Result
found at: ' + index + ' on:' + this);
12                  return index;
13          }
14);
```

jQuery-AOP provides many options in terms of functions. These functions can be used when necessary within the RIAs development. jQuery-AOP has features that are capable of providing extra functionality. For instance, these features 1) are able to add a new functionality to an application, 2) are able to solve problems of development or design, 3) can modify the RIA behavior or even 4) can disable the RIA operation, adding only a few functions and without modifying the original source code.

To better understand the functionality of an advice after the method, let us suppose an application with user data, such as address, phone numbers, and more. Let us assume also that the registration form requires a large amount of data that must be manually entered by the user. The problem is when the user changes some data and the Done button is not clicked, because if a failure occurs, the information will be lost and the user would have to rewrite the data. To avoid this, it is possible to use an advice after the method, this way, it is possible to add the functionality to save the information each time a field in the form is changed by the user. Also, the application can send a message to inform the user that the data has been modified. With this, it is possible to prevent the loss of information and time. This is just one example that depicts the possible uses of AOP support in RIAs, particularly in the use of advices after the method.

3.1.3. AOP Support in Qooxdoo

Qooxdo version 1.1 has a static class named Aspect (qx.core.Aspect) which is the only class that provides the AOP support. This class shows a very basic AOP support, the class permits joining functions before or after each call to a function. This class includes two static methods; the first is for the advice and the second for the wrap (qooxdoo.org, 2014).

Classes, which define own aspects must add an explicit require/requirement (require() is used to load files) to this class in the header comment using the following code:

```
#require(qx.core.Aspect)
#ignore(auto-require)
```

Qooxdoo supports Dynamic Crosscutting, and the elements supported are presented in Table 5.

Table 5. Elements for AOP support in Qooxdoo (qooxdoo.org, 2014)

AOP Elements Supported
• Join Point
• Pointcut
• Advice (before and after)

Adding an advice after or before a method

addAdvice (Function fcn, String position?, String type?, (String | RegExp) name?)

This function registers a function to be called just before or after each time one of the selected functions is called. Parameters to this function are presented in Table 6 (qooxdoo.org, 2014).

In this case, the Aspect class provides the ability to add advices, which may be executed before or after the method as it is needed. For Qooxdoo, the AOP functionality is of great help, since the same function provides the ability to use an advice after or before a method. By using this functionality, Qooxdoo can solve many problems that require the execution of a function, either before or after another specific function. This other function must be previously specified in the advice parameters.

3.2. JavaScript-Based Frameworks for RIAs Development without AOP Support

Out of the eight JavaScript based frameworks analyzed in this book, merely three of them account for AOP support. This means that the remaingin five do not have AOP support. These five frameworks, as well as their versions, are presented below.

3.2.1. AOP Support in Mootools

Mootools (version 1.3) has no AOP support, and in contrast to another framework, it does not have an extension or plugin to give AOP support. However, some efforts and developments are being done, although but they still lack of maturity to be released or published.

3.2.2. AOP Support in Prototype

Prototype (version 1.7) neither has AOP support, nor includes extensions or some plugin to give AOP support. However, some researches and developments are carried out to solve this. However, they still lack of the maturity in order to be released or published.

3.2.3. AOP Support in Sencha ExtJS

Sencha ExtJS (version 3.3) has no AOP support, and no extension or plugin have been developed yet to give AOP support.

3.2.4. AOP Support in Rico

Rico (version 2.0) has neither AOP support nor an extension or plugin to provide AOP support.

Table 6. Parameters of addAdvice function

Function fcn parameter	It is a function to be called right before or after any of the selected functions is called.
position (default: "after") parameter	Before or after, it defines whether the function is called before or after the main function.
type (default: null) parameter	It refers to the type of function. Only one of the following values is allowed: "member", "static", "constructor", "destructor", "property" or "", null is handled identical to "".
name (default: null) parameter	It refers to a pattern to match names. It is not necessary to have the same name, it can also be but only a part that coincides with it.

3.2.5. AOP Support in X-Library

X-Library (version 4.2) has no AOP support or any extension or a plugin to give AOP support.

It is important to mention the framework version reviewed, because the possibility that in future versions of these frameworks AOP capabilities can be added is not discarded.

4. AOP SUPPORT ON NON-JAVASCRIPT-BASED FRAMEWORKS

In the case of non-JavaScript-based frameworks for developing RIAs, there are four important frameworks, which are AdobeFlex™, JavaFX™, Silverlight™ and OpenLaszlo™. For each framework, the AOP support is presented below.

4.1. AOP Support in Adobe Flex™

Adobe Flex™ (Flex™ 4) has not AOP support but there are some alternatives regarding Adobe Flex™ development. For instance, a framework called Swiz can be used when specific AOP techniques are required.

Swiz (version 1.4) is a framework for Adobe Flex™, Adobe AIR™, and Adobe Flash™ that aims to bring complete simplicity to RIA development. Swiz provides:

- Inversion of Control / Dependency Injection
- Event handling
- A simple life cycle for asynchronous remote method invocations
- A framework that is decoupled from an application code.
- Compatibility with both Flex™ and non-Flex™ AS3 projects

Swiz represents best practices learned from the top RIA developers in some of the best consulting firms in the industry. Therefore, Swiz is simple, lightweight, and extremely productive.

The popular Swiz framework provides the new AOP support, as well as a new way of greatly reducing barriers by simplifying AOP. Swiz AOP gives the powerful ability to easily configure a new functionality into an existing code, instead of muddying up fundamental business logic. It is an extremely powerful methodology that Swiz makes very easy to work with (Swiz Framework, 2014).

Although it is important to mention that this Swiz project is currently being developed to provide AOP support for Flex, it is also important to mention that it still exists in a beta version, and it is developed by third-parties and not by Adobe™ itself.

4.2. AOP Support in JavaFX™

JavaFX™ (version 2.1) has not AOP support; nevertheless, independent projects have been carried out in order to provide that support. An example of these ongoing projects is the Spring™ Framework.

The Spring™ Framework (version 3.2) is a lightweight solution and a potential one-stop-shop for building enterprise-ready applications. However, Spring™ is modular, and this enables to use only those parts to be needed, without having to bring in the rest. The Spring Framework supports declarative transaction management, remote access to the logic through RMI (Remote Method Invocation) or web services, and various options for data persistence. It offers a full-featured MVC framework, and enables to integrate AOP transparently into the software. Spring's AOP module provides an AOP Alliance-compliant aspect-oriented programming implementation, which permits defining, for example, method-interceptors and pointcuts to cleanly decouple the code that implements functionality to be separated. Behavioral information can be incorporated into the code by using source level metadata functionality. Una funcionalidad de metadatos a nivel de código

In the same case of Adobe Flex™, this framework is developed by third-parties and their capabilities mentioned are not included in JavaFX™ by default, and the AOP support for JavaFX™ is only provided by Spring™ framework (Springsource.org, 2014).

4.3. AOP Support in Silverlight™

Silverlight™ (version 5.1.) has not AOP support, and there are no frameworks or plugins to give AOP support yet. It is important to remark that some research and developments are being done, although they still lack of support and maturity to be published or released.

4.4. AOP Support in OpenLaszlo™

OpenLaszlo™ (version 4.9) has not AOP support, and no framework or plug-in to give AOP support has been provided yet. As it is the case of some of the aforementioned frameworks, research and developments are being performed to solve this issue, but they still of readiness to be published or released.

5. CONCLUSION

Most of the AOP-based research and developments have been carried out by using specialized programming languages. Most of these languages have been used for developing desktop applications. So far, few contributions have been done in Web applications development. But in recent years, developers needed to add AOP support for Web programming languages, which is why some contributions have been proposed. An example of this is the recent inclusion of AOP features into frameworks for developing RIAs.

Another important aspect is the contribution of other works to supplement frameworks through the use of plugins. Two specific cases are Adobe Flex™ and JavaFX™. Although the AOP features are limited, contributions to offer AOP support on new programming languages are increasing. For this reason, we believe that programming languages for Web development could implement AOP features. The AOP support on RIAs provides benefits such as: 1) reducing development time and costs, 2) extending the functionality of the applications and 3) preventing errors and failures due to modifications in the original code.

Finally, it is known that Reusability is crucial in any software development, including Web development, since it saves a great amount of development time and avoids possible errors and mishaps. Therefore, the implementation of AOP in software development is an excellent bonus since AOP is greatly useful in cases of reusability. Moreover, it is possible to improve both maintenance and extensibility of systems and, of course, of RIAs. This will reduce development time and will also improve the systems developed.

REFERENCES

Barbosa, D. A., Honório, L. M., Leite da Silva, A. M., & Lopes, C. (2009). Concepts of Aspect-Oriented Modeling Applied to Optimal Power Flow Problems. In *Proceedings of Intelligent System Applications to Power Systems,* (pp. 1-6). IEEE. doi:10.1109/ISAP.2009.5352929

Bebjak, M., Vranic, V., & Dolog, P. (2007). Evolution of Web Applications with Aspect-Oriented Design Patterns. In *Proceedings of AEWSE*. AEWSE.

Dolog, P., Vrani'c, V., & Bielikov'a, M. (2001). Representing change by aspect. *ACM SIGPLAN Notices, 36*(12), 77–83. doi:10.1145/583960.583970

Ekabua, O. O. (2012). Using Aspect Oriented Techniques to Build-in Software Quality. *International Journal of Computer Science Issues, 9*(4).

Fayad, M. E., & Adam, A. (2001). Thinking objectively: An Introduction to Software Stability. *Communications of the ACM, 44*(9), 95–98. doi:10.1145/383694.383713

Harmon, J. E. (2008). *Dojo: Using the Dojo JavaScript Library to Build Ajax Applications.* Addison-Wesley Professional.

Hmida, M. M. B., Tomaz, R. F., & Monfort, V. (2005). Applying AOP concepts to increase Web services flexibility. In *Proceedings of Next Generation Web Services Practices.* IEEE.

Holmes, J. (2012). *Taking Abstraction a step further.* Retrieved April, 2014, from https://weblogs.java.net/blog/2004/09/29/taking-abstraction-one-step-further

Holzinger, A., Brugger, M., & Slany, W. (2011). Applying aspect oriented programming in usability engineering processes: On the example of tracking usage information for remote usability testing, In *Proceedings of the International Conference on e-Business (ICE-B 2011)* (pp. 1-4). Seville, Spain: IEEE.

jquery-aop. (2014). *API Reference.* Retrieved April, 2014, from http://code.google.com/p/jquery-aop/wiki/Reference

Kulesza, U., Sant'Anna, C., Garcia, A., Coelho, R., Von Staa, A., & Lucena, C. (2006). Quantifying the Effects of Aspect-Oriented Programming: A Maintenance Study. In *Proceedings of Software Maintenance,* (pp. 223-233). IEEE.

Li, H., Zhang, J., & Wang, L. (2010). The research and application of web-based system with Aspect-Oriented features. In *Proceedings of Computer Engineering and Technology (ICCET),* (pp. V4-480). IEEE.

Lippert, M., & Lopes, C. V. (2000). A study on exception detection and handling using aspect-oriented programming. In *Proceedings of the 2000 International Conference on Software Engineering* (pp. 418-427). IEEE.

Ortiz, G., Bordbar, B., & Hernandez, J. (2008). Evaluating the Use of AOP and MDA in Web Service Development. In *Proceedings of Internet and Web Applications and Services,* (pp. 78-83). IEEE. doi:10.1109/ICIW.2008.24

Patel, S. V., & Pandey, K. (2009). SOA Using AOP for Sensor Web Architecture. In *Proceedings of Computer Engineering and Technology,* (vol. 2, pp. 503-507). IEEE. doi:10.1109/ICCET.2009.152

Ponnalagu, K., Narendra, N. C., Krishnamurthy, J., & Ramkumar, R. (2007). Aspect-oriented Approach for Non-functional Adaptation of Composite Web Services. In *Proceedings of Services,* (pp. 284-291). IEEE. doi:10.1109/SERVICES.2007.18

qooxdoo.org. (2014). *API Documentation.* Retrieved April, 2014, from http://demo.qooxdoo.org/current/apiviewer/#qx.core.Aspect

Resendiz, M. P., & Aguirre, J. O. O. (2005). Dynamic invocation of Web services by using aspect-oriented programming. In *Proceedings of Electrical and Electronics Engineering,* (pp. 48-51). IEEE.

Ruengmee, W., Silva, R. S., Bajracharya, S. K., Redmiles, D. F., & Lopes, C. V. (2008). XE (eXtreme editor) -bridging the aspect-oriented programming usability gap. In *Proceedings of the 2008 23rd IEEE/ACM International Conference on Automated Software Engineering* (pp. 435-438). IEEE Computer Society. doi:10.1109/ASE.2008.67

Springsource.org. (2014). *Spring Framework Reference Documentation.* Retrieved April, 2014, from http://static.springsource.org/spring/docs/3.2.x/spring-framework-reference/pdf/spring-framework-reference.pdf

Swiz Framework. (2014). *Getting Started with Swiz AOP.* Retrieved April, 2014, from http://swizframework.org/post.cfm/getting-started-with-swiz-aop

Tarta, A. M., & Moldovan, G. S. (2006). Automatic Usability Evaluation Using AOP. In *IEEE International Conference on Automation, Quality and Testing.* IEEE *Robotics, 2,* 84–89.

Verheecke, B., Vanderperren, W., & Jonckers, V. (2006). Unraveiliny crossoutting concerns in Web services middleware. *Software, IEEE, 23*(1), 42–50. doi:10.1109/MS.2006.31

Xu, Y., & Huang, H. (2009). A Petri Net-Based Model for Aspect-Oriented Web Service Composition. In *Proceedings of Management and Service Science,* (pp. 1-4). IEEE. doi:10.1109/ICMSS.2009.5305764

Xu, Y., Tang, S., Tang, Z., Xu, Y., & Xiao, R. (2007). Constructing Web Service Flows with Reusable Aspects. In *Proceedings of Internet and Web Applications and Services,* (pp. 21-21). IEEE. doi:10.1109/ICIW.2007.27

Zhang, J., Meng, F., & Liu, G. (2009). Research on Multi-tier Distributed Systems Based on AOP and Web Services. In *Proceedings of Education Technology and Computer Science,* (Vol. 2, pp. 203-207). IEEE. doi:10.1109/ETCS.2009.307

ADDITIONAL READING

Alexander, R. (2003). The Real Cost of Aspect Oriented Programming. *Software, IEEE, 20*(6), 91–93. doi:10.1109/MS.2003.1241373

Holzinger, A. (2005). Usability engineering methods for software developers. *Communications of the ACM, 48*(1), 71–74. doi:10.1145/1039539.1039541

Jacobson, I., & Ng, P.-W. (2005). *Aspect-Oriented Software Development with Use Cases.* Addison-Wesley Professional.

Kiczales, G., Lamping, J., Mendhekar, A., Maeda, C., Lopes, C., Loingtier, J. M., & Irwin, J. (1997). Aspect-oriented programming. In Ecoop'97: Object-Oriented Programming (pp. 220-242). Berlin: Springer-Verlag.

Laddad, R. (2003). *AspectJ in Action: Practical Aspect-Oriented Programming.* Manning Publications.

KEY TERMS AND DEFINITIONS

Advice: The code to be executed at a join point that has been previously selected by a pointcut. Advice can execute before, after, or around the join point.

Aspect-Oriented Programming: A new programming paradigm that describes a development methodology for separating crosscutting concerns during the software development.

Crosscutting: The implementation of the weaving rules by the compiler is called crosscutting. There exist two types of crosscutting defined as static and dynamic crosscutting.

Join Point: It is an identifiable point in the execution of a program. It could be a call to a method or an assignment to a member of an object.

Model-Driven Architecture: It is a software development architecture.

Pointcut: It is a program construct that selects join points and collects context at those points.

Usability Engineering: It is an engineering field that refers the interaction between a person and a computer, and the development of interfaces that allow this interaction.

Chapter 7
Design Patterns Support for RIAs Development

ABSTRACT

In Chapter 7, a review of Design Patterns proposed by GOF classification is presented. GOF classifies Design Patterns in Creational Patterns, Structural Patterns, and Behavioral Patterns. Some implementation examples of GoF Design Patterns are presented by using both JavaScript-based frameworks and non-JavaScript-based frameworks for RIAs development. Additionally, the chapter also presents a comparative analysis that summarizes the review of the capabilities of the RIA frameworks in the context of GoF Design Patterns support between JavaScript-based RIA frameworks and non-JavaScript-based RIA frameworks. Finally, this chapter also mentions how to solve different programming problems by using Design Patterns. Throughout the chapter, GOF Design Patterns and their classification are used.

1. INTRODUCTION

Design Patterns generally arise by the need of solving problems of software development in a systematic way. A Design Pattern is a formal description of a problem and its solution. Design Patterns must have a simple and descriptive name that can be readily used when referring to the pattern. A pattern should document the problem, its solution and the consequences of using it. Design Patterns can be used to assist in solving related problems to software development. From this perspective, a Design Pattern is a reusable solution that can be applied to common problems in software design.

A Design Pattern systematically names, motivates, and explains a general design that addresses a recurring problem in the design of object-oriented systems. It describes the problem, the solution, in the moment of applying the solution and its consequences. The solution is a general agreement of the objects and classes that solve the problem. The solution is customized to solve the problem in a particular context. (Gamma et al., 1994)

A well-known Design Pattern on Web applications development is MVC (Model-View-Controller). The MVC pattern separates the domain modeling, the presentation and the actions based on the user input into three classes: 1) Model, 2) View and 3) Controller. MVC pattern is a funda-

DOI: 10.4018/978-1-4666-6437-1.ch007

mental Design Pattern for the separation of user interface logic from business logic. Fortunately, the emergence of Web applications has helped to solve some of the ambiguity because the separation between the view and the controller is apparent.

In Software Engineering field, the Design Patterns were classified by the GoF in three types: 1) Creational patterns, 2) Structural patterns, 3) Behavioral patterns.

Creational Design Patterns are Design Patterns that deal with object creation mechanisms, trying to create objects in a manner suitable to the situation. All the creational patterns define the best possible way in which an object can be created considering reuse and changeability. These describe the best way to handle instantiation (Christiansson et al., 2008).

Structural Design Patterns are Design Patterns that ease the design by identifying a simple way to realize relationships among entities. These patterns describe how objects and classes can be combined to form structures. It is important to distinguish between object patterns and class patterns. The difference is that class patterns describe relationships and structures with the help of inheritance. While object patterns describe how objects can be associated and aggregated to form larger, more complex structures (Christiansson et al., 2008).

Behavioral Design Patterns are Design Patterns that identify common communication patterns between objects and realize these patterns. These patterns are focused on the interactions among cooperating objects. The interactions between cooperating objects should be such that they are communicating while maintaining as loose coupling as possible. The loose coupling is the key to n-tier architectures. From this context, the implementation and the client should be loosely coupled in order to avoid hard-coding and dependencies (Christiansson et al., 2008).

The Design Patterns are very important on RIAs (Rich Internet Applications) development. In particular, Design Patterns are employed on frameworks for RIA development. In this chapter, a review and analysis about the Design Patterns support on JavaScript-based frameworks and non-JavaScript-based frameworks for RIAs development are presented. It should be noted that the GoF classification was used for this review and analysis.

2. DESIGN PATTERNS

Design Patterns are classified into 3 categories according to GoF, Creational, Structural and Behavioral Patterns. In the following subsections, the description and the UML class diagram representing the structure of each Design Pattern are presented.

2.1. Creational Patterns

Examples of Design Patterns located in this category are Abstract Factory, Builder, Factory Method, Prototype and Singleton patterns. These design patterns are described below in detail.

Abstract Factory

The abstract factory pattern is a software Design Pattern that provides a way to encapsulate a group of individual factories that have a common theme. This pattern separates the details of implementation of a set of objects from their general usage. Factories and products are the key elements into Abstract Factory pattern. This pattern captures how to create families of related objects without carry out the instantiation process of classes. It is most appropriate when the number and general kinds of product objects stay constant, and there are differences in specific product families (Gamma et al., 1994).

A factory is the location or a concrete class in the code at which objects are constructed. The intent in employing the pattern is to insulate the creation of objects from their usage. This allows

Figure 1. UML class diagram for Abstract Factory pattern

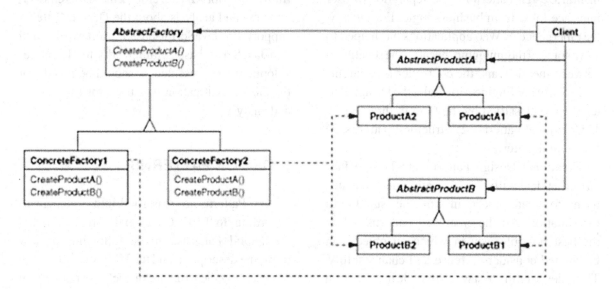

for new derived types to be introduced with no change to the code that uses the base class. Use of this pattern makes it possible to interchange concrete implementations without changing the code that uses them, even at runtime. However, employment of this pattern, as with similar Design Patterns, may result in unnecessary complexity and extra work in the initial writing of code.

In Figure 1, the UML class diagram representing the behavior of the Abstract Factory pattern is presented. This UML class diagram comes from the book entitle *Design Patterns* (Gamma et al., 1994).

Builder

The Builder pattern is an object creation software Design Pattern. Unlike the Abstract Factory pattern and the Factory Method pattern whose intention is to enable polymorphism, the intention of the Builder pattern is to find a solution to the telescoping constructor anti-pattern. The telescoping constructor anti-pattern occurs when the increase of object constructor parameter combination leads to an exponential list of constructors. Instead of using numerous constructors, the Builder pattern

uses another object, a Builder object that receives each initialization parameter step by step and then it returns the resulting constructed object at once (Gamma et al., 1994).

The intention is to abstract steps of construction of objects so that different implementations of these steps can construct different representations of objects. Often, the Builder pattern is used to build products in accordance with the Composite pattern.

In Figure 2, the UML class diagram representing the behavior of the Builder Pattern is depicted. In this figure, the elements that participate in this pattern can be identified.

Prototype

The Prototype pattern is used in software development when the type of objects to create is determined by a prototypical instance, which is cloned to produce new objects. Prototype pattern is used when a system should be independent of how its products are created, composed, and represented; and

Figure 2. UML class diagram for Builder pattern

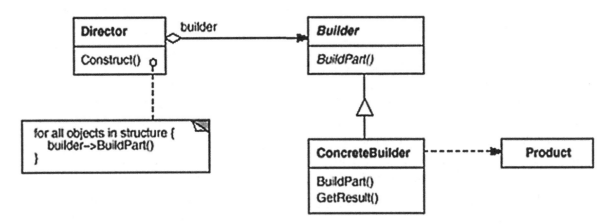

- When the classes, to be instantiated, are specified at run-time, for example, by dynamic loading; or
- To avoid building a class hierarchy of factories that parallels the class hierarchy of products; or
- When instances of a class can have one of only a few different combinations of state. It may be more convenient to install a corresponding number of prototypes and clone them rather than instantiating the class manually, each time with the appropriate state (Gamma et al., 1994).

The Prototype pattern specifies the kind of objects to create using a prototypical instance. Prototypes of new products are often built prior to full production (Gamma et al., 1994).

In Figure 3, the UML class diagram representing the behavior of the Prototype pattern is presented.

Figure 3. UML class diagram for Prototype pattern

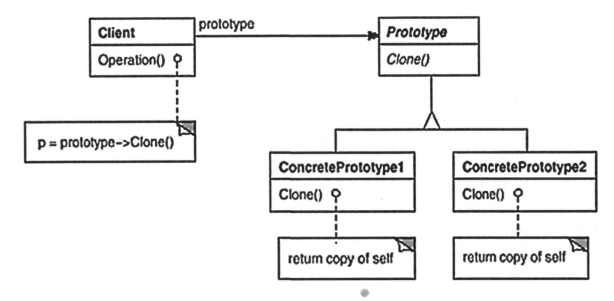

Singleton

Singleton pattern is a Design Pattern that restricts the instantiation process of a class to one object. This is useful when exactly one object is needed to coordinate actions across the system. The concept is sometimes generalized to systems that operate more efficiently when only one object exists, or that restrict the instantiation to a certain number of objects. The term comes from the mathematical concept of a singleton (Gamma et al., 1994).

The implementation process of a Singleton pattern must satisfy the single instance and global access principles. It requires a mechanism to access the singleton class member without creating a class object and a mechanism to persist the value of class members among class objects. The Singleton pattern is implemented by creating a class with a method that creates a new instance of the class if one does not exist. If an instance already exists, it simply returns a reference to that object.

In Figure 4, the UML class diagram representing the behavior of the Singleton pattern structure is depicted.

2.2. Structural Patterns

Some examples of Structural Design Patterns are Adapter, Bridge, Composite, Decorator, Facade, Flyweight and Proxy patterns. For practical purposes, the most representative patterns are described.

Composite

Composite pattern is a partitioning Design Pattern. The composite pattern describes that a group of objects are to be treated in the same way as a single instance of an object. The intent of a composite is to "compose" objects into tree structures to represent part-whole hierarchies. Implementing the composite pattern lets clients treat individual objects and compositions uniformly (Gamma et al., 1994).

Composite pattern can be used when clients should ignore the difference between compositions of objects and individual objects (Gamma et al., 1994). If programmers find that they are using multiple objects in the same way, and often have nearly identical code to handle each of them, then Composite pattern is a good choice; it is less complex in this situation to treat primitives and composites as homogeneous.

In Figure 5 the Composite Pattern is represented through a UML class diagram where its components can be observed.

Figure 4. UML class diagram for Singleton pattern

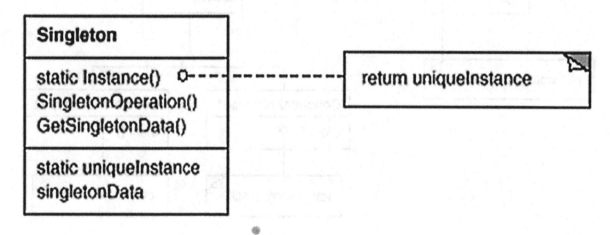

Figure 5. UML class diagram for Composite pattern

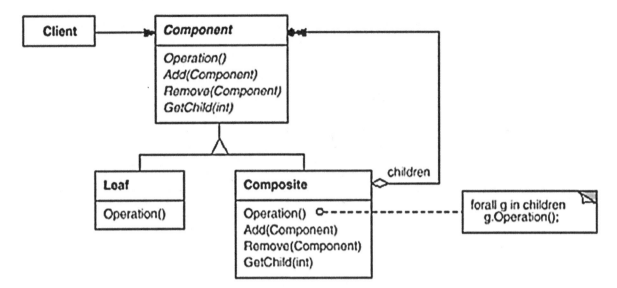

Façade

The Facade pattern (or façade pattern) is a software Design Pattern commonly used with object-oriented programming. The name is by analogy to an architectural facade. A facade is an object that provides a simplified interface to a larger body of code, such as a class library. A facade can:

- Make a software library easier to use, understand and test, since the facade has convenient methods for common tasks;
- Make the library more readable, for the same reason;
- Reduce dependencies of outside code on the inner workings of a library, since most code uses the facade, thus allowing more flexibility in developing the system;
- Wrap a poorly-designed collection of APIs with a single well-designed API (as per task needs).

The Façade pattern provides a unified interface to a set of interfaces in a subsystem. Façade pattern defines a higher-level interface that makes the subsystem easier to use.

This Design Patterns allow structuring a system into subsystems, this situation helps to reduce complexity in software design. A common design goal is to minimize the communication and dependencies between subsystems. One way to achieve this goal is to introduce a facade object that provides a single, simplified interface to the more general facilities of a subsystem (Gamma et al., 1994).

In Figure 6, the behaviour of the Facade pattern is depicted by a UML class diagram.

Flyweight

A flyweight is an object that minimizes memory use by sharing as much data as possible with other similar objects. It is a way to use objects in large numbers when a simple repeated representation would use an unacceptable amount of memory. Often some parts of the object state can be shared, and it is common practice to hold them in external data structures and pass them to the flyweight

Figure 6. UML class diagram for Facade pattern

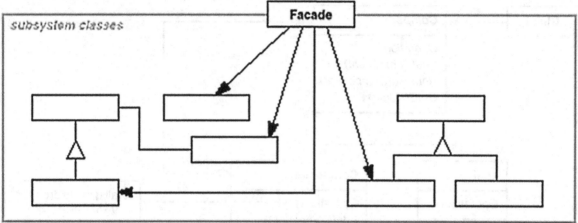

objects temporarily when they are used (Gamma et al., 1994).

A classic example usage of the Flyweight pattern is the data structures for graphical representation of characters in a word processor. It might be desirable to have, for each character in a document, a glyph object containing its font outline, font metrics, and other formatting data, but this would amount to hundreds or thousands of bytes for each character. Instead, for every character there might be a reference to a flyweight glyph object shared by every instance of the same character in the document; only the position of each character (in the document and/or the page)

Figure 7. UML class diagram for Flyweight pattern

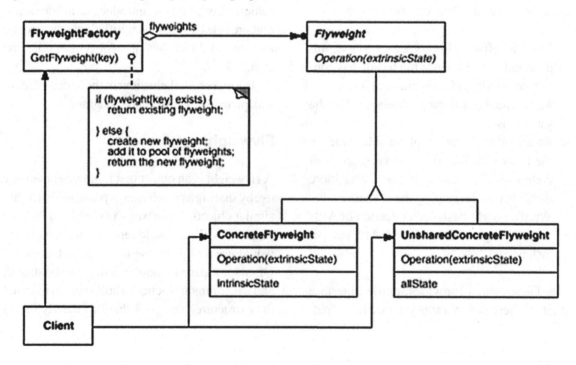

would need to be stored internally. In other contexts the idea of sharing identical data structures is called hash consing.

In Figure 7, the UML class diagram for the Flyweight Pattern is presented. In this UML class diagram, all clases involved in the the structure of this pattern can be observed.

Proxy

A proxy is a class functioning as an interface to something else. The proxy could interface to anything: a network connection, a large object in memory, a file, or some other resource that is expensive or impossible to duplicate. A well-known example of the Proxy pattern is a reference counting pointer object (Gamma et al., 1994). In situations where multiple copies of a complex object must exist, the Proxy pattern can be adapted to incorporate the Flyweight pattern in order to reduce the application's memory footprint. Typically, one instance of the complex object and multiple proxy objects are created, all of which contain a reference to the single original complex object. Any operations performed on the proxies are forwarded to the original object.

Once all instances of the proxy are out of scope, the complex object's memory may be deallocated.

In Figure 8, the UML class diagram for Proxy Pattern is depicted.

2.3. Behavioral Patterns

Some examples of Behavioral Design Patterns are Chain of Responsibility, Command, Interpreter, Iterator, Memento, Observer, State, Strategy, Template Method, Visitor and Mediator patterns. For practical purposes, the most representative patterns are presented.

Iterator

The Iterator pattern is a Design Pattern in which an iterator is used to traverse a container and access the container's elements. The Iterator pattern decouples algorithms from containers; in some cases, algorithms are necessarily container-specific and thus cannot be decoupled. The essence of the Iterator Pattern is to "provide a way to access the elements of an aggregate object sequentially without exposing its underlying representation" (Gamma et al., 1994).

Figure 8. UML class diagram for Proxy pattern

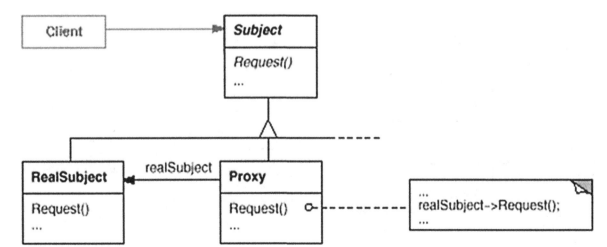

Figure 9. UML class diagram for Iterator pattern

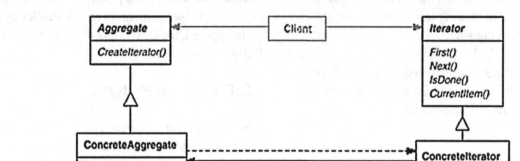

For a better understanding, the UML class diagram about the structure of the Iterator pattern is depicted in Figure 9.

Observer

The observer pattern is a software Design Pattern in which an object, called the subject, maintains a list of its dependents, called observers, and notifies them automatically of any state changes, usually by calling one of their methods. It is mainly used to implement distributed event handling systems. The Observer pattern is also a key part in the familiar model–view–controller (MVC) architectural pattern. In fact the Observer pattern was firstly implemented in Smalltalk's MVC based user interface framework. The Observer pattern is implemented in numerous programming libraries and systems, including almost all GUI toolkits (Gamma et al., 1994).

The essence of the Observer Pattern is to "define a one-to-many dependency between objects so that when one object changes state, all its dependents are notified and updated automatically" (Gamma et al., 1994).

Figure 10. UML class diagram for Observer pattern

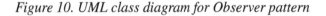
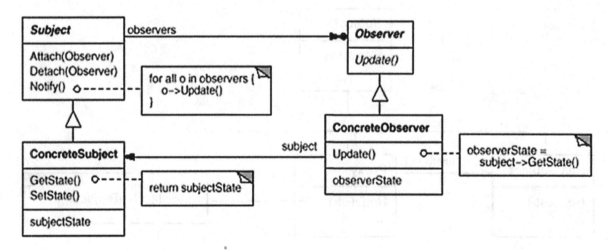

In Figure 10, the UML class diagram representing the behavior of the Observer pattern is depicted.

State

The State pattern, which closely resembles Strategy Pattern, is a behavioral software Design Pattern, also known as the objects for states pattern. This pattern is used in computer programming to encapsulate varying behavior for the same routine based on an object's state object. This can be a cleaner way for an object to change its behavior at runtime without resorting to large monolithic conditional statements (Gamma et al., 1994).

An example of this pattern is a drawing program. The program has a mouse cursor, which at any point in time can act as one of several tools. Instead of switching between multiple cursor objects, the cursor maintains an internal state representing the tool currently in use. When a tool-dependent method is called (say, as a result of a mouse click), the method call is passed on to the cursor's state. Each tool corresponds to a state.

As can be seen in Figure 11, the UML class diagram for State Pattern is depicted. This figure describes the main structure for this pattern.

Strategy

The Strategy pattern (also known as the Policy pattern) is a software Design Pattern that enables an algorithm's behavior to be selected at runtime. The Strategy pattern defines a family of algorithms, encapsulates each algorithm, and makes the algorithms interchangeable within that family (Gamma et al., 1994). For instance, a class that performs validation on incoming data may use a strategy pattern to select a validation algorithm based on the type of data, the source of the data, user choice, and/or other discriminating factors. These factors are not known for each case until run-time, and may require radically different validation to be performed. The validation strategies, encapsulated separately from the validating object, may be used by other validating objects in different areas of the system (or even different systems) without code duplication. The essential requirement in the programming language is the ability to store a reference to some code in a data structure and retrieve it.

The UML class diagram for Strategy Pattern is depicted in Figure 12.

Figure 11. UML class diagram for State pattern

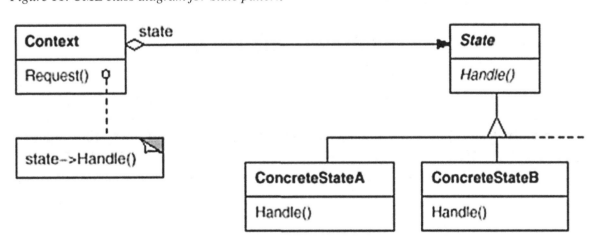

Figure 12. UML class diagram for Strategy pattern

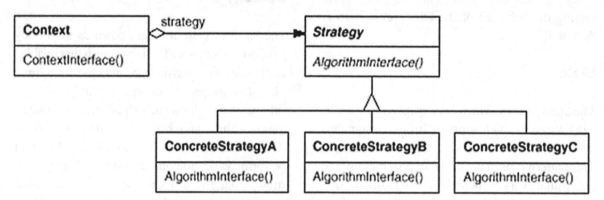

Mediator

The Mediator pattern defines an object that encapsulates how a set of objects can interact. This pattern is considered to be a Behavioral Design Pattern due to it can alter the behavior of the program is running (Gamma et al., 1994).

Usually a program is made up of a number of classes. So the logic and computation are distributed among these classes. However, as more classes are developed in a program, especially during maintenance and/or refactoring, the problem of communication between these classes may become more complex. This makes the program harder to read and maintain. Furthermore, it can become difficult to change the program, since any change may affect code in several other classes. By using Mediator pattern, communication between objects is encapsulated with a mediator object. Objects no longer communicate directly with each other, but instead communicate through the mediator. This reduces the dependencies between communicating objects, thereby lowering the coupling.

The essence of the Mediator Pattern is to "define an object that encapsulates how a set of objects interact. Mediator promotes loose coupling by keeping objects from referring to each other explicitly, and it lets you vary their interaction independently" (Gamma et al., 1994).

In Figure 13, the UML class diagram for Mediator Pattern is depicted.

Figure 13. UML class diagram for Mediator pattern

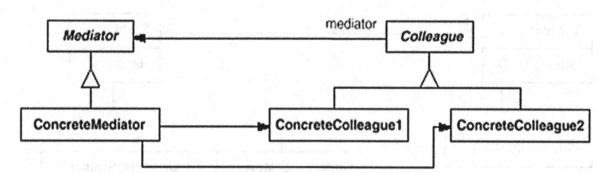

3. DESIGN PATTERNS SUPPORT INTO JAVASCRIPT-BASED FRAMEWORKS

Design patterns are effective solutions to reduce time development problems and to improve the effectiveness solutions indices. It is important to remark that not all programming languages and RIAs frameworks are able for Design Patterns support. Today, developers are more concerned about these issues, and they have developed new features that offer the support for the Design Patterns implementation in different frameworks such as JavaScript-based Frameworks. There are several JavaScript-based frameworks for RIAs development such as Dojo, jQuery, Mootools, Qooxdoo, Prototype, Rico, Sencha ExtJS, X-Library, GWT, Cappuccino, SproutCore, Spry, midori and YUI Library to mention but a few. In this chapter, only eight JavaScript-based frameworks are analyzed, Dojo, jQuery, Mootools, Qooxdoo, Prototype, Rico, Sencha ExtJS and X-Library. The following subsections explain in detail the scope of the Design Patterns support provided by each one of these frameworks.

3.1. Design Patterns Support in Dojo

Dojo is a powerful JavaScript-based framework included in Dojo Toolkit. Table 1 shows the Design Patterns supported in Dojo.

Table 1. Design Patterns supported in Dojo (Harmon, 2008)

Creational Patterns	Structural Patterns	Behavioral Patterns
Singleton	Not reported	Observer

In Table 2, an analysis of Design Patterns supported by the Dojo framework is presented.

A representative example of one of the Design Patterns supported by Dojo is presented below.

Observer Pattern

An observer is a structural pattern that enables publish/subscribe functionality. This is accomplished by an autonomous object, publisher that allows other objects to attach or detach their subscription as they like. The pattern does not impose any limit to the number of observers that can attach, or subscribe themselves for notification on future changes in the publisher's state. This pattern can be used when an object wants to publish information and many objects will need to receive that information. The benefits are makes for a loose coupling between publisher and subscriber as the publisher does not need to know who or how many subscribers there will be. The consequences about this pattern are, for example, in a complex scenario there may be problems to determine whether the update to the publisher is of

Table 2. Analysis of the Design Patterns supported by Dojo framework (Harmon, 2008)

Design Patterns	
Creational Patterns	
Singleton	The singleton pattern is supported in the constructors of the type: **dojo.declare(className: String, superclass: Function|Function[ ], props: Object);**
Behavioral Patterns	
Observer	The observer Design Pattern within the Dojo framework is evident in the *Listeners classes/methods*, listeners are event provided by the programming language, a representative example would be the use of the connect() function. **dojo.connect (null, "function1", null, "function2");** This function has a listener by using the Observer Design Pattern, and which remains alert at all time and when it detects that function1 was executed, the function2 is immediately executed.

Table 3. Design Patterns supported in jQuery (Osmani, 2010)

Creational Patterns	Structural Patterns	Behavioral Patterns
Builder Prototype	Composite Facade Flyweight Proxy	Iterator Observer Strategy

relevance to all subscribers or just some of them. Sending an update signal to all subscribers might impose a communication overhead of information not needed (Christiansson et al., 2008).

To better depict the use of the Observer Design Pattern, the following practical example is presented. Let us suppose there are several Web applications or RIAs from different domains that they are managed by the same company. In addition, these applications are used for publishing news coming from the same source. The problem is that RIAs administrators would have to post the news on each one of the different applications. This situation causes loss of time and therefore loss of money, plus the possibility to generate variations or mistakes. One solution to this problem is the use of the Observer Design Pattern, this Design Pattern works with a structure publish / subscribe, in this case the main source of news is the Publisher or main subject and every website that require publishing the news are subscribers or observers. When the subject changes must be notified this change to the observers so that they can change in turn.

3.2. Design Patterns Support in jQuery

jQuery is a JavaScript-based library used by developers. The use of Design Patterns in jQuery has been increased according to the needs of Web development. jQuery has support for different Design Patterns. Table 3 shows the Design Patterns supported in jQuery.

In Table 4, an analysis of the Design Patterns supported by jQuery is presented.

A representative example of one of the Design Patterns supported by jQuery is presented below.

Facade Pattern

This Design Pattern provides a unified interface to a set of interfaces in a subsystem. It defines a higher-level interface that makes the subsystem easier to use. The Facade pattern design can be used to make a software library easier to use and understand, since the Facade has convenient methods for common tasks. For the same reason, it can make code that uses the library more readable. A final usage scenario is where several poorly-designed APIs can be wrapped with a single well-designed API. The main benefit with the Facade pattern is that very complex method calls and code blocks can be combined into a single method that performs a complex and recurring task. Besides making code easier to use and understand, it reduces code dependencies between libraries or packages, making programmers more apt to consideration before writing new code that exposes the inner workings of a library or a package. Also, since the Facade makes a weak coupling between the client code and other packages or libraries it allows vary the internal components since the client does not call them directly. One drawback is that there are much less control of what goes on beyond the surface. Also, when some classes require small variations to the implementation of Facade methods, this might end up in a mess (Christiansson et al., 2008).

A representative example of the Facade Design Pattern is all function libraries or frameworks like jQuery itself, which are very useful because they are not required to know how to work internally the API functions provided just enough to know call that function and see how it works in general. In the same way developers use the Facade Design Pattern to develop their own APIs, i.e. an experienced developer who works with Web ap-

Table 4. Analysis of the Design Patterns supported in jQuery (Osmani, 2010)

	Design Patterns
	Creational Patterns
Builder	The Builder Pattern abstracts the steps involved in creating objects, so different implementations of these steps have the ability to construct different representations of objects. An example of how jQuery utilizes this pattern is presented below. This example allow showing an element which can be append to the document body in order to be constructed by using a string definition. 1 $('< div class= "foo"> bar < /div>');
Prototype	The Prototype Pattern is used when the objects that need to be created are determined by a prototypal instance that is cloned to produce the new objects. Essentially this pattern is used to avoid creating a new object in a standard manner when this process may be expensive or overly complex. In the following code sample which extends the jQuery.fn object for a minimal plugin, underlying prototypal code makes this possible: 1 $.fn.plugin = function(){ } 2 $('#container').plugin();
	Structural Patterns

Composite	The Composite Pattern describes a group of objects that can be treated in the same way by a single instance such as only one object. By implementing this pattern, both individual objects and compositions are treated in a uniform way. In jQuery, when actions are being accessed or performed on a single DOM element or a group of DOM elements, they can be treated in a uniform manner. This is demonstrated by the following sample below:
	1 $('#someDiv').addClass('active'); // a single element
	2 $('div').addClass('active'); // a collection of elements

Facade	The Facade Pattern is quite commonly used with OOP (Object-oriented programming) where a facade is an object which provides a simpler interface to a larger piece of code, by example for using a function of a class library. Facades can be frequently found across the jQuery library and make the methods easier to use and understand, but also more readable. The following functions are facades for jQuery's $.ajax(): 1 $.get(); 2 $.post(); 3 $.getJSON(); 4 $.getScript();

Flyweight	The Flyweight Pattern is a Design Pattern where an object attempts to minimize the amount of memory used by sharing as much information as possible with other objects that are similar in nature. It is a way to utilize objects in large numbers when a simple repeated representation may use an amount of memory deemed unacceptable. There are often aspects of an object state that can be shared and it is commonplace that these are stored in external data structures that are passed to the flyweight objects temporarily when needed.
	In this function the userConfig is shared. This example uses inheritance to define the object containing all info about user Config. This makes easier to save memory.
	1 $.fn.plugin = function(userConfig){
	2 userConfig = $.extend({
	3 content: 'Hello user!'
	4 }, userConfig);
	5 return this.html(useConfig.content);
	6 });

Proxy	The Proxy Pattern - a proxy is basically a class that functions as an interface to something else. The proxy can be an interface for anything: a file, a resource, an object in memory, something else that is difficult to duplicate. jQuery *.proxy()* function takes as input a function and returns a new one that will always have a particular context. This is similar to the idea of providing an interface such as the Proxy pattern. 1 $.proxy(function(){ }, obj);
	Behavioral Patterns
Iterator	The Iterator Pattern is a Design Pattern where iterators (objects that allow traversing through all the elements of a collection) sequentially access the elements of an aggregate object without needing to expose its underlying form. Iterators encapsulate the internal structure of how that particular iteration occurs, in the case of jQuery is *.each()* iterator, that is actually able to use the underlying code behind .each() to iterate through a collection, without needing to see or understand the code working behind the scenes that is providing this capability. 1 //Here jQuery makes use of it is event system on top of DOM events 2 $('.button').click(function(){ }) 3 $('.button').trigger('click', function(){ })

continued on following page

Table 4. Continued

Design Patterns	
Observer	The Observer pattern is where a subject (the object) keeps a list of its dependents, which are known as observers, and notifies them automatically of any changes in state. This is commonly done by calling one of their methods. The Observer pattern can be considered a subset of PubSub (publish/subscribe pattern). jQuery uses its event system on top of DOM events, as can be seen in the following function. 1 $('.button').click(function(){}) 2 $('.button').trigger('click', function(){})
Strategy	The Strategy Pattern is a pattern where a script may select a particular algorithm at runtime. The purpose of this pattern is that it is able to provide a way to clearly define families of algorithms, encapsulate each as an object and make them easily interchangeable. The biggest benefit this pattern offers is that it allows algorithms to vary independent of the clients that utilize them. An example of this is *toggle()* that allows to bind two or more handlers to the matched elements, to be executed on alternate clicks. The strategy pattern allows for alternative algorithms to be used independent of the client internal to the function. 1 $('#container').toggle(function(){}, function(){});

plications of the same type, for example, need to perform the same functions on a recurring basis, causing loss of time, money and possible errors in the source code. However if all these functions are grouped into a library or API, these functions can be used without worrying about developing them whenever the need just using the function invocation These resources are used in the RIAs development. Another important application of Facade Design Pattern in RIAs development arises from the need to manage a complex system comprised of a series of subsystems and to the possibility of independently accessing these subsystems, because this way the Design Pattern should be able to implement an efficient communication mechanism between the various subsystems that compose the complex system and in turn provide communication with one or more of the subsystems, thus achieving a system more independent, portable and reusable

3.3. Design Patterns Support in Mootools

Mootools is a compact JavaScript-based framework designed for the intermediate to advanced JavaScript developers Table 5 shows the Design Patterns supported in Mootools.

Table 5. Design Patterns supported in Mootools (mootools.net, 2013)

Creational Patterns	Structural Patterns	Behavioral Patterns
Singleton	Not reported	Not reported

In Table 6, an analysis of the Design Patterns supported by the Mootools framework is presented.

A representative example of one of the Design Patterns supported by Mootools is presented below.

Singleton Pattern

The Singleton pattern provides the possibility to control the number of instances (mostly one) that are allowed. This pattern can be used when only one instance or a specific number of instances of a class are allowed. Facade objects are often Singletons because only one Facade object is required. The benefits of this pattern are for example, controlled access to unique instance, reduced name space, allows refinement of operations and representations, among others. The Drawback of Singleton pattern is also considered an anti-pattern by some people, who feel that it is overused, introducing

Table 6. Analysis of the Design patterns supported by the Mootools framework (mootools.net, 2013)

Design Patterns
Creational Patterns

Singleton	Mootools has a Singleton class which performs the function of the Singleton Design Pattern. An example of the use of the Singleton pattern is depicted:
	1 var MySingleton = new Class.Singleton({
	2 initialize: function(){
	3 // code here
	4 },
	5 method1: function(){
	6 // code here
	7 },
	8 method2: function(){
	9 // code here
	10 }
	11 });

unnecessary limitations in situations where a sole instance of a class is not actually required (Christiansson et al., 2008).

An example of the Singleton Design Pattern could be when the access to a Web application or RIA is allowed in a limited way, i.e., test application which allows users to access only once or a limited number of times, It is useful this pattern because once the user has accessed or the user has exhausted the allowed accesses should be denied access to the application. It is possible to do with the Singleton pattern. It is noteworthy that this pattern has other applications with the same or greater benefit than described above.

3.4. Design Patterns Support in Prototype

Prototype is a popular JavaScript-based framework and one of the most used by developers. Table 7 shows the Design Patterns supported by Protype.

Table 7. Design Patterns supported in Prototype (prototypejs.org., 2013)

Creational Patterns	Structural Patterns	Behavioral Patterns
Singleton Builder	Not Reported	Observer

Table 8 presents an analysis of the Design Patterns supported by Prototype.

A representative example of one of the Design Patterns supported by Prototype is presented below.

Builder Pattern

The Builder pattern can be used to ease the construction of a complex object from simple objects. The Builder pattern also separates the construction of a complex object from its representation so that the same construction process can be used to create another composition of objects. This pattern is used: 1) when the algorithm for creating a complex object should be independent of the parts that make up the object and how they are assembled, 2) when the construction process must allow different representations for the object that is constructed, 3) when clients need to be insulated from the knowledge of the actual creation process and/or resulting product. The benefits about use of this pattern is that the built object is shielded from the details of its construction, code for construction is isolated from code for representation and both are easy to replace without affecting the other, it gives control over the construction process and it gives the possibility to reuse and/or change the process and/or product independently. The

Table 8. Analysis of the Design patterns supported by the Prototype framework (prototypejs.org., 2013)

Design Patterns	
Creational Patterns	
Singleton	An example of the use of the Singleton pattern in Prototype is through the SlideShow object, since the SlideShow object is created as a Singleton.
Builder	The createSlide() function works as a constructor, since each time the Builder.node function is invoked, a new element is created. 1 var newSlide=Builder.node("div", { className: "slide" 2 }); Also, Prototype has functions of a **Proxy** element and has the possibility to define an **Iterator** element, i.e. it also uses these two design patterns.
Behavioral Patterns	
Observer	The Snippet element acts as an Observer, according to the following source code: 1 new Form.Element.Observer("favColor",2,function(el,value){ 2 show($F("name")+" likes...",value); 3 });

drawback is the need flexibility in creating various complex objects (Christiansson et al., 2008).

An example of the Builder Design Pattern would be the construction of a house where the onstruction process has the following order: the floor, walls and ceiling, assume that the client requests to the builder two houses: wood house and brick house. Although the materials are different, the construction process is exactly done in the same way, firstly the floor, then the walls and finally the ceiling. So the construction is isolated from any other factor. This design pattern is useful on RIAs development where is necessary to build applications with the same structure but with different elements. A specific example of the Builder Design Pattern on RIAs development could be the automatic development of Websites. For doing this, the structure of Websites only should be defined, for example all Websites will be composed of a header, a body divided into two columns and a footer, and then the Builder will be responsible for automatically developing Websites without giving much importance to the contents of each one of the sections of the Websites developed.

Table 9. Design Patterns supported in Qooxdoo (qooxdoo.org, 2013)

Creational Patterns	Structural Patterns	Behavioral Patterns
Singleton	Not reported	Not reported

3.5. Design Patterns Support in Qooxdoo

Qooxdoo is a powerful JavaScript-based framework for developing advanced JavaScript applications. Table 9 shows the Design Patterns supported in Qooxdoo.

In Table 10 presents an analysis of the the Design Patterns supported in Qooxdoo.

The Singleton Design Pattern has already been defined and discussed above; it is a pattern that is widely used in all kinds of applications. This pattern fulfills important tasks and very helpful in RIAs development.

3.6. Design Patterns Support in Rico

The Rico framework does not report Design Patterns support (version 2.0).

Table 10. Analysis of the Design patterns supported by the Qooxdoo framework (qooxdoo.org, 2013)

Design Patterns	
Creational Patterns	
Singleton	Qooxdoo uses the class define () to create a Singleton type instance, the following source code exemplifies the use of the Singleton pattern. 1 qx.Class.define("qx.test.Cat", { 2 type: "singleton" 3 ... 4 });

Table 11. Design Patterns support in Sencha ExtJS (sencha.com., 2013)

Creational Patterns	Structural Patterns	Behavioral Patterns
Singleton	Not reported	Observer State

3.7. Design Patterns Support in Sencha ExtJS

Sencha ExtJS is a powerful JavaScript-based framework for developing Rich Internet Applications. Table 11 shows the Design Patterns supported in Sencha ExtJS.

The Table 12 presents an analysis of the Design Patterns supported by Sencha ExtJS.

A representative example of one of the Design Patterns supported by Sencha ExtJS is presented below.

State Pattern

The State pattern allows an object to alter its behavior when its internal state changes. By using inheritance and letting subclasses represent different states and functionality that can be switched during runtime. This is a way for an object to partially change its type at runtime. This pattern can be used, 1) when a "context" class is needed to be defined in order to present a single interface to the outside world. By defining a State abstract base class and 2) when different "states" of a state

Table 12. Analysis of the Design patterns supported by Sencha ExtJS framework (sencha.com., 2013)

Design Patterns	
Creational Patterns	
Singleton	The Singleton pattern is supported in Sencha ExtJS through a ToolTip type called QuickTip. To use a QuickTip, it is necessary to activate it by using a QuickTip instance. 1 <div id="tip4" class="tip-target" ext:qtitle="Informacion" ext:qtip="Este es un 2 ejemplo de QuickTip">QuickTip</div> To enable a QuickTip, the following statement is used: Ext.QuickTips.init ()
Behavioral Patterns	
Observer	By using Sencha ExtJS, there are multiple methods of Listener types, these methods have their specific function and they are known as observers. This is an application of the Observer design pattern, the following source code is a small example: 1 this.addListener('render',this.onRender,this,{ct:this.ct,position:this.position});
State	The State Design Pattern is very used and it also appears in Sencha ExtJS. It is used to save the state of a component and to switch among states. The following source code is an example of the use of the State Design Pattern: 1 Ext.state.Manager.setProvider(new Ext.state.CookieProvider()); In this example, a Manager state is created; through the setProvider method a new CookieProvider object is created. This means that the application state is saved in a cookie on the client-side, which in turn is read to enable the actual state of the component.

machine as derived classes of the State base class need to be presented. The benefits about use of this pattern are 1) cleaner code when each state is a class instead, and 2) use a class to represent a state, not a constant, among others. The Drawbacks are: generates a number of small class objects, but in the process, simplifies and clarifies the program, and eliminates the necessity for a set of long, look-alike conditional statements scattered throughout the code (Christiansson et al., 2008).

An example of this pattern can be the change of the language of a Web application. Let us suppose a RIA in two or more langauge in which the user can choose what language to use. For each language, a state is defined and the state of application is changing from one state to another according to the langauge selected.

3.8. Design Patterns Support in X-Library

The X-Library framework does not report Design Patterns support (version 4.2).

3.9. Summary of Design Patterns Support into JavaScript-Based Frameworks

Every day the JavaScript-based frameworks have more Design patterns implemented in their source code. This is because Design Patterns help to developers to solve different problems in a relatively simple way in order to obtain most effective solutions achieving better software development in less time. Table 13 provides an overview of Design Patterns supported by each one of the JavaScript-based frameworks analyzed.

4. DESIGN PATTERNS SUPPORT INTO NON-JAVASCRIPT-BASED FRAMEWORKS

Design Patterns are also of great help and importance for Web frameworks for non-JavaScript-based frameworks. This section presents a review of the Desing Pattern support of the following non-JavaScript-based frameworks: AdobeFlex™, JavaFX™, Silverlight™ and OpenLaszlo™. The Design Patterns support for each one of these frameworks is presented below.

Table 13. Design Patterns involved on JavaScript-based frameworks

Framework	Creational Patterns	Structural Patterns	Behavioral Patterns
Dojo	Singleton	Not reported	Observer
jQuery	Builder Prototype	Composite Facade Flyweight Proxy	Iterator Observer Strategy
Mootools	Singleton	Not reported	Not reported
Prototype	Singleton Builder	Not reported	Observer
Qooxdoo	Singleton	Not reported	Not reported
Rico	Not reported	Not reported	Not reported
Sencha Ext JS	Singleton	Not reported	Observer State
X-Library	Not reported	Not reported	Not reported

Table 14. Design patterns supported by Adobe Flex™ (Fain et al, 2010)

Creational Patterns	Structural Patterns	Behavioral Patterns
Singleton	Proxy	Mediator

4.1. Design Patterns in Adobe Flex™

Adobe Flex™ is a productive framework for Rich Internet Applications. Table 14 shows the Design Patterns supported in Adobe Flex™.

The table 15 presents an analysis of the Design Patterns supported by Adobe Flex™.

It is noteworthy that Adobe Flex™ has support for other Design Patterns that do not belong to the GoF classification and thus are not described in this chapter. These Design Patterns are: Data Transfer Object, Asynchronous Token and Class Factory.

A representative example of one of the Design Patterns supported by Adobe Flex™ is presented below.

Proxy Pattern

A Proxy is a structural pattern that provides a stand-in for another object in order to control access to it. This pattern can be used, 1) when the creation of one object is relatively expensive it can be a good idea to replace it with a proxy that can make sure that instantiation of the expensive object is kept to a minimum, 2) when Proxy pattern implementation allows for login and authority checking before one reaches the actual object that is requested and, 3) when can provide a local representation for an object in a remote location. One of the Proxy benefits is that this pattern gives the ability to control access to an object, whether it is because of a costly creation process of that object or security issues. The Proxy drawbacks are that introduces another abstraction level for an object, if some objects accesses the target object directly and another via the proxy there is a chance that they get different behavior this may or may not be the intention of the creator (Christiansson et al., 2008).

Table 15. Analysis of the Design Patterns supported by Adobe Flex™ (Fain et al, 2010)

	Design Patterns
	Creational Patterns
Singleton	The singleton Design Pattern can be represented as follows: **var model: AppModelLocator.getInstance AppModelLocator = ();** Flex provides an element called Cairngorm singleton that can communicate with the server and ensure a single instance, it is represented by the following code: **service = ServiceLocator.getInstance () getHTTPService ('loadEmployeesService.')** Flex provides the ability to implement the Singleton Design Pattern, also provides elements already included in the source code that fulfill the same function and have already been tested.
	Structural Patterns

Proxy	In ActionScript can be wrapped the class XYZ in mx.util.ObjectProxy, which will be a proxy that controls access to XYZ properties.
	import mx.utils.ObjectProxy
	var person:Person = new Person;
	var personProxy:ObjectProxy = new ObjectProxy(person);
	There is one line in PersonProxy.mxml that wraps up the instance of the class Person into an ObjectProxy.

	Behavioral Patterns
Mediator	Mediator Design Pattern is one of the most useful for any programming environment due to it includes special components for communication in event-driven environment such as Flex. In Flex, Mediator Design Pattern is implemented in components classified as Layouts and Navigators. For example, in a Flex-based application where a Panel component has a TabNavigator component and the TabNavigator component has TextInput and Button components. The TahNavigator component acts as a mediator among Panel component and the TextInput and Button components. In most cases, Mediator Design Pattern is represented by a container-type component.

One of the most common uses of the Proxy pattern is the proxy security. This proxy is used to add security access to an existing object, and in this case the proxy will determine whether the client can access the object of interest. The Proxy pattern is widely used in RIAs and Web applications to provide security for applications. Also, it is widely used in Flex and ActionScript through to the mx.util.ObjectProxy class. Another example for the Proxy pattern is, let us suppose that an application must be quickly deployed but it contains large images which makes the download process to be very slow, then it requires the implementation of the Proxy pattern because with this pattern is possible to present to the user an interface in which images are deployed on demand when the user chooses and only if the user is agreed, the images will be downloaded. Even in some cases, the user can have the option to choose whether downloading all images or one by one.

4.2. Design Patterns in JavaFX™

The Design Patterns support of the GoF classification in JavFX™ is not reported. However, there is the possibility of manually implementing these patterns, i.e. the developer has the possibility of implementing these patterns by codifying them. This can be done by developing functions with the Design Patterns architectures, i.e. Design Patterns architectures can be implemented if the developer requires it through the programming language that they are using. It is also well known that JavaFX™ uses the MVC Design Pattern (Model-View-Controller) o MVP Design Pattern (Model-View-Presenter); however these Design Patterns are not explained in this chapter because they do not belong to the GoF classification.

4.3. Design Patterns in Silverlight™

Silverlight™ does not report the Design Patterns support of the GoF classification. However, Silverlight™ uses the MVC Design Pattern and the MVVM Design Pattern (Model-View-View Model).

4.4. Design Patterns in OpenLaszlo™

It is important to notice that OpenLaszlo™ does not report Design Patterns support for GoF classification.

5. CONCLUSION

Design patterns are very important and helpful for developers. Well-implemented Design Patterns can help the developer to: 1) solve complex problems with simple solutions, 2) Reuse ideas, 3) Reduce development time 4) Reduce production costs, 5) Apply best practices development, among other benefits.

As can be noticed, not all frameworks have an extensive Design Patterns support; however development companies as well as the developers are working on the implementation of Design Patterns in the most used frameworks in order to achieve a more efficient programming.

It can be observed; JavaScript-based frameworks have a greater implementation of Design Patterns. This situation is due to several reasons, including: 1) the level of maturity of the frameworks, 2) programming language, and 3) development communities. The JavaScript-based frameworks have a high level of maturity by using JavaScript as a programming language so the learning curve is reduced. Furthermore, JavaScript-based frameworks have a great number of developer communities continuously working in adding new features on these frameworks. Non-JavaScript-based frameworks have some limitations such as the use of proprietary programming languages and paid licenses. Another important detail is the constant evolution in programming languages such as the case JavaFX™ where from one version to another, there are too many changes on syntax and components, making them incompatible among versions. These factors make that developers have to learn new features. Another factor is that JavaScript-based frameworks are mainly focused on business logic where information is exchanged between a database and a user interface. The non-JavaScript-based frameworks are based on the presentation for developing graphical user interfaces in terms of page layout, page transitions and page control elements.

REFERENCES

Christiansson, B., Forss, M., Hagen, I., Hansson, K., Jonasson, J., & Jonasson, M. et al. (2008). *GoF Design Patterns - with examples using Java and UML2. Logica Java Architects Training Crew.* Authors.

Fain, Y., Rasputnis, V., & Tartakovsky, A. (2010) *Enterprise Development with Flex* (p. 688). O'Reilly Media.

Gamma, E., Helm, R., Johnson, R., & Vlissides, J. (1994). Design Patterns. In Elements of reusable Object-Oriented Software. Addison Wesley.

Harmon, J. E. (2008). Dojo: Using the Dojo JavaScript Library to Build Ajax Applications. Addison-Wesley Professional.

Mootools.net. (2013). *API Documentation.* Retrieved January, 2013, from http://mootools.net/docs/core

Osmani, A. (2010). *Essential JavaScript & jQuery Design Patterns For Beginners.* Addy Osmani.

prototypejs.org. (2013). *API Documentation.* Retrieved January, 2013, from http://prototypejs.org/learn

qooxdoo.org. (2013). *API Documentation.* Retrieved January, 2013, from http://demo.qooxdoo.org/current/apiviewer/#qx.core.Aspect

sencha.com. (2013). *API Documentation.* Retrieved January, 2013, from http://docs.sencha.com/extjs/4.1.3/

ADDITIONAL READING

Gamma, E., Helm, R., Johnson, R., & Vlissides, J. (1994). Design Patterns. In Elements of reusable Object-Oriented Software. Addison Wesley.

KEY TERMS AND DEFINITIONS

Behavioral Patterns: Design Patterns that identify common communication patterns between objects and realize these patterns. These patterns are focused on the interactions among cooperating objects.

Class Diagram: A type of UML diagram, and a type of static structure diagram that describes the structure of a system by showing its classes, their attributes, operations (or methods), and the relationships among objects.

Creational Patterns: Design Patterns that deal with object creation mechanisms, trying to create objects in a manner suitable to the situation.

Design Patterns: A proven solution a common and recurring problem, this solution is designed for a particular context.

MVC: A software architectural pattern. The MVC pattern separates the domain modeling, the presentation and the actions based on the user input into three classes, Model, View and Controller.

Structural Patterns: Design Patterns that ease the design by identifying a simple way to realize relationships among entities, and describe how objects and classes can be combined to form structures.

UML: A general-purpose modeling language in the software engineering field; UML is designed to provide a standard way to visualize the design of a system, and is supported by the OMG (Object Management Group).

Chapter 8
UI Patterns Support on RIAs Development

ABSTRACT

In Chapter 8, a review of UI patterns supported by using non-JavaScript-based frameworks and JavaScript-based frameworks for RIAs development is presented. For this purpose, the UI Patterns are classified in Transitional Patterns, Lookup Patterns, and Feedback Patterns. Additionally, this chapter presents a series of applications samples depicting the use of not only UI controls but also non-visual functions or classes (as applicable) for implementing the supported UI patterns. These applications are intended to clarify the differences and similarities between UI controls and UI patterns. Finally, the chapter presents a comparative analysis that summarizes the review of the capabilities of the RIA frameworks in the context of rich UI design both for JavaScript-based frameworks and non-JavaScript-based frameworks.

1. INTRODUCTION

RIAs (Rich Internet Applications) design involves two main stages: 1) application structure design and 2) GUIs (Graphic User Interfaces) design which, in turn, is composed of three subtasks: a) layouts design, b) GUI controls design and c) interactions design (Neil, 2009).

Layouts design covers the arrangement of visual elements, i.e., GUI controls across the screen. In this sense, there are common ways to arrange the RIAs' GUI controls, namely canvas, vertical and horizontal layouts. In fact, most of the RIA frameworks consider these standard layouts; thereby, Web 2.0 community has outlined a set of screen patterns that can be used at this design level,

and they can be implemented as a combination of GUI controls containers such as panels, forms and the aforementioned layouts.

GUI controls design covers the design of the GUI controls that allows applications to communicate the required user interactions. Typically, RIA frameworks offer both a set of simple GUI controls acting as application building blocks and a set of look and feel customization mechanisms. However, most of the RIA frameworks also offer the possibility of adding custom GUI controls built from simple controls.

In another hand, interactions design implies the usage of patterns aimed at achieving effective user experiences, i.e., rich interactions. In this sense, most of the RIA frameworks offer simple GUI

DOI: 10.4018/978-1-4666-6437-1.ch008

controls that natively implement interaction patterns, e.g., progress bar (progress indicator pattern) and accordion (expand/collapse pattern) in Adobe Flex™ or JavaFX™. However, some interaction patterns require more development time and effort in order to be implemented. Therefore, it is not easy to understand the differences between GUI controls and interaction patterns. Interaction design patterns are commonly used to ease the interaction between users and Web 2.0 applications by bringing more intuitive and responsive user experiences, i.e., rich user experiences; in short, they allow developers to encourage users to engage with applications. The most popular interaction patterns from the point of view of the authors are described below.

- **Brighten and Dim:** it is actually considered a pair of interaction design patterns intended to focus user attention on an area of the GUI by brightening there at the same time that the rest of the GUI is dimmed to indicate that is not in use. The most common technique to achieve this consists on displaying a non-dimmed overlay over a dimmed background which is called lightbox effect.
- **Expand/Collapse:** it allows keeping additional contents hidden until the user needs them; it is also useful in cases where the content length exceeds the length of the area of the GUI intended to display them.
- **Animation:** it is a means for clarifying user interactions by mimicking object transitions from the real world. This pattern is closely related to the drag and drop interaction pattern because it is commonly used to clarify where objects came from and are going.
- **Spotlight:** it is one of the major mechanisms for notifying users about changes occurred on applications. It consists on temporarily focus the user attention on changes

in the GUI even when these changes are explicitly triggered by users.

- **Auto Complete:** it allows users to save time on filling out forms which is overused among Internet search engines such as Google™, Bing™ and Yahoo! ™ with the aim of optimizing searches by providing real-time term suggestions for creating searches starting from previous entries. At this point, this pattern is known as live suggest.
- **Live Preview:** in the context of form submission, it is used to prevent mistakes by providing real-time feedback about form inputs. It can also be used in the context of e-commerce as a means for showcasing customizable products such as clothes and cars.
- **Progress Indication:** it is a means for keeping the user informed about the progress of a lengthy operation running in background; it is also used to simply indicate the user that must wait for an operation to be completed; i.e., as an indication of a busy application.
- **Periodic Refresh:** it is useful to maintain the content of an application up-to-date; in this sense, the new content can be loaded either automatically or on demand as is broadly used by some microblogging websites such as Twitter™ and Facebook™.

According to the above, this chapter is aimed at reviewing the support for implementing the interaction design patterns outlined above among popular non-JavaScript-based and JavaScript-based RIA frameworks not only in terms of GUI controls but also in terms of non-visual classes. This systematic review is finally summarized in a comparative analysis of the capabilities of the RIA frameworks in the context of rich GUI design. In addition, the differences and similarities between GUI controls and interaction design patterns are intended to be explained by using sample applications. For practical purposes, the source code used for implement these sample applications is not presented in its entirety. In fact, only two implementations for each RIA framework are included in this chapter. Despite this issue, all the interaction design patterns above described are covered in terms of sample implementations.

2. UI PATTERNS SUPPORT INTO JAVASCRIPT-BASED FRAMEWORKS

Because most of the JavaScript-based RIA frameworks are available under open source software licenses; they take advantage of the developer communities contributing to implement the features that are absent. From this prespective, some of the interaction design patterns analyzed in this chapter that are not closely related to standard GUI controls are fully implemented by third-party plug-ins by using HTML controls and the CSS style sheet language, hence the importance to cover these third-party extensions. This is because interaction patterns are actually a set of design principles and best practices for delivering rich user experiences.

It is important to notice that the sample implementations presented in this chapter are based on demo applications provided as part of the official documentation of the related JavaScript-based RIA frameworks.

2.1. UI Patterns in Dojo

Brighten and Dim

Dojo provides a lightbox component as part of the *Dojox* package. This component inherits properties and methods from the *Digit Dialog* class which is a modal pop-up dialog box. As can be inferred, *Digit* is the Dojo's GUI library. In its basics, the *Dojox Lightbox* widget allows converting links containing title and href attributes into widgets; in fact, it can be used either programmatically or inline. Figure 1 depicts the usage of the *Dojox Lightbox* and *ThumbnaillPicker* widgets on developing an image gallery. *ThumbnailPicker* is actually a layout that displays a series of images either horizontally or vertically and it provides controls to page through the images.

Figure 1. Implementing the brighten and dim interaction design pattern by using the Dojox Lightbox and ThumbnailPicker widgets

Expand/Collapse

Dojo has a layout container called *Accordion-Container* which implements the expand/collapse interaction design pattern. In fact, Dojo provides a complete set of layouts as part of the *Digit* package. For instance, the *AccordionContainer* layout holds a set of panes where each pane is in turn an instance of the *ContentPane* layout which is the most basic Dojo layout and it contains a title area. Furthermore, like the Dojo *TabContainer* and *StackContainer* layouts, the *AccordionContainer* layout displays only one pane at a time. Figure 2 depicts the usage of the Dojo *AccordionContainer* layout.

Animation

In its basics, the animation interaction design pattern can be used as means to incorporate effects to RIAs, i.e., visual or audible changes that occur over a period of time. In this sense, Dojo has a subpackage called *Fx* which provides effects targeting DOM nodes; these effects include fade, slide and wipe effects. As part of the *Dojox* package, Dojo also has a subpackage providing additional effects such as highlights and resizes. Every Dojo effect is built on top of the base effect functionality provided by the *_base/fx* subpackage which comprises the *animateProperty()* function, a function that allows animating changes of CSS properties. Figure 3 depicts the usage of the Dojo *animateProperty()*, *slideTo()*, *fadeIn()* and *fadeOut()* functions on animating text and image nodes.

Figure 2. Implementing the accordion interaction design pattern by using the Dojo AccordionContainer layout

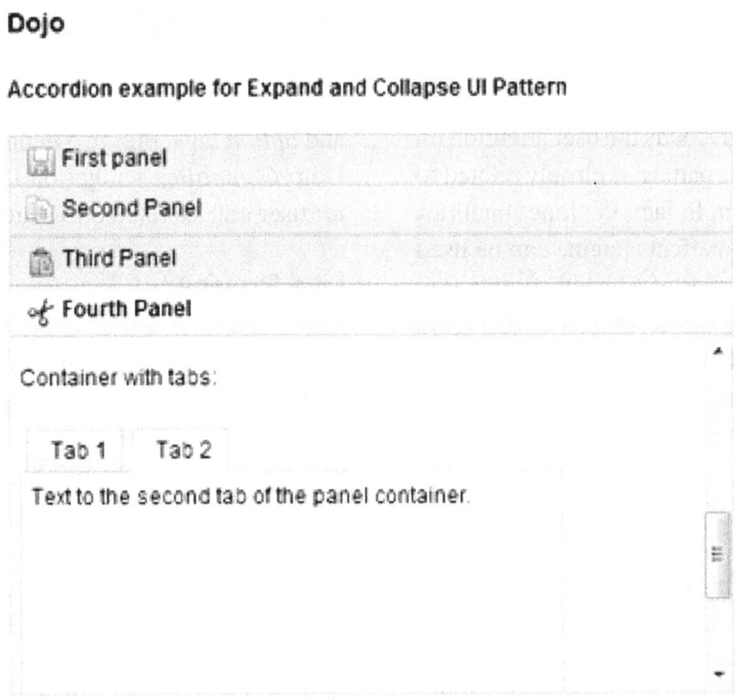

Figure 3. Implementing the animation interaction design pattern by using the Dojo Fx engine

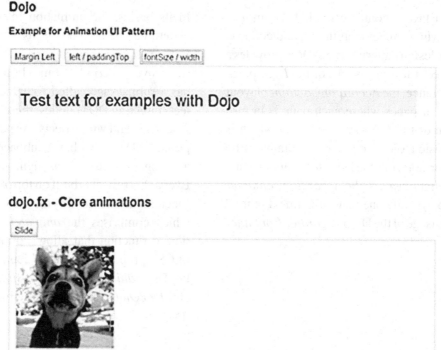

Spotlight

The spotlight interaction design pattern is commonly used to simply highlight an area of a GUI in order to temporarily focus the user attention on it. In this context, this pattern is closely related to the animation pattern. In fact, the functionalities provided by the Dojo effects engine can be used to animate the properties of a layout container in order to highlight certain areas on a GUI. Figure 4 depicts the usage of the Dojo *animateProperty( )* function on animating the border color and size of a Dojo *ContentPane* layout.

Auto Complete

As part of the *Dijit* package, Dojo has a widget called *ComboBox* which is a hybrid between the HTML *select* and *input* controls. Despite its name, the Dojo *ComboBox* widget displays partially matched values for an entry in a pop-up below a

text box as the user types. As usual on instantiating *Dijit* widgets, the *ComboBox* widget can be used either programmatically or declaratively; the latter approach implies the usage of the HTML *select* and *option* tags. Figure 5 depicts the usage of the Dojo *ComboBox* widget on suggesting matches for user entries related to states names.

Live Preview

Dojo provides form validation facilities by means of the *Form* class as part of the *Digit* package. In fact, it has a set of form controls with built-in support for client-side form validation. For instance, the *DateTextBox* widget is a date entry widget that allows either typing or choosing a date from a calendar. It automatically validates the typed entries against locale-specific internationalization (i18n) rules; additionally, it allows validating entries against developer-provided constraints like min and max values. As can be inferred, these form

Figure 4. Implementing the spotlight interaction design pattern by using the Dojo animateProperty() function

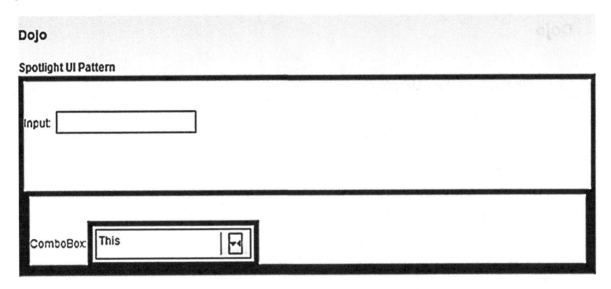

Figure 5. Implementing the auto complete interaction design pattern by using the Dojo ComboBox widget

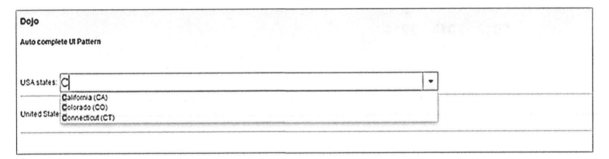

widgets are typically used in conjunction with the *Digit Form* class which is the equivalent of the HTML *form* tag and it provides the *isValid()* and *validate()* methods to prevent invalid form from submitting. Figure 6 depicts the usage of the Dojo *DateTextBox* widget in the context of a Dojo *Form*. In addition, a snippet of the corresponding source code is depicted in Figure 7.

Progress Indication

Dojo provides both a widget called *BusyButton* which implements the simplest form of the

progress indication pattern and a widget called *ProgressBar* which implements the most complex form of the progress indication pattern. In detail, the *BusyButton* widget is part of the *Dojox* package and it is intended to be used in the context of form submission; it allows displaying a custom label during a configurable timeout. On the other hand, the *ProgressBar* widget is part of the *Digit* package and it allows giving dynamic feedback on the progress of long-running JavaScript operations. Figure 8 depicts the usage of the Dojo *BussyButton* widget. In addition, a snippet of the corresponding source code is depicted in Figure 9.

Figure 6. Implementing the live preview interaction design pattern by using the Dojo DateTextBox widget

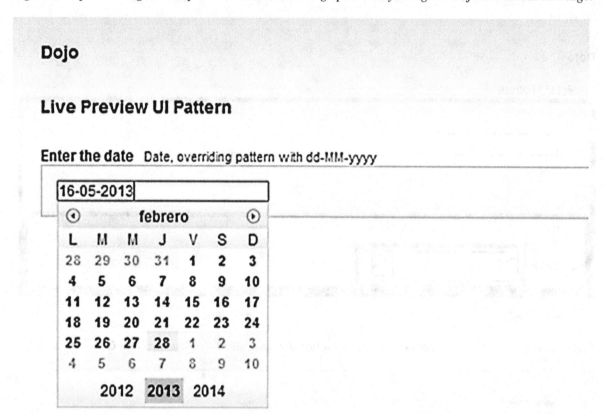

Figure 7. Snippet of the Dojo-based source code used for implementing the live preview interaction design pattern

```
1    <link id="themeStyles" rel="stylesheet" href="../../../dijit/themes/tundra/tundra.css">
2    <script type="text/javascript" src="../../../dojo/dojo.js" djConfig="isDebug: true,
3    parseOnLoad: true, extraLocale: ['de-de', 'en-us']"></script>
4    <script type="text/javascript" src="../_testCommon.js"></script>
5    <script type="text/javascript">
6        dojo.require("dijit.dijit");
7        dojo.require("dijit.form.DateTextBox");
8        dojo.require("dijit.form.Form");
9        dojo.require("dojo.date.locale");
10       dojo.require("dojo.parser");
11       function eventHandler(e){
12           console.log(this.domNode.getAttribute('widgetId') + ' ' + arguments[0].type);
13       }
14   </script>
15   …
16   <form id="form1" dojoType='dijit.form.Form' action="" name="example" method=""
17   onSubmit="return this.validate()">
18       <div class="dojoTitlePaneLabel">
19           <label for="pattern">Enter the date</label>
20           <span class="noticeMessage">Date, overriding pattern with dd-MM-yyyy</span>
21       </div>
22       <div class="testExample">
23           <input id="pattern" name="noDOMvalue" type="text"
24   dojoType="dijit.form.DateTextBox" constraints="{datePattern:'dd-MM-yyyy', strict:true}">
25       </div>
26   </form>
```

Figure 8. Implementing the progress indication interaction design pattern by using the Dojo BusyButton widget

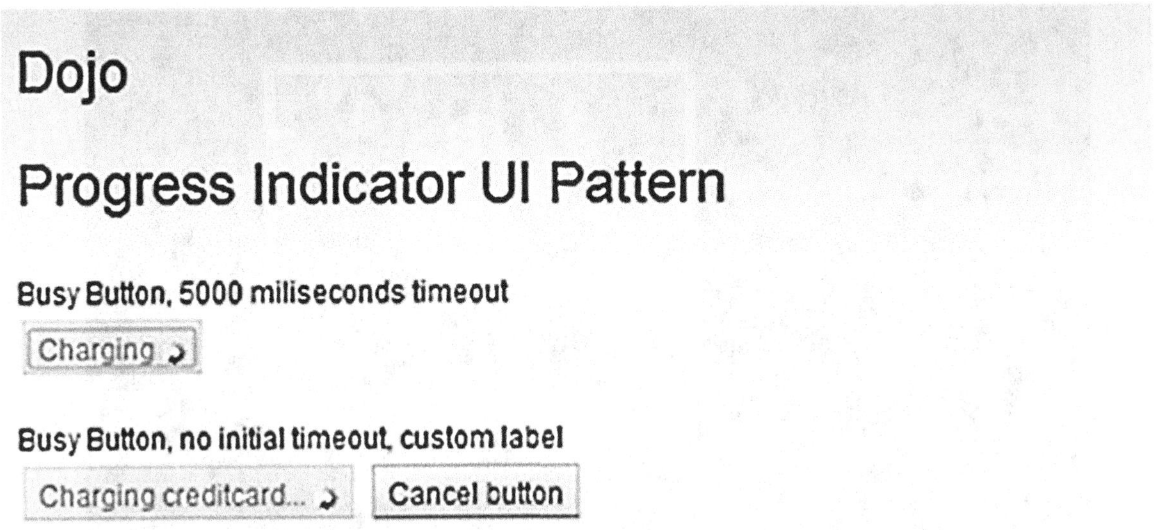

Dojo

Progress Indicator UI Pattern

Busy Button, 5000 miliseconds timeout

Charging ⤴

Busy Button, no initial timeout, custom label

Charging creditcard... ⤴   Cancel button

Figure 9. Snippet of the Dojo-based source code used for implementing the progress indication interaction design pattern

```
1   <script type="text/javascript" src="../../../dojo/dojo.js" djConfig="parseOnLoad: true,
2   isDebug: true"></script>
3   <style type="text/css">
4       @import url(../../../dojo/resources/dojo.css);
5       @import url(../../_static/js/dojo/../dojox/form/resources/BusyButton.css);
6       @import url(../../../dijit/themes/tundra/tundra.css);
7   </style>
8   <script type="text/javascript">
9       dojo.require("dojox.form.BusyButton");
10  </script>
11  ...
12  <p> Busy Button, 5000 miliseconds timeout <br/>
13      <button dojoType="dojox.form.BusyButton" busyLabel="Charging" timeout="5000"
14  >Click</button>
15  </p>
```

2.2. UI Patterns in jQuery

Brighten and Dim

jQuery UI is a GUI framework built on top of jQuery, which defines a level of interaction design patterns as part of its components architecture. In fact, it is a set of GUI interactions, effects, widgets and themes. However, it does not include the brighten and dim pattern so that a plug-in providing this functionality must be used. Figure 10 depicts the usage of the version 5 of the jQuery *lightbox* plug-in available at http://leandrovieira.com/projects/jquery/lightbox/ on developing an image gallery. In addition, a screenshot of this application is depicted in Figure 10. In addition, a snippet of the corresponding source code is depicted in Figure 11.

Figure 10. Implementing the brighten and dim interaction design pattern by using the jQuery lightbox plug-in

Figure 11. Snippet of the jQuery-based source code used for implementing the brighten and dim interaction design pattern

```
1   <script type="text/javascript" src="js/jquery.js"></script>
2   <script type="text/javascript" src="js/jquery.lightbox-0.5.js"></script>
3   <link rel="stylesheet" type="text/css" href="css/jquery.lightbox-0.5.css" media="screen" />
4   <script type="text/javascript">
5       $(function() {
6           $('#gallery a').lightBox();
7       });
8   </script>
9   …
10  <div id="gallery">
11      <ul>
12          <li>
13              <a href="photos/image1.jpg" title="Lightbox 1">
14                  <img src="photos/thumb_image1.jpg" width="72" height="72" alt="" />
15              </a>
16          </li>
17          …
18      </ul>
19  </div>
```

Auto Complete

The jQuery UI framework has a native GUI widget called autocomplete which uses a simple JavaScript-based array provided by means of the source option as data source. Figure 12 depicts the usage of the jQuery autocomplete widget. Here the suggestions are tags for cities names. In addition, a snippet of the corresponding source code is depicted in Figure 13.

Figure 12. Implementing the auto complete interaction design pattern by using the jQuery autocomplete widget

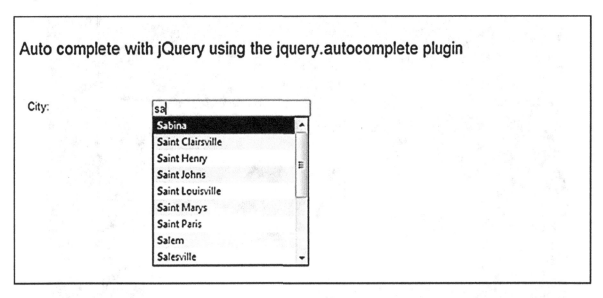

Figure 13. Snippet of the jQuery-based source code used for implementing the auto complete interaction design pattern

```
1    <script type="text/javascript" src="../lib/jquery.js"></script>
2    <script type="text/javascript" src="../lib/jquery-ui.js"></script>
3    <link rel="stylesheet" type="text/css" href="main.css" />
4    <script type="text/javascript">
5        $(function() {
6            $("#suggest1").autocomplete({
7                source: cities
8            });
9        });
10   </script>
11
12   <div class="ui-widget">
13       <p>
14           <label for="suggest1">City:</label>
15           <input type="text" id="suggest1" />
16       </p>
17       ...
18   </div>
```

2.3. UI Patterns in Mootools

Brighten and Dim

MooTools is a JavaScript-based framework primarily addressing Ajax manipulation and visual effects. In fact, the MooTools animation engine which relies on the classes of the *Fx* package is a major component of MooTools. According to the above, MooTools does not have native widgets. However there are several third-party MooTools plugins available on Internet. For instance, the official MooTools website lists different categories of third-party plug-ins, including widgets. In this sense, there is a variety of plug-ins implementing the brighten and dim interaction design pattern mainly by means of the lightbox effect technique. A popular plug-in called *Videobox* provides a

Figure 14. Implementing the brighten and dim interaction design pattern by using the MooTools Videobox plug-in

Figure 15. Snippet of the MooTools-based source code used for implementing the brighten and dim interaction design pattern

```
1    <script type="text/javascript" src="js/mootools.js"></script>
2    <script type="text/javascript" src="js/swfobject.js"></script>
3    <script type="text/javascript" src="js/videobox.js"></script>
4    <link rel="stylesheet" href="css/videobox.css" type="text/css" media="screen" />
5    ...
6    <div>
7        <a href="http://www.youtube.com/v/MrXfbyj26Vk?version=3&amp;hl=es_MX" rel="vidbox"
8    id="flvvideo" title="Mootools y Videobox" >Video</a>
9    </div>
```

means to show videos by using overlays; it is a lightbox for videos. Figure 14 depicts the usage of the MooTools *Videobox* plugin on implementing the brighten and dim interaction design pattern. In addition, a snippet of the corresponding source code is depicted in Figure 15.

Animation

Outside the context of implementing drag-and-drop gestures, the animation interaction design pattern can be used on a variety of scenarios mimicking object transitions from the real world. In this sense, animating the value of a single CSS property is the most basic kind of animation in JavaScript-based RIA frameworks. As part of the

Figure 16. Implementing the animation interaction design pattern by using the MooTools Tween class

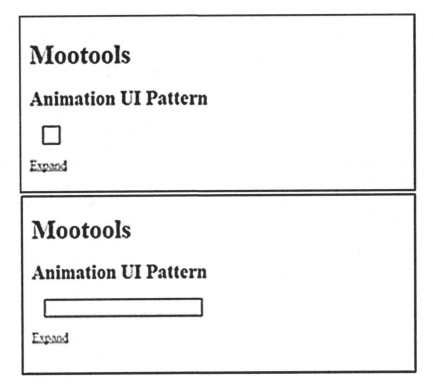

Figure 17. Snippet of the MooTools-based source code used for implementing the drop animation interaction design pattern

```
1    <script type="text/javascript" src="js/mootools.js"></script>
2    <script type="text/javascript">
3        var myFx = new Fx.Tween('one_one_div ', {
4            duration: 'long',
5            transition: 'bounce:out',
6            link: 'cancel',
7            property: width
8        });
9        document.id('myLink').addEvent('click', function(event){
10           event.stop();
11           myFx.start(140);
12       });
13   </script>
14   …
15   <div id="one_one_div" style="border: 1px solid; height: 20px; width: 20px;"></div>
```

MooTools *Fx* package, there are a set of classes providing support for simple and complex CSS-based animations, including the *Tween* and *Morph* classes. The hierarchy of *Fx* classes starts with a class called *Fx* which defines methods for starting, pausing and canceling effects. In detail, the *Tween* class is used to transition any CSS property from one value to another, i.e., to implement a tween effect. Furthermore, the *Morph* class is used to animate multiple CSS properties at once. For animating a single CSS property by using the MooTools *Tween* class, the name of the property to be animated as well as the starting and target values must be passed to the *start()* method. Figure

16 depicts the usage of the MooTools *Tween* class on implementing the animation interaction design pattern. In addition, a snippet of the corresponding source code is depicted in Figure 17.

2.4. UI Patterns in Prototype

Brighten and Dim

Prototype and Script.aculo.us do not provide native support for pop-up dialog windows or boxes as the primary mean for achieving the brighten and dim interaction design pattern. However, there are several Prototype plug-ins implementing the brighten and dim interaction pattern by means of the so-called lightbox effect technique. For instance, the *Lightbox Slideshow* plug-in is a script used to overlay images on the current Web page and it is available at http://www.justinbarkhuff.com/lab/lightbox_slideshow/. As usual among other lightbox plug-ins, the *Lightbox Slideshow* plug-in implements an animation aimed at resizing the pop-up window from a point to full-size when the *initialize()* method is called. The *initialize()* method can receive an object specifying optional configuration options such as the duration of the resize animation and the speed of the image resizing. Finally, it is important to notice that this plug-in can also be used to navigate and display groups of images. Figure 18 depicts the usage of the Prototype *Lightbox Slideshow* plug-in on implementing the brighten and dim interaction design pattern. In addition, a snippet of the corresponding source code is depicted in Figure 19.

Expand/Collapse

Because Prototype primarily addresses Ajax and DOM manipulation it does not include GUI components as part of its core (Raymond & Pereira, 2006). In fact; it is commonly used in conjunction with Script.aculo.us, a JavaScript-based library built on top of Prototype, which adds GUI

components, visual effects and behavior classes. As can be inferred, the Script.aculo.us behavior classes are equivalent to the jQuery UI interaction classes and they can be directly mapped to the interaction design patterns level of rich GUI design. Nevertheless, Script.aculo.us does not have a GUI control or layout container implementing the expand/collapse interaction design pattern to date; hence, a third-party plug-in must be used. In this sense, there is a lot of Prototype plug-ins publicly available over Internet. For instance, the plug-in repository available at http://www.prototype-plugins.com/ lists a plug-in called *e24TabMenu* which implements a tab navigator container able to expand and collapse. Figure 20 depicts the usage of the Script.aculo.us *e24TabMenu* plug-in on implementing the expand/collapse interaction design pattern. In addition, a snippet of the corresponding source code is depicted in Figure 21.

Animation

Script.aculo.us provides a set of classes that allows adding rich behaviors to Web applications; these classes called behavior classes include the *Draggable* and *Droppables* classes. It also has a *Sortable* class which adds additional built in support for drag-and-drop operations to layout containers. The *Draggable* class is used to enable a DOM element to be dragged; for that purpose, a new instance of the *Draggable* class must be created. The *Droppables* class is a static class used to enable a DOM element to react when a draggable element is dropped onto it; for that purpose, the *Droppables.add()* method must be used. Although the usage of the Script.aculo.us *Draggable* and *Droppables* classes does not require handling mouse events, they accept callback functions associated to typical drag-and-drop mouse events as part of their configuration options. Finally, it is important to notice that the *Draggable* class implements a drag animation consisting in changing the opacity of the element is being dragged.

Figure 18. Implementing the brighten and dim interaction design pattern by using the Prototype Lightbox Slideshow plug-in

Figure 19. Snippet of the Prototype-based source code used for implementing the brighten and dim interaction design pattern

```
1    <link rel="stylesheet" href="css/lightbox.css" type="text/css" media="screen" />
2    <script type="text/javascript" src="PyS/Librerias/prototype.js"></script>
3    <script type="text/javascript" src="PyS/Librerias/scriptaculous.js"></script>
4    <script src="PyS/Librerias/lightbox.js" type="text/javascript"></script>
5    <table border="0">
6        <tr>
7            <th><a href="imagenes/dg1.png" rel="lightbox"><img src="imagenes/dp1.png"/></a>
8            <center><b>Velociraptor</b></center></th>
9            ...
10       </tr>
11   </table>
```

Figure 20. Implementing the expand/collapse interaction design pattern by using the Script.aculo.us e24TabMenu plug-in

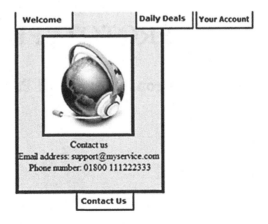

153

Figure 21. Snippet of the Prototype-based source code used for implementing the expand/collapse interaction design pattern

```
1    <script type="text/javascript" src="../PyS/Librerias/prototype.js"></script>
2    <script type="text/javascript" src="../PyS/Librerias/scriptaculous.js"></script>
3    <script type='text/javascript' src='../PyS/Librerias/menujs/e24tabmenu.js'></script>
4    <script type="text/javascript">
5        function initApp() {
6            oe24TabMenu = new e24TabMenu('menu', { mode: 'uppertabs', duration: 1.0,
7    transition: Effect.Transitions.sinoidal });
8        }
9        Event.observe(window, 'load', initApp, false);
10   </script>
11   …
12   <div id="page">
13       <div id="menu">
14           <div id="item_bn" class="menutarget">
15               <div class="gallery">
16                   <center><img src="imagenes/logo.png" />
17                   <br>Welcome to <b>BuysAll.com</b>
18                   <br>Buys All Store</center>
19               </div>
20           </div>
21           …
22       </div>
23   </div>
```

Figure 22. Implementing the drop animation interaction design pattern by using the Script.aculo.us Draggable and Droppable classes

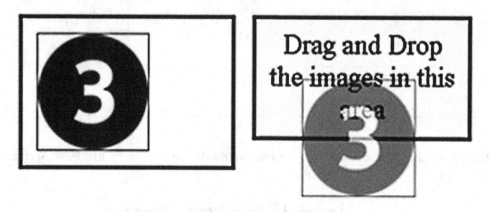

PROTOTYPE

Drop animation UI Pattern

Figure 23. Implementing the drop animation interaction design pattern by using a Qooxdoo List widget

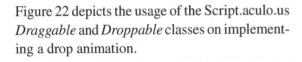

Figure 22 depicts the usage of the Script.aculo.us *Draggable* and *Droppable* classes on implementing a drop animation.

2.5. UI Patterns in Qooxdoo

Animation

Qooxdoo provides support for drag-and-drop operations as part of its event-driven programming model. Thus, any Qooxdoo widget can be configured to be used as a sender (drag source), receiver (drop target) or both. For that purpose, the draggable and droppable properties must be enabled on the target widget. In addition to the typical mouse event handling, the supported drag operations must be specified on a drag source by means of the *addAction( )* method inherited from the *DragDrop* event handler class. In this sense, the supported drag operations are copy, move and alias. This configuration automatically enables a drop animation based on a custom mouse cursor represented by the *DragDropCursor* widget. In addition to this feedback mechanism, Qooxdoo automatically displays a snapshot of the item is being dragged. Figure 23 depicts a sample Qooxdoo-based RIA implementing the drag-and-drop gesture over a *List* widget.

Progress Indication

Under the category of indication widgets, Qooxdooo provides a simple progress bar widget. This widget called *ProgressBar* is designed to display the current percentage of completion of a lengthy JavaScript operation so that it is a kind of determinating progress bar. It only exposes two setter methods: one method that sets the maximum value of the progress bar and one method that sets the current value of the progress bar. It is important to notice that, unlike other progress bar implementations, the Qooxdoo *ProgressBar*

Figure 24. Implementing the progress indication interaction design pattern by using the Qooxdoo ProgressBar widget

widget does not allow to display a label besides the progress value. Figure 24 depicts the usage of the Qooxdoo *ProgressBar* widget on implementing the progress indication interaction design pattern.

2.6. UI Patterns in Rico

Expand/Collapse

Unlike the other JavaScript-based RIA frameworks providing support for the expand/collapse interaction design pattern, Rico does not have a native accordion control or layout container; the *Rico.Accordion* class is actually a simple script used to transform a set of HTML <*div*> tags into an accordion GUI control. In detail, the *Rico.Accordion* class allows adding the event handlers necessary to manage the expand and collapse behaviors to the corresponding *div* elements. In this sense, each one of the accordion panes must be represented by using a pair of *div* elements: one representing the pane header and one representing the pane content. Figure 25 depicts the usage of the *Rico.Accordion* class on implementing the expand/collapse interaction design pattern. In addition, a snippet of the corresponding source code is depicted in Figure 26.

Animation

Rico provides a set of classes that allows RIAs to support drag-and-drop operations. In detail, these classes include a predefined object called *dndManager* which allows easily defining draggable (drag source) objects as well as objects acting as drop zones (drop targets) by using the *registerDraggable()* and *registerDropZone()* methods, respectively. For that purpose, Rico provides the *Rico.Draggable* and *Rico.DropZone* classes. It is important to notice that, unlike most of the JavaScript-based RIA frameworks, Rico does not require handling the mouse events involved on a drag-and-drop gesture. In addition, Rico implements a drop animation consisting in changing the look and feel of the drop zone while a draggable object is being dragged. Figure 27 depicts the usage of the *Rico.Draggable* and *Rico.DropZone* classes on implementing a drop animation. In addition, a snippet of the corresponding source code is depicted in Figure 28.

Figure 25. Implementing the expand/collapse interaction design pattern by using the Rico.Accordion class

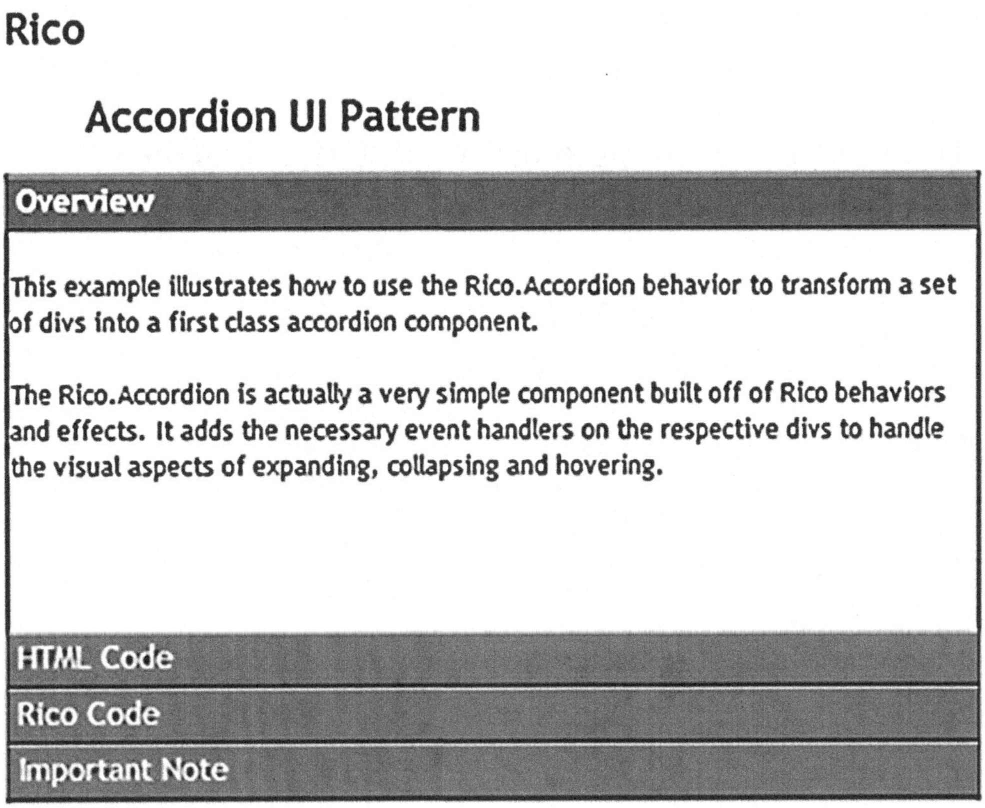

Rico

Accordion UI Pattern

Overview

This example illustrates how to use the Rico.Accordion behavior to transform a set of divs into a first class accordion component.

The Rico.Accordion is actually a very simple component built off of Rico behaviors and effects. It adds the necessary event handlers on the respective divs to handle the visual aspects of expanding, collapsing and hovering.

HTML Code

Rico Code

Important Note

Figure 26. Snippet of the Rico-based source code used for implementing the expand/collapse interaction design pattern

```
1   <script src="../../src/rico.js" type="text/javascript"></script>
2   <script type='text/javascript'>
3       Rico.loadModule('Accordion');
4       Rico.onLoad(function() {
5           new Rico.Accordion($$('div.panelheader'), $$('div.panelContent'),
6   {panelHeight:200, hoverClass: 'mdHover', selectedClass: 'mdSelected'});
7       });
8   </script>
9
10  <div style='clear:both;'>
11      <div id="accordionExample">
12          <div>
13              <div  class="panelheader">
14                  Overview
15              </div>
16              <div class="panelContent">
17                  <br>This example illustrates how to use the Rico.Accordion behavior to
18  transform a set of divs into a first class accordion component.<br><br>
19              </div>
20          </div>
21          ...
22      </div>
23  </div>
```

Figure 27. Implementing the drop animation interaction design pattern by using the Rico.Draggable and Rico.DropZone classes

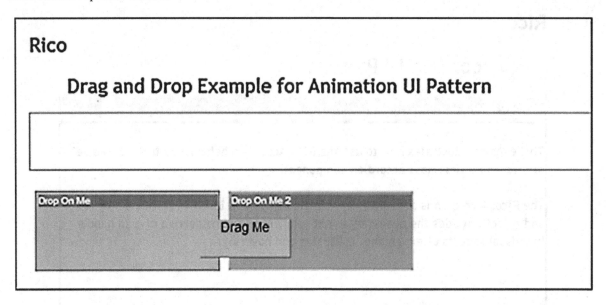

Figure 28. Snippet of the Rico-based source code used for implementing the drop animation interaction design pattern

```
1    <script src="../../src/rico.js" type="text/javascript"></script>
2    <script type='text/javascript'>
3        Rico.loadModule('Corner','DragAndDrop');
4        Rico.onLoad(function() {
5            Rico.Corner.round('explanation');
6            dndMgr.registerDraggable(new Rico.Draggable('test-rico-dnd','dragme'));
7            dndMgr.registerDropZone(new Rico.Dropzone('droponme'));
8            dndMgr.registerDropZone(new Rico.Dropzone('droponme2'));
9        });
10   </script>
11   ...
12   <div style="padding:5px;border:1px solid #5b5b5b;height:50px;clear:both;">
13       <div class="box" style="background:#f7a673" id="dragme">Drag Me</div>
14   </div>
15   <p><table style="margin-bottom:8px" cellspacing="3" cellpadding="3">
16       <tr>
17           <td>
18               <div id="droponme" class="simpleDropPanel" style="background:#ffd773">
19                   <div class="title">Drop On Me</div>
20               </div>
21           </td>
22           ...
23       </tr>
24   </table>
```

2.7. UI Patterns in Sencha Ext JS

Brighten and Dim

Sencha Ext JS provides support for implementing pop-up dialog boxes mainly by means of a utility class called *MessageBox* which allows creating different kinds of pop-up dialog boxes including confirmation, alert as well as indefinite and definite progress dialog boxes. All these dialog

Figure 29. Implementing the brighten and dim interaction design pattern by using the Ext JS Message-Box class

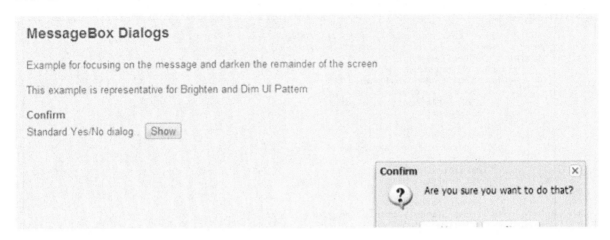

Figure 30. Implementing the expand/collapse interaction design pattern by using the Ext JS Accordion class

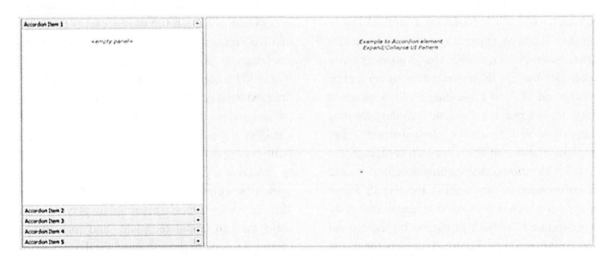

boxes are created as modal by default; optionally, they can be created as non-modal by properly setting the modal property of the object passed to the *MessageBox show( )* method. Furthermore, an Ext JS *MessageBox*-based dialog box can be displayed either as fully-decorated or as non-decorated dialog box by properly settling the *title* and *closeable* properties. In addition, the Ext JS *MessageBox* class fully implements the brighten and dim interaction design pattern because it au-

tomatically dims the entire GUI before a dialog box is displayed. Figure 29 depicts the usage of the Ext JS *MessageBox* class on creating a simple confirmation dialog box.

Expand/Collapse

Like Dojo, Sencha Ext JS has a layout container implementing the expand and collapse interaction design pattern. This container called *Accordion*

Figure 31. Snippet of the Ext JS-based source code used for implementing the expand/collapse interaction design patter

```
1    <link rel="stylesheet" type="text/css" href="../../resources/css/ext-all.css"/>
2    <script type="text/javascript" src="../../adapter/ext/ext-base.js"></script>
3    <script type="text/javascript" src="../../ext-all.js"></script>
4    <script type="text/javascript">
5        Ext.onReady(function() {
6            var item1 = new Ext.Panel({
7                title: 'Accordion Item 1',
8                html: '&lt;empty panel&gt;',
9                cls:'empty'
10           });
11           …
12           var accordion = new Ext.Panel({
13               region:'west',
14               margins:'5 0 5 5',
15               split:true,
16               width: 210,
17               layout:'accordion',
18               items: [item1, item2, item3, item4, item5]
19           });
20       });
21   </script>
```

layout is a set of panes using an expandable accordion style; it is based on a stacked layout because it allows expanding only one pane at a time. Nevertheless, unlike the Dojo *Accordion* container, the Ext JS *Accordion* container can be configured to allow expanding multiple panes at once; for that purpose, the multi property must be properly settled. Moreover, as usual among other implementations of the accordion container, the Ext JS *Accordion* container only accepts one kind of component as direct child: the Ext JS *Panel* container which is composed of header and body sections and it has built-in support for the expand and collapse effects. Figure 30 depicts the usage of the Ext JS Accordion class. In addition, a snippet of the corresponding source code is depicted in Figure 31.

Animation

Sencha Ext JS has an extensive classes hierarchy abstracting all the concepts involved on a drag-and-drop operation. These classes are organized into a package called *DD* and they all stem from an interface called *DragDrop* which defines base functionality of items that can be drag sources or drop targets. In detail, the *DragDrop* interface has event handlers for all the mouse events typically involved on a drag-and-drop gesture, including start drag, on drag, on drag over and on drag out. It should be noticed that any item intended to be dragged must be allowed to be dragged by settling the *draggable* property. Furthermore, both the Ext JS *grid* and *tree* GUI components incorporate built-in support for the drag-and-drop operation by means of a plugin providing functionality for View-based classes. In this sense, the Ext JS *View* class provides a mechanism for displaying data using custom layout templates and formatting. Figure 32 depicts the usage of the Ext JS *grid. DragDrop* plug-in on implementing the drop animation interaction design pattern.

Spotlight

Sencha Ext JS can implement the spotlight interaction design pattern by means of a native GUI component. In fact, it has a GUI component called *Spotlight* as part of the *UX* package. In detail, the Ext JS *Spotlight* component is used to restrict user input to a particular GUI section by dimming all other application content. Although this behav-

Figure 32. Implementing the drop animation interaction design pattern by using the Ext JS grid.DragDrop plug-in and the Ext JS grid widget

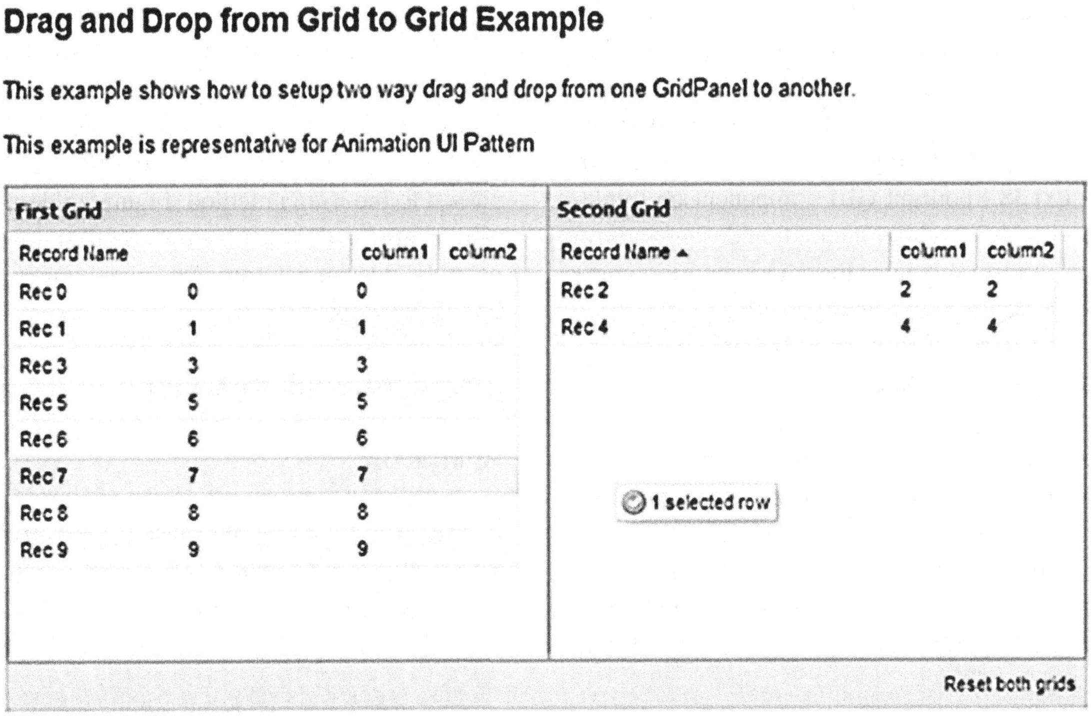

Drag and Drop from Grid to Grid Example
This example shows how to setup two way drag and drop from one GridPanel to another.
This example is representative for Animation UI Pattern
First Grid
Record Name
column1
column2
Rec 0 0 0
Rec 1 1 1
Rec 3 3 3
Rec 5 5 5
Rec 6 6 6
Rec 7 7 7
Rec 8 8 8
Rec 9 9 9
Second Grid
Record Name
column1
column2
Rec 2 2 2
Rec 4 4 4
1 selected row
Reset both grids

Figure 33. Implementing the spotlight interaction design pattern by using the Ext JS Spotlight widget

Spotlight
This is an example for Spotlight UI Pattern
Start
Demo Panel
Some panel content goes here!
Next Panel
Demo Panel
Some panel content goes here!
Next Panel
Demo Panel
Some panel content goes here!
Done

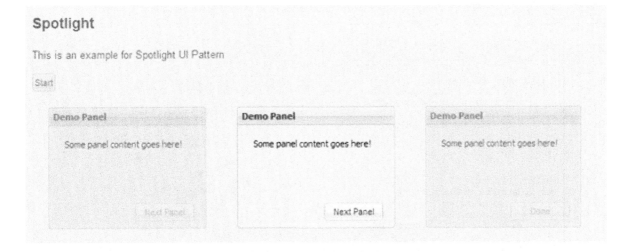

ior is similar to the brighten and dim interaction pattern, the Ext JS *Spotlight* component is most suitable for situations where the user is not able to interact with a certain GUI section before a change in another section is committed. In addition, the dimming effect can be configured during a specified period of time by properly settling the *duration* property. Figure 33 depicts the usage of the Ext JS Spotlight GUI component on implementing the spotlight interaction design pattern. In addition, a snippet of the corresponding source code is depicted in Figure 34.

Progress Indication

Since version 2.3.0 of Sencha Ext JS, there is a component called ProgressBar which supports both the determinate and indeterminate modes. In determinate mode, a bar that fills based on a value is used whereas in indeterminate mode, a bar that displays a repeating pattern is used. The

determinate mode is manual which means that the progress value must be manually updated via the *updateProgress()* method. As can be inferred, an Ext JS-based indeterminate progress bar is automatic and it runs indefinitely by simply calling the *wait()* method; optionally, it can run for a specified period of time by properly setting the *duration* and *interval* parameters of the object passed to the *wait()* method. Figure 35 depicts a sample application displaying a set of indeterminate and determinate progress bars by using the Ext JS *ProgressBar* class.

2.8. UI Patterns in X-Library

Animation

X-Library defines a function called *xEnableDrag()* which allows adding the dragging behavior to any DOM element. It also defines a function called *xEnableDrop()* which is used to enable DOM ele-

Figure 34. Snippet of the Ext JS-based source code used for implementing the spotlight interaction design pattern

```
1    Ext.onReady(function() {
2        var spot = Ext.create('Ext.ux.Spotlight', {
3            easing: 'easeOut',
4            duration: 300
5    })
6
7    Ext.define('DemoPanel', {
8        extend: 'Ext.panel.Panel',
9        ...
10        toggle: function(on) {
11            var btns = this.dockedItems.last(),
12            btn = btns.items.first();
13            if(btn) {
14                btn.setDisabled(!on);
15            }
16        }
17    });
18
19    var p1, p2, p3;
20    var updateSpot = function(id) {
21        if (typeof id == 'string') {
22            spot.show(id);
23        } else if (!id && spot.active) {
24            spot.hide();
25        }
26        p1.toggle(id == p1.id);
27        p2.toggle(id == p2.id);
28        p3.toggle(id == p3.id);
29    };
```

Figure 35. Implementing the progress indication interaction design pattern by using the Ext JS ProgressBar class

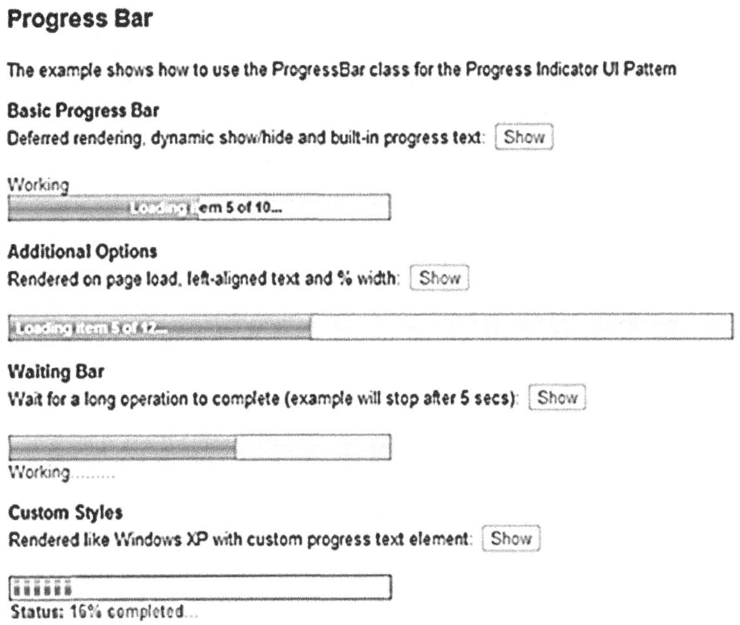

Progress Bar

The example shows how to use the ProgressBar class for the Progress Indicator UI Pattern

Basic Progress Bar
Deferred rendering, dynamic show/hide and built-in progress text: [Show]

Working
[Loading item 5 of 10...]

Additional Options
Rendered on page load, left-aligned text and % width: [Show]

[Loading item 5 of 12...]

Waiting Bar
Wait for a long operation to complete (example will stop after 5 secs): [Show]

[   ]
Working.........

Custom Styles
Rendered like Windows XP with custom progress text element: [Show]

[¡¡¡¡¡¡]
Status: 16% completed...

Figure 36. Implementing the drop animation interaction design pattern by using the X-Library xEnable-Drag() and xEnableDrop() functions

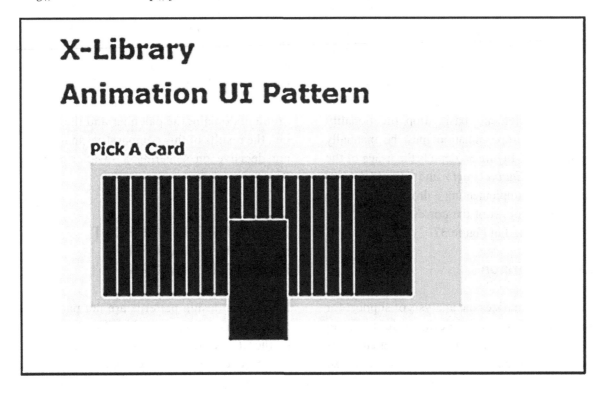

Figure 37. Snippet of the X-Library-based source code used for implementing the drop animation interaction design pattern

```
1   <script type="text/javascript" src="../x.js"></script>
2   <script type="text/javascript" src="../lib/xenabledrag.js"></script>
3   <script type="text/javascript" src="../lib/xconsole.js"></script>
4   <script type="text/javascript">
5       window.onload = function() {
6           var i, e, p = xGetElementById('parent');
7           for (i = 0; i < 20; ++i) {
8               e = document.createElement('div');
9               e.className = 'child';
10              p.appendChild(e);
11              xEnableDrag(e, onDragStart);
12          }
13      };
14
15      function onDragStart(ele, mouseX, mouseY, xEventObj) {
16          var x = xPageX(ele), y = xPageY(ele);
17          document.body.appendChild(ele);
18          ele.style.float = 'none';
19          ele.style.position = 'absolute';
20          xMoveTo(ele, x, y);
21          xConsole.log('x:' + x + ', y:' + y);
22      }
23  </script>
```

ments to receive drop events from drag-enabled objects. In detail, the *xEnableDrag()* function must receive a reference to the object to be dragged and it optionally receive the functions to handle the mouse events underlying to the drag start, on start and drag end events. According to the above, the *xEnableDrag()* function implements basic drag functionality, i.e., the functionality to position the object is being dragged by capturing the position of the mouse in terms of the x and y coordinates. Like the *xEnableDrag()* function, the *xEnableDrop()* function implements basic drop functionality so that any drop animation must be manually implemented. Figure 36 depicts the usage of the X-Library *xEnableDrag()* and *xEnableDrop()* functions on implementing a drop animation. In addition, a snippet of the corresponding source code is depicted in Figure 37.

2.9 Comparison

Table 1 summarizes the analysis of support for implementing interaction design patterns among JavaScript-based RIA frameworks, which is performed in this chapter. It covers the eight most popular patterns (see section 1) as well as the Dojo, jQuery, MooTools, Prototype, Qooxdoo, Rico, Sencha Ext JS and X-Library frameworks.

This comparison is intended to determine which JavaScript-based RIA framework provides the broadest support for implementing interaction design patterns, taking as sample the eight most popular patterns (see section 8.1). Nevertheless, the selection of one of these framework relies also on features internal to the development project to be carried out such as the problem domain, the calendar and the budget, i.e., the results of this comparative analysis are not decisive on selecting a JavaScript-based RIA framework.

3. UI PATTERNS SUPPORT INTO NON-JAVASCRIPT-BASED FRAMEWORKS

Interaction design patterns are not part of the components architecture of the RIA frameworks neither JavaScript-based nor non-JavaScript-based. Therefore, the rich design levels de-

Table 1. UI Patterns Support on JavaScript-based Frameworks

Framework	Transitional Patterns	Lookup Patterns	Feedback Patterns
Sencha	Brighten and Dim Expand/Collapse Animation Spotlight	Not reported	Progress Indicator
Prototype	Brighten and Dim Expand/Collapse Animation	Not reported	Not reported
Dojo	Brighten and Dim Expand/Collapse Animation Spotlight	Auto Complete	Live Preview Progress Indicator Periodic Refresh
jQuery	Brighten and Dim	Auto Complete	Not reported
MooTools	Brighten and Dim Animation	Not reported	Not reported
Qooxdoo	Animation	Not reported	Progress Indicator
Rico	Expand/Collapse Animation	Not reported	Not reported
X-Library	Animation	Not reported	Not reported

scribed at the beginning of this chapter can be partially mapped to the components architecture of the non-JavaScript-based RIA technologies'. For instance, the Adobe™ Flex's official Integrated Development Environment (IDE) groups components according to category in: 1) GUI controls, 2) layouts, 3) navigators and 4) charts. In this case, a navigator is a special type of GUI controls container, which can take other containers as children. A chart, on the other hand, is a special type of simple GUI control representing a way to deliver rich data visualizations, and they enable quick and efficient data analysis.

This section treats a set of sample RIAs that allows contextualizing the usage of the interaction design patterns analyzed in this chapter to common scenarios involving data from cloud services APIs of popular Web 2.0 websites, namely YouTube™, Twitter™ and last.fm™.

3.1. UI Patterns in Adobe™ Flex

Brighten and Dim

The Flex Alert control, which is similar to the JavaScript Alert control, represents the easiest way to achieve the brighten and dim interaction pattern; it displays a modal pop-up dialog box that can contain a title, a message, an icon and a pair of buttons. In fact, this control implements the "brighten and dim" interaction pattern by dimming down the Web page or window (background) and showing a non-dimmed pop-up dialog box over the background. However, Flex provides developers with other mechanisms for building custom pop-up windows, namely the SkinnablePopUpContainer and TitleWindow layout containers. In any case, these containers appear as pop-up windows on top of their parent containers; therefore, they are not defined as part of the MXML code of their parents, but rather as custom MXML components, possibly in external MXML files. In detail, the TitleWindow container consists of a title bar, a caption and status area in the title bar, a content area,

Figure 38. Implementing the brighten and dim interaction pattern by using the ActionScript Skinnable-PopUpContainer class

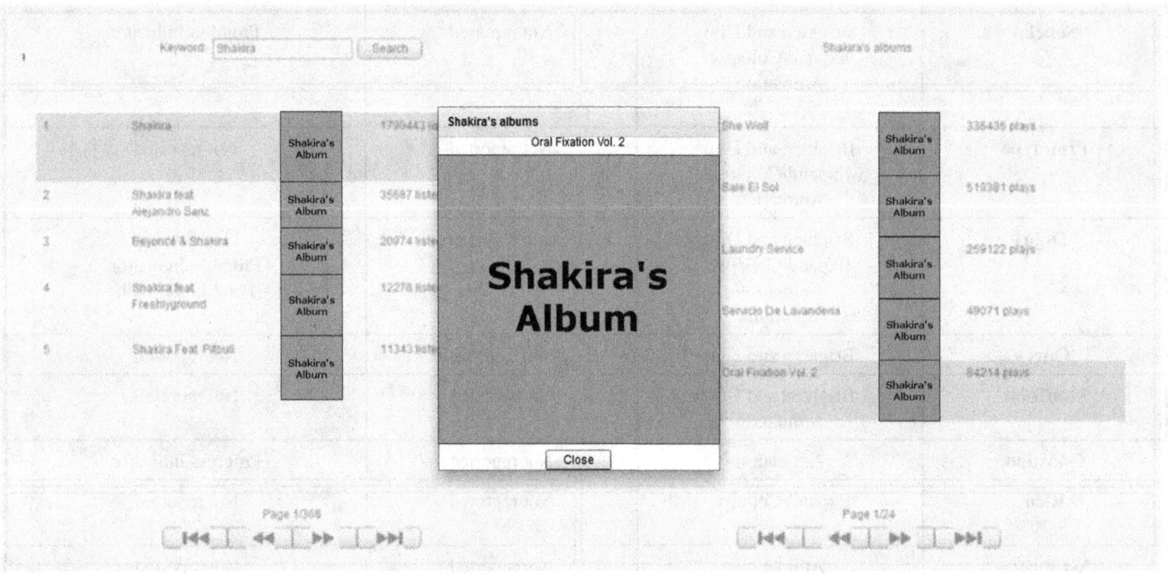

a border and an optional close button, whereas the SkinnablePopUpContainer is a lightway container used for simple pop-ups. Furthermore, although both containers can be modal or non-modal, only the TitleWindow container supports dragging. In any case, the parent container is automatically dimmed when the pop-up window is defined as modal. Figure 38 depicts the implementation of the brighten and dim interaction pattern by means of the SkinnablePopUpContainer.

Expand/Collapse

The expand/collapse interaction pattern, which is a means for keeping additional content hidden until the user needs them, is one example of interaction pattern closely linked to a specific GUI control in many RIA frameworks. For instance, Flex includes the Accordion navigator container, which defines a sequence of child panels and displays only one panel at a time. Each panel defines, in turn, a navigation button that allows users to navigate it. Because the Flex Accordion is a navigator container, it is not possible to directly

nest controls within it. In detail, it is part of the Flex MX components architecture; therefore, its direct children must be MX containers although it also accepts one Spark container, namely the NavigatorContent container. In general, accordions are useful for working with large forms. In this sense, figure 8.39 depicts the use of the Flex Accordion navigator container for implementing an on-line curriculum vitae application, which comprises five different kinds of information by means of five separate forms.

Animation

Flex list-based controls such as DataGrid and List controls include built-in support for the drag-and-drop interaction pattern. In addition, these controls include support for the drop animation interaction pattern. Furthermore, manual support for drag and drop operations can be added to any Flex non-list-based control by: 1) handling the involved events such as dragEnter and dragDrop and 2) using specific ActionScript classes like the DragSource, which contains the data being

Figure 39. Implementing the expand/collapse interaction pattern by using the Adobe™ Flex Accordion navigator container

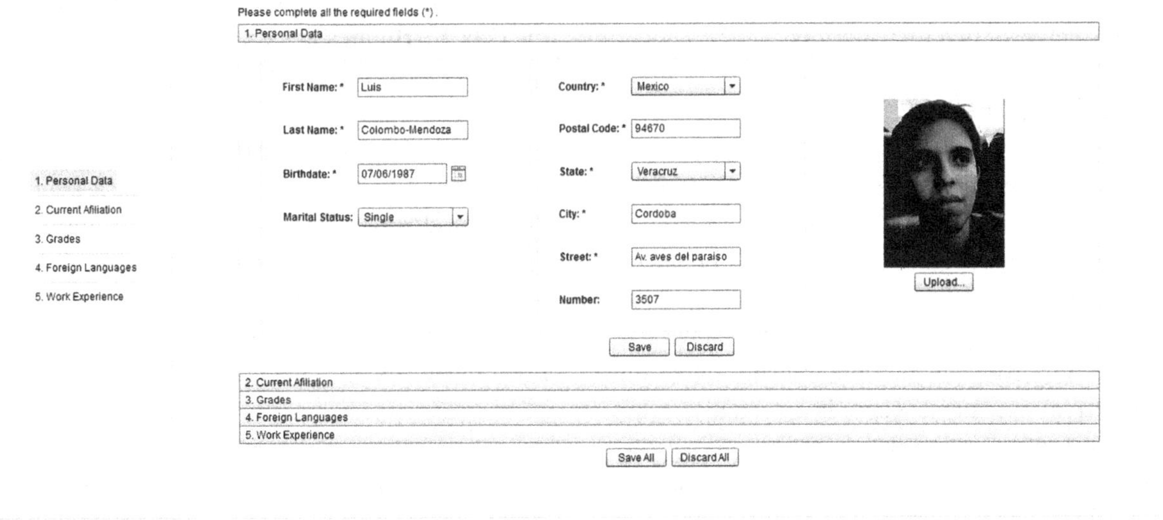

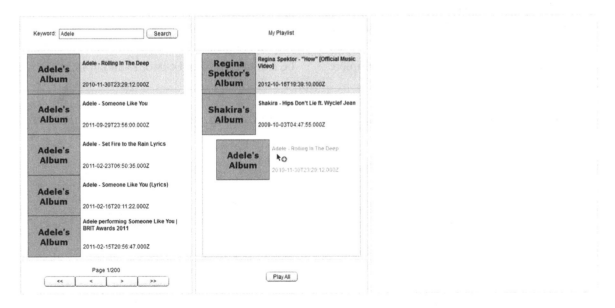

Figure 40. Implementing the drag-and-drop and drop animation interaction patterns by using the Adobe Flex™ List control

dragged. In the case of the drag and drop built-in support, drag and drop operations need to be properly enabled by using the dragEnabled and dropEnabled properties of the involved list-based controls. Furthermore, for dragging and dropping data between different list-based controls the only requirement is that the structure of the data providers matches. The dropEnabled property also activates a default drop animation which indicates that the intended drop target is a valid drop target by changing the border color of the list-based control and using a custom mouse cursor. The figure 8.40 depicts a screenshot of a Flex application that allows dragging and dropping YouTube™ video results between two List controls.

Auto Complete

The auto complete interaction pattern defines a way of displaying matching values for a user input as the input is typed. Commonly, this behavior is implemented by using a text box control for user input in conjunction with a drop-down list control that contains possible matches based on the current user input. There is not a native GUI control implementing this behavior among the non-JavaScript-based RIA frameworks although there are few approaches. For instance, Flex includes a ComboBox control and a DropDownList control, which basically let the user select an item from a predefined set of items. The ComboBox control, in detail, contains a prompt area that lets the user types input in order to either select a predefined item or enter a new item. Thus, Flex developers can implement the auto complete

interaction pattern either by building a custom MXML or ActionScript control or by taking advantage of third-party controls. In fact, the use of a third-party auto complete control based on the Flex TextInput and List controls is depicted in Figure 41. It is important to notice that, this is a custom ActionScript control based neither on the ComboBox control nor the DropDownList control but on the List control, which is not a control that drop-downs; therefore, it also uses the Flex PopUpAnchor control for displaying the list of matching values as a pop-up below the text box.

Live Preview

Form validation can be considered the primary use for the live preview interaction pattern, which allows users to known beforehand how appropriate are their entries. In this sense, unlike traditional Web applications, RIAs can provide immediate feedback to users as they modify their entries on the client instead of until they submit their entries to the server. Flex includes both an event dispatcher base class called *Validator*, which can be extended to build custom validators, and a set

Figure 41. Implementing the auto complete interaction pattern by using a third-party ActionScript control

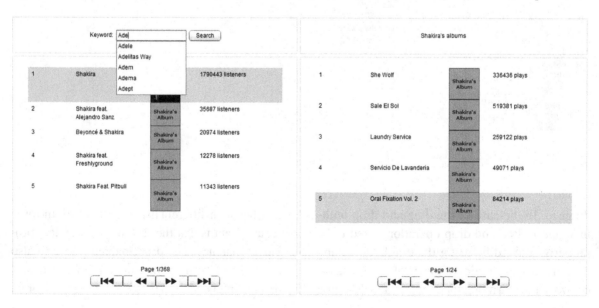

of predefined validator controls for ensuring that typical data such as credit card numbers, zip codes and phone numbers represent valid patterns. In general, Flex validators can be additionally used to make a field required by using the *required* property. In the case of custom Flex validators, the *Validator doValidation()* method must be overridden to include custom validation logic, possibly to match regular expressions against entries. In any case, it is necessary to set: 1) the *source* property of the validator to the name of the control where the user input will occur and 2) the *property* property of the validator to the name of the property that the validator should check. In addition, a custom error message to be displayed if the validation fails must be settled to the *errorMessage* property of the control where the user input will occur; otherwise, a default error message will be displayed. By default, the border color of the involved control is changed to red and a warning icon is displayed beside the error message. It is important to notice that there are two main approaches to trigger validations in Flex: 1) as result of a change in the control where the user input will occur or 2) as result of a change

in a third control, e.g., a "submit" button. Figure 42 depicts the use of the Flex number validator for implementing the live preview interaction pattern. In addition, a snippet of the corresponding source code is depicted in Figure 43.

Periodic Refresh

The periodic refresh interaction pattern is an example of interaction pattern not related to a particular GUI control. It is a means for bringing fresh content (content possibly produced by a community of users) to an application without direct user request. It can be used in conjunction with an interaction pattern related to the displaying of additional content. Typically, the behavior behind the periodic refresh interaction pattern is related to a scheduled task, i.e., a task that is executed every certain time mainly as a background process. In this sense, there is an ActionScript Timer class acting as an interface to the timers, which let applications run code on a specified time sequence. It exposes common timer functions such as *start()*, *stop()* and *reset()* as well as common timer properties like delay, i.e., the period of time between execu-

Figure 42. Implementing the live preview interaction pattern by using the Flex number validator

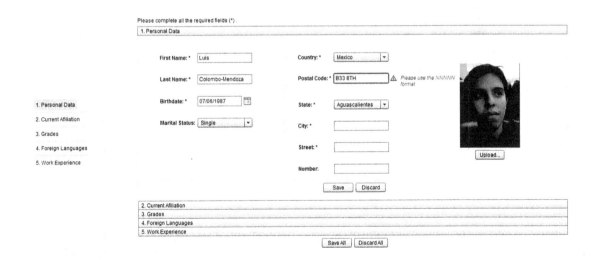

Figure 43. Snippet of the Flex-based source code used for implementing the live preview interaction design pattern

```
1    <fx:Script>
2        protected function validationFailsHandler():void{
3            postal.errorString = "Please use the NNNNN format.";
4        }
5        ...
6    </fx:Script>
7    <fx:Declarations>
8    <s:NumberValidator trigger="{postal}" invalid="validationFailsHandler()"
9    triggerEvent="change" domain="int" maxValue="99999"/>
10   </fx:Declarations>
11   ...
12   <mx:Accordion width="87.5%" height="75%" borderColor="0xE6E6E6">
13       <s:NavigatorContent label="1. Personal Data" width="90%" height="90%">
14           <s:layout>
15               <s:HorizontalLayout horizontalAlign="center" verticalAlign="middle"/>
16           </s:layout>
17           <s:HGroup horizontalAlign="center" verticalAlign="middle"  width="100%"
18   height="100%">
19               <s:BorderContainer borderColor="0xE6E6E6" width="33%" height="100%">
20                   <s:Form width="290">
21                       ...
22                       <s:FormItem label="Postal Code: *    ">
23                           <s:TextInput id="postal"/>
24                       </s:FormItem>
25                       ...
26                   </s:Form>
27               </s:BorderContainer>
28           </s:HGroup>
29       </s:NavigatorContent>
30   </mx:Accordion>
```

Figure 44. Implementing the periodic refresh interaction pattern by using the ActionScript Timer class

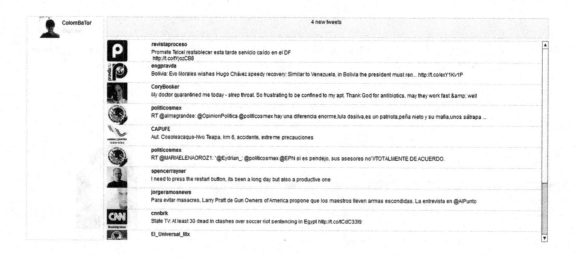

tions. Figure 44 depicts the implementation of the periodic refresh interaction pattern in conjunction with the more content invitation pattern in a Flex application. This application is inspired by the Twitter™'s look and feel, and behavior. In fact, it uses the ActionScript Timer class to search for

Figure 45. Snippet of the Flex-based source code used for implementing the periodic refresh interaction design pattern

```
1    private function onGetHomeTimeLine(event:Event):void {
2        var list:XMLList = new XMLList(new XML(loader.data).status);
3        listCol = new XMLListCollection(list);
4        ...
5        minuteTimer = new Timer(30000);
6        minuteTimer.addEventListener(TimerEvent.TIMER, onTick);
7        minuteTimer.start();
8        for(index;indice<listCol.length;index++){
9            row=new Object();
10           row.id=listCol[index].id.toString();
11           ...
12           data.addItem(row);
13       }
14       tweets.dataProvider = data;
15   }
16   private function onTick(event:TimerEvent):void {
17       getHomeTimeline(true);
18   }
```

new tweets in the timeline of a user logged into Twitter™ every 30 seconds; it also uses a Flex List control to display the timeline and a Flex Label control to inlay an invitation message on top of the GUI to discover new tweets when they arrive. In addition, a snippet of the corresponding source code is depicted in Figure 45.

3.2. UI Patterns in JavaFX™

Expand/Collapse

Besides the implementation of complex forms, another typical usage of the expand/collapse interaction pattern is the implementation of applications containing different kinds of information to be displayed, e.g. product catalogs, which commonly display one kind of product at a time. The JavaFX™ application depicted in Figure 46 is an example of a RIA that provides static content through an accordion control. As Flex, JavaFX™ includes a native accordion control, which is actually a group of *TitledPane* controls. As can be inferred, unlike the Flex *Accordion* control, the JavaFX™ *Accordion* control must contain one specific type of control as direct child. The *TitledPane* control is a panel with a title that can be opened and closed, and it can encapsulate any

node either a control or a layout container. The title of a *TitledPane* control is settled by using the *setText()* method whereas the content is added by using the *setContent()* method. Furthermore, a titled pane can be used as standalone control, i.e., they can be used outside of an accordion.

Progress Indication

The progress indication interaction pattern is another example of interaction pattern implemented by most non-JavaScript RIA frameworks in a native way. It allows keeping the user informed about the progress of a lengthy process such as an upload, a searching or a loading operation. In its simplest form, this pattern is used to inform that an application is currently busy with a lengthy process; hence that there is a busy control among the non-JavaScript-based RIA frameworks, namely, the Flex Busy control, which is limited to be used in mobile applications. It is important to notice that this section is only focused on the simplest form of the progress indicator interaction pattern. JavaFX™ 2.2 includes a ProgressIndicator class and a ProgressBar subclass. Whereas the Progress-Bar class visualizes the progress as a completion bar, the ProgressIndicator class visualizes the progress as a pie chart. Both controls provide

Figure 46 Implementing the expand/collapse interaction pattern by using the JavaFX™ Accordion control

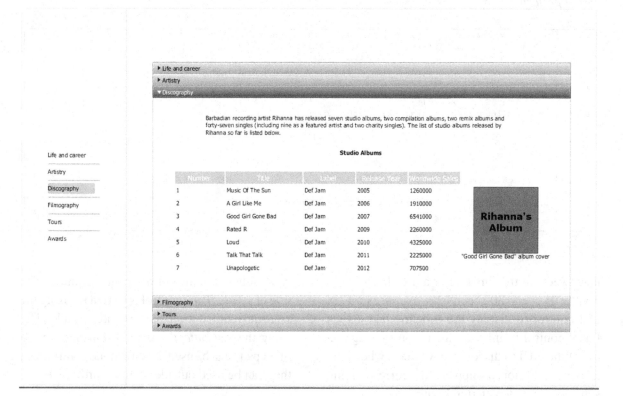

the capabilities to indicate that a particular task is processing and to detect how much of the task has been already done. In this sense, the percentage of the progress is indicated by setting a value between 0 and 1 to the *progress* variable through the *setProgress()* method. A negative value for the *progress* variable indicates that the progress is in an indeterminate mode. In that case, controls remain in indeterminate mode until the length of the task is determined, i.e., they indicate that an operation is in progress without specifying the current percentage of progress. As can be inferred, this approach can be used to display JavaFX™ ProgressBar and ProgressIndicator controls as busy indicator controls. Figure 47 depicts the implementation of the progress indicator interaction pattern by using the JavaFX™ ProgressIndicator control. In addition, a snippet of the corresponding source code is depicted in Figure 48.

Brighten and Dim

Unlike Flex and Silverlight™, JavaFX™ 2.2 has no common support for alert-like dialog boxes; this feature is currently under development, and it is on the JavaFX™ 3.0 roadmap. Therefore, developers may create their own implementations, possibly by using or extending the JavaFX™ *Stage* class. The *Stage* class is the top level JavaFX™ container, and it inherits from the JavaFX™ *Window* class which is also the parent of other classes like the *PopupWindow* class. The *PopupWindow* class is, in turn, the parent of the *Popup* and *PopupControl* classes which are special window-like containers for *scene graphs*, and they are typically used for tooltip-like notifications and drop down boxes. Although the *PopupWindow* class seems to be the best choice for implementing pop-up dialog boxes, a *PopupWindow* window has no decorations, i.e., it does not include a title bar. Therefore, in cases

Figure 47. Implementing the progress indication interaction pattern by using the JavaFX™ ProgressIndicator control

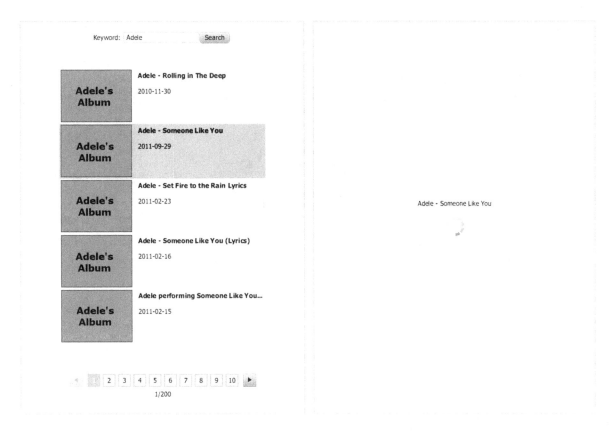

Figure 48. Snippet of the JavaFX™-based source code used for implementing the progress indication interaction design pattern

```
1    cell.addEventFilter(MouseEvent.MOUSE_PRESSED, new EventHandler<MouseEvent>() {
2        @Override
3        public void handle(MouseEvent event) {
4            ...
5            currentVideo.setText(((Title)((Video)table.getSelectionModel().getSelectedItem())
6    .getTitle()).getTitle());
7            progress.setVisible(true);
8            event.consume();
9        }
10   });
11   Label currentVideo = new Label("-");
12   javafx.scene.control.ProgressIndicator progress=new
13   javafx.scene.control.ProgressIndicator();
14   progress.setStyle("-fx-progress-color:CCCCCC;");
15   progress.setVisible(false);
16   boxRight.getChildren().addAll(currentVideo,progress);
```

where a title bar is required, to style a JavaFX™ *PopupWindow* window in order to add a title bar can be a time-consuming task. On the other hand, a *Stage* window has decorations by default; it can be defined as a modal or non-modal window. The image 49 depicts a JavaFX™ application

Figure 49. Implementing the brighten and dim interaction pattern by using the JavaFX™ Stage class

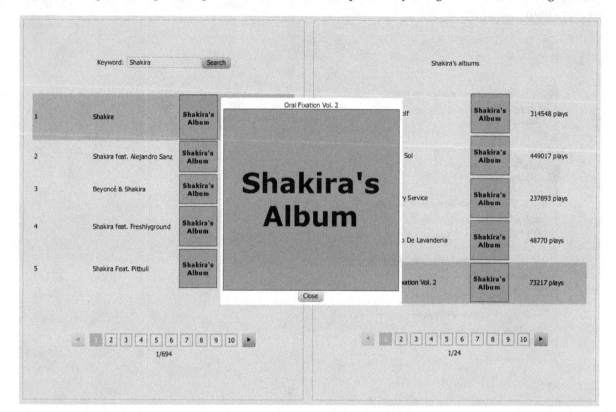

that uses the *Stage* class for displaying a modal pop-up dialog box including a full-size image of the thumbnail selected from a list. It is important to notice that, unlike the Flex *SkinablePopUp-Container* container, the JavaFX™ *Stage* class does not have the functionality to automatically dim the parent container (background) of a *Stage* window. For that purpose, the sample application uses a JavaFX™ *ColorAdjust* effect to adjust the saturation of the background.

Spotlight

A spotlight provides a means to subtly notify the user of a change in a GUI. Because this interaction pattern can be applied to different kinds of objects, notification can be accomplished in many ways. Therefore, there is not a GUI control closely linked to the spotlight interaction pattern among

the non-JavaScript-based RIA frameworks. A common approach is to display status messages over the area of the GUI that has changed and gradually fade out them as the time passes. For that purpose, it is not necessary to implement a mechanism to pop up a "window" with the notification message. This task can be simply accomplished by using a label control and positioning it over the GUI employing absolute positioning, i.e., explicitly setting the values for its x and y coordinates. The JavaFX™ application depicted in figure 50 uses a JavaFX™ *HBox* layout to build a custom notification message comprising a text message and an image. This application allows users to search for YouTube™ videos; it displays video results by pages of five results and allows adding up to five videos to a video playlist. Each time a video is added to the playlist, a notification message is displayed at the top right of the GUI. Notification messages are removed after five seconds; however, they are faded away every second in order to distinguish between new and old messages. The aforementioned behavior is implemented by using the JavaFX™ *Timeline* class and the inherited *setOpacity()* method of the *HBox* class, which specifies how solid or transparent a node appears by using a value between 0 and 1. In addition, a snippet of the corresponding source code is depicted in Figure 51.

Animation

Unlike Flex, JavaFX™ does not include controls with built-in support for the drag-and-drop gesture. Thus, JavaFX™ developers must implement the drag-and-drop gesture by hand. This task involves not only the handling of the events related but also the implementation of the drop animation, i.e., the change in the appearance of the target control to provide a hint to the user where the data can be dropped. In this sense, the source control must at least implement a handler for the MouseEvent. *DRAG_DETECTED* event in order to start the drag-and-drop gesture by calling to the *startDragAndDrop()* method inherited from the *Node* class. A handler for the *DragEvent.DRAG_OVER* event must be implemented to specify which control accepts the data, because after the drag-and-drop operation is started, any control that the mouse is dragged over is a potential target to drop the data. In addition, the target control must implement a handler for the *DragEvent.DRAG_DROPPED* event, which is triggered when the mouse button is released on the gesture target; this handler must complete the drag-and-drop gesture by calling the *setDropCompleted()* method. Figure 52 depicts the implementation of the drag-and-drop gesture in a sample application that allows users to drag and drop YouTube™ video items between two video lists. Each video item comprises a JavaFX™ *ImageView* control showing a thumbnail of the video. The video lists are implemented by using the JavaFX™ *TableView* control. The sample ap-

Figure 50. Implementing the spotlight interaction pattern by using the JavaFX™ Timeline class

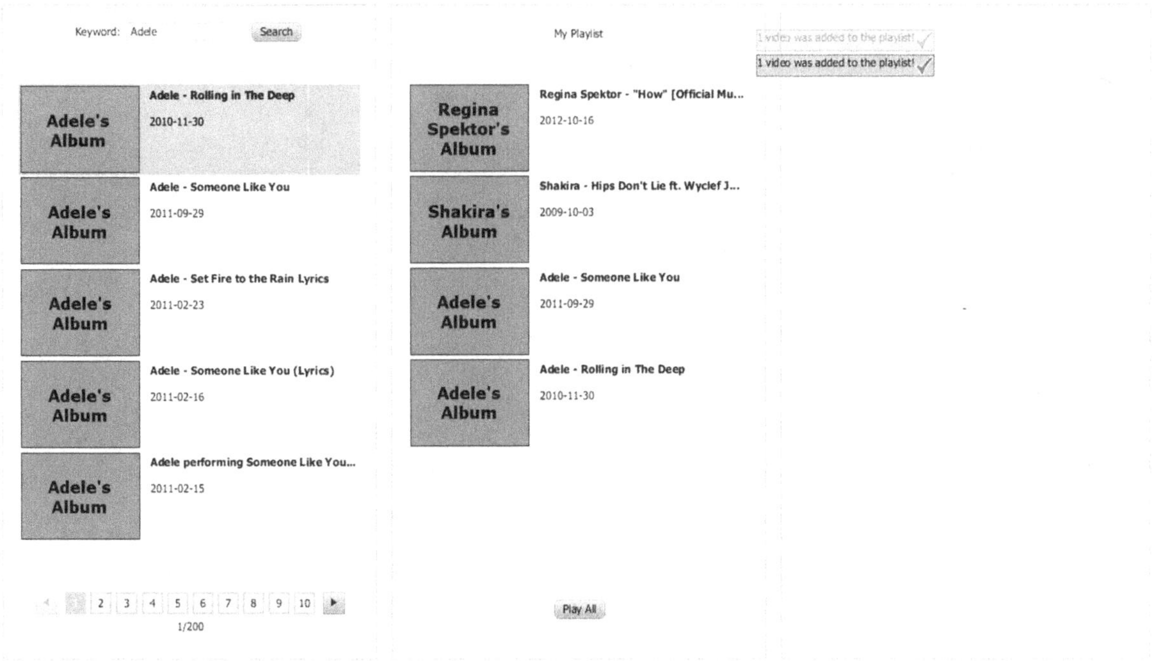

Figure 51. Snippet of the JavaFX™-based source code used for implementing the spotlight interaction design pattern

```
1   public void displaySpotlight(){
2       spotCount++;
3       final HBox spot = new HBox();
4       …
5       spot.setLayoutX(boxCenter.getLayoutX()+boxCenter.getWidth()-(spot.getWidth()+10));
6       spot.setLayoutY(boxCenter.getLayoutX()+spotCount*(spot.getHeight()+25));
7       spot.setStyle("-fx-background-color:CCCCCC; -fx-border-color:gray; -fx-dash-
8   style:dashed;");
9           ((Group)stage.getScene().getRoot()).getChildren().add(spot);
10
11      Timeline fiveSecondsWonder = new Timeline(new KeyFrame(Duration.seconds(5), new
12  EventHandler<ActionEvent>() {
13          @Override
14          public void handle(ActionEvent event) {
15              try {
16                  stop();
17                  ((Group)stage.getScene().getRoot()).getChildren().remove(spot);
18                  spotCount--;
19              }
20              catch(Exception e) {}
21          }
22      }), new KeyFrame(Duration.seconds(3), new EventHandler<ActionEvent>() {
23          @Override
24          public void handle(ActionEvent event) {
25              spot.setOpacity(0.5);
26          }
27      }));
28
29      fiveSecondsWonder.setCycleCount(Timeline.INDEFINITE);
30      fiveSecondsWonder.play();
    }
```

Figure 52. Implementing the drop animation interaction pattern in a JavaFX™ TableView control

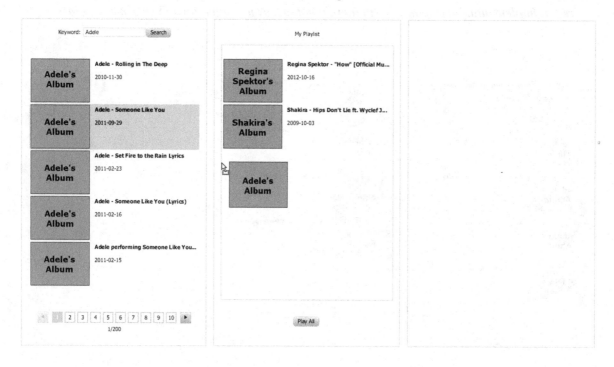

plication implements a drop animation by changing the border color of the target table and moving over the GUI a snapshot of the video thumbnail is being dragged. The snapshot is positioned over the GUI by using the *x* and *y* properties of the *DragEvent* class as the *ImageView* control is dragged. It is important to notice that, JavaFX™ 2.2 has no support for custom drag and drop cursors on Windows.

3.3. UI Patterns in Silverlight™

Expand/Collapse

Unlike Flex and JavaFX™, Silverlight™ has no native support for the expand/collapse interaction pattern, i.e., it has no a native accordion control. Nevertheless, there is an accordion control as part of the Silverlight™ Standard Development Kit (SDK), which is released by the Silverlight™ Toolkit open source project. This *Accordion* class inherits from the Windows™ *ItemsControl* class; therefore, it can be used to present a collection of items. In fact, the Silverlight™ Toolkit *Accordion* control consists of a set of collapsible panels where each panel is actually an *AccordionItem* control. The title of each *AccordionItem* control is settled through the *Header* property whereas the content is settled by using the *Content* property. The elements to be displayed in an accordion panel can either be added as direct children or be added by using templates. In this sense, the Silverlight™ Toolkit *Accordion* control exposes a *HeaderTemplate* property and a *ContentTemplate* property, which are commonly used when a data binding operation is involved, and they allows setting the *AccordionItem Header* and *Content* properties, respectively. Unlike Flex and JavaFX™ *Accordion* controls, if the items added to a Silverlight™ Toolkit *Accordion* control are not of type *AccordionItem*, they are wrapped inside *AccordionItem* controls at runtime. Furthermore, the Silverlight™ Toolkit *Accordion* control allows expanding more than one panel at a time by properly setting the *Se-*

lectionMode property; this non-standard behavior can be useful in specific cases. In addition, this control can display its panels using a horizontal layout besides the typical vertical layout. Figure 53 depicts the use of the Silverlight™ Toolkit *Accordion* control in the implementation of the expand/collapse interaction pattern.

Progress Indication

A Silverlight™ application can implement the progress indicator interaction pattern either by using the Silverlight™ native *ProgressBar* control or by using the Silverlight™ Toolkit *BusyIndicator* control. As Flex and JavaFX™ *ProgressBar* controls, the Silverlight™ *ProgressBar* control can be used as a bar that fills based on a value (determinate) or as a bar that displays a repeating pattern (indeterminate) by setting a value to the *IsInDeterminate* property. The indeterminate style is useful as a replacement of the busy indicator control, which is the control used in this chapter as a means to implement the progress indicator interaction pattern. The *BusyIndicator* control, on the other hand, is used as a wrapper control for the content that causes the application enters a busy state. By doing this, the content is disabled while the busy indicator is shown; a visual effect aimed at completing the feedback to be provided to users is also applied to the disabled content. The implementation of the progress indicator interaction pattern by using the Silverlight™ Toolkit *BusyIndicator* control is depicted in Figure 54.

Brighten and Dim

Besides the support for JavaScript alert pop-up boxes, Silverlight™ provides two different native controls that developers can use in order to implement custom pop-up boxes: *PopUp* and *ChildWindow* controls. The Silverlight™ *PopUp* control is commonly used to temporary display additional content like help information; it is positioned on top of an existing Silverlight™

Figure 53. Implementing the expand/collapse interaction pattern by using the Silverlight™ Toolkit Accordion control

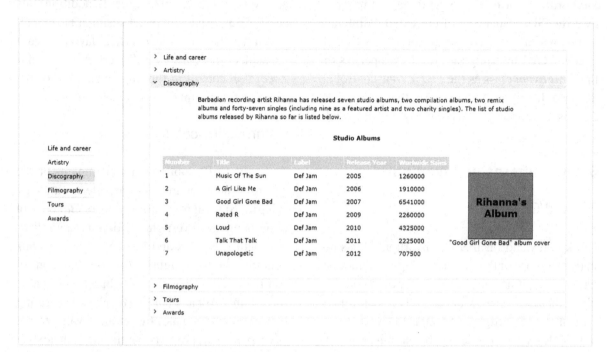

control, i.e., within the bounds of another control. The content of the Silverlight™ *PopUp* control is settled using its *Child* property; it can accept a set of controls grouped in a container like a Silverlight™ *Group* control. The Silverlight™ *ChildWindow* control, on the other hand, provides a window that is displayed over a parent window as a modal pop-up, i.e., a child window that blocks interaction with the parent window. This control does not only dim the parent window like the Flex *SkinnablePopUpContainer* container, but actually comprises a dimmed overlay that covers the parent window. Furthermore, unlike the Silverlight™ *PopUp* control, the Silverlight™ *ChildWindow* control comprises decorations, i.e., a title bar including a close button. Therefore, in cases where the implementation of a modal pop-up box is required, the *ChildWindow* control seems to be the most suitable choice. In addition, this control let developers implement the brighten and dim interaction pattern saving time and effort as is depicted in Figure 55.

Animation

Silverlight™ has no native controls with built-in support for the drag-and-drop gesture. Nevertheless, there is a series of Silverlight™ Toolkit wrapper controls that add default drag-and-drop functionality to the controls nested inside of them: *TreeViewDragDropTarget, ListBoxDragDropTarget* and *DataGridDragDropTarget*. In fact, there is almost one Silverlight™ Toolkit *DragDropTarget* control for each Silverlight™ native control aimed at displaying data. A Silverlight™ Toolkit *DragDropTarget* control automatically initiates a drag-and-drop operation when an item is dragged over it. Furthermore, when an item is dropped onto a Silverlight™ Toolkit *DragDropTarget* control, it is automatically added to the control nested inside of the *DragDropTarget* control. Although a Silverlight™ Toolkit *DragDropTarget* control automatically displays a snapshot of the item while is being dragged, a custom drop animation can be implemented by hand. In this sense, with

Figure 54. Implementing the progress indicator interaction pattern by using the Silverlight™ Toolkit BusyIndicator control

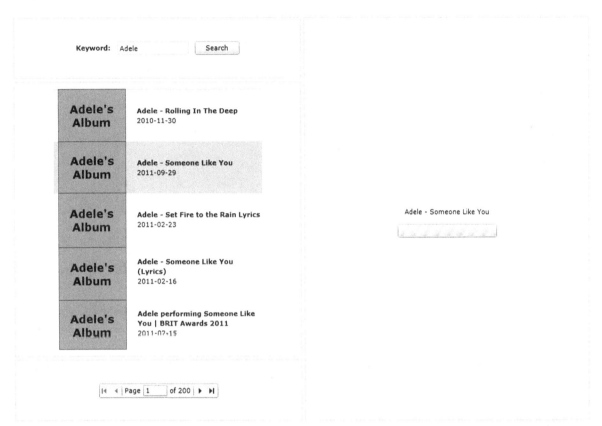

Figure 55. Implementing the brighten and dim interaction pattern by using the Silverlight™ ChildWindow control

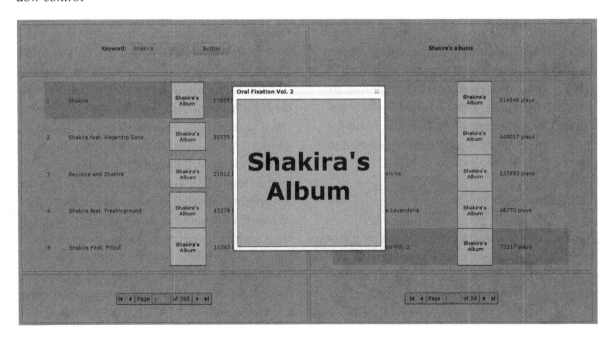

Figure 56. Implementing the drop animation interaction pattern by using the Silverlight™ Toolkit DataGridDragDropTarget control

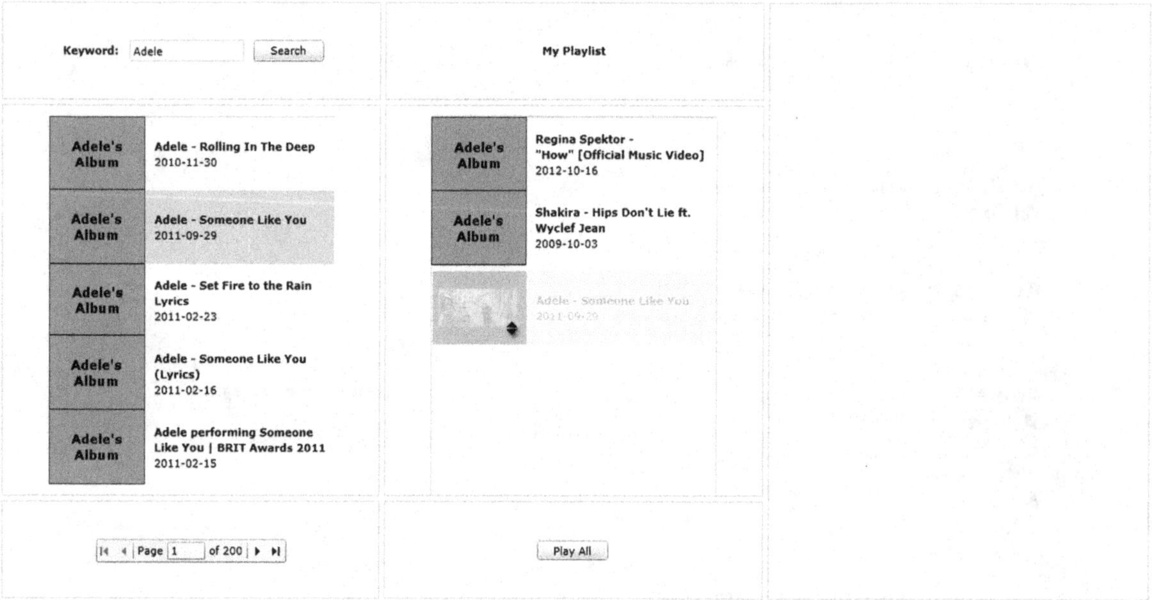

the aim of indicating that a control can or cannot accept a drop operation, its *AllowDrop* property must be properly settled. Figure 8.56 depicts the implementation of the drag-and-drop gesture in the sample application that allows users to drag and drop YouTube™ video items between two video lists. Each video list is implemented by using a Silverlight™ *DataGrid* control wrapped inside a Silverlight™ Toolkit *DataGridDragDropTarget* control. This sample application complements the drop animation provided by the Silverlight™ Toolkit *DataGridDragDropTarget* control by changing the border color of the target Silverlight™ *DataGrid* control. In addition, a snippet of the corresponding source code is depicted in Figure 57.

Auto Complete

The auto complete interaction pattern is probably the most largely used interaction pattern. Search engines like Google™ and Bing™ use this interaction pattern to provide lists of suggestions users can choose from without having to finish typing search keywords. The Silverlight™ SDK has an *Auto-CompleteBox* control that uses an items collection to generate a list of suggestions to be displayed in a drop-down list. Unlike other similar controls like the combo box, the auto-complete box filters the list of suggestions on the fly as the user types into its text box area. In this sense, the Silverlight™ Toolkit *AutoCompleteBox* uses a "starts with" filter pattern by default; however, it defines other alternative patterns such as "contains" or "equals". The filter function to be used is settled through the *FilterMode* property. Furthermore, this control exposes an *IsTextCompletionEnabled* property, which allows the control to automatically display in the text box the first possible match as is achieved by the Google™ auto-complete box. Finally, the Silverlight™ Toolkit *AutoCompleteBox* control can display not only text strings as suggestions but also complex items composed of images and text strings, for example. For that purpose, the *Item-Template* property must be settled to a container like the Silverlight™ *StackPanel* control. Figure

Figure 57. Snippet of the Silverlight™-based source code used for implementing the drop animation interaction design pattern

```
1    <data:DataGridDragDropTarget>
2        <sdk1:DataGrid x:Name="VideosGrid"...>
3            <sdk1:DataGrid.Columns>
4                <sdk1:DataGridTemplateColumn Header="Image" Width="130">
5                    <sdk1:DataGridTemplateColumn.CellTemplate>
6                        <DataTemplate>
7                            <Image Source="{Binding Filename}" Height="85"/>
8                        </DataTemplate>
9                    </sdk1:DataGridTemplateColumn.CellTemplate>
10               </sdk1:DataGridTemplateColumn>
11               ...
12           </sdk1:DataGrid.Columns>
13       </sdk1:DataGrid>
14   </data:DataGridDragDropTarget>
15   ...
16   <data:DataGridDragDropTarget DragLeave="DataGridDragDropTarget_DragLeave_1"
17   Drop="PlaylistGrid_Drop_1" DragEnter="PlaylistGrid_Drag_1"...>
18       <sdk1:DataGrid AllowDrop="True" x:Name="PlaylistGrid"...>
19           <sdk1:DataGrid.Columns>
20               <sdk1:DataGridTemplateColumn Header="Image" Width="100">
21                   <sdk1:DataGridTemplateColumn.CellTemplate>
22                       <DataTemplate>
23                           <Image Source="{Binding Filename}"/>
24                       </DataTemplate>
25                   </sdk1:DataGridTemplateColumn.CellTemplate>
26               </sdk1:DataGridTemplateColumn>
27               ...
28           </sdk1:DataGrid.Columns>
29       </sdk1:DataGrid>
30   </data:DataGridDragDropTarget>
```

Figure 58. Implementing the auto complete interaction pattern by using the Silverlight™ Toolkit Auto-CompleteBox control

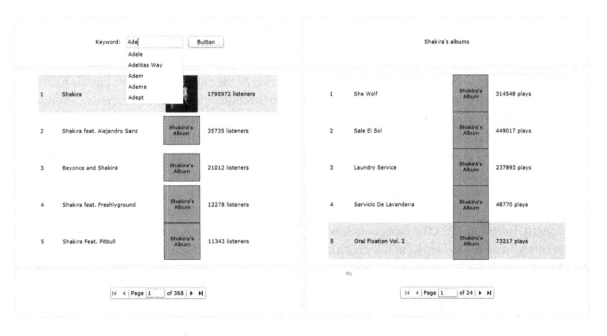

Figure 59. Snippet of the Silverlight™-based source code used for implementing the auto complete interaction design pattern

```
1   <controls:ObjectCollection x:Key="words">
2       <clr:String>Adele</clr:String>
3       <clr:String>Adelitas Way</clr:String>
4       <clr:String>Adem</clr:String>
5       <clr:String>Adema</clr:String>
6       <clr:String>Adept</clr:String>
7   </controls:ObjectCollection>
8   ...
9   <sdk:AutoCompleteBox Style="{StaticResource autoComplete}" Name="box"
10  ItemsSource="{StaticResource words}" HorizontalAlignment="Center" Height="22"
11  VerticalAlignment="Center" Width="120" BorderBrush="#FFCCCCCC" Margin="10,0"/>
```

58 depicts the use of the Silverlight™ Toolkit *AutoCompleteBox* control in the implementation of a Last.fm™-based search engine. In addition, a snippet of the corresponding source code is depicted in Figure 59.

3.4. UI Patterns in OpenLaszlo™

Expand/Collapse

OpenLaszlo has a GUI component called *tabslider* which implements the expand/collapse interaction pattern; it is actually a container because it is used to arrange child components as sequences of tab panes.

These tab panes are defined by using the *tabelement* class, a kind of view that can be opened and closed under the coordination of a parent *tabslider* and it comprises basically a content area and a title area. The *tabslider* component allows customizing the sliding animation implemented by default in terms of the desired duration; for that purpose, the *slideduration* property inherited from the *basetabslider* class must be properly settled. The title of a *tabelement* object is settled by using the *text* property inherited from the *basecomponent* class. Finally, it is important to notice that the OpenLaszlo *tabslider* component is similar to the JavaFX™ *Accordion* component in the sense that both accept only one kind of object as direct child. Figure 60 depicts the use of the OpenLaszlo *tabslider* container on implementing the on-line

curriculum vitae application previously addressed in this chapter. In addition, a snippet of the corresponding source code is depicted in Figure 61.

Brighten and Dim

OpenLaszlo has an extensive window classes hierarchy starting with a base class which is extended by a class called *windowpanel* that provides common behavior for various window-like classes and it represents a fully-decorated (title bar and close button) draggable panel. At the third hierarchy level, the functionality provided by the *windowpanel* class is extended by a class called *window* specifically by means of the resizable capability; in addition, there is a class called *modaldialog* which includes built-in support for modal pop-up windows. At the end of the *window* classes hierarchy, the functionality provided by the *modaldialog* class is extended by a class called alert which allows displaying modal alert dialog boxes, i.e., modal pop-up dialog boxes displaying text messages (alert messages) and confirmation buttons only. According to the above, the *modaldialog* class seems to be the most suitable way to implement custom modal pop-ups. In this sense, unlike the Flex *SkinnablePopUpContainer* container, the OpenLaszlo *modaldialog* class can be declared as part of the code of its parent container; in fact, it is typically instantiated inside the top-most view in an OpenLaszlo application, the *canvas* container. Additionally, it is important to notice

Figure 60. Implementing the expand/collapse interaction pattern by using the OpenLaszlo tabslider container

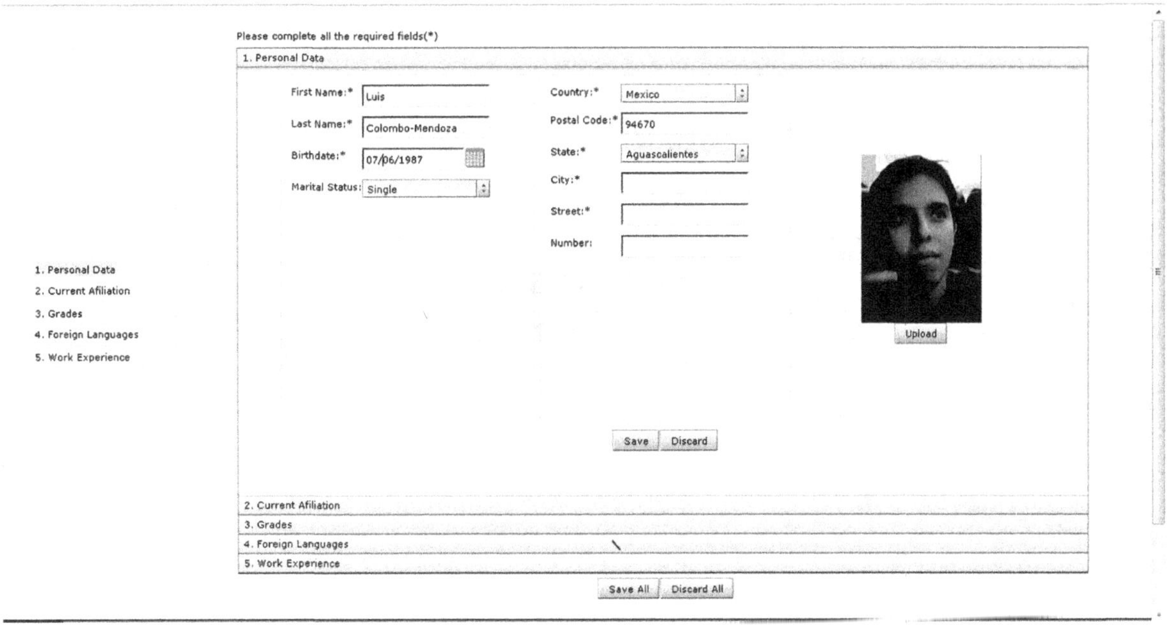

Figure 61. Snippet of the OpenLaszlo-based source code used for implementing the expand/collapse interaction design pattern

```
1    <tabslider width="1000" height="600" slideduration="300" align="center" yoffset="-25">
2        <tabelement text="1. Personal Data">
3            <simplelayout axis="y" spacing="5"/>
4            <hbox spacing="5" align="center" width="900">
5                <view bgcolor="0xE6E6E6" height="400" width="33%">
6                    <simplelayout axis="y" spacing="5" inset="1"/>
7                    <form bgcolor="white" width="99%" height="398" align="center" >
8                        <hbox>
9                            <text width="85">First Name:*</text>
10                           <edittext width="150"></edittext>
11                       </hbox>
12                       ...
13                   </form>
14               </view>
15               ...
16           </hbox>
17           ...
18       </tabelement>
20       <tabelement text="2. Current Afiliation"/>
21       <tabelement text="3. Grades"/>
22       <tabelement text="4. Foreign Languages"/>
23       <tabelement text="5. Work Experience"/>
24   </tabslider>
```

that, unlike the Flex *SkinablePopUpContainer* container and the Silverlight™ *ChildWindow* component, the OpenLaszlo *modaldialog* class does not have the functionality to automatically dim the parent container (background) of a modal pop-up window. Therefore, the *bgcolor* (background color) and *opacity* properties inherited from the OpenLaszlo *view* class can be used

Figure 62. Implementing the brighten and dim interaction pattern by using the OpenLaszlo modaldialog class

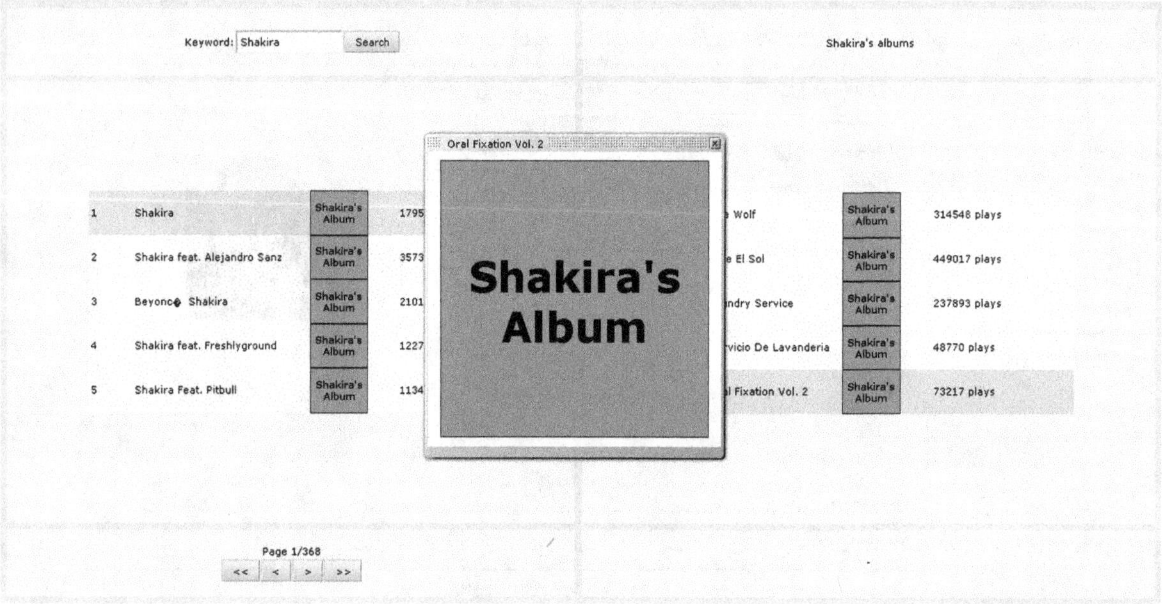

Figure 63. Snippet of the OpenLaszlo-based source code used for implementing the brighten and dim interaction design pattern

```
1    <modaldialog name="albumDialog"
2    title="${parent.parent.view1.vbox1.view2.view3.vbox2.grid1.title}" align="center"
3    valign="middle" width="345" closeable="true">
4        <image src="${parent.parent.view1.vbox1.view2.view3.vbox2.albumsGrid.selected}"/>
5    </modaldialog>
6    ...
7    <headerlessGrid name="albumsGrid" sizetoheader="false" datapath="myData2:/*" align="center"
8    width="455" rowheight="48" height="240" valign="middle" showvscroll="false">
9        <handler name="onselect" method="onSelectHandler"/>
10       <method name="onSelectHandler">
11           this.setAttribute('title',this.getSelection()[0].p.childNodes[0].childNodes[0].data);
12           canvas.albumDialog.open();
13       </method>
14       <gridtext editable="false" datapath="position()" width="50" resizable="false"
15   sortable="false" showheader="false"/>
16       ...
     </headerlessGrid>
```

for this purpose. In this sense, the OpenLaszlo *view* class is the base class for anything that is displayed on the *canvas* container. Figure 62 depicts a screenshot of an OpenLaszlo application that uses the *modaldialog* class for displaying a modal pop-up dialog box including a full-size image of the thumbnail selected from a grid. In addition, a snippet of the corresponding source code is depicted in Figure 8.63.

Animation

As usual among non-JavaScript based RIA frameworks, OpenLaszlo has no native controls with built-in support for the drag-and-drop gesture. However, it provides a utility class called *drag-state* which extends the *state* class and it is similar to the Silverlight™ Toolkit *XDragDropTarget* controls in the sense that it can be used to make the view where it is nested draggable. In fact, the *dragstate* class is used to add standard dragging behavior to any view; this requires the handle of the *mousedown* and *mouseup* mouse events over the element is being dragged (the parent view) in order to activate and deactivate the dragging state. Nevertheless, this standard functionality does not involve the definition of both a drag source and a drop target as opposed to the implementation of manual support for the drag-and-drop operation in Adobe™ Flex. A complex scenario requiring the abstraction of drag sources and drop targets on an OpenLaszlo application may suppose more development time and effort especially if the elements to be manipulated are customized GUI controls such as the rows of a *grid* control which can contain virtually any other GUI control. In this sense, there are some third-party libraries built on top of the *dragstate* class, which are available at the official OpenLaszlo forum (http://forum.openlaszlo.org) and they support different GUI controls such as lists and grids. In this chapter, a library extending the *grid* calss is used to develop a sample application that allows dragging rows comprising text and images between two different grids; this library is available at http://forum.openlaszlo.org/showthread.php?t=5707.

The aforementioned library allows displaying a snapshot of the grid row is being dragged; in fact, it creates a copy of each of the elements composing the row and it properly positions them over the parent view by capturing the position of the mouse in terms of the x and y coordinates. Nevertheless, it only supports text so that the functionality aimed at rendering images must be manually added. Finally, it should be noticed that this library implements the drop animation interaction pattern by using icons indicating that the intended drop target is an invalid drop target. Figure 64 depicts the implementation of the drag-and-drop gesture in the sample application that allows users to drag and drop YouTube™ video items between two video grids.

Live Preview

In the context of client-side form validation, the live preview interaction pattern represents a distinctive feature of RIAs because it involves client-side data computation which is commonly considered one of the four standard features of RIAs (Toffetti et al., 2011). In this sense, Open-Laszlo does not have validation components as part of its core but as part of the incubator classes package, i.e., a set of classes that have been not fully integrated into the product although they have been contributed to the OpenLaszlo project. In fact, as part of the distribution of OpenLaszlo version 4.9.0, a set of validation classes are included within the incubator directory. In detail, the OpenLaszlo validation classes include four predefined validators: string validator, number validator, e-mail validator and date validator as well as a base validation class that can be extended in order to implement customized validators by means of the *iserror* and *errorstring* properties. In their basic form, the OpenLaszlo validators can be used to make fields required by using the *required* and *requiredErrorstring* properties inherited from the *basevalidator* class. Furthermore, the *numbervalidator* class, for instance, can be used to enforce a value type either integer or real as well as a minimum and a maximum value; in this sense, it exposes a *domain*, *minvalue* and *maxvalue* properties as well as four error message properties. It is important to notice that only the *minvalue* and *maxvalue* properties must be properly settled in order to use this number validator because the other properties have default values. Finally, it should be noticed that all the OpenLaszlo validators display error and success icons in addition to the aforementioned error messages; both feedback indicators can be customized. Figure 65 depicts the use of the OpenLaszlo *numbervalidator* class on implementing the live preview interaction pattern in the context of ZIP code validation.

Figure 64. Implementing the drop animation interaction pattern by using a third-party library built on top of the OpenLaszlo dragstate class

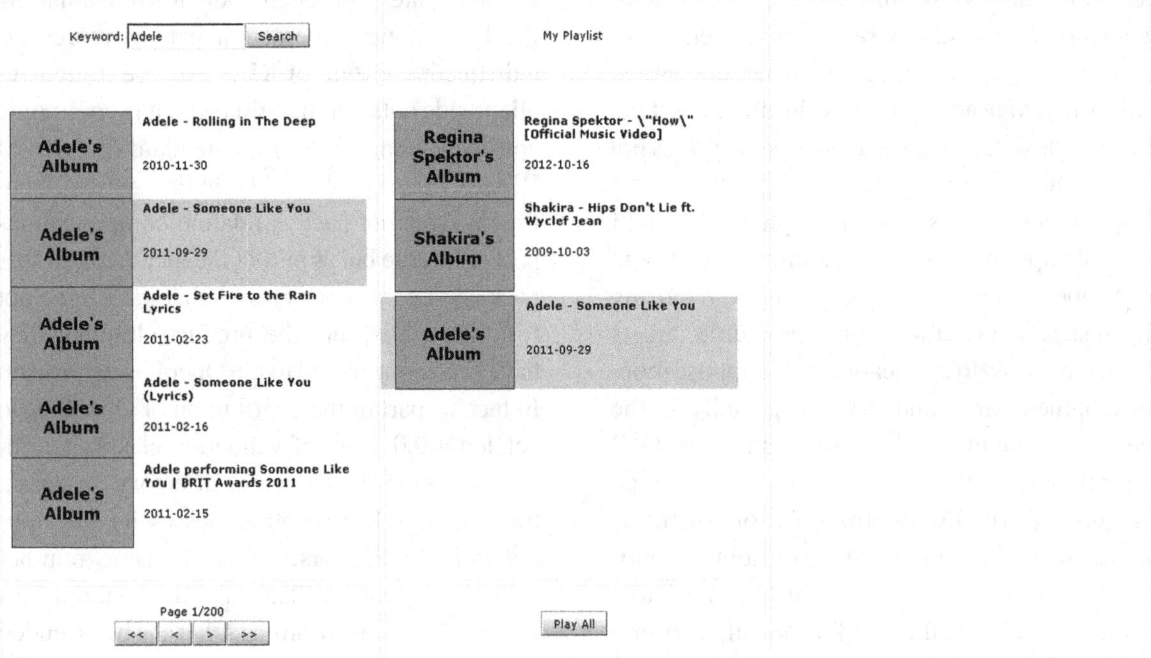

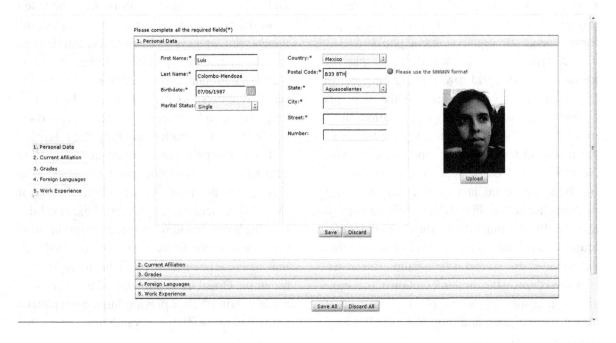

Figure 65. Implementing the live preview interaction pattern by using the OpenLaszlo numbervalidator class

3.5. Comparison

Table 2 summarizes a comparison of the support for implementing interaction patterns among non-JavaScript-based RIA frameworks. It is important to notice that this comparison is based on the analysis performed in this chapter; therefore, it only covers the Flex, JavaFX™ and Silverlight™ frameworks as well as the eight interaction patterns outlined at the beginning of this chapter.

It is important to notice that some interaction patterns, namely spotlight, live preview and periodic refresh, are not related to a specific GUI control, i.e., they can be implemented in a variety of ways. Therefore, the support for these interaction patterns does not depend on a particular framework capability. Moreover, there are other interaction patterns, namely animation and auto-complete, that can be implemented more easily by using non-native controls instead of native controls. This is the reason behind the decision to analyze non-native controls.

4. CONCLUSION

As it was explained thought this chapter, for the interaction design patterns that are not closely related to a particular GUI control or set of GUI controls, there is no only one way to implement them. In fact, the design patterns analyzed in this chapter provide generic solutions to common interaction problems in the context of user tasks where the solutions provided are high-level abstractions, i.e., solutions not at design level but at implementation level.

According to the above, the implementations addressed in this chapter are the most suitable implementations for practical purposes and they are certainly neither the only ones nor the most optimal. At the same time, these implementations are intended to serve as a comparative analysis of the capabilities of the RIA frameworks covered in this chapter mainly in terms of the GUI components and containers provided.

Due to the nature of JavaScript-based RIA frameworks, many different third-party implementations for a feature that is not natively included

Table 2. Support for interaction patterns into non-JavaScript-based RIA frameworks

Framework	Transitional Patterns	Lookup Patterns	Feedback Patterns
Flex	Brighten and Dim Expand/Collapse Animation Spotlight	Auto Complete (no native)	Live Preview Progress Indicator Periodic Refresh
JavaFX™	Brighten and Dim Expand/Collapse Animation Spotlight	Unknown	Live Preview Progress Indicator Periodic Refresh
Silverlight™	Brighten and Dim Expand/Collapse (no native) Animation (no native) Spotlight	Auto Complete (no native)	Live Preview Progress Indicator Periodic Refresh
OpenLaszlo	Brighten and Dim Expand/Collapse Animation Spotlight	Auto Complete (incubator classes)	Live Preview (incubator classes) Periodic Refresh

into its core can be found over Internet. This also applies to design principles and best practices like interaction design patterns; therefore, the sample applications presented throughout the first part of this chapter are primarily intended to exemplify the wide range of possibilities in this regard.

In the specific case of the non-JavaScript-based RIA frameworks, the interaction patterns analyzed in this chapter are implemented as part of common Web 2.0 scenarios; this contextualization allows developers to understand the associations between the three stages of the RIAs design task, which are outlined at the beginning of this chapter.

REFERENCES

Neil, T. (2009). *Designing Rich Applications*. Slideshare Website. Retrieved May 28, 2012, from http://www.slideshare.net/theresaneil/designing-rich-applications

Raymond, S., & Pereira, S. (2006). *Prototype Quick Reference*. O'Reilly Media, Inc.

Toffetti, G., Comai, S., Preciado, J. C., & Linaje, M. (2011). State-of-the Art and trends in the Systematic Development of Rich Internet Applications. *Journal of Web Engineering, 10*(1), 70–86.

ADDITIONAL READING

A Pattern Library for Interaction Design. (n.d.). *Patterns in Interaction Design*. Retrieved May 25, 2013, from http://www.welie.com/patterns/index.php

Mahemoff, M. (2006). *Ajax Design Patterns*. O'Reilly Media.

Neil, T. (n.d.). *RIA Screen Layouts*. Technology. Retrieved from http://www.slideshare.net/theresaneil/ria-screen-layouts

Tidwell, J. (2011). *Designing Interfaces* (2nd ed.). O'Reilly Media.

User Interface Design Patterns. (n.d.). *UI Patterns Library*. Retrieved May 25, 2013, from http://ui-patterns.com/

Yahoo Design Pattern Library. (n.d.). *Yahoo! Developer Network*. Retrieved May 25, 2013, from http://developer.yahoo.com/ypatterns/

KEY TERMS AND DEFINITIONS

Cascading Style Sheet (CSS): A style sheet language used for describing the look and formatting of a document written in a markup language. While most often used to style web pages and interfaces which are written in HTML and XHTML, the language can be applied to any kind of XML document, including plain XML, SVG and XUL.

Graphic User Interface (GUI): A part of the system software that acts as a user interface, i.e. it provides a mechanism for the user to interact with a software, these mechanisms can be text, images and other graphics.

Hypertext Markup Language (HTML): Markup language for developing Web pages. It is a standard that is the reference for the development of Web pages in different versions, it defines a basic structure and a code (HTML code).

Image Gallery: A representation of images, which can present in various formats and styles, in this case is handled in the context of Web applications development.

Lightbox: A UI Pattern, and is a technique that shows a modal dialog and allows to focus on the dialogue itself as the most representative feature is that obscure the rest of screen and being able to focus on the user's attention on a particular task.

User Interface Design Pattern: UI design patterns are solutions to common user interface problems.

Web 2.0: Web applications that allow to share information, interoperability, user-centered design and the collaboration with the World Wide Web.

Chapter 9
Case Studies Using JavaScript–Based Frameworks

ABSTRACT

In development of thin-client applications, it is a common practice to use server-side technologies in order to create data and business logic back-ends and client side-technologies to create lightweight HyperText Markup Language (HTML)-based front-ends. In the development of Web 2.0 applications, the data and business logic back-ends are typically built on top of third-party Web services. In this context, Simple Object Access Protocol (SOAP) has been traditionally used as the standard communication protocol for eXtensible Markup Language (XML)-based Web services. This chapter presents a review of the support for invoking SOAP-based Web services using Java; then, it discusses the development, using jQuery, Prototype, Dojo, and Java Server Pages (JSP), of different thin-client applications based on third-party SOAP Web services by means of a series of case studies to exemplify the use of some User Interface (UI) patterns for accomplishing rich design principles such as stay on the page and use transitions.

1. INTRODUCTION

Case studies are very important to present real and practical applications about a particular topic. RIAs (Rich Internet Applications) are taking a more important role on Web development, since enterprises are concerned about improving their Web applications to be accessible and have a good presentation. There are several technologies for developing RIAs, such as Adobe™ Flex™ or Microsoft™ Silverlight™ to mention but a few, but they represent a high cost of development by having to pay expensive development licenses or purchasing their expensive development suites. Usually, users cannot afford these high costs; because the best option is to use open source alternatives, and, in the RIAs development, JavaScript-based frameworks are the best solution.

It is very important for a developer to increase the development options; and JavaScript could be a formidable option, since it reduces both costs and learning curve. There are different JavaScript-based frameworks such as Dojo, jQuery, Mootools, Qooxdoo, Prototype, Rico, Sencha™ ExtJS™, X-Library, GWT (Google Web Toolkit™), Cappuccino, SproutCore, Spry, midori and YUI Library, among others. This chapter presents four different applications developed by using JavaScript-based

DOI: 10.4018/978-1-4666-6437-1.ch009

technology. The JavaScript-based frameworks used for the development of these applications are jQuery, Prototype and Dojo. These frameworks were selected according to 1) their usefulness for developing JavaScript-based applications in particular and 2) the ability to use two frameworks at once without causing development problems between them. The case studies using JavaScript-based frameworks include different important factors about RIAs development, such as multimedia support, AOP (Aspect Oriented Programming) support, design patterns support, and UI (User Interface) patterns support.

Applications developed in this chapter were chosen because they enable to easily illustrate the use and features of the JavaScript-based frameworks, as well as the characteristics of RIAs, such as avoiding page changes and keeping the focus on the main screen, among some others.

The RIAs developed were:

1. A world atlas that is a system for displaying information about all countries in the world. This application uses multimedia support for displaying related videos and improving the user experience. It also permits loading information on the same Web page. This application exemplifies the use of UI patterns, specifically interaction patterns, through the use of elements such as progress indicator.
2. A document indexing system enabling to search and display results in just one interface. This application provides information about indexed files showing elements such as a tag cloud and a reputation system in order to exemplify the UI patterns implementation.
3. An e-procurement system of medical supplies implemented in a hospital. This application searches for medical supplies of different US (United States) providers. For doing this task, the main interface was designed to show results within a LightBox element in order to avoid page changes and keep the user's attention on the same interface. Also,

auto complete and accordion elements were included to show the UI patterns support.

4. A meta-search engine that represents a search engine showing results in the same input interface. The carrousel element was used to exemplify the implementation of UI patterns and an example of the use and implementation of AOP support is presented.

The chapter presents a brief state-of-the-art analysis of each sample application. The analysis is aimed at emphasizing the distinguishing features of the applications developed.

2. DEVELOPING SOAP WEB SERVICES-BASED APPLICATIONS

SOAP (Simple Object Access Protocol) is a simple and lightweight mechanism for exchanging structured and typed information between peers in a decentralized and distributed environment using XML (eXtensible Markup Language). It consists of three parts:

1. The SOAP envelope construct defines an overall framework for expressing what is in a message, who should deal with the message, and weather the message is optional or mandatory.
2. The SOAP encoding rules define a serialization mechanism that can be used to exchange instances of application-defined data types.
3. The SOAP RPC (Remote Procedure Call) representation defines a convention that can be used to represent remote procedure calls and responses.

SOAP messages are fundamentally one-way transmissions from a sender to a receiver; however, they are often combined in order to implement patterns such as request/response. According to the above, SOAP messages can take advantage of the well-known connection model and message exchange pattern defined by HTTP in such a way that a correlation between a SOAP message sent in the body of an HTTP request message and a SOAP message returned in the corresponding HTTP response can be inferred.

A SOAP message is an XML-based document that consists of a mandatory SOAP envelope, an optional SOAP header, and a mandatory SOAP body. The header is a generic mechanism for adding features to a SOAP message in a decentralized manner without prior agreement between the communicating parts. The body is a container for mandatory information intended for the ultimate recipient of the message.

Thus, the information that can be added to the body of a SOAP message is regulated by another kind of XML-based document: a WSDL (Web Services Description Language) document. WSDL is an XML-based format specifying a grammar for describing services as a set of network endpoints operating on messages containing either document-oriented or procedure-oriented information. A WSDL document defines services as collections of network endpoints known as ports; a single port is defined as the combination of a network address and a concrete protocol and data format specification for a particular port type; a porttype is defined as an abstract set of operations supported by one or more end points; an operation is defined as an abstract description of a an action supported by the service in terms of messages; and a message is defined as an abstract definition of the data being communicated. The aforementioned concepts actually correspond to elements in a WSDL document.

In the context of developing SOAP Web services-based applications, it is a mandatory requirement to resolve the URL of the WSDL document describing the intended Web service. Once the URL is resolved, the operations of interest can be determined. Then, the input and output parameters can be identified by means of their names and data types. Basically, these are the early steps in developing SOAP Web services-based applications.

2.1. Invoking SOAP-Based Web Services Using JavaScript-Based RIA Frameworks

In the development of thin-client applications, it is a common practice to use server-side technologies, such as PHP (PHP Hypertext Preprocessor), JSP (Java Server Pages) and ASP.NET™, in order to create data and business logic back-end and client side-technologies like JavaScript to create lightweight HTML-based front-ends. In this chapter, three case studies addressing the development of thin client applications based on JSP, HTML and JavaScript are presented. These applications take advantage of public SOAP-based Web services; thereby, they can be viewed as SOAP-based Web service clients.

Since the applications discussed in this chapter are thin client applications, Web services invocations should occur at server-side. Table 1 summarizes different options for developing SOAP-based Web service clients in Java. These options include both high-level solutions – such as built-in APIs and third-party frameworks implementing these APIs – and low-level solutions, such as Java core networking classes. It is important to notice that, this chapter does not consider another approach related to the use of command line tools for automatically generating Web services client stubs.

In the case of thick-client applications comprising HTML/JavaScript-based front-ends, SOAP-based Web services can be called by using the JavaScript *XMLHttpRequest* object. This means that Web services invocations are treated as asynchronous HTTP requests, which rules out the possibility that other transport protocol, such as SMTP (Simple Mail Transfer Protocol) and XMPP (eXtensible Messaging and Presence Protocol) could be used. In fact, the JavaScript *XMLHttpRequest* object is used to send HTTP and

Table 1. Options for developing SOAP-based Web service clients in Java

API/Framework/Class	Description	Packages	Transport Protocol	SOAP Version
JAX-WS	It is a technology for building Web services and clients that communicate using XML. JAX-WS implements support for both message-oriented and RPC-oriented Web services. It is part of the Java EE (Java Platform Enterprise Edition) platform.	javax.xml.ws javax.xml.ws.handler javax.xml.ws.handler.soap javax.xml.ws.http javax.xml.ws.soap javax.xml.ws.spi javax.xml.ws.spi.http javax.xml.ws.wsaddressing	HTTP, JMS (Java Message Service), IN-VM (Virtual Machine), TCP (Transmission Control Protocol) and other via the JAX-WS commons project (SMTP, Grizzly and custom).	1.1 and 1.2
JAX-RS	It is a Java API (Application Programming Interface) that provides support for creating Web services according to the REST (Representational State Transfer) architectural style. JAX-RS implements support for Java annotations, and this makes it easy for developers to build RESTful Web services. JAX-RS is part of the Java EE platform.	javax.ws.rs javax.ws.rs.client javax-ws.rs.container javax.ws.rs.core javax.ws.rs.ext	HTTP	-
Apache Axis2/Java	It is the Java implementation of the Apache Axis2™ Web services/SOAP/WSDL engine. It allows developers to create, deploy, and run Web services.	See API documentation online	HTTP and others via Axis2 Transports: JMS, SMTP, POP3 (Post Office Protocol 3), TCP, SMS (Short Message Service), UDP (User Datagram Protocol), XMPP	1.1 and 1.2
Apache CXF™	It is an open-source Web services framework that allows developers to build and develop Web services using a variety of message protocols, such as SOAP, XML/HTTP, RESTful HTTP, and CORBA (Common Object Request Broker Architecture).	See API documentation online	HTTP, JMS, IN-VM (local), UDP, custom and others via Camel transport for CXF (SMTP/POP3, TCP and XMPP)	1.1 and 1.2
HttpURLConnection	It represents a communication link between a Java application and a URL with support for HTTP-specific features.	java.net	-	-

Figure 1. Initial user interface to world atlas application

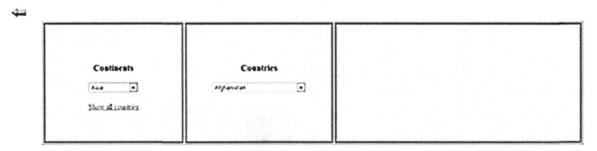

HTTPS (HyperText Transport Protocol Secure) requests to Web servers behind the scenes. In the context of JavaScript-based frameworks, this task can be done by using functions that encapsulate the *XMLHttpRequest* such as the *ajax()* function in the case of jQuery, the *Ajax.Request* object in the case of Prototype and the *dojo/request/xhr* function in the case of Dojo.

The JAX-WS API, as a part of the Java EE SDK (Software Development Kit), does not provide support for the extra transport protocols mentioned in Table 1. In fact, the implementations for these transport protocols are part of an open source services stack called Metro. More specifically, they are part of the JAX-WS commons project. Metro is part of the Glassfish project; nevertheless, it can be used with other application servers or servlet containers such as Apache Tomcat™.

Apache Axis2/Java is an implementation of the JAX-WS API, whereas Apache CXF™ is an implementation of both the JAX-WS and JAX-RS APIs. Hence, SOAP-based Web services can be created by adopting any of these high-level approaches. This also applies for RESTful Web services because of the WSDL 2.0 HTTP Binding specification. WSDL 2.0 HTTP Binding defines a way to implement REST with Web services and it is implemented by Apache Axis2/Java.

An own implementation based on core networking classes – such as the HTTPURLConnection class and other classes related to system input and output through data streams – involves creating the entire SOAP messages, either as hand-coded string variables or by using an API for XML parsing and validation such as JAXP (Java API for XML Processing) and JDOM. The use of an API for XML parsing must be also required in order to process the responses from the Web services.

3. DEVELOPING A WORLD ATLAS

A world atlas is a great collection of maps, and as an application, it is a useful tool which displays information from different countries. A world atlas can display information ranging from same maps, currency, language, and even flags. It can also include additional information such as videos.

Figures 1 and 2 describe the main user interfaces of the world atlas developed in this case study. Unlike other world atlas applications publicly available on the Internet, the application developed in this case study integrates videos as additional media resources. The videos contain valuable information about locations visualized on maps. Free video searches are also possible because the application provides independent video search functionality.

There are some similar applications to the world atlas developed in this chapter. Similar applications include websites and mobile applications available on online digital application stores

Figure 2. General user interface for displaying information, which presents the maps and the multimedia support, to mention a few

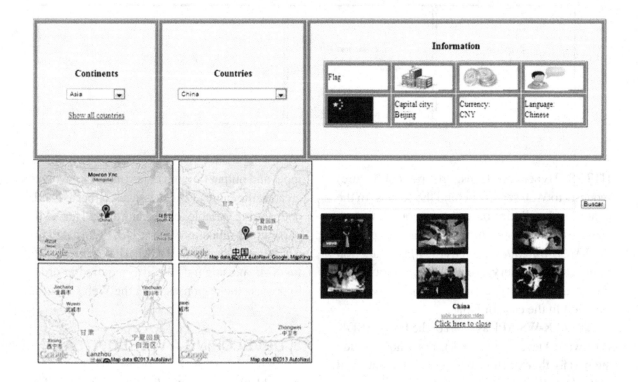

such as Google Play™ store, iTunes Store™ and Windows™ MarketPlace. Table 2 summarizes the features of the most representative applications according to ratings given by users in the aforementioned application stores.

In Figure 1, the two first squares contain information while the rest of interface is empty. It is only filled out when the information to be displayed is required.

This application is structured as follows:

1. Section 1 represents the option to select a continent. The values allowed are: Africa, Antarctica, Asia, Europe, Oceania, and The Americas. These values are retrieved from the Web Service *CountryInfoService* (Country Info Service, 2013) available at http://web-services.oorsprong.org/websamples.coun-tryinfo/CountryInfoService.wso?WSDL by using the property *ListOfContinentsByName*. This section provides a list of continents and the periodic refresh interaction pattern is used as a means for updating the information requested. Once a change in the input information has happened, an automatic update is done in the list of countries of section 2 with the information coming from section 1.

2. Section 2 contains a list of countries that appears after choosing the continent in section 1. If a country is selected, then the relevant information about that country is displayed on sections 3, 4, and 5 as shown in Figure 2. If a change in the countries list in section 2 has occurred, automatic updates are carried out in sections 3, 4 and 5.

Table 2. State-of-the-art analysis of World Atlas applications

Name	Application Type	Description	Features
World Atlas Atlas of the World	Web application	It is an educational resource for world maps, atlases, and in-depth geographical information.	It has a rich user interface that permits selecting the continent to be explored directly from a world map. All maps are based on a platform called Graphic Maps and they are partially available to be used by third-party applications. Among the geographical information provided by World Atlas, there are facts, flags, geographical statistics, travel information, weather, time zones and geographic information such as landforms and waterbodies.
World Atlas	Native mobile application (Android™)	It is a free and fully featured atlas application developed by Mindbeach™. It integrates information from diverse sources such as Wikipedia™, Wikitravel™, Google Maps™, Weather Undergound™, the CIA's (Central Intelligence Agency's) World Factbook, and others.	It displays a country flag gallery organized continents and it permits selecting the flag of the country to be explored in a map. World Atlas provides country and capital political maps based on the Google Maps™ mapping service. Besides geographic information, it provides Olympics data and a quiz application. It must be mentioned that this application is considered to be a hybrid mobile application, since the information from sources such as Wikipedia™ and Wikitravel™ is displayed by embedding the corresponding Web pages from these Websites into a native mobile container.
National Geographic Word Atlas	Native mobile application (Apple™ iOS)	It is a high-resolution atlas application developed by National Geographic Society, National Geographic™ World Atlas is optimized for Retina Display-based iPhone™ and iPad™ devices.	It displays an interactive 3-D globe that permits selecting the country to be explored. Maps provided by National Geographic™'s World Atlas are based on the Microsoft™ Bing™ Maps platform. Unlike other world atlas applications, this application integrates distance and travel time measurement tools. Moreover, it provides a drag-and-drop pin functionality that enables users to place spot markers and save them in the cloud.

3. Section 3 displays information related to the selected country of section 2. This information includes flag, language, currency, and the capital city of the country.
4. Section 4 shows the map of the selected country (however, these maps are different versions provided by Google Maps™ API (Application Programming Interface) such as hybrid and satellite, to mention but a few (Google Developers–GoogleMaps, 2013)).
5. Section 5 presents a list of related videos for a selected country obtained from YouTube™ (Google Developers–Youtube, 2013). In this section, the expand/collapse interaction pattern is implemented, since the video player is displayed when a particular video is selected. Additionally, the user has the ability to hide the full video section.

All sections of the application have taken advantage from the progress indicator interaction pattern by using a progress bar element. It must be noticed that sometimes the behavior of the progress bar element cannot be detected due to the loading speed of the application. For this reason, Figure 3 depicts the behavior of the progress indicator pattern in the context of the world atlas application.

To achieve this functionality, Web services such as JAX-WS (Java API for XML Web Services) are used. In this case JAX-WS version 2.2 was used. JAX-WS is included in any version of the NetBeans™ IDE. The Web service used for this application is *CountryInfoService* and it is available at http://webservices.oorsprong.org/websamples.countryinfo/CountryInfoService.wso?WSDL. This Web service has methods that

Figure 3. User interface displaying a progress bar element when a list of countries is displayed by selecting a continent

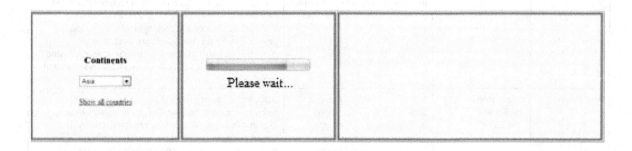

Table 3. Web Service description of CountryInfoService

Operation	Description
ListOfContinentsByName	Returns a list of continents ordered by name
ListOfContinentsByCode	Returns a list of continents ordered by code
ListOfCurrenciesByName	Returns a list of currencies ordered by name
ListOfCurrenciesByCode	Returns a list of currencies ordered by code
CurrencyName	Returns the name of the currency
ListOfCountryNamesByCode	Returns a list of all stored countries ordered by ISO (International Organization for Standarization) code
ListOfCountryNamesByName	Returns a list of all stored countries ordered by country name
ListOfCountryNamesGroupedByContinent	Returns a list of all stored countries grouped per continent
CountryName	Searches the country on the database by passing the ISO country code
CountryISOCode	This function tries to found a country based on the passed country name
CapitalCity	Returns the name of the capital city given a country code
CountryCurrency	Returns the currency ISO code and name given the country ISO code
CountryFlag	Returns a link to a picture of the country flag
CountryIntPhoneCode	Returns the international phone code for the past ISO country code
FullCountryInfo	Returns a structure with all the stored country information given the ISO country code
FullCountryInfoAllCountries	Returns an array with all countries and all the language information stored
CountriesUsingCurrency	Returns a list of all countries that use the same currency code. Pass a ISO currency code
ListOfLanguagesByName	Returns an array of languages ordered by name
ListOfLanguagesByCode	Returns an array of languages ordered by code
LanguageName	Finds a language name based on the ISO language code
LanguageISOCode	Finds a language ISO code based on the language name

permit performing specific functions as shown in Table 3. Only two methods are not used in this application. These methods are: *CountryISOCode* and *FullCountryInfo*.

In order to use Web services, the developer should review each operation available. This allows him or her to choose the operation that best suits the needs of the project. It must also meet required parameters since sometimes it depends on the choice of operation used.

This application was developed by using JSP (Java Server Pages) and Web services. AJAX (Asynchronous JavaScript And XML) and Prototype framework were used for implementing the periodic refresh and progress indicator interaction patterns. Web services were used to present the information when necessary, since storing the information is not required. However, the inaccessibility of Web services may cause some drawbacks, such as the application interruption. A possible solution to this is the use of databases, which store all necessary information to avoid connection errors with Web services. A recommended use of this application is the implementation of markers on the maps provided by Google Maps™. This increases the functionality of the world atlas by displaying relevant information when the marker is clicked.

4. DEVELOPING A DOCUMENT INDEXING SYSTEM

Today search engines have become more popular and crucial when a user is browsing the Internet. A variety of search engines are readily available. However, the most popular search engine is Google™, owned by Google Inc.

There are different ways of developing a search engine system. An API that can be used for full-text indexing and searching is Apache™ Lucene™. Lucene™ is a high-performance, full-featured text search engine library written entirely in Java. It is a technology suitable for nearly any application that requires full-text search, especially cross-platform. (lucene, 2013). Lucene™ is complemented with Apache™ TIKA™, which is a toolkit for detecting and extracting metadata and structured text from various documents using existing parsing libraries. The document types supported include: HTML (HyperText Markup Language), XML (eXtensible Markup Language), DOC, XLS, PPT (Microsoft™ Office formats), and PDF (Portable Document Format), among others (Apache Tika, 2013).

Document indexing is the process by which data stored in a document and data about the document itself is captured with the aim of making it searchable. There are two ways in which data from a document is made searchable. The first is by using full text indexing while the other way concerns entering "data about the data" – such data is called 'metadata'. The first method uses OCR (Optical Character Recognition) or text extraction to capture text from within the document. The second method of indexing captures details about the document under various fields and stores this data to help locate the document when needed. This is done by the document indexing software itself (sohodox.com, 2013).

The RIAs presented in this chapter integrate a variety of elements that exemplify the use and implementation of UI patterns. For instance, the application developed in this case study is a document indexing and search system that supports DOCX, XLSX, PPTX, TXT, HTML, and PDF file extensions. It also integrates a rating system aimed at enabling users to indicate the usefulness of the documents retrieved by assigning ratings. Likewise, tag-based search functionality is also integrated into this application so that documents can be tagged.

Due to security and privacy concerns, file indexing and search systems for local usage are not available as online public Web applications but as desktop applications. Nevertheless, there are some online public services providing indexing and search functionalities for files publicly

Table 4. File indexing and search systems state-of-the-art analysis

Name	Application Type	Description	Supported File Extensions	Features
DocFetcher	Desktop application	It is a free open-source desktop search engine. It is a multiplatform application that runs on Windows™, Linux™ and Mac OS™ X	Microsoft™ Office formats, OpenOffice.org formats PDF, TXT, RTF (Rich Text Format), MP3, JPG, PST and others.	DocFetcher allows for searching documents using a Query Syntax that supports phrase search, wildcards, fuzzy search, and proximity search, among other features. It also supports regex-based expressions for indexing exclusion. Search results can be filtered by file size, location, and file type.
FindThatDoc	Web application	It is a free service for searching files from the Internet. It was developed by Find That File LLC (Limited Liability Company).	47 file types and more than 558 file extensions. See detailed information online.	FindThatDoc supports video, audio, document, fonts, compressed, bittorrent, and software file categories. In FindThatDoc search results can be filtered by file extension and source type, including Web, FTP (File Transport Protocol), direct connect, USENET, and eMule. FindThatFile has a database of over 300 million files.
Docjax	Web application	It is a free search engine for documents and e-books available on the Internet. It was developed by IJAX LC (Limited Company)	PDF, DOC, XLS and PPT.	Docjax allows for searching for documents by keyword. Search results can be filtered by file extension; documents can be previewed and downloaded. The preview mode is based on a lightbox-type control. Docjax provides top-n lists including most viewed and most downloaded file lists.

available on the Internet. The features of some well-known file indexing and search systems, whether Web applications or desktop applications, are summarized in Table 4.

The user interface shown in Figure 4 is used to find indexed files in a specific location. The search can be performed in two different ways: 1) by entering a keyword in a text box or 2) by clicking a concept of the word cloud. To initiate a search, the user must index the documents by clicking the "Indexing" option in order to index and store documents in a folder. The user can return to the initial interface by clicking in "OK" button in the dialog box as shown in Figure 5.

Searches are only performed on documents that were indexed, i.e., the index is built with information from the documents in the indexed folder. Figure 6 shows an interface where some results were displayed by entering the keyword "chapter".

The interface presented in Figure 6 is structured in three sections:

1. This section shows the files found from a search. These files are presented with a file type's icon. When the "see" option is clicked in a document, a lightbox-type element is displayed with the file description. For doing this action, a jQuery *fancy box* element is used and, in this element, the information of the selected file is displayed. To implement this element the style sheet *jquery.fancybox-1.3.1.css* is used and JavaScript files *jquery.easing* and *jquery.fancybox-1.3.1.pack.js-1.3.pack.js* are also used. This is shown in Figure 7.

2. This section defines the search parameters, in this case, the file types to be searched.

3. This section displays a cloud tag which is implemented by using style sheets and da-

Figure 4. Main user interface of the information search engine

Figure 5. Message of indexing process

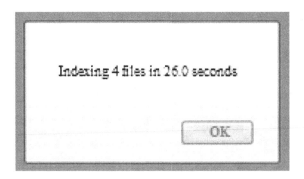

tabase to store the labels assigned to each one of the files. Section 2 and 3 are implemented within an accordion-like element by using jQuery functions located in *jquery. ui.accordion.js* style sheet.

The interface for displaying information represented in Figure 7 is structured in four sections:

1. In this section the name and icon of the selected file are presented.

2. In this section, the file information, such as size and name is displayed. The section also provides a link to download the file.
3. This section is used to add tags to the file and also displays the labels previously added. The labels added to the files are listed in section 3 of Figure 6.
4. This section is a ranking system where a file is evaluated by using a star ranking question element as a means to implement the animation interaction pattern. The star ranking question element allows the respondent to interactively rate criteria based on different categories defined by the row and column headers. Each star represents the equivalent numeric value for that rating. To implement the star ranking question element, it is necessary to include the following style sheets: *crystal-stars.css?v =2.0.3b38* and *jquery.ui.stars.js?v=3.0.0b38*. It must be mentioned that the star-ranking element uses a database to store votes and rate each one of the indexed files.

Figure 6. User interface where the results found are displayed

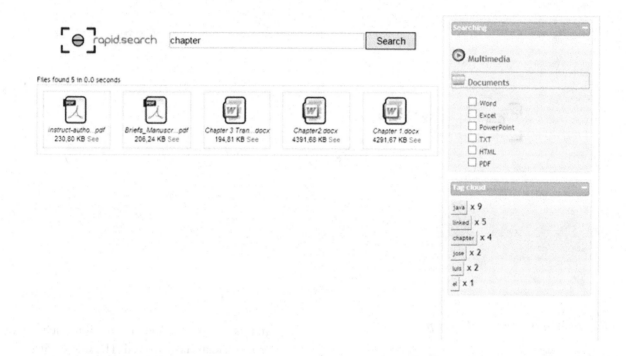

Figure 7. User interface displaying information of a selected file

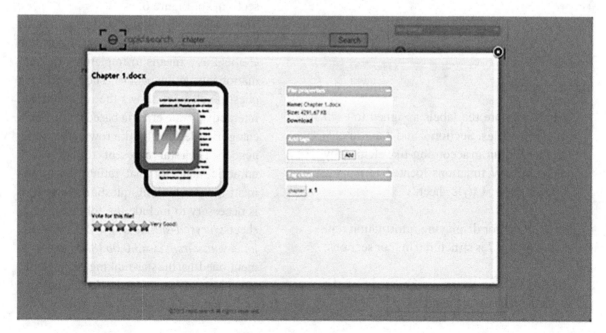

Section 2 and 3 are implemented in an accordion element representing the expand/collapse interaction pattern by using jQuery functions located in *jquery.ui.accordion.js* style sheet. The application was developed under JSP technology. The indexing system was performed by using Lucene™ and TIKA™. AJAX and jQuery framework were also used. Each section of this application was developed with jQuery functions.

5. DEVELOPING AN E-PROCUREMENT SYSTEM OF MEDICAL SUPPLIES

The application developed in this case study is an e-procurement application that helps hospitals, clinicians, and doctors in the process of upgrading their medical equipment. The application, in fact, displays a list of potential medical suppliers given a name state and a ZIP code. This application only displays on US suppliers that offer several medical equipment and supplies. To find potential suppliers, the application provides a set of user interfaces and automatic queries to search for the available suppliers in the US. Queries were performed by using Web services and the support of a database compliant.

There are some solutions for supply chain management as part of complete application suites providing business intelligence facilities. Nevertheless, for the purposes of the state-of-the-art analysis summarized in Table 4, authors of this book merely considered some public online services that provided functionality similar to the functionality provided by the application developed in this section.

The user interface shown in Figure 8 is structured in three sections:

Table 5. Healthcare e-procurement applications state-of-the-art analysis

Name	Application Type	Description	Features
Medicare.gov's Quality Care Finder	Web application	As part of the official Website for the US social insurance program called Medicare, the Quality Care Finder application allows for searching and comparing hospitals, doctors, nursing homes, supplies providers, home health services, facility providers, and other health providers in U.S.	Medicare.gov's Quality Care Finder allows for searching for healthcare providers by location. For this purpose, a city name, state name or ZIP code must be entered regardless of the type of provider being searched. However, different search functionality is provided for each type of provider supported by Medicare.gov's, because search results can be filtered by using a set of filters that are displayed according to the type of provider. For instance, in the case of hospital searches, results can be filtered by hospital's name and type. In addition to the typical list view, search results can also be displayed using a map view that relies on Google Maps™'s maps.
Blue Shield of California's Find a Provider application	Web application	The Blue Shield of California's Find a Provider application is a B2C (Business-to-consumer) e-procurement solution in the healthcare industry. It is intended to provide Californians with access to healthcare plans based on healthcare providers, such as doctors, dentists, vision care professionals, facility providers, pharmacies, and equipment and supplies providers.	In Blue Shield of California's Find a Provider, healthcare providers can be searched by location by entering a city name or ZIP code. For this purpose, the desired supplier category must be previously indicated; otherwise, a category is selected by default. Additionally, advanced searches can be performed according to the selected category. For instance, in the case of the doctor category, doctors can be searched by name, specialty, genre, and language.

Figure 8. User interface of the e-procurement system of medical supplies

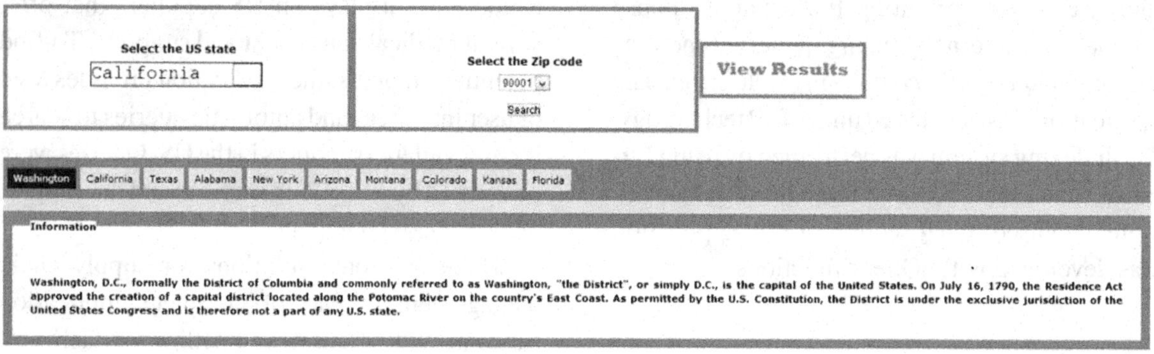

1. In this section, the selection of the US state name is required in order to execute a search. An *AutoComplete* element of the Dojo framework is used to perform this task. Also, it is required to include style sheets *tundra.css* and *dojo.css*, as well as the JavaScript files *testCommon.js* and *dojo.js*. Once the Select element is changed, then call to the function is invoked.

2. This section shows the ZIP codes available for the selected state in Section 1. The "Search" button should be clicked. Next, the "View Results" button should be also clicked. The Periodic Refresh and Progress Indicator elements were implemented to perform this task. The elements were implemented by using the Prototype framework. This section uses a ZIP codes database of each one of states of the US. When "View Results" option is clicked, a lightwindow element is opened as it is shown in figure 9. The JavaScript files *prototype.js*, *scriptaculous.js?load=effects*, and *lightwindow.js* were required and *lightwindow.css* style sheet is used to implement the lightwindow element.

3. This section shows a series of tabs with information about each one of the US states. This section uses a tabs element by using Prototype framework. Style sheets and *fabtabulous.js* JavaScript file were required for implementing this element. After click-

ing the "View Results" button in Figure 8, the information is presented as shown in Figure 9. This interface shows all available providers given a US ZIP code. If this user interface is closed, the focus is returned to the main user interface.

4. In this section, an accordion element was used. This element was intended to implement the Expand/Collapse interaction pattern and it was inserted into a lightwindow element that is used to implement the Brighten and Dim Interaction pattern. This section also uses a progress indicator element to show the progress of data loading. For doing this, Prototype framework and Scriptaculous were used. Also, some files were required, such as *accordion_glam.css* style sheet and *prototype.js*, *accordion.js* and *scriptaculous.js* JavaScript files.

JSP and Web services technologies were used for this application. The *medicareSupplier* Web service was implemented in order to obtain information about medical supplies, (Medicare Supplier, 2013). This Web service is located inhttp://www.webservicex.net/medicareSupplier.asmx?WSDL, and it has various operations as described in Table 6. The *GetSupplierByZipCode* method was the only method not used in this application.

Figure 9. User Interface displaying results of medical supplies located in a ZIP code selected

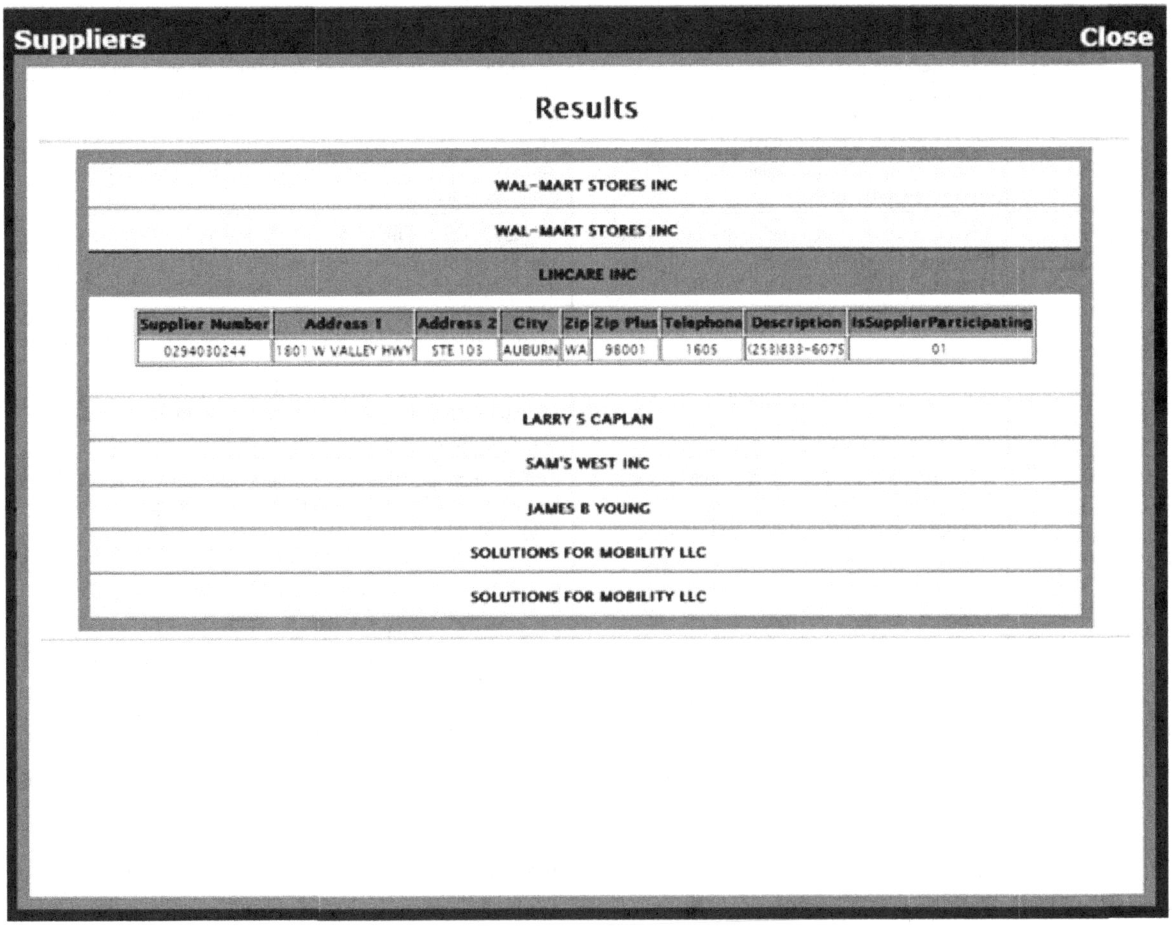

Table 6. Description of the medicareSupplier Web service

Operation	Description
GetSupplierByZipCode	Gets Supplier details given a ZIP code
GetSupplierByCity	Gets Supplier details given a city
GetSupplierBySupplyType	Gets Supplier details given a supply type

6. DEVELOPING A MASHUP: A META-SEARCH ENGINE

A mashup is a technique for building applications that combines data from multiple sources to create an integrated experience. Many mashups available are hosted as websites on the Internet, providing visual representations of publically available data (Holmes, 2013).

The application developed in this case study is a mashup that incorporates a search engine for using Web services provided by Amazon™ and eBay™. It was designed to perform a search on the same interface in two different Web sites i.e., it is capable of searching products in two of the

Table 7. Amazon™/eBay™ mashups state-of-the-art analysis

Name	Description	Features
WishMindr™	It is a free online service developed by WRIGHTLABS, LLC. It allows for creating and sending universal gift wish lists for any occasion. WishMindr relies on ShopStyle™, eBay™ Finding, eBay™ Shopping, and Amazon™ Product Advertising APIs.	WishMindr™ not only allows for searching for products on ShopStyle™, eBay™, and Amazon™ at the same time, it also permits adding products to wish lists regardless of their source. These wish lists can be further sent via e-mail by creating Yahoo! ™ and Gmail™ contact lists and setting up automatic reminder e-mails.
Oskope	It is a free visual search engine that allows for browsing and organizing items from Amazon™, eBay™, Flickr™, Fotolia, and YouTube™ services intuitively.	To start a search with Oskpe, it is necessary to select a service. This means that searches are not performed on all services at the same time. Search results are images and can be displayed using five different layouts: pile, stack, grid, list, and graph. Thereby, images need to be clicked in order to obtain detailed information about results. Detailed information is displayed using a lightbox-type control. Additionally, search results can be filtered by category, subcategory and keyword. In fact, random search results are displayed at the beginning.
5th village	It is a free Pinterest-like visual search engine for Amazon™, eBay™, and Shopstyle™ online shopping services. It is also an Instagram client.	At the beginning, 5th village displays random clothing search results from ShopStyle™. In order to search for products on eBay™ and Amazon™, it is necessary to click the proper link from a navigation bar. In both cases, daily deals are showed as response. In the case of eBay™, search results can be refined by category and subcategory only; they can also be sorted by price, date and popularity. In the case of Amazon™, search results can be refined by category and keyword; price filters can also be added to result lists. In any case, search results primarily consist of images, and they can be loaded on demand. Finally, if an image is clicked, a redirect to the corresponding Website is performed.

largest online sales websites, such as eBay™ and Amazon™ through the same interface.

There are some publicly available Websites providing functionality similar to the functionality provided by the mashup developed in this chapter. Table 7 summarizes the features of some Websites integrating Amazon™ and eBay™ Web services.

Figure 10 shows the main user interface. A product/service category can be selected by clicking an icon in the carousel element; next, a keyword must be entered in a text box. Finally, the user must select the website where he/she wants to find products or services. In Figure 10, Section 1 displays a Carousel element that is used to implement the animation interaction pattern. The Carousel element was implemented by using jQuery framework. The JavaScript files: *jquery-1.2.3.min.js, jquery.simplemodal.js, cloud-carousel.1.0.5.js* and *clod-carousel.1.0.5.min.js*

were used to perform this task. When an option from the carousel element is chosen, information is displayed as shown in Figure 11.

In Figure 11, if a product is selected, it is possible to see the details as shown in Figure 12. A lightbox-type element is used for this feature.

To deploy the lightbox element (in this case a pop-up window by using jQuery functions), the following files are required separately: *popup.css* and *styles.css* style sheets; and *simplemodal.js* jQuery file. The contents of the window are obtained from invoking Web services provided by Amazon™ and eBay™.

To illustrate the implementation of the AOP support, an example was implemented in this application. The AOP support can be used, for instance, to add a login method or to modify the logic business in an application previously designed. In these cases, case the AOP support

Figure 10. User interface for searching products and services in Amazon™ and eBay™

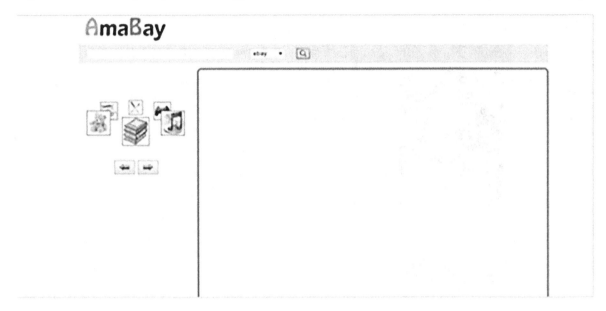

Figure 11. User Interface displaying a list of products found on eBay™

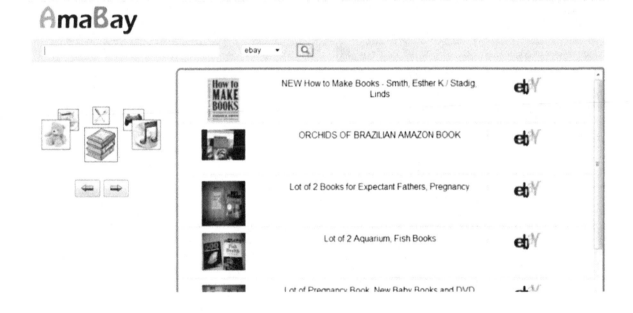

is used to modify the search process in the application, and it is implemented to verify that the user knows what category is conducting the search. This prevents from avoid showing incorrect results. The implementation of AOP support is explained below.

For this example, *dojo.connect* function is used at the source code as shown:

```
dojo.connect(null,"funcion",null,"get
Categories")
```

Figure 12. Information details of a selected product

Figure 13. AOP support to modify the search process

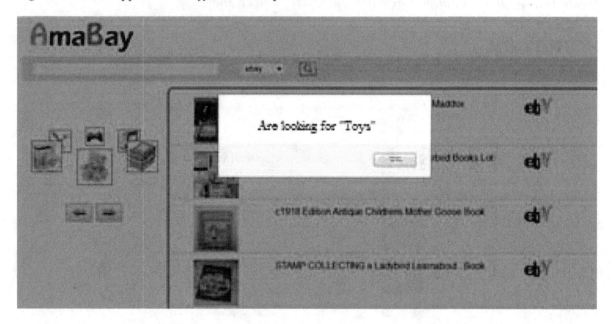

This snippet allows modifying the search process for toys. In this case, a dialog box is introduced as shown in Figure 13.

This application is a PHP Web-based system where Web services provided by Amazon™ and eBay™ were also used. Carrousel and lightbox elements were implemented by using the jQuery framework. AOP support was implemented by using Dojo functions. In this particular case, Web services cannot be changed instead of using a database because the information must be obtained from Amazon™ and eBay™ directly.

Table 8. Web Service description of AWSECommerceService (common request parameters)

Operation	Description
AssociateTag	It is an alphanumeric token that uniquely identifies an associate. By using this token, Amazon™ identifies the associate to have privilege for a sale. Valid values: An alphanumeric token distributed by Amazon™ that uniquely identifies an associate.
AWSAccessKeyId	It is an alphanumeric token that uniquely identifies a seller. Valid value: Access Key ID distributed by Amazon™.
ContentType	It specifies the response format of the content. For example, to transform a Product Advertising API response into HTML, *ContentType* must be set to text/html.
MarketplaceDomain	It specifies the marketplace domain where the request will be directed.
MerchantId	An optional parameter that can be used to filter search results and offer listings to only include items sold by Amazon™. By default, the API will return items sold by various merchants including Amazon™.
Operation	It specifies the Product Advertising API operation to be executed. Valid value: A Product Advertising API operation, for example, *ItemLookup*.
Service	It specifies the Product Advertising API service. Valid value: *AWSECommerceService*
Validate	It prevents that an operation to be executed. If the *Validate* parameter is set to true, the request can be tested without actually executing it. Default: false. Valid Values: true, false
Version	The version of the Product Advertising API software and WSDL (Web Services Description Language) to be used. By default, the 2011-08-01 version is used. Default: 2011-08-01. Valid values: Valid WSDL version date, for example, 2011-08-01.
XMLEscaping	It specifies whether responses are XML encoded in a single pass or in a double pass. By default, *XMLEscaping* is single, and Product Advertising API responses are encoded only once in XML. Default: single. Valid values: single, double

Table 9. eBay API description (principal all-specific input fields for FindProducts method)

Operation	Description
AvailableItemsOnly	If true, the operation only retrieves data for products that have been used to pre-fill active listings on the specified eBay site. If false, it retrieves all products matching the query. Default: false.
CategoryID	It includes an identifier in the request to restrict the query to a specific category. The request requires a single one of these three elements: *QueryKeywords*, *ProductID*, or *CategoryID*, and can only include one of the three. Max length: 10.
DomainName	A domain to search in. This is similar to searching for a section of a catalog. If not specified, the product search is conducted across all domains.
HideDuplicateItems	It specifies whether or not to remove duplicate items from search results. When it is set to true, and there are duplicate items for an item in the search results, the subsequent duplicates will not appear in the results. Default: false.
MaxEntries	It specifies the maximum number of products to be returned per page in a single call. Min: 1. Max: 20. Default: 1.
PageNumber	It specifies what page of data will be returned in the call. Min: 1. Max: 2000. Default: 1.
ProductID	It is used to retrieve product details for one specific product. The identifier as a string is specified, and the type attribute is used to indicate the nature of the identifier. Max length: 4000.
QueryKeywords	One or more keywords to search for. When a keyword search is used, eBay searches the product catalogs for matching words in the product title, description, and/or item specifics, and it returns a list of matching products. Max length: 350.

The Amazon™ Web service used is *AWSECommerceService* (Amazon Web Services, 2013) and is described in Table 8. The eBay API (Ebay developers program, 2013) is available at http://svcs.ebay.com/services/search/FindingService/v1. The principal all-specific input fields for *FindProducts* method are described in Table 9.

7. CONCLUSION

The JavaScript-based frameworks are of great importance in Web applications development, particularly in RIAs development. These frameworks permit easily incorporating different RIAs features. RIAs seek to improve both user experience and productivity, and for this to be done, it is necessary to incorporate different features such as avoiding reloading pages continuously and the indiscriminate use of links in the Web applications to communicate with the server. In those cases, RIAs work in a particular way, i.e. a RIA downloads all available information in a single call to the server, but this information is presented to the user until it is needed. The applications developed in this chapter incorporated some important features with the aim of presenting the typical interaction mechanisms of RIAs, and making it clear to the user. However, other features were also incorporated into the applications, reducing limitations of traditional Web applications. Therefore, both user experience and productivity were improved. The JavaScript-based frameworks allow for integration with other technologies such as AJAX, Web services, and databases, among others. They also allow for the development of mashup-style applications, which permits the enrichment of user interfaces in a more dynamic way by integrating information from different data sources. These Web applications are easy to use and they avoid that the applications were developed with different programming languages and different JavaScript-based frameworks (even a combination of them) in order to enrich the information navigating among Web pages, also information

is quickly and cleanly displayed through the use of AJAX technology.

REFERENCES

Amazon Web Services. (2013). *Amazon Web Services*. Retrieved March, 2013, from http://aws.amazon.com/es/

Apache Tika. (2013). *A content analysis toolkit*. Retrieved March, 2013, from http://tika.apache.org/

Country Info Service. (2013). *Country Info Service*. Retrieved March, 2013, from http://webservices.oorsprong.org/websamples.countryinfo/CountryInfoService.wso

Ebay Developers Program. (2013). *Ebay API*. Retrieved March, 2013, from http://developer.ebay.com/common/api/

Google Developers – GoogleMaps. (2013). *API Google Maps*. Retrieved March, 2013, from https://developers.google.com/maps/?hl=es

Google Developers – Youtube. (2013). *Youtube API Resources*. Retrieved March, 2013, from https://developers.google.com/youtube/

Holmes, J. (2013). Enterprise Mashups. MSDN Architecture Journal. *MSDN Architecture Center*. Retrieved March 2013, from http://msdn.microsoft.com/en-us/architecture/bb906060.aspx

Lucene (2013). *Apache Lucene Core*. Retrieved March, 2013, from http://lucene.apache.org/core/

Medicare Supplier. (2013). *MediCareSupplier*. Retrieved March, 2013, from http://www.webservicex.net/medicareSupplier.asmx

sohodox.com. (2013). *Document Indexing: The Key to Finding Documents Quickly*. Retrieved May, 2013, from http://www.sohodox.com/articles/document-indexing-the-key-to-finding-documents-quickly#sthash.CdBNBeue.dpuf

ADDITIONAL READING

Atlases. (2013). Geography and maps. *Library of congress and illustrated guide*. Retrieved March, 2013, from http://www.loc.gov/rr/geogmap/guide/gmillatl.html

KEY TERMS AND DEFINITIONS

Aspect Oriented Programming: A new programming paradigm that describes a development methodology for separating crosscutting concerns during the software development.

Document Indexing System: A document indexing system is a software tool that enables data stored in documents and data about documents themselves to be captured with the aim of making them searchable.

E-Procurement System: A software tool for B2B, B2C or B2G purchase and sale of supplies and services through the Internet.

Interaction Design Pattern: A kind of user interface pattern aimed at achieving effective user experiences, i.e., rich interactions.

Mashup: A mashup is a Web application that integrates data from multiple sources to provide a unique service.

Rich Internet Application (RIA): Applications that are deployed over the Web; this type of applications combines features and functionality of Web applications and desktop applications.

Thin Client Application: An application that relies on a client/server architecture, and it executes most of its business logic operation on the server-side.

Chapter 10
Case Studies Using Adobe™ Flex

ABSTRACT

REpresentational State Transfer (REST) is an architectural style that has recently emerged as a new approach to develop and deliver Web services. In fact, a great number of companies, such as eBay™, Twitter™, and Amazon.com™, have adopted REST to deliver Web services and Web feeds. This chapter offers a review of the support for consuming RESTful Web services in Adobe™ Flex™; then, it presents two case studies about the development of third-party RESTful Web services-based Rich Internet Applications (RIAs) using Adobe Flex™ along with HyperText Markup Languages (HTML) and JavaScript. The case studies presented in this chapter are intended to explain the common prerequisites for using RESTful Web services Application Programming Interfaces (APIs) as well as the particular implementation details, including the challenges and alternatives facing the capabilities and limitations of the target technologies. In addition, they exemplify the use of some User Interface (UI) patterns.

1. INTRODUCTION

Adobe™ Flex is a free and open source application framework for building Web and desktop Rich Internet Application (RIAs) as well as RIAs for diverse mobile devices by using a common code base[1]. Adobe™ Flex includes the Macromedia FleX Markup Language (MXML) and Action-Script programming languages. MXML is an XML-based language used for the design of application GUIs. ActionScript is an object-oriented language used for the definition of client-side application logic. MXML and ActionScript are compiled together into a single SWF file. Flex-based Web application runs in a Web browser through the Adobe™ Flash™ Player plugin. On the other hand, AIR™ is a cross-operating system runtime that allows building and deploying ActionScript or JavaScript-based RIAs outside the browser and on mobile devices.

According to Adobe™, Flash™ Player is approximately installed on 1.3 billion of desktop computers across Web browsers and operating systems. This fact represents the largest market share in the RIA market. In addition, Flex is a mature technology, and it has a huge developer community officially supported by Adobe™[2] as well as an open source community as part of the

DOI: 10.4018/978-1-4666-6437-1.ch010

Apache Incubator™ project[3]. Besides the capabilities and limitations inherent to the technologies, the above factors must be considered in order to adequately select a technology for developing RIAs. From this perspective, Flex can be a great option against other non-JavaScript-based application frameworks.

Considering that Web services have become a means to allow third-party developers to build on top of the infrastructure of Internet-connected companies, this chapter presents two case studies of the development of Representational State Transfer (REST) Web services-based RIAs by using Flex along with HTML and JavaScript. REST is an architectural style that has recently emerged as a new approach to develop and deliver Web services. In fact, a great number of companies such as eBay™, Twitter™ and Amazon.com™ have adopted REST to deliver Web services, as well as Web feeds.

Other application samples, case studies and showcase applications in diverse domains can be found online at http://www.adobe.com/devnet/flex/samples.html. In addition, the Tour de Flex desktop application available at http://www.adobe.com/devnet/flex/tourdeflex.html provides over 200 running samples, each one includes source code, links to documentation, resources and other details.

2. DEVELOPING REST WEB SERVICES-BASED APPLICATIONS

Representational State Transfer (REST) is a hybrid architectural style derived from several of network-based architecture styles and combined with additional constraints that defines a uniform connector interface. REST was stemmed from a PhD dissertation by Roy Fielding in 2000 (Fielding, 2000). Basically, it refers to a stateless client/server architecture where Web services and any other kind of reachable object such as document or image files are viewed as resources. Resources are identified by their Uniform Resource Identifiers (URIs) and they can be accessed through a standard transfer protocol such as the HyperText Transfer Protocol (HTTP) by using the GET, POST, PUT, and DELETE methods. In fact, requests and responses to actions over resources are based on transferring representations to capture the current or intended state of the resources ("REST application programming," 2010).

A REST-based (Application Programming Interface) API is a URI or a collection of URIs that can manage create, read, update and delete (CRUD) operations. Typically, a REST-based API exposes a base URI which is a URI common to all resources and serves as the entry point to the API. Moreover, REST-based APIs are programming language independent because they are accessible from any language that has an HTTP client library, including ActionScript, Java and PHP ("REST application programming," 2010).

Two of the most important issues to consider for developing REST Web services-based applications are: 1) the HTTP methods supported by the target API and 2) the available response formats. The second aspect affects the way of processing the response in order to display data to the user. Many REST-based APIs support JSON, RSS or Atom-formatted responses besides the XML-based responses which unlike the aforementioned do not imply the necessity of third-party libraries to be processed. Furthermore, RSS and Atom-formatted responses can be manipulated without requiring much effort by using standard XML-based client libraries because RSS and Atom syndication formats are XML-based dialects.

2.1. Invoking Rest-Based Web Services by Using Flex™

Conceptually, since REST-based Web services can be accessed through standard HTTP methods, any class that wraps HTTP requests can be used to consume REST-based Web services. The main features of the ActionScript classes that allow developers to achieve the aforementioned purpose are described in Table 10.1. These classes are available as part of the Flex Standard Development Kit (SDK). Basically, there are two options: 1) the HTTPService class and 2) the URLRequest class.

On the one hand, the HTTPService class can be also used in MXML because there is an HTTPService component as part of the mx.rpc. http.mxml package. When the HTTPService component is used, all the parameters to be sent to the destination URL must be specified under a unique mx:request tag under the corresponding mx:HTTPService tag. In any case, the resultant data can be accessed through the lastResult property according to the data type specified by the resultantFormat property. Moreover, this class allows programming at a higher level of abstraction than the URLRequest + URLLoader approach. Therefore, it can represent the best option for non-expert developers. On the other hand, there is not an equivalent MXML component for the URLRequest class. Furthermore, it must be used in conjunction with an ActionScript class responsible of sending the HTTP request, handling the corresponding HTTP response and providing developer-friendly access to the received data. For instance, when the URLRequest class is used in conjunction with the URLLoader class, the data to be transmitted with the destination URL must be assigned to the URLRequest's data property whereas the data received in the response can be accessed through the URLLoader's data property. Furthermore, the HTTP method to be used for sending the request must be specified through the URLRequest's method property which, unlike the HTTPService's method property, only supports the GET and POST HTTP methods.

3. CASE STUDIES

The following two sections explain both: 1) the prerequisites related to the use of the REST-based APIs involved and 2) the implementation details,

including challenges and alternatives facing the capabilities and limitations of the technology as well as the best practices and design patterns to be used in the development of a Vimeo™ and YouTube™-based meta-search engine for videos and a Yahoo!™-based forecast system, respectively. These applications were developed by using the Flex 4.5 application framework available at http://www.adobe.com/devnet/flex/flex-sdk-download. html and the Flash™ Builder 4.6 Standard development tool available at http://www.adobe.com/products/flash-builder-standard.html.

The weather forecast system is a desktop application that lets users both search for locations such as countries, states and towns by name as well as get Yahoo!™-based weather information for a selected location including current conditions and two-day forecast. The matches are paged displaying up to ten results per page. Additionally, by using Google Maps™ a map is displayed in order to complement the weather information of the selected location.

These applications implement different interaction design patterns proposed by Bill Scot and Theresa Neil (Scott & Neil, 2009), namely the inline paging, progress indicator and dialog overlay (lightbox effect) interaction patterns. This kind of GUI design pattern enables traditional Web applications to incorporate rich interactions aimed at improving user experiences.

3.1. Developing a Meta-Search Engine for Videos

A meta-search engine involves scanning information from two or more available sources simultaneously. This kind of search engine can cope with the common drawbacks of the traditional search tools such as the lack of accuracy in search results as well as the rapid and continuous growth of information resources. A meta-search can also be considered as a mashup involving two or more different types of search tools ("Search engine

Table 1. ActionScript classes useful for invoking REST-based Web services

Class	Description and Uses	Package	Result Format	Parameter Format	HTTP Method
HTTPService	It represents an HTTP request-response transaction. It allows calling HTTP-based Web services and accessing information retrieved from server-side scripts[4].	mx.rpc.http	Object, Array object, xml (XMLNode object), flashvars (name-value pairs into an Object), text (String object) and e4X (XML object).	Name-value pairs (Object)	GET, POST, HEAD, OPTIONS, PUT, TRACE and DELETE.
URLRequest	It captures all the information required to set up an HTTP request. URL request objects are used in conjunction with Loader, URLLoader, URLStream or FileReference objects to manage HTTP responses[5].	flash.net	-	Raw binary data (ByteArray object), URL-encoded variables (URLVariables object) and text (String object).	GET and POST.
Loader	It loads local and external SWF files or image (JPG, PNG, or GIF) files[6].	flash.display	The contents of the loaded file are made available as raw binary data (ByteArray object).	-	-
SWFLoader	It loads and displays local and external SWF files. It allows loading one Flex application into a host Flex application[7].	mx.controls. SWFLoader	-	-	-
URLLoader	Like HTTPService class, it allows sending requests to server-side scripts and accessing the information returned. It also lets loading data from local and external XML documents or text files[8].	flash.net	Text (String object), raw binary data (ByteArray object) and URL-encoded variables (URLVariables object).	-	-
URLStream	It provides low-level access for downloading data as the data arrives, instead of waiting until the entire file is completed as with URLLoader class[9].	flash.net	The contents of the downloaded file are made available as raw binary data (ByteArray object).	-	-
FileReference	It provides a means for downloading and uploading files between a user's computer and a server. It allows opening operating system dialog boxes that prompt the users to select either a location for saving or a file for uploading, accordingly[10].	flash.net	-	-	-

mashup," 2007). Websites such as Dogpile, Kayak and Ixquick are well-known meta-search tools.

3.1.1. Description of the REST-Based APIs Used

According to ProgrammableWeb.com website, the two most popular APIs for video-sharing are Vimeo™ and YouTube™ APIs[11]. These APIs also offer video-searching facilities. Therefore, in this case study, a meta-search engine for YouTube™ and Vimeo™ videos was developed. Both, YouTube™ and Vimeo™ are video-sharing websites where users can upload, share, search and view videos. These websites are also considered video-centered social networking websites because of the rating and commenting facilities. Moreover, according to the Alexa rank, these websites are the third[12] and the one hundred and twentieth[13] most popular websites on the world, respectively. The main features of the APIs used in this case study are described in Table 2.

Regarding to the requirements of using the above data APIs, it is important to notice that every call made to the Vimeo™ Advanced API must be authorized by using the version 1.0 of the OAuth protocol because this API comprises methods that require read/write access over private data, which implies Vimeo™ users to be authenticated in order to grant these permissions to external applications. In addition, Vimeo™ offers another data API called Simple API which is read-only and lets getting public information about users, videos, user groups, channels and other kind of data entities without requiring external applications to be authorized. On the other hand, the YouTube™ Data API requires users to be authenticated by using the version 2.0 of the OAuth protocol to only perform actions affecting information related to YouTube™ accounts.

With the aim of simplifying the OAuth authorization process, both the Vimeo™ and YouTube™ websites offer demo OAuth access tokens and secrets for every application registered. This is the approach used in this case study because the explanation of the OAuth flows is out of the scope of this chapter.

Therefore, the only requirement of using the Vimeo™ Advanced API is to obtain the OAuth access token and secret by registering some information about the application to be developed on the Vimeo™ website. Regarding to the result formats supported by the above APIs, it is important to notice that, the YouTube™ Data API is part of the Google™ Data APIs protocol which is a standard way of reading and writing data on the Web, and it is based on the Atom 1.0 and RSS 2.0 syndication formats. Therefore, the data from the YouTube™ Data API can be mainly retrieved as Atom or RSS feeds.

In fact, this API is conceived as a set of several types of feeds such as video, channel and playlist feeds rather than as a set of API methods or services. On the other hand, the Vimeo™ Advanced API provides simple XML-based responses by default, which can be easily processed without requiring third-party client libraries.

Regarding to the player APIs, both Vimeo™ and YouTube™ websites offer a JavaScript Player API besides an ActionScript player API; however, this API also involves embedding the Flash™ object enscapsulated on a SWF file, in an HTML Web page. The only difference is that the functions are made available via JavaScript or ActionScript by adding a *version* parameter indicating the required version of the API to a common URI. The chromeless version of the YouTube™ player requires more development effort compared with the embedded version of the YouTube™ player as well as with the Vimeo™ player because the chromeless YouTube™ player does not include playback controls. Thus, custom controls must be developed by using either JavaScript or ActionScript, which implies calling the functions of the corresponding API in order to set up the standard playback functions, namely play, pause and stop. In short, a video player with built-in controls can be the best option for non-

Table 2. REST-based APIs used for developing a meta-search engine for videos

API	Description	Base URI	Supported Result Format	Supported HTTP Methods	Official Libraries
Vimeo™ Advanced API	It allows applications to perform actions normally executed on the Vimeo website, including to search for videos and users, to retrieve information about videos and users, to delete existing videos and upload new videos, to manage comments on videos, to create and delete albums and channels of videos, to add and remove videos from albums, to subscribe and unsubscribe users from channels, to allow users to join and leave groups of users, among others actions. All the requests sent to this API must be authorized[14].	http://vimeo.com/api/rest/v2?method=METHOD Target method: vimeo.videos.search	XML, JSON, JSOP and PHP	GET and POST	PHP
Vimeo™ ActionScript Player API (client library)	It lets developers to control the Vimeo™ video player through ActionScript functions by loading it into Flash™/Flex applications. This version of the Vimeo™ player API is called Moogaloop and consists of a single ActionScript class that allows easily adding video support to Flash™/Flex applications. The functions available via the Moogaloop API are: to set the color and dimensions of the player, besides the common playback functions[15].	-	-	-	-
YouTube™ Data API 2.0	It allows applications to carry out the actions that a user can directly carry out on the YouTube™ website, including to search for videos, to retrieve video feeds, comments, playlists, subscriptions and user profiles, and to upload or update existing videos. In addition, this API lets applications to create playlists, subscriptions and other account-specific entities by sending authorized requests[16].	https://gdata.youtube.com/feeds/api/FEED Target feed: videos	JSON, JSON-IN.SCRIPT, JSONC, RSS and Atom	GET, POST, PUT and DELETE	Java, .NET, PHP, Python, Objective-C, JavaScript (Google™ APIs)
YouTube™ ActionScript 3.0 Player API (SWF player)	It lets developers to control the YouTube™ video players by loading them into Flash™/Flex applications and making calls to their ActionScript functions. There are two versions of the YouTube™ player: 1) a player that has standard built-in controls and 2) a player that does not display any control. The former is known as embedded player whereas the latter is known as chromeless player. Besides the common playback functions, this API allows playing videos in playlists and retrieving playlist information[17].	http://www.youtube.com/apiplayer?version=3 (chromeless player) http://www.youtube.com/v/VIDEO_ID?version=3 (embedded player)	-	-	-

skilled developers. Moreover, it is important to notice that the Vimeo™ ActionScript Player API actually is a client library composed of a unique class. Although a URI is not explicitly exposed, internally the Vimeo™ ActionScript Player API uses the http://api.vimeo.com/moogaloop_api. swf *URI* for loading the player by using the ActionScript Loader class.

3.1.2. Implementation Details

The first aspect to be evaluated in the development of applications based on Web services APIs that require applications to be authorized for making calls is the necessary type of application. This aspect determines the method to be used in order to authorize applications. In the case of Web applications authorization by using OAuth, a callback URI is used that enables servers to redirect users to their applications once the credentials have been successfully interchanged. On the other hand, in the case of native desktop and mobile applications, a pin is used that is retrieved from the server and it is displayed as HTML content once the credentials have been successfully interchanged. Typically, this pin is manually entered by the user in the application, and it is added to each of the calls made to the API as an access token.

This case study covers the development of a Web meta-search engine that scans data from two different data sources: the YouTube™ Data API and the Vimeo™ Advanced API. Behind this desired functioning there is a key principle: concurrency, i.e. the capability of simultaneously executing multiple sets of code instructions. This capability is related to a typical feature of RIAs, which enables applications to make parallel requests to different sources both in a synchronous and in an asynchronous way (Preciado et al., 2005). In ActionScript, each function that loads data into a SWF file such as the URLLoader's load function and the HTTPService's send function is asynchronous. It means that the results of this kind of actions are returned at an indeterminate time. In addition, the ActionScript Worker class provides a means for executing the application's code in multiple linear blocks of execution steps known as execution threads. In this sense, a worker object represents a virtual instance of the application runtime usually intended to execute code in the background at the same time that other operations are running in the main application thread which implicitly is a worker object usually responsible

for updating the screen. However, this execution model is not completely accurate for the desired functioning of the meta-search-engine. Thus, the asynchronous execution of the calls made to the REST-based APIs is only considered here.

In order to select a component for displaying the results returned by the YouTube™ Data API and the Vimeo™ Advanced API, the Flex List and DataGrid components are analyzed below. The former displays a scrollable list of data items. The latter can be considered as a scrollable list that can display more than one column of data with an extra row of column headings above the list. It represents the primary way to display data in Flex-based applications, and it is easy of using because allows arranging large amounts of data without a lot of code. It also provides useful features such as column sorting and cell editing. Adobe™ discourages using the DataGrid component on mobile devices. It is a best practice to write much code compatible across Web, desktop and mobile platforms as possible in order to reduce the effort necessary to perform future migrations. In this sense, although the meta-search engine developed in this case study is a Web tool, the List control is used with the aim of maintaining compatibility across the AIR™ platforms. In this sense, considering that all the list-based components use an item renderer to control the display of the data items in the list, a custom item renderer that enables the List to display a group of data items in a single cell must be defined. In detail, these data items are the title, upload date and thumbnail of each video entity returned by the REST-based Web services used.

In order to display HTML-based content in a Flex-based AIR™ application, the HTML component or the HTMLLoader class can be used. The former, which is part of the MX component architecture, is not available for developing Web and mobile applications. On the other hand, the latter is part of the AIR™ SDK, and it defines a type of display object that is a container for HTML-based content giving close integration and script bridging between ActionScript and JavaScript. Nevertheless, the features of the HTMLLoader class are only supported by desktop operating systems; thereby, this class cannot be used for developing mobile applications. There is another class called StageWebView which provides a simple means to display HTML-based content on devices where the HTMLLoader class is not supported. However, this class is not a display object and cannot be added to any Flash™ display object; therefore, the size and position of the rendering area defined by this class must be manually controlled which can require more development effort. In fact, there are third-party client libraries over Internet intended to provide a developer-friendly way to integrate this class in any Flex application[18,19]. Moreover, regardless of the application type, it is possible to display HTML content directly in a Web browser by using the navigateToURL ActionScript function.

One of the features that distinguish RIAs from traditional Web applications is the possibility of avoiding screen refreshments and blink experiences, which is well-known as visual continuity (Preciado et al., 2005). In this sense, RIAs change the content and appearance of their GUIs based on the user interaction without affecting the visual continuity. Or instance, Flex-based applications can define view states, i.e. particular views of their components by using the State class. Each custom view state can modify the default view state by adding or removing child components, by setting style and property values or by defining state-specific event handlers. In this case study, several custom view states representing the stages in the execution of the application are defined: 1) when the data are being retrieved from the Web services, 2) when the data have been displayed, 3) when the video players are being loaded and 4) when the video players have been loaded. In addition, because the user can select one of the two available sources, namely the Vimeo™ Advanced API and the YouTube™ Data API in order to search for videos, the aforementioned view states are specialized to support this behavior. In detail, the default view state of the meta-search engine only comprises a search box, a button and both check boxes. The custom view states representing the stages where the data have been loaded, add a busy indicator to the default view state for indicating that a long-running operation is in progress. This component implements a type of feedback

Figure 1. Search results from YouTube™ displayed

Figure 2. Loading search results from both Vimeo™ and YouTube™

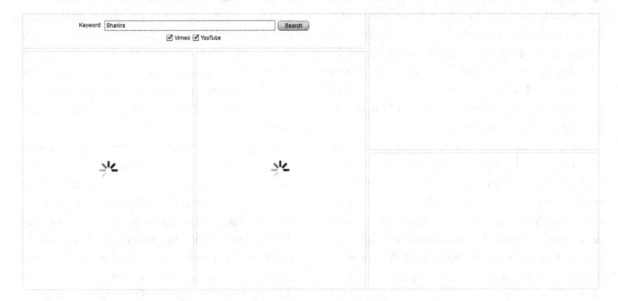

pattern known as progress indicator which provides a means to design reactive GUIs. Although Flex provides a BusyIndicator component as part of the Spark components architecture, it can only be used in AIR™ mobile applications.

Therefore, in this case study, an animated GIF file containing a rotating spinner is used. Figure 1 depicts the stage where the search results are displayed from only one source. Figure 2 depicts the stage where the search results from both sources are being retrieved.

Finally, in order to embed the YouTube™ and Vimeo™ players into the Flex-based application, the SWFLoader and SpriteVisualElement components are respectively used. Although the Vimeo™ Player class internally loads a SWF file, it inherits properties and functions from the Sprite class which is a basic display list building block appropriate for Graphical User Interface (GUI) objects that do not require timelines. Therefore, the SpriteVisualElement component must be used to add the Vimeo™ player class to the tree of MXML components. Figure 3 depicts the stage where the YouTube™ video player is being loaded. Figure

4 depicts the stage where both video players have been loaded.

3.2. Developing a Weather Forecast System

Weather forecasting is the application of science and technology to predict the state of the atmosphere for a given location. Web services have becoming more and more necessary in the área of meteorology because they allows gathering all the information from sensors and other measuring instruments about current weather conditions and bringing the weather forecasts to the people through the Web (Rambadt, 2009). Websites such as The Weather Channel's weather.com, National Weather Service's weather.gov, and AccuWeather. com are popular weather forecast websites.

3.2.1. Description of the REST-Based APIs Used

According to ProgrammableWeb.com website, the Weather Channel™'s Weather API and the National Weather Service's National Digital

Figure 3. Loading the YouTube™ video player

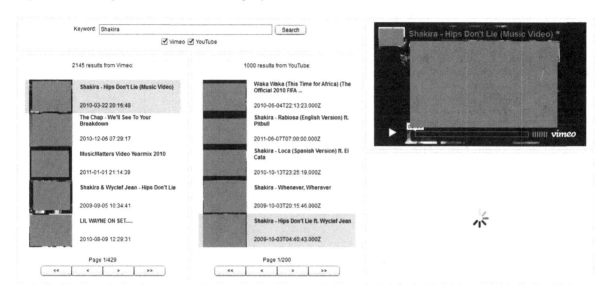

Figure 4. Video players loaded

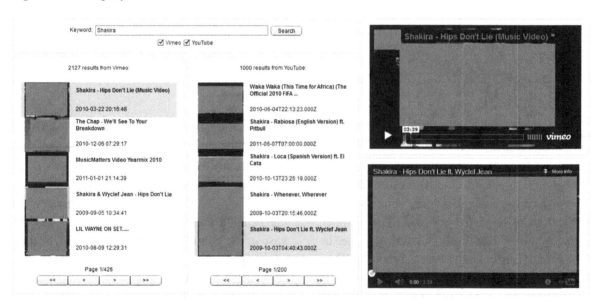

Forecast Database SOAP Web service are the two most popular weather APIs. Nevertheless, for the purpose of this case study and with the aim of providing not only weather information but also geographical information about a given location, the Yahoo! GeoPlanet™ API and the Yahoo!™ Weather RSS Feed were considered. In fact, the former provides an open infrastructure for geo-referencing data on Internet. On the other hand, the latter, is the fifth most popular weather API according to ProgrammableWeb.com[20]. Finally, in order to complement the geographical information provided, the Google Maps™ API was used for embedding the maps of the given locations. The

Table 3. REST-based APIs used for developing a weather forecast system

API	Description	Base URI	Supported Result Format	Supported HTTP Methods	Official Libraries
Yahoo! GeoPlanet™	It is a resource for managing all geo-permanent named places on earth. It enables getting collections of resources such as continents, oceans, seas and countries as well as places matching a query string. It also allows getting a place resource starting from a Where On Earth ID (WOEID)[21].	http://where.yahooapis.com/ v1	XML, JSON and GeoJSON	GET	-
Yahoo! ™ Weather RSS Feed	It enables getting up-to-date weather information about wind, atmospheric conditions and astronomical conditions for specific locations starting from their WOEID[22].	http://weather.yahooapis.com/ forecastrss	RSS	GET	-
Google Maps™ JavaScript API v3	It lets embedding Google Maps™ in any Web page. It is applicable to application for both desktop and mobile devices. This API provides diverse utilities for manipulating maps just like on the Google Maps™ website, and it also lets adding content such as zoom controls, position markers and polylines to the maps through a variety of services[23].	http://maps.google.com/maps/ api/js	-	-	-

main features of the APIs used in this case study are described in Table 3.

Regarding to the requirements of using the Yahoo!™ APIs, an application ID must be obtained by registering some information about both the application to be developed and the developer at the Yahoo!™ Developer Network website. In this sense, it is necessary to use a Yahoo!™ ID to sign into Yahoo!™; a Facebook™ or Google™ account can be alternatively used. The Yahoo! GeoPlanet™ Web service is in accordance with the REST architectural elements; therefore, it comprises collections of resources such as places, continents, oceans, seas and countries. Subsets of these collections can be retrieved by using filter parameters. For instance, the places collection, which is the collection used in this case study, can be filtered by using the name, WOEID and type filters. Additionally, other name-value pair pa-

rameters related to paging and required languages and result formats can be specified. In fact, the application ID must be added to the base URI of the Yahoo! GeoPlanet ™ Web service as a mandatory name-value pair parameter, filter parameters can be additionally added to the base URI. In the case of the Yahoo!™ Weather RSS Feed, instead of the application ID, the WOEID of the location for which the weather forecast is required must be added to the base URI as a mandatory parameter. In the case of Google Maps™, an API for Flash™ is offered; however, it is officially deprecated in favor of the JavaScript API. Actually, the API for Flash™ has a client library composed of two SWC files: an SWC file for using within a Flex application and an SWC file for use within a Flash™ CS3 application. This client library requires the usage of an API key which had to be specified as a property of a Map MXML component. The

JavaScript API also requires the usage of an API key which can be obtained in the Google™ APIs Console accessing with a Google™ account.

Regarding to the result formats supported by the above APIs, the Yahoo! GeoPlanet™ Web service has support for three different formats: XML, JSON and GeoJSON. The latter is a dialect of JSON that can be used to represent geographical features. On the other hand, the Yahoo!™ Weather RSS Feed returns RSS 2.0 feeds in response to requests.

3.2.2. Implementation Details

A feed from Yahoo!™ Weather RSS Feed has an element containing current conditions data and an element containing two-day forecast data for a given location. These data are also provided together as HTML-based content ready to be displayed. The HTML-based content can be the easiest way to display the weather information in a Flex-based application; however, because this information comprises images for depicting the textual descriptions of conditions, the HTML-based content cannot be properly displayed in MXML components such as the HTML component. In this sense, the simple data is used in this case study to build textual HTML strings to be displayed by using the MXML Text component. The Text component is part of the Flex MX components architecture, and it allows displaying multiline noneditable text which can be formatted by using HTML tags. The images, in turn, are displayed by using the Image MXML component which allows importing local or remote images files at runtime. In addition, the units used for measuring the temperature can be changed at runtime from Fahrenheit to Celsius or vice versa by using the Flex CheckBox component. When the degrees units are specified also all other units such as speed units in the case of wind velocity are properly changed from English units to metric units and vice versa.

In order to retrieve data from external sources by using the HTTPService class, result and fault event listeners must be settled up. A result event is a type of event represent by the ResultEvent class, which indicates an RPC operation has successfully returned a result whereas a fault event is a type of event represented by the FaultEvent class, which is dispatched when a RPC call has a fault. From a usability perspective, error messages are the means of informing to users about unexpected conditions. In this sense, the Flex Alert component represents the primary way to keep the user informed about what is going on. The Alert component is a modal pop-up dialog box that can contain a title, a message, an icon and buttons. In fact, this component implements the dialog overlay interaction design pattern which is a replacement of the old style Web browser pop up (Scott & Neil, 2009). In this case study, the Alert component is used for displaying error messages related to the faults occurring when the REST-based Web services are called. In addition to the error messages, the Alert component is used to display information messages related to the searches that do not return matches. Figures 5-6 depict the use of the dialog overlay interaction pattern for displaying error messages.

Typically, when a collection of resources is requested to a REST-based API, the response contains an element describing the amount of results returned by the query. These data can be retrieved in order to calculate the amount of result pages to be offered to the user. Nevertheless, some APIs calculate the amount of available result pages starting from a parameter that indicates the amount of results required in the response. This parameter must be added to the base URI along with the parameter that indicates the amount of results to be skipped, i.e. the index of the first matching result that must be included in the response. Nevertheless, some APIs calculate the start index by themselves. In these cases, a parameter indicating the result page to be returned by the API must be added to the base URI. In this case

Figure 5. "No matching places found" error message

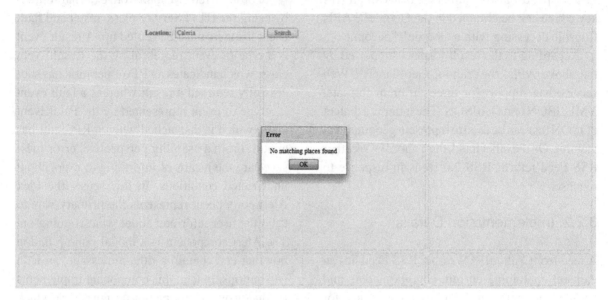

Figure 6. "No weather information available for this location" error message

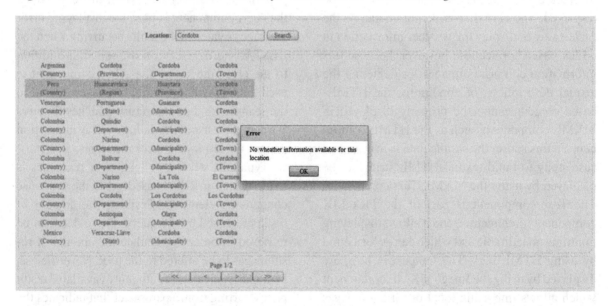

study, once the amount of available result pages has been calculated, a pagination bar that allows navigating through the result pages is displayed. This pagination bar is based on the Flex Button-Bar component which defines a horizontal row of related buttons with a common appearance, and it implements the inline paging interaction pattern proposed by Bill Scot and Theresa Neil. An inline paging experience can be created by only switching the area of search results and leaving the rest of the application stable. Figure 7 depicts the use of the inline paging interaction pattern to let users navigate through the results returned by the Yahoo! GeoPlanet™ Web service.

Figure 7. Using the inline paging interaction pattern

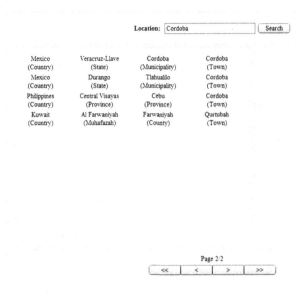

Figure 8. Weather information displayed

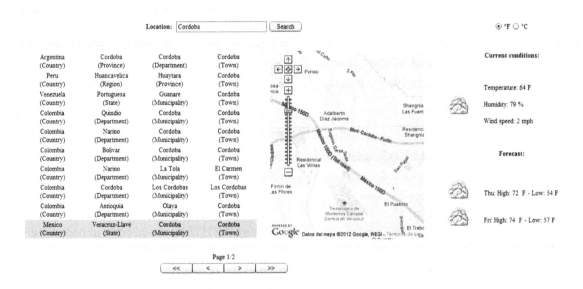

Finally, in order to embed the maps of the given locations into the weather forecast system, a container for HTML-based content must be used. For this purpose the HTML component, the HTMLLoader class and the StageWebView class are available because the weather forecast system is a Flex desktop application. In this case study, the HTMLLoader class was used with the aim of enabling a script bridge between the JavaScript definitions in the Google Maps™ JavaScript API and the ActionScript definitions in the Flex-based application. In detail, the Google Maps™ JavaScript API is loaded into a local HTML Web page by specifying the http://maps.google.com/

maps/api/js URI in the src attribute of the HTML *script* element. Then, the HTML Web page is loaded into an HTMLLoader object by passing a URLRequest object to the load function which not only displays the HTML-based content but it also loads all the JavaScript definitions contained. The maps are loaded by calling a JavaScript function through the HTMLLoader's window property which represents a global JavaScript object for the content loaded into the HTMLLoader object. This JavaScript function receives the latitude and longitude coordinates of the location to be displayed on the map. These coordinates are returned as part of the Yahoo! GeoPlanet™ Web service responses. Figure 8 depicts a screenshot of the weather forecast system displaying the weather information and Google Maps™ map for a given location.

4. CONCLUSION

Flex uses the Remote Procedure Call (RPC) protocol to provide great integration with server-side technologies like PHP, Microsoft ASP.NET and Java. These technologies can be used in conjunction with SQL databases to develop data-intensive RIAs. Moreover, ActionScript classes such as URLRequest and URLLoader and MXML components such as HTTPService also can be used to access REST-based Web services. These ActionScript classes allow formatting the data returned in the Web services responses according to the formats specified in the requests. For this purpose, ActionScript XML, XMLNode and Object classes can be used. In addition, there is an ActionScript JSON built-in parser as part of the Flash™ Player 11 API. Atom and RSS-formatted responses can be manipulated by using the ActionScript XML or XMLNode classes because these syndication formats are XML dialects. Moreover, the ActionScript Array class can be used to format responses with the aim of binding the data to MXML components such as the DataGrid and List components. In fact, these components use an Array wrapper object such as an ArrayCollection or ArrayList object as data provider.

The AIR™ API provides great integration with other client-side technologies such as HTML and JavaScript. Regarding to the HTML support there are different MXML components that allows easily displaying HTML-formatted strings like the HTML, Text, Label and TextArea components of the MX components architecture. However, the last two components are deprecated in favor of the corresponding Spark Label and TextArea components which require more effort in order to display the HTML content, namely the use of TextFlow objects. In fact, the ActionScript TextFlow class is responsible for managing all the text added to the text-based components supporting the Adobe™'s Text Layout Framework text engine. ActionScript classes such as HTMLLoader and StageWebView, on the other hand, allows both loading HTML-formatted strings as well as loading local and remote HTML Web pages. In addition, these classes load the JavaScript definitions within the HTML Web pages, and they allow both calling JavaScript functions and passing values between ActionScript and JavaScript. Moreover, unlike the HTMLLoader class, the StageWebView class is supported on mobile devices besides desktop operating systems. Nevertheless, unlike the HTMLLoader class, the StageWebView class requires more effort in order to display the HTML-based content because it is not a display object. Therefore, the size and position of the rendering area defined by this class must be manually controlled. It is important to notice that, neither the HTMLLoader class nor the StageWebView class can be used for developing Web applications. Therefore, the script bridging between ActionScript and JavaScript must me enabled by adding the JavaScript definitions to the HTML wrapper used for displaying the Flex Web application and accessing it via the ActionScript ExternalInterface class.

REFERENCES

Fielding, R. T. (2000). *Architectural styles and the design of network-based software architectures.* (PhD dissertation). University of California, Irvine, CA.

Preciado, J. C., Linaje, M., Sanchez, F., & Comai, S. (2005). Necessity of methodologies to model Rich Internet Applications. In *Proceedings of the Seventh IEEE International Symposium on Web Site Evolution* (pp. 7–13). Washington, DC: IEEE Computer Society. doi:10.1109/WSE.2005.10

Rambadt, M. (2009). *Monitoring of Web Services Using UNICORE 6 as an Example.* (MS thesis). Aachen University of Applied Sciences, Aachen, Germany. Retrieved November 30, 2012, from http://www.ibm.com/developerworks/aix/library/au-aem_rest/

Scott, B., & Neil, T. (2009). *Designing Web Interfaces: Principles and Patterns for Rich Interactions.* O'Reilly Media.

Search Engine Mashup. (2007, July 6). *EurekAlert.org*. Retrieved November 16, 2012, from http://www.eurekalert.org/pub_releases/2007-07/ip-sem070407.php

ADDITIONAL READING

Accesing JavaScript Functions. (n.d.). *Adobe™ help*. Retrieved November 23, 2012, from http://help.adobe.com/en_US/flex/using/WS2d-b454920e96a9e51e63e3d11c0bf626ae-7fe8.html

Neil, T. (2009). Designing Rich Applications. *Slideshare™ Website*. Retrieved May 28, 2012, from http://www.slideshare.net/theresaneil/designing-rich-applications

Noble, J., Anderson, T., Braithwaite, G., Casario, M., & Tretola, R. (2010). *Flex 4 Cookbook*. O'Reilly Media.

Richardson, L., & Ruby, S. (2007). *Restful Web Services*. O'Reilly Media.

Tomayko, R. (2004). How I Explained REST to My Wife. *Ryan Tomayko website*. Retrieved November 23, 2012, from http://tomayko.com/writings/rest-to-my-wife

Using WebService Components. (n.d.). *Adobe™ help*. Retrieved November 23, 2012, from http://help.adobe.com/en_US/Flex/4.0/AccessingData/WS2db454920e96a9e51e63e3d11c0bf69084-7fdb.html

KEY TERMS AND DEFINITIONS

Application Programming Interface Client Library: A wrapper for a RESTful API; it is written in a specific programming language.

Desktop RIA: A kind of out-of-browser RIA that can consistently run on multiple operating systems.

Interaction Design Pattern: A kind of user interface pattern aimed at achieving effective user experiences, i.e., rich interactions.

Meta-Search Engine: A type of search engine that relies on other search engines so that the result of a query is the result of aggregating the responses from the underlying search engines.

Representational State Transfer-Based Web Service: A Web service that adheres to the Representational State Transfer (REST) constraints. REST is a hybrid architectural style derived from several network-based architecture styles and combined with additional constraints that defines a uniform connector interface. It is a new approach to develop and deliver Web services.

Rich Internet Application: Applications that are deployed over the Web; this type of applications combines features and functionality of Web applications and desktop applications.

Web Feed: A document that contains content items and the links to the sources of the items on the Web. It is used to deliver frequently updated content from RESTful APIs to developers. The two major Web feed formats are RSS and Atom.

ENDNOTES

[1] http://www.adobe.com/products/flex.html

[2] http://www.adobe.com/devnet/flex.html

[3] http://incubator.apache.org/flex/index.html

[4] http://help.adobe.com/en_US/FlashPlatform/reference/actionscript/3/mx/rpc/http/HTTPService.html

[5] http://help.adobe.com/en_US/FlashPlatform/reference/actionscript/3/flash/net/URLRequest.html

[6] http://help.adobe.com/en_US/FlashPlatform/reference/actionscript/3/flash/display/Loader.html

[7] http://help.adobe.com/en_US/FlashPlatform/reference/actionscript/3/mx/controls/SWFLoader.html

[8] http://help.adobe.com/en_US/FlashPlatform/reference/actionscript/3/flash/net/URLLoader.html

[9] http://help.adobe.com/en_US/FlashPlatform/reference/actionscript/3/flash/net/URLStream.html

[10] http://help.adobe.com/en_US/FlashPlatform/reference/actionscript/3/flash/net/FileReference.html

[11] http://www.programmableweb.com/apis/directory/1?apicat=Video

[12] http://www.alexa.com/siteinfo/youtube.com

[13] http://www.alexa.com/siteinfo/Vimeo.com

[14] https://developer.vimeo.com/apis/advanced

[15] https://developer.vimeo.com/player/as-api

[16] https://developers.google.com/youtube/2.0/developers_guide_protocol_audience

[17] https://developers.google.com/youtube/flash_api_reference

[18] http://soenkerohde.com/2010/11/air-mobile-stagewebview-uicomponent/

[19] http://www.judahfrangipane.com/blog/2011/01/16/stagewebview-uicomponent/

[20] http://www.programmableweb.com/apis/directory/1?apicat=Weather

[21] http://developer.yahoo.com/geo/geoplanet/guide/

[22] http://developer.yahoo.com/weather/

[23] https://developers.google.com/maps/documentation/javascript/tutorial

Chapter 11
Case Studies Using JavaFX™

ABSTRACT

JavaFX™ 2.0 is the evolution of the Java programming language as a rich client platform. JavaFX™ platform provides multiple advantages to Java developers and companies that are part of the Java ecosystem, including the ability to leverage existing Java skills and development tools, as well as extending Swing applications, thus providing a migration path towards more modern and flexible User Interface (UI) technologies. This chapter first goes in depth on the JavaFX architecture and describes the benefits of using JavaFX to develop highly interactive Web applications; then, it presents four case studies on the development of JavaFX™-based Rich Internet Applications (RIAs) built on top of popular social networking services. For each case study, reviews of some similar real world implementations publicly available on the Internet are provided.

1. INTRODUCTION

JavaFX™ 2.0 is the evolution of the Java programming language as a rich client platform. It was designed to provide a modern Java-based environment that shortens the development time and eases the deployment of data driven business and enterprise client applications. The JavaFX™ platform enables application developers to easily create and deploy Rich Internet Applications (RIA) that behave consistently across multiple platforms. Built on Java-based technology, the JavaFX™ platform provides a rich set of graphics and media API with high performance hardware-accelerated graphics and media engines that simplify the development of data-driven enterprise client applications. JavaFX™ platform provides multiple

advantages to Java developers and companies that are part of the Java ecosystem, including the ability to leverage existing Java skills and development tools, as well as extending Swing applications, thus providing a migration path towards more modern and flexible UI technologies.

The JavaFX™ API enables developers to create UIs that seamlessly work across different devices. The common profile of the JavaFX™ API includes classes that function on both the desktop and mobile devices. However, additional classes and packages can be used from the desktop profile to take advantage of specific functionality that can enhance desktop applications.

JavaFX™ was announced on May 2007 at the "World Wide JavaOne Developer" conference by Sun Microsystems in order to help content

DOI: 10.4018/978-1-4666-6437-1.ch011

developers and application developers to build Rich Internet Applications on mobile devices, desktops, televisions and other consumer devices. At December 4, 2007 was launched the first version of this technology that initially consisted of JavaFX™ Mobile platform and JavaFX™ Script language. JavaFX™ 2.0 has new features which its predecessor lacked; the main features are listed below:

- **Java APIs for JavaFX™:** The APIs set are designed to be friendly with different Java Virtual Machine-based programming languages such as JRuby and Scala. Due to JavaFX™ capabilities are available through Java APIs, tools such as IDE, code refactoring, debuggers and analyzers can be used to develop JavaFX™-based applications.
- **A New Graphics Engine:** It handles modern graphics processing units (GPU). The basis of this new engine is a hardware accelerated graphics pipeline, called Prism, which is coupled with a windowing toolkit, called Glass. The graphics engine is the basis for current and future developments for rich graphics in a simple and fast way.
- **A New Multimedia Engine:** It supports playback of multimedia content on the Web. It provides a stable and low latency that is based on the GStreamer multimedia.
- **A Web Component:** It provides the ability to embed HTML-based content within a JavaFX™ application by using the WebKit HTML rendering technology. The view of hardware acceleration is available by using Prism.
- **An Updated Browser Plugin:** It allows loading JavaFX™ applets based on Prism.
- **Miscellaneous Components:** A wide variety of integrated controls for user interfaces, including graphics, tables, menus and panels. Furthermore, it provides an API to allow others to contribute their own user

interface controls for the user community can use them.

In the following section, the main components of the JavaFX architecture are described. This chapter presents four case studies of the development of JavaFX-based RIAs built on top of popular social networking websites. In detail, this chapter addresses the development of three photo albums based on Flickr™, Picasa™ and Photobucket™ websites, respectively. In addition, the development of a search engine for movies based on Rotten Tomatoes™ website is finally addressed.

2. JAVAFX™ ARCHITECTURE

The JavaFX™ platform is a rich client platform (RCP) built on Java-based technology and designed to allow developers to easily build and deploy Rich Internet Applications having a consistently behavior across platforms.

The Figure 1 presents the architectural components of the JavaFX™ platform which describes each component and how they are interrelated (Debnath, 2012).

JavaFX™ 2.0 is comprised of several subcomponents, including a high-performance graphics engine named Prism. Prism is the byproduct of the Mozilla Labs experiments to bridge the gap in user experience between Web and desktop applications. JavaFX™ also includes the Glass window toolkit, a media engine and a Web engine. It is responsible for showing windows (including Stage, Popup, among others), managing the event queue, passing events up to JavaFX™, and setting up timers.

- *The JavaFX™ public API* provides freedom and flexibility in creating rich client applications. Since JavaFX™ 2.0 includes the capabilities of Java platform; it can leverage the power of Java features such as annotations, multi-threading, generics, and

Figure 1. The architectural components of JavaFX™

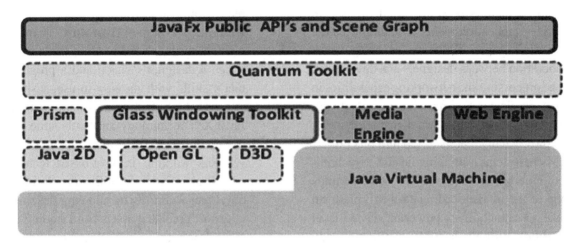

the extended Java collection library. Most of the API and programming model have been directly ported as a lineage of its predecessor, while some APIs such as Layout and Media have been optimized and simplified in response to the feedback from previous users.

- *Scene graph* is the starting point of JavaFX™ 2.0 application. It is responsible for rendering user interfaces and handling user input through various visual elements represented as hierarchical tree of nodes. Each item in the scene graph is called a node and has one parent and zero or more children. The javafx.scene API simplifies working with rich UIs.
- *The Quantum Toolkit* connects Prism and Glass Windowing Toolkit together to make them available to the JavaFX™ layer above them in the stack and it also manages the threading rules related to rendering versus events handling.
- *Prism* is responsible for rasterization and rendering of JavaFX scenes and processes rendering jobs. It can run on both hardware and software renderers, including 3-D.
- *Glass Windowing Toolkit's* main responsibility is to provide native operating servic-

es, such as managing the windows, timers and surfaces. It serves as the platform-dependent layer that connects the JavaFX™ platform to the native operating system. The Glass toolkit is also responsible for managing the event queue.

- *The Media Engine* component has been completely designed for JavaFX™ 2.0 to increase stability, improve performance and provide consistent behavior across platforms.
- *The Web Engine* component is based on Web Kit, an open source Web browser engine that supports HTML5, CSS, JavaScript, DOM and SVG. It enables developers to implement features such as rendering HTML content, support history, back and forward navigation, execute JavaScript command and event handling in their Java applications.

The JavaFX™ tools suite offers creative solutions for both developers and designers. There is a JavaFX™ Script plugin with language support for NetBeans™ IDE. The plugin enables development of JavaFX™ applications within the cross-platform NetBeans™ tools suite. In addition, Project Nile is a set of easy-to-use plugins for Adobe™ Photoshop and Adobe™ Illustrator that allow designers to export graphical assets to JavaFX™ applications. This tool simplifies the designer/developer workflow, enabling better collaboration between designers and developers.

The processing and networking capabilities in today's mobile handsets have the potential to deliver a new class of rich, Internet-enabled content. To allow content creators to tap into this power, Sun Microsystems is bringing JavaFX™ technology to mobile devices. JavaFX™ Mobile builds on top of the market-leading Java ME platform to take advantage of its powerful, device-level capabilities. With the Java ME platform already running on over 2 billion handsets, Sun is well positioned to establish JavaFX™ Mobile as the leading technology for rich Internet applications (RIAs) on mobile devices. The content created for JavaFX™ technology is capable of running on all the screens of different devices. This means people building content based on JavaFX™ technology for desktop, mobile phone, or other consumer devices will be able to deploy their content more broadly than with any other platform.

There are a large number of requirements for RIAs that are not met by any platform, and Sun is positioned to address these challenges. JavaFX™ technology offers a number of unprecedented advantages (Features of JavaFX):

- **Built on Java:** JavaFX™ is not starting from scratch; it is built on the Java platform (Java SE and Java ME) and leverages all the power and capabilities of the Java platform.
- **Across Devices and Screens:** JavaFX™ applications run across multiple devices and screens, including browser, desktop, mobile, TV, and more. The same JavaFX™ Script applications that run in the browser can also be deployed unmodified on the desktop.
- **Open Source:** JavaFX™ is the only non-proprietary rich client environment with

many components of the technology already available in open source.
- **Designer/Developer Workflow:** There remains a distinct need to close the gap between a designer's vision and a programmer's skills with an easy-to-use, visually accurate, high-performance suite of tools. JavaFX™ technology and tools suite empower designers to collaborate with developers working in Java-based technology. Project Nile simplifies the designer/developer workflow by allowing designers to export graphical assets from leading designer tools to JavaFX™ applications. A JavaFX™ Designer tool is planned for release in the future. The JavaFX™ Designer tool will provide a comprehensive visual design environment to allow designers to author rich, Internet-enabled content and applications without necessarily knowing the underlying JavaFX™ Script language or the specifics of the Java platform.

3. BENEFITS OF USING JAVAFX™

While Rich Internet Applications apply across a broad lattice of industries and uses, one of their primary virtues is to allow a company to reduce the complexity that stands between where they are today with their traditional Web applications and where they want to be. RIAs are consistently bringing companies closer to their vision of their application, closer to their customers, and closer to the business impact they believed the Internet could actually have on their overall business. This is expressed most clearly in what RIAs have allowed or enabled companies to do (Duhl, 2003). Companies have considered and chosen JavaFX because they believe they could:

- Develop new kinds of applications with features or capabilities that would be extremely difficult or impossible for a developer to create using traditional Web technologies.

- Engage, guide and listen to their customers on-line more intimately or more closely to how they would do it in person to increase loyalty, improve service, deepen the customer relationship, distinguish the company, or guide product development.

- Create compelling, attractive Web sites using audio, video, text and graphics that generate leads, increase sales, simplify communication and create a unique online experience worth returning to.

- Simplify typically complex processes like registration, configuration or purchasing leading to increased leads, sales, bookings, time on the site and repeat visits.

- Present information to their employees, management and partners in clear, innovative, intuitive and effective ways to increase productivity, information sharing, decision-making and competitive advantage.

- Provide an engaging, highly interactive presentation layer to underlying Web Services.

- Reduce bandwidth costs associated with frequent page refresh for high traffic sites.

- Dramatically increase sales of their products and services through their Internet channel.

- Build an engaging, highly interactive Web site or application at a reduced cost compared to using alternative Web technologies.

At a high level, RIAs can improve the overall client experience and provide the continuity that is lacking in many of today's websites. When a user arrives at a website and he is faced with the task of finding a product/service, there are really two ways this can be accomplished, by browsing or searching. If the site has a relatively small or highly focused product/service offering, then browsing can be an effective way to navigate. However, if

the retailer offers a wide variety of products, particularly ones with very different characteristics, then searching may be a more effective option. For example, in a typical HTML-based website, if a consumer searches for a product, the rigid page-by-page model means that he/she will be delivered to a new page where the search results are displayed. If he/she clicks on a specific product, then a second page is launched with the product detail. Getting back to the original search results generally means hammering on the browser's back button or re-submitting the search. With an RIA, the search function can launch results on the same page and then use modal window to display detailed product information. This keeps the context of the search visible and allows the consumer to adjust criteria on the fly and update his/her search (Simmons, 2007).

In addition, specific RIA-driven tools can be used to enhance the user experience on websites, these include (Simmons, 2007):

- **Product Selectors:** If a retailer only offers a handful of products, the location process is easy. However, when websites offer hundreds or thousands of different options, drilling down to find a specific item, in a specific color or size can be challenging. Product selectors help users sift through large volumes of data and easily narrow results down to just their area of focus. By using sliders, check boxes, color swatches, product comparisons and other customizations, users can search for products and then selectively narrow results to exactly find the right fit. The enhanced ability to customize views on-the-fly and provide real-time visual representations of the selected products also significantly enhances the user's shopping experience. An example of this feature is presented by using the sliders in the "Find a Diamond" application on the Amazon.com™ website.

- **Configurators:** As retailers provide customers with more personalized options, the complexity of buying an item increases significantly. Configurators allow users to build and configure their own products and to immediately visualize the customizations that they have made. Since RIAs allow page updates, they are perfect for this type of implementation as they allow images to change on-the-fly to reflect additions and updates. Configurators are very useful for complex products that offer many options and exceptions. They can be used to strategically show accessory dependencies and to up-sell additional features to clients. Product configurators can lead to both better conversion ratios and larger order sizes (thanks to the concept of bundles and add-ons that users can easily add with a few clicks). An example of this feature is presented by using sports uniform creator from Teamwork™ website.

- **Integrated Video**: Another way that retailers can enhance their website with rich media is through the addition of integrated video. Many fashion retailers are exploring adding captured video from fashion shows to their sites for consumers to view at their leisure. This presentation of complete looks, often with overlays that provide detailed product info and a "buy it now" option, encourages the purchase of multiple items at once. In addition to fashion, integrated video can also be used to: 1) leverage advertising footage, 2) blend in lifestyle elements (such as sports footage) to make the website more sticky, 3) provide guidance, how-to's or instructions for the products. An example of this feature is presented by using the RL Style Guide that is a mini application that is embedded into the Ralph Lauren™ website.

- **Visualization:** Similar to the above examples, visualization tools allow users to re-ally see what they are buying. For example, if a retailer sells rugs and flooring, it may be challenging to drive buyers through the purchase process without seeing a sample and showing them how the floor will look in their home. Visualization tools allow users to choose a room that is similar to theirs, or even upload a photo of their own room, and virtually apply the floor to exactly see how the room will look. Tools such as this not only get the consumer more involved with a brand, and therefore more committed to the sale; they also increase conversion and reduce returns. An example of this feature is presented by browsing the Shaw Floors Idea™ Gallery website.

- **Add-Ons:** These add-ons can complement a retail strategy by adding more touch points and providing dedicated customers with the opportunity to further engage with a brand. From notifying users when new products are added to the site, to pushing out special offers or even collecting client information, these desktop widgets can provide a new level of interaction and relationship building. An example of this feature is presented by installing eBay™ Desktop that runs off the user's desktop and updates whenever an internet connection is available.

- **Full Site Revamp:** A final option for adding richness for a website in order to enhance the user experience comes with a full site revamp. If a retailer has a proprietary solution in place that does not have an open architecture, it may be challenging to embrace some of the other options presented.

These features were taken into account in order to develop a set of Web-based applications by using the JavaFX™ programming language. In the following sections, different case studies of using

Table 1. Third-party Flickr APIs

Actionscript	C	Java	PHP	Ruby
Flasrh **AS3 Flickr Lib**	Flickrcurl	Flickrj Flickr-jAndroid Jickr	phpFlickr Phlickr PEAR::Flickr_API	Flickraw Flickr.rb RFlickr

JavaFX™ as a way of building highly interactive Web applications are presented.

4. DEVELOPING A PHOTO ALBUM BY USING FLICKR™

Flickr™ is an image hosting and video hosting website, web services suite, and online community that was created by Ludicorp™ in 2004 and acquired by Yahoo! ™ in 2005. Flickr™ is a great website for hosting family photos, vacation photographs, weddings photos, or any image collection intended to be shared with friends or family. Flickr™ popularity is largely due to its ability to manage images using tools that allow authors to label their pictures and explore and comment on other users' images. The Flickr™ API is available for non-commercial use by outside developers. Commercial use is possible by a prior arrangement (USF College of Education, n.d.).

The Flickr™ API is available in three request formats: 1) REST, 2) XML-RPC and 3) SOAP. In addition, the Flickr™ API has support for five different response formats: 1) REST, 2) XML-RPC, 3) SOAP, 4) JSON and 5) PHP.

To perform an action by using the Flickr™ API, a request must be built and sent it to an entry point. This request includes some parameters and methods to be invoked. The invocation result is a formatted response. All the requests include some parameters; some examples of them are listed below.

- **method:** This mandatory parameter is used to specify the method call.

- **api_key:** This mandatory parameter is used to specify the API key to be used.
- **format:** This optional parameter is used to specify a response format.

A usage example is presented in the following URL:

```
http://api.flickr.com/ser-
vices/rest/?method=search&api_
key=A3344DSLÑSDS&format=JSON
```

The parameters, format responses and error codes for each method are listed in the API documentation available at the Flickr™ website. Furthermore, there are some Flickr™ APIs developed by third parties, however Flickr™ is not responsible of their operation. Some of these APIs are listed in Table 1.

For developing a JavaFX™-based photo album, the flickr.photo.search method is required. This method returns a list of photos matching some criteria. Only photos visible to the calling user are returned. To return private or semi-private photos, the caller must be authenticated with 'read' permissions, and have permission to view the photos. Unauthenticated calls will only return public photos. Some parameters for this method are listed in table 2.

A usage example is presented in the following URL:

```
http://api.flickr.com/servic-
es/rest/?method=flickr.photos.
search&api_key=c953fff5d22c9cd6f
57d7501d04d1921&text=Giner&per_
page=10&page=3
```

Table 2. Parameters for the Flickr API fllickr.photo.search method

Parameter	Mandatory	Default value	Description
api_key	Yes	None	Application key assigned in the registration process
user_id	No	None	If this parameter is specified, then the application searches photos by this user
Tags	No	None	It returns photos that match the tags delimited by commas
text	Yes	None	It allows searching text on the photos located in the title, description and tags
min/max_upload_date	No	None	It specifies time periods in which the pictures were uploaded
licence	No	All	It specifies the license type
sort	Yes	date-posted-asc	It specifies the list order to be returned. It can be date-posted, date-taken, interestingness and relevance
privacy_filter	No	1	It returns photos that match a desired level of privacy applied when the user was authenticated
bbox	No	None	It is used to define geo-tag photos as coordinates
safe_search	No	3	Safe Search, 1 for safe, 2 for moderate
media	Yes	All	Filter by media type. The allowed values are all, photos and videos
per_page	Yes	100	Number of photos to be returned per page. Maximum value is 500
page	Yes	1	The results page to be returned

Regarding to implementation details, all the sample applications developed in this chapter implement some interaction design patterns (see chapter 8). For instance, they implement the brighten and dim interaction design pattern by means of the so-called lightbox effect technique. The lightbox effect is used to focus the user's attention on a pop-up dialog box (a dialog overlay) by dimming down the parent window (background). At the same time, it allows reinforcing modality; in fact, it is commonly used with modal pop-up boxes, i.e., pop-up dialog boxes that do not enable users to interact with their parent windows. In addition, the sample applications developed throughout this chapter also implement the inline paging interaction design pattern because they show a set of search results (a page of results) at a time, i.e., they allow switching between sets of search results while keeping the remain of the application (search panel) stable.

In addition, these sample applications exemplify other factors affecting three of the distinguishing features of RIAs, namely, enhanced GUI, client and server-side business logic and sophisticated mechanisms for client-server communication (Toffetti et al., 2011). In fact, taking advantage of the JavaFX™ support for client-side business logic and the Java SE support for asynchronous HTTP requests, these sample RIAs implement a single-page navigation model in order to preserve the visual continuity of their GUIs.

In detail, the photo albums developed in this chapter are composed of three main components: 1) a search panel, 2) a results panel and 3) a modal pop-up box by using the lightbox technique. The pop-up dialog box is a JavaFX™ *VBox* layout which actually has the same size that the top level container of the application, the *Stage* container. In this case, the modality is not an issue because it is achieved by overlaying a pop-up dialog box that actually has the same size than the parent window so that the user can not interact with the parent window until the pop-up dialog box is removed. In detail, the pop-up dialog box displays a centered full-size image of the thumbnail selected from the results panel. This full-size image is based on the JavaFX™ *ImageView* control. In addition, the background color of the pop-up dialog box is settled to black and, at the same time, the opacity is adjusted to 0.5 by using the *opacity* property inherited from the JavaFX™ *Node* class in order to make the pop-up dialog box translucent. The results panel is composed of a JavaFX™ *TilePane* layout arranging results (thumbnails) in eight columns and five rows where each cell contains an *ImageView* control displaying the corresponding thumbnail. The results panel also contains a JavaFX™ *HBox* layout which in turn contains the typical paging controls (next and previous controls); these paging controls are actually JavaFX™ *Button* controls. It should be noticed that, although JavaFX™ provides a *Navigation* control which has built-in functions for navigating through multiple pages of content, the sample applications developed in this chapter use a custom navigation control representing a lightweight version of the JavaFX™ *Navigation* control. In fact, the JavaFX™ *Navigation* control comprises both a content area and a navigation area; the navigation area contains in turn a next page button, a previous page button, a selected page label as well as a configurable set of page indicator buttons which directly allows navigating to a particular page of content.

The functionality of the photo albums developed in this chapter describes a workflow where the functions are executed in a sequential way as follows: 1) a keyword is entered into the text field and the search button is clicked, 2) the corresponding URI is generated and the request is sent to the underlying Web service engine, 3) the document containing the corresponding results is loaded and it is properly processed in order to retrieve the data to be presented to the user; the relevant data (thumbnails) are displayed on the results panel, 4) the user selects a result from the results panel and a modal pop-up box containing more detailed information (a full-size image) about the result is automatically displayed.

It is important to notice that all the sample applications preferably use the XML-based result format to retrieve data from the underlying Web services engine. Finally, it should be noticed that, unlike JavaFX™ version 1.x, JavaFX™ version 2.x does not have special support for synchronous and asynchronous HTTP requests as a means to invoke REST-based Web services. At this point, standard Java features must be used for this purpose. In this sense, the analysis of the Java APIs related to HTTP request/response handling is out of the scope of this chapter and it is not subsequently addressed.

In the specific case of the Flickr™-based photo album developed in this section, it allows users to search for images hosted on Flickr™ and it displays both a thumbnail and a full-size image for each result retrieved. The initial state of the GUI of the Flickr™-based photo album developed by using JavaFX™ is depicted in Figure 2. This GUI is composed of the aforementioned search and results panels. In addition, unlike the other photo albums developed in this chapter, the search panel of the Flickr™-based photo album includes a set of sort fields that allows retrieving search results sorted by date, relevancy and interestingness. Figure 3 depicts the usage of the Flickr™-based photo album on searching dog images by entering the "mastin napolitano" keyword. Finally, the usage of the Flickr™-based photo album on displaying the full-size image of a thumbnail (image entitled "Mi nena") selected from the results panel is depicted in Figure 4. This functionality represents the second state of the GUI of the Flickr™-based photo album.

Figure 2. Main GUI of the photo album developed for Flickr™

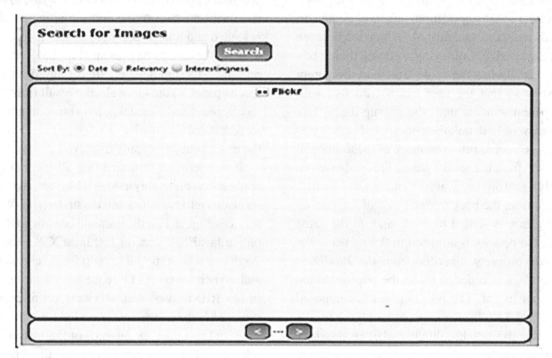

Figure 3. Searching dogs images on Flickr™ by using the photo album developed entering the "mastin napolitano" keyword

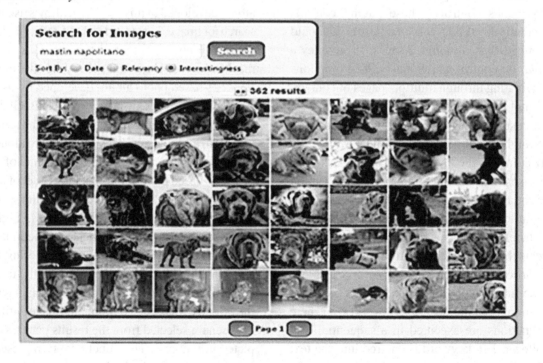

Figure 4. Preview of an image hosted on Flickr™ by using the photo album developed

Some examples of other similar Flickr™-based Tools are listed below:

- **Flickr's Badge Maker** (http://flickr.com/badge_new.gne): It allows creating either an HTML-based or Flash™-based badge for a website.
- **fd's Flickr Toys** (http://bighugelabs.com/flickr/): This website has a great collection of different tools that can be used with a Flickr™ account. It allows creating motivational posters, a magazine cover, and more.
- **Preloadr** (http://preloadr.com/): An image editing tool for Flickr™ images. Preloadr allows adjusting the brightness, color balance, sharpness, and more. It can also be used to crop images. Preloadr uses a Flickr™ account.

5. DEVELOPING A PHOTO ALBUM BY USING PICASA™

Picasa™ is an image organizer and image viewer for organizing and editing digital photos, plus an integrated photo-sharing website, originally created by a company named Lifescape™. Since 2004, this web application was owned by Google™. The Picasa™ Web Albums Data API allows for websites and programs to integrate with Picasa™ Web Albums, enabling users to create albums, upload and retrieve photos, comment on photos, and more. Some developers have done some actions with the API which are listed below:

- Created applications to easily upload photos from devices, desktop applications, and other web services.
- Created full-featured mobile clients for browsing and uploading to Picasa™ Web Album.
- Integrated Picasa™ Web Album with blogging software to easily show Picasa™ Web Album albums and photos.
- Used Picasa™ Web Album to power digital photo frames.

Picasa™ offers two APIs (Indiana University, 2009):

- **Picasa Button API:** This API allows adding own button to Picasa™ and enables end users to export images from Picasa™ into another application or service with one click. The Picasa™ user interface (UI) includes custom buttons which can open image files in local applications and upload the selected image files to the web by using the Picasa™ Web Uploader.

- **Picasa Web Uploader API:** In combination with the Picasa™ Button API, this API allows users to upload photos to a web service after seeing a webpage preview of the images they have chosen to upload. Uploader API. The Picasa™ Web Uploader (PWU) enables end users to upload photos from Picasa™ to online services such as web-based email, blogging, gallery display, and photo printing services. With PWU, end users can interact with a dynamic web UI and preview images before sending photo data. PWU is a stateless API, which gives the developers and IT administrators the ability to control what images are uploaded (and at what sizes) via server settings. This API has support for uploading video files.

In order to exemplify the capabilities of JavaFX™, a sample RIA by using the Picasa™ Web albums API was developed in this section. This application allows users to search for images hosted on Picasa™ and it displays both a thumbnail and a full-size image for each result retrieved. As all the photo albums developed in this chapter, this application has the structure and functionality previously described in section 11.4. Table 3 summarizes the parameters for the search method of the Picasa™ Web albums API.

Figure 5 depicts the usage of the Picasa™-based photo album on searching images by entering the "pico de orizaba" keyword. In addition, the usage of the Picasa™-based photo album on displaying the full-size image of a thumbnail (image entitled "Pico de Orizaba 154") selected from the results panel is depicted in Figure 6. As for the other photo albums developed in this chapter, this functionality represents the second state of the GUI of the Picasa™-based photo album.

Some examples of other similar Flickr™-based Tools are listed below:

- **PicPush:** (http://blog.350nice.com/wp/products/picpush) A multimedia syndication application for Android. It au-

Table 3. Parameters for the Picasa™ Web albums API search method

Parameter	Mandatory	Default value	Description
Access	Yes	Public	This represents the element visibility
Alt	No	Atom	This allows a kind of alternative representation
Bbox	No	None	This returns results for a geographic zone of geo-tagged photos
Fields	No	None	It filters some features to be displayed in the response
Imgmax	No	Variable	It specifies the photo maximum size
Kind	Yes	All	It specifies the elements to be searched
L	No	None	It specifies the place where photos can be found .
max-results	Yes	100	Maximum number of result to be displayed
start-index	Yes	0	It represents the index of the first result to be displayed
Tag	No	Variable	It allows filtering photos according to a specific tag
Thumbsize	No	None	It specifies the thumbnail size

Figure 5. Searching images on Picasa™ by entering "Pico de Orizaba" keyword

Figure 6. Preview of an image hosted on Picasa™ by using the photo album developed

tomatically shares pictures and videos to Shutterfly™, PhotoBucket™, SmugMug™, Facebook™, Gallery™, Picasa™ and Flickr™.

- **Picasa Mobile:** (http://imprologic.com/picasa/android/) A mobile application for Android-based devices, which allows browsing and managing Picasa™ Web albums and photos. It also allows browsing and uploading local photos directly from the mobile device's camera as well as from the SD card.

- **Web Albums:** (http://www.webalbumsapp.com/) A Picasa™ Web albums and photos viewer and manager application for iOS-based devices. It also allows uploading not only photos but also videos both locally stored and captured by using the built-in camera feature. It supports offline browsing and it is Google+-compatible.

- **Picasa Tool:** (https://play.google.com/store/apps/details?id=larry.zou.colorfullife&hl=en) A multi-platform mobile application (Android and BlackBerry Tablet OS) for browsing and managing Picasa™ Web albums and photos as well as Google+™ photos either online or offline. It has photo editor capabilities including image size alteration and special effects.

6. DEVELOPING A PHOTO ALBUM BY USING PHOTOBUCKET™

Photobucket™ is an image hosting, video hosting, slideshow creation and photo sharing website. It was founded in 2003 by Alex Welch and Darren Crystal and received funding from Trinity Ventures™. It was acquired by Fox Interactive Media™ in 2007. In December 2009, Fox's parent company, News Corp sold Photobucket™ to Seattle mobile imaging startup Ontela™. Ontela™

Table 4. Third-party Photobucket™ APIs

Programming Language	API
C#	* Photobucket C#.NET * PhotobucketNet * Silverlight 2
PHP	* Zend_Service_Photobucket library * PHP5 Fluent library
Actionscript	* Actionscript 3 Photobucket API Library
Java	* Photobucket Java API
Pyhon	* Photobucket Python API
Javascript	* OAuth for WebOS
Ruby	* BitBucket Ruby
Objective-C	* BitBucket Objective-C

then renamed itself Photobucket Inc. and continues to operate as Photobucket™.

Photobucke™t provides multiple options for connecting applications or websitse to media on Photobucket™. Photobucket™ API provides API calls to connect applications to Photobucket™. It is useful when an application that requircs Photobucket™ is not displayed on the Photobucket™ interface.

Furthermore, there are some Photobucket™ APIs developed by third parties, however Photobucket is not responsible for their operation. Some of these APIs are listed in Table 4.

The Photobucket™ API allows a set of operations for:

- Uploading images.
- Uploading video.
- Getting all recent media (videos and images) for:
  ○ A specific user.
  ○ All users.
  ○ Group albums.
- Searching media matching a specific term or terms in:
  ○ One user's account.
  ○ All user accounts.
  ○ Group albums.

- Getting all details associated with one piece of media, such as:
  ◦ Link URLs.
  ◦ Thumbnail URL.
- Updating titles, descriptions, and tags.

The Photobucket™ API uses REST (Representational State Transfer) for requests and responses, so that domain-specific data can be transferred over HTTP without an additional messaging layer such as SOAP or session tracking via HTTP cookies. The REST Request Format is a simple HTTP GET, POST, PUT, or DELETE action. Any object that is associated with a user must use the URL provided by Photobucket™, via the login process or via the Get User URL method. Any object not associated with a user can use an anonymous request, sent to http://api.photobucket.com. The REST response format is a simple XML-based block that includes the action in a <method> tag: HTTP GET, POST, PUT, or DELETE. The response format can be specified in the request. The default response format is XML. All responses are wrapped in a "response envelope" that contains:

- "status" The response status.
- "format" The current format.
- "method" The method that was used to request.
- "timestamp" The timestamp of the request.
- "content" - The contents of the response.

The Search method is one of the main methods of the Photobucket™ API. This method provides a set of operations which are listed below:

- **Search Images:** It allows searching for images.
- **Search Videos:** It allows searching for videos.
- **Search Group Albums:** It allows searching group albums for images and videos.

- **Get Featured Home Page Categories**: It gets categories featured on the home page by Photobucket™.
- **Get Featured Group Albums:** It gets a list of featured group albums.
- **Get Find Stuff Category Names:** It gets the category names for the Find Stuff page.
- **Get Find Stuff Category Media:** It gets media in a specific category or featured media for all categories.
- **Follow a Search Term:** It allows searching for a term and follow the results.
- **Stop Following a Search Term:** It stops following a search term.
- **Get Search Term Following Status:** It determines if a user is following a particular search term.

These operations involved on the Search method contain parameters in order to customize a particular search. Some of these parameters are listed in Table 5.

In order to exemplify the capabilities of JavaFX, a sample RIA by using the Photobucket™ API was developed in this section. This application allows users to search for images hosted on Photobucket™ and it displays both a thumbnail and a full-size image for each result retrieved. As all the photo albums developed in this chapter, this application has the structure and functionality previously described in section 11.4; nevertheless, it includes a sorting field that allows retrieving results sorted by date, restricting the results to the last 7 days.

Figure 7 depicts the usage of the Photobucket™-based photo album on searching images by entering the "gatitos" keyword. In addition, the usage of the Photobucket™-based photo album on displaying the full-size image of a thumbnail (image entitled "Gatitos") selected from the results panel is depicted in Figure 8. As for the other photo albums developed in this chapter, this functionality represents the second state of the GUI of the Photobucket™-based photo album.

Table 5. Parameters for the Photobucket™ API search method

Parameter	Mandatory	Default value	Description
Identifier	No	None	Search term. If a search term is not entered, or is "-", recent images are returned
Num	No	20	Number of results to be returned (recent). Maximum of 100
Perpage	No	20	Number of results to be returned for main search type. Maximum of 100
Page	No	1	Page number to be displayed (1 indexed)
Offset	No	(page-1)*-Perpage	Beginning offset of results
Secondaryperpage	No	5	Number of images to be showed, per page, for secondary search type
Recentfirst	No	False	It shows images from the last seven days

Figure 7. Searching images on PhotoBucket™ by entering the "gatitos" keyword

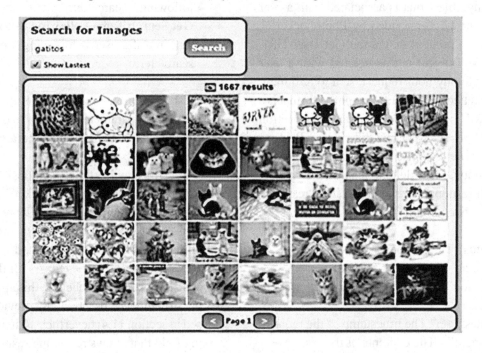

Some examples of other similar Photobucket™-based tools are listed below:

- **FotoFlexer:** (http://fotoflexer.com/) A web application (and Facebook™ application) that lets making high quality, near-Photoshop quality alterations to photos. The website evolved as a place for MySpace™ users to store and share photos.

- **Photobucket Mobile:** (http://photobucket.com/mobile) The official Photobucket™ mobile application. Thus, it lets performing most of the tasks a user can perform directly on the Photobucket™ website. In fact, it allows managing Photobucket™ accounts for locally uploading stored photos and videos, downloading photos from albums and so on.

Figure 8. Preview of an image hosted in PhotoBucket™ by using the photo album developed

- **Snapbucket:** (http://photobucket.com/ mobile) A photo editing multi-platform (Android and iOS-based mobile devices) mobile application developed by Photobucket.com, Inc. It is not only a photo editing tool; it also lets sharing the snaps by using Twitter™, Facebook™, e-mail, SMS and Photobucket™.
- **JustPictures!:** (https://play.google. com/store/apps/details?id=com. justpictures&hl=en) A multi-platform photo viewer application for Android-based mobile devices. It allows browsing and synchronizing photo albums from Picasa™, Flickr™, Smugmug™, Photobucket™, Tumblr™ and other Web 2.0 websites; it also supports locally stored photos.

7. DEVELOPING A ROTTEN TOMATOES™-BASED SEARCH ENGINE FOR MOVIES

Rotten Tomatoes™ is a website devoted to reviews, information, and news of films, widely known as a film review aggregator. The API gives access to Rotten Tomatoes' wealth of movie information, allowing anyone to build applications and widgets enriched with Rotten Tomatoes™ data. Using the API, users can, for example:

- Search for movies and retrieve detailed movie information, like cast, directors, and movie posters
- Access to the Rotten Tomatoes ™Score (aggregation of critic's scores) and the Audience Score
- Get the current box office movies, new releases, and upcoming movies

The Rotten Tomatoes™ API is RESTful web service that was designed to be easy to explore and use. The base URI to access all resources is

Table 6. Operations of the Rotten Tomatoes™ API

Operator	Description
Movies Search	The movies search endpoint for plain text queries. It allows searching for movies
Lists Directory	It displays the top level lists available in the API. There are movie lists and DVD lists available
Movie Lists Directory	It shows the movie lists available
Box Office Movies	It displays top box office earning movies, sorted by most recent weekend gross ticket sales
In Theaters Movies	It retrieves movies currently available in theaters
Opening Movies	It retrieves current opening movies
Upcoming Movies	It retrieves upcoming movies. The results are paginated if they go past the specified page limit
DVD Lists Directory	It shows the DVD lists available
Top Rentals	It retrieves the current top DVD rentals
Current Release DVDs	It retrieves current release DVDs. The results are paginated if they go past the specified page limit
New Release DVDs	It retrieves new release DVDs. The results are paginated if they go past the specified page limit
Upcoming DVDs	It retrieves new release DVDs. The results are paginated if they go past the specified page limit
Movie Info	It provides detailed information on a specific movie specified by Id. The movies search endpoint can be used or peruse the lists of movies/DVDs to get the urls to movies
Movie Cast	It pulls the complete movie cast for a movie
Movie Clips	It provides related movie clips and trailers for a movie
Movie Reviews	It retrieves the reviews for a movie. The results are paginated if they go past the specified page limit
Movie Similar	It shows similar movies for a movie
Movie Alias	It provides a movie lookup by an id from a different vendor. It only supports IMDb™ lookup at this time

http://api.rottentomatoes.com/api/public/v1.0. By using the base URI, a developer will be able to reach and manipulate without reading through multiple pages of documentation. This is accomplished by linking related resources and providing instructions on how to use each representation (link templates) in the response itself

The main operations of the Rotten Tomatoes™ API are listed in Table 6.

In order to exemplify the capabilities of JavaFX™, a sample RIA by using the Rotten Tomatoes™ API was developed. This application allows users to search for movies listed on Rotten Tomatoes™ and it displays detailed information about a particular movie including the poster and the similar movies. In detail, it is composed of four main components: 1) a search panel, 2) a results panel, 3) a details panel and 4) a modal pop-up box by using the lightbox technique. Unlike the pop-up dialog box developed for the photo albums analyzed in previous sections of this chapter, the pop-up dialog box developed for this sample RIA displays a list of other movies related to the movie is being displayed on the details panel. Both the pop-up dialog box and the results panel are based on the JavaFX™ *VBox* layout and they arrange both the movie poster and the movie title in a single column per each result. The movie titles are based on the JavaFX™ *Label* control whereas the movie posters are based on the JavaFX™ *ImageView* control. On the other hand, the details panel uses a JavaFX™ *HBox* layout to horizontally arrange the full-size movie poster and the detailed movie information which includes the release date, the film rating (Motion Picture Association of America's rating system) and the synopsis. The movie information is displayed using simple label controls. It is important to notice that, unlike other GUI controls used to display non-editable text such as the Adobe™ Flex *Label*, the JavaFX™ *Label* can be used to display multiline text labels. For this purpose, the *setWrapText( )* method which is directly inherited from the *Labeled* class must be used. The details panel also contains a JavaFX™ *Button* control which is in charge of displaying the modal pop-up box showing the movies related to the movie selected from the results panel.

The functionality of the search engine for videos developed in this section describes a workflow where the functions are executed in a sequential way as follows: 1) a keyword is entered into the text field and the search button is clicked, 2) the corresponding URI is generated and the request is sent to the underlying Rotten Tomatoes™ engine, 3) the document containing the corresponding results is loaded and it is properly processed in order to retrieve the data to be presented to the user, 4) the relevant data (thumbnail of movie posters and movie titles) are displayed on the results panel, 5) the user selects a result from the results panel and the corresponding detailed information is displayed on the details panel (a full-size movie poster, the release date, the film rating and the synopsis) and 6) the "show similar movies" button on the details panel is clicked and a modal pop-up box is displayed listing movies similar to the movie is being reviewed.

The initial state of the GUI of the Rotten Tomatoes™-based search engine developed by using JavaFX™ is depicted in Figure 9. This GUI is composed of the aforementioned search, results and details panels. Figure 10 depicts the usage of the Rotten Tomatoes™-based search engine on searching movies by entering the "the avengers" keyword. In addition, the usage of this sample application on displaying detailed information related to a previewed movie ("Marvel's The Avengers") is depicted in Figure 11. Finally, the usage of the Rotten Tomatoes™-based search engine on displaying the list of movies related to a particular movie ("Marvel's The Avengers") is depicted in Figure 12. Unlike the photo albums developed in previous sections, the second state of the GUI of the Rotten Tomatoes™-based search engine is represented by this latter functionality.

Some examples of other similar Rotten Tomatoes™-based tools are listed below:

Figure 9. Main GUI of the search engine for movies based on Rotten Tomatoes™

Figure 10. Searching movies on Rotten Tomatoes™ by using the search engine developed, entering the "the avengers" keyword

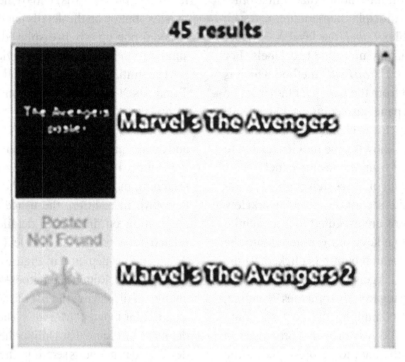

Figure 11. Displaying detailed information about the "Marvel™'s The Avengers" movie by using the search engine developed

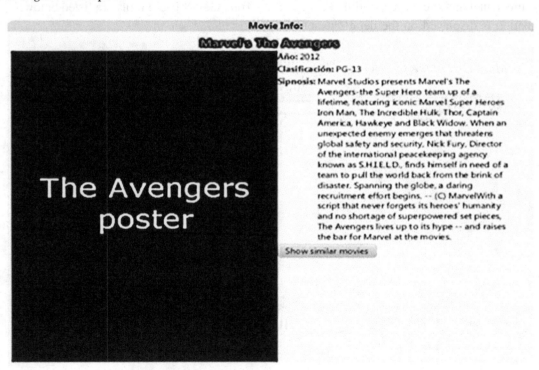

Figure 12. Displaying the list of movies related to the "Marvel™'s The Avengers" movie by using the search engine developed

- **Flixster Mobile:** (http://community.flixster.com/wap/apps) A multi-platform mobile application for streaming and downloading full-length movies. It also allows watching trailers of movies coming soon as well as getting critic reviews from Rotten Tomatoes™. In addition, it lets users browse showtimes and buy tickets at specified theatres.
- **Worth Watching:** (https://play.google.com/store/apps/details?id=com.moubry.worthwatching&hl=en) A mobile application for Android-based devices. It allows searching for movies and getting lists of now playing movies, opening soon movies and new DVD releases. It retrieves critic and audience scores as well as critic consensus from Rotten Tomatoes™.
- **TomatoFlix:** (http://rive.rs/projects/tomatoflix) A Google ™Chrome extension that lets getting Rotten Tomatoes™ critic and audience scores for Netflix™ movies while navigating the Netflix™ website.

- **On Demand Movie Reviews:** (http://www.ondemandmoviereviews.com/) A XFINITY On Demand/Rotten Tomatoes™ mash-up. It allows viewing Rotten Tomatoe™s critic and audience scores for XFINITY On Demand movies. It allows filtering reviews by movie genre, year of publication and film rating; it also lets sorting reviews by using diverse criterion including Rotten Tomatoes™ scores.

8. CONCLUSION

RIA represents the transition of web applications from the simple, thin client model to a model that provides the user experience of a desktop client/server application while leveraging the ubiquity of the Internet. Most of the standard features of RIAs can be implemented by using the capabilities of popular non-JavaScript-based RIA frameworks. For instance, the JavaFX™ framework offers: 1) a set of GUI controls intended to improve user interactions, 2) a multimedia engine supporting some container and compression formats, delivery technologies and media types, 3) a graphics engine supporting both 2-D and 3-D scene graphs and hardware acceleration and 4) a Web engine based on the Webkit Web browser engine, which provides great integration with Web technologies such as HTML5, CSS and JavaScript.

As it can be inferred from the case studies addressed throughout this chapter, it is possible to take advantage of the aforementioned capabilities in order to implement most of the distinguishing features of RIAs, especially the features related to the relevant factors on RIAs development outlined in chapter 4, namely, GUI patterns support, design patterns support and multimedia support. In addition, under the understanding that the typical architecture of RIAs has a service back-end as part of its business logic layer, the case studies addressed in this chapter exemplify the support for REST-based Web services as a new mean of delivering Web services and feeds.

REFERENCES

Debnath, M. (2012, May 3). *JavaFX 2.0: A Platform for Rich Enterprise Client Apps*. Retrieved November 26, 2012, http://www.devx.com/Java/Article/48067

Duhl, J. (2003). *Rich Internet Applications*. Framingham, MA: IDC, Inc.

Indiana University. (2009). *Google Picasa 3: The Basics*. Retrieved from http://ittraining.iu.edu/free/picba.pdf

Simmons, A. (2007). *Enhancing eCommerce ROI through Rich Internet Applications (RIAs)*. Montreal, Canada: Integration New Media, Inc.

Toffetti, G., Comai, S., Preciado, J. C., & Linaje, M. (2011). State-of-the Art and trends in the Systematic Development of Rich Internet Applications. *Journal of Web Engineering*, *10*(1), 70–86.

USF College of Education. (n.d.). *Online Photo Sharing with Flickr*. Retrieved from http://fcit.usf.edu/laptop

ADDITIONAL READING

Dea, C. (2011). *JavaFX 2.0: Introduction by Example*. Fremont, CA: Nielsen Norman Group.

Weaver, J., Gao, W., Chin, S., Iverson, D., & Vos, J. (2012). *Pro JavaFX 2: A Definitive Guide to Rich Clients with Java Technology*. Apress. doi:10.1007/978-1-4302-6873-4

KEY TERMS AND DEFINITIONS

Application Programming Interface Client Library: A wrapper for a RESTful API; it is written in a specific programming language.

Enterprise Rich Client Application: A type of rich client application specifically designed to provide business value in the context of an organization rather than a single end user.

Interaction Design Pattern: A kind of user interface pattern aimed at achieving effective user experiences, i.e., rich interactions.

Rich Client Application: An application that relies on a client/server architecture, and it executes most of its business logic operation on the client-side. For that reason, rich client applications are commonly delivered as desktop-like applications.

Rich Internet Application: Applications that are deployed over the Web; this type of applications combines features and functionality of Web applications and desktop applications.

Search Engine: A software tool designed to search for information and files. It is usually available on the Internet.

User Experience: The quality of the interaction between a user and a software application.

Chapter 12
Multi-Device RIAs Development

ABSTRACT

Web 2.0 applications are becoming ubiquitous applications (i.e., applications that can be accessed by anyone, anywhere, anytime, using any device). A key element of these ubiquitous applications is mobile devices. In fact, the involvement of mobile devices such as smartphones and tablet computers in the development of Web 2.0 applications has resulted in a new kind of Rich Internet Application (RIA) that can run on a variety of devices starting from the same code base, and it is known as multi-device RIA. The term multi-device RIA embraces not only mobile applications but also other kinds of out-of-browser applications such as cross-platform desktop applications as well as the traditional cross-browser Web applications. This chapter formalizes the concept of multi-device RIA, and then it presents an overview of the capabilities of several multi-device development frameworks. This review is finally summarized in a comparative analysis.

1. INTRODUCTION

In recent years, Web applications are becoming a common usage thanks to the great variety that they have. The new trends on RIAs development are basically divided into two aspects: 1) the cloud computing which enables the applications to be distributed and; 2) incursion of RIAs on mobile devices. The second aspect has the greatest interest in this chapter due to the large number of mobile device users and because users have greater access to mobile devices than an Internet-connected personal computer.

A mobile device is a small and hand-held computing device. Cell phones, smartphones, tablet computers and PDAs are examples of mobile devices, which can differ in the quality and range of features. For classification purposes, these devices are categorized by levels of functionality made by T38 DuPont Global Mobility Innovation Team in 2005. Under this classification, three types are well-known: 1) Limited Data Mobile Device, 2) Basic Data Mobile Device and 3) Enhanced Data Mobile Device. A mobile device with an operating system embedded almost as powerful as one of a desktop computer is included in the third category. In fact, modern mobile operating systems integrate the features of a desktop operating system with the support for touchscreen, Bluetooth, GPS, video camera, audio recorder, music player, among others.

DOI: 10.4018/978-1-4666-6437-1.ch012

Therefore, there are mobile devices with different operating systems and hardware features for all needs and budgets. This chapter presents a systematic review of multi-device RIAs development.

2. MULTI-DEVICE RIAS

Mobile devices such as smartphones and tablet computers have recently been involved in RIAs development because of the ubiquitous requirements of Web 2.0 applications (Kappel et al., 2003). In this sense, RIAs are known as multi-device RIAs. This term covers RIAs that run as cross-browser Web applications, cross-platform desktop applications and applications for diverse mobile devices.

The operating systems on mobile devices have increased in number of ways in the last couple of years. These devices are becoming more integrated with the same functionalities of a small computer. Among the variety of operating systems for mobile devices are: Android™ developed by Google™ Inc.; iOS™ developed by Apple™ Inc.; and Windows™ Phone developed by Microsoft™ to mention but a few. A brief description of the most popular mobile operating systems is presented below.

- **Android™** is a mobile operating system based on a modified Linux kernel. It was initially developed by Android™ Inc, which was purchased by Google™ in August 2005. Android™ is currently developed by a consortium of diverse hardware, software and telecommunication companies such as the Open Handset Alliance, which is led by Google™. Google™ released the Android™ source code as open source, under the Apache License V. 2. Nowadays, Android™ has the major smartphone market share worldwide, it also runs in tablet computers. Applications for Android™-

based devices are usually developed in the Java programing language by using the Android™ SDK.

- **Apple™ iOS**, formerly called iPhone™ OS, is a mobile operating system developed and distributed by Apple™ Inc. It is based on the XNU hybrid kernel which is used by the Mac OS X operating system, also property of Apple™ Inc. iOS was released under a proprietary software license, which restricts the installation to Apple™ hardware devices such as iPod Touch, iPhone, iPad and Apple™ TV. Apple™ Inc. allows third-party developers building Objective-C applications for iOS and Mac OS X operating systems by using the Xcode Integrated Development Environment (IDE) which can be only installed on Mac OS X desktop computers. However, deploying third-party applications on Apple™ devices is only possible after of paying an Apple™ developer program fee.

- **Windows™ Phone** is a mobile operating system developed by Microsoft™. It is the successor of the Windows™ Mobile platform, which was primarily aimed at the enterprise market. The latest version is called Windows™ Phone 8, which is based on the Windows™ NT hybrid kernel. Windows™ Phone was released under a proprietary software license and it is used by multiple manufacturers such as HTC Corporation, Samsung Electronics and Nokia Corporation in multiple smartphones. Moreover, Microsoft™ provides two frameworks for developing applications for Windows™ Phone-based devices: the Silverlight™ framework, which allows developing XAML-based RIAs and the XNA framework, which allows building video games for all Microsoft™ gaming platforms.

- **Symbian™** is a mobile operating system based on a real-time kernel. It is the successor of the Symbian™ OS mobile operating system developed by Symbian Ltd, which was acquired by Nokia™ Corporation. Symbian™ was created by integrating software assets such as Symbian™ OS as its core and the S60 platform for mobile phones contributed by Nokia™. Although the Symbian™ OS source code was published under an Eclipse Public License (EPL) in February 2010, it is currently released under a proprietary software license. Symbian™ remains a core part of Nokia's phone portfolio even though Nokia™ is transitioning to Windows™ Phone mobile operating system.

- **BlackBerry™ OS** is a mobile operating system developed by Research In Motion (RIM) Company. It has a kernel based on the Java Virtual Machine (JVM). BlackBerry™ OS is aimed to be run in smartphones of the RIM's BlackBerry™ line. Unlike the BlackBerry™ OS, which was released under a proprietary software license, RIM launches a series of open SDKs for developing BlackBerry™ OS applications, such as a native SDK for C/C++, an SDK for Java, an SDK for HTML5/JavaScript and an SDK for Adobe™ AIR. This platform also supports the development of applications for the BlackBerry™ PlayBook tablet, which run another operating system called BlackBerry™ Tablet OS.

- **Bada™** is a mobile operating system developed by Samsung™ Electronics. It is based on a configurable kernel architecture, which allows the use of either the Linux kernel or the real-time operating system kernel. Bada™ is extensively used in the Samsung™'s Wave line of smartphones. Samsung launched Bada™ under a proprietary software license. It also provides an open SDK for developing C/C++-based, Flash™-based and HTML/JavaScript-based applications for Bada™-based devices.

- **MeeGo™** is a free and open source operating system based on the Linux kernel, which merges the efforts of Intel™'s Moblin and Nokia™'s Maemo former operating systems and it is sponsored by the Linux Foundation. MeeGo™ was released under a GNU General Public License (GPL) V. 2. It was presented as an operating system ready to be run on netbooks, handsets, In-Vehicle Infotainment (IVI) systems, smart TVs and media phones. The main feature of MeeGo™ is the support of the x86 microprocessor instruction set architectures. In September 2011, the Linux Foundation announced that MeeGo was canceled in favor of a new project called Tizen.

- **HP™ webOS™** is a mobile operating system based on the Linux kernel initially developed by Palm™ Inc., which was acquired by Hewlett-Packard™ (HP™) in April 2010. It was released under both a proprietary software license and an Apache License V. 2. HP™ webOS™ is used on HP™'s smartphones such as the HP™ Pre 3 and the HP™ Veer, as well as on the HP™ TouchPad tablet. HP™ provides an SDK for developing HP™ webOS™ applications. It includes a framework called Enyo for developing HTML/JavaScript-based applications; also it includes libraries for developing C/C++-based applications.

RIAs for mobile devices have the same features and they are basically similar as those developed for desktop computers with the difference that RIAs for mobile devices must be properly seen on mobile Web browsers. Today, mobile applications have a wide market since the user wants to perform more activities from his or her mobile device and from anywhere he or she is. A mobile application is a software application written for a mobile device that performs a specific task, e.g. a calendar viewer, a contact list manager, a music player, among others. These applications commonly come preinstalled on devices; also they are publicly distributed and can be downloaded by users from application stores on Internet. There are basically two kinds of applications for mobile devices; (1.) native applications that are applications written for a specific device's hardware and operating system and (2.) Web-based applications. Firstly, all mobile applications were almost developed in a native way but nowadays Web-based applications are more commonly developed due to the extensive use and because it is not required to modify the source code on which they run. RIAs are also part of these Web-based applications which do not require a Web browser.

3. MULTI-DEVICE DEVELOPMENT FRAMEWORKS

Today, there are various frameworks for mobile applications, these frameworks are software platforms designed to support the development of mobile applications that are written as embedded dynamic Web sites and they can take advantage of the native capabilities of the device like geographical data or contact list. The following sections describe some of these frameworks.

3.1. PhoneGap™

It is a free framework for developing mobile applications, and it was contributed to the Apache Software Foundation (ASF) under a project called Apache Cordova; therefore, it was released as open source under the Apache License v. 2. The main objective of PhoneGap™ is the development of embedded applications. Nitobi was the original creator of PhoneGap™, and it is one of the main contributors in the development of this framework; however, there is a global community that also contributes to the project, including IBM™, Mi-

crosoft™ and RIM™ companies. In October 2011, Adobe™ acquired Nitobi enabling the team to be exclusively focused on the PhoneGap™ project.

The ease of use is one of the advantages of this framework because it does not require learning new programming languages, and it uses more known Web development technologies such as HTML and JavaScript. In terms of IDEs, the DreamWeaver™ CS 5.5 tool which is also owned by Adobe™ can be integrated with PhoneGap™. Similarly, other IDEs for device-specific programming languages such as XCode and Eclipse Classic can be used.

PhoneGap™ is one of the most popular frameworks for cross-platform development. In fact, it has been recently used by companies such as Panasonic™ Corporation, Wikipedia Foundation, Inc. and British Broadcasting Corporation (BBC™).

Moreover, there are some books published about PhoneGap™, for instance, a book entitled PhoneGap Mobile Application Development Cookbook written by Matt Gifford; a book entitled Beginning PhoneGap written by Rohit Ghatol and Yogesh Patel; and a book entitled PhoneGap Beginner's Guide written by Andrew Lunny, member of the PhoneGap development team.

The main capabilities as well as the platforms supported by this framework are presented in Tables 1 and 2, respectively. In addition, more information such as user manuals and technical documentation can be found at phonegap.com website.

3.2. Application Craft™

Application Craft™ is a cloud-based cross-platform framework for developing desktop and mobile applications. It was created by a United Kingdom company founded by Freddy May, by using pure Web technologies. Similarly, applications built on top of this framework can use the same Web standards, namely JavaScript, HTML5 and CSS3.

Application Craft™ consists of a unique Web browser-based visual IDE integrating a drag &

Table 1. Platforms for mobile applications supported by PhoneGap™

iOS™	Android™	BlackBerry™	Palm WebOS™	Symbian™	Windows™ Mobile	Others
Yes	Yes	Yes	Yes	Yes	Yes	-

Table 2. Main capabilities of PhoneGap™

Enterprise data synchronization	No
Multi-Threaded Applications	No
File uploading	Yes
Image Library Browsing	Unknown
In Application Email	Unknown
Application distribution support	No
Self-contained, no web required	Yes
Web Services	Unknown
Mobile APIs support	Unknown
Able to access the web for data	Yes
Geolocation support	Yes
Vibration support	Yes
Accelerometer support	Yes (BlackBerry requires OS 4.7)
Sound (play) support	Yes
Sound (record) support	Yes
Camera support	Yes
XMPP support	Yes
File system IO support	Yes
Gesture / Multi-touch support	Yes
Native date/time picker support	Unknown
SMS support	Yes
Telephone support	Yes
Maps support	Yes
Orientation change support	Yes
Contact support	Yes
SQLite support	Yes (not possible on BlackBerry)
Native Language Application Development support	No
Graph Library Support	Unknown

drop GUI designer, a code editor and a building tool for compiling HTML/JavaScript source code into mobile binaries. The building tool relies on a cloud service called AC Mobile Build which is based on the open source Apache Cordova project.

Regarding licensing, Application Craft™ is available as a 14-day unrestricted free trial, which can be upgraded to a lifetime edition for a per month charge. It is also released under an enterprise edition which enables developers to host the framework on the enterprises' servers. This framework is most notably used by Coca-Cola™ Enterprises and New Dimension Technology, (NDTec™) Ltd. that is a software provider for construction professionals based in South Africa.

So far, the existence of books published about this framework is unknown, however on the official website can be downloaded the manuals and the user guides needed to understand the functioning of Application Craft™.

The main capabilities as well as the platforms supported by this framework are presented in Tables 3 and 4, respectively. In addition, more detailed information can be found at application-craft.com website.

3.3. iUI™

IUI™ is a framework for developing mobile applications. This framework is free, and it is distributed under an open source MIT license. It was initially released by Joe Hewitt whit the aim of providing a GUI library for iPhone development. Nevertheless, it has support for almost all mobile platforms, the Kernel code of the framework is very light, and it has a lot of extensions and themes.

Table 3. Platforms for mobile applications supported by Craft™

iOS™	Android™	BlackBerry™	Palm WebOS™	Symbian™	Windows™ Mobile	Others
Yes	Yes	Yes	Yes	Yes	Yes	Tablet, desktop and Web environments

Table 4. Main capabilities of Craft™

Enterprise data synchronization	Yes
Multi-Threaded Applications	Unknown
File uploading	Yes
Image Library Browsing	Yes
In Application Email	Yes
Application distribution support	Yes
Self-contained, no web required	Yes
Web Services	Unknown
Mobile APIs support	Yes
Able to access the web for data	Yes
Geolocation support	Yes
Vibration support	Yes
Accelerometer support	Yes
Sound (play) support	Yes
Sound (record) support	Yes
Camera support	Yes
XMPP support	Yes
File system IO support	Yes
Gesture / Multi-touch support	Yes
Native date/time picker support	Unknown
SMS support	Yes
Telephone support	Yes
Maps support	Yes
Orientation change support	Yes
Contact support	Yes
SQLite support	Yes (not possible on BlackBerry)
Native Language Application Development support	No
Graph Library Support	Yes

The main purpose of iUI™ is to minimize the need for manual code entry providing the user with all the basics for creating Web-based applications by using the JavaScript, HTML and CSS3 Web standards. In this sense, it is possible to use an already available HTML editor to create most of iUI-based applications. Furthermore, unlike other frameworks for cross-platform development, the source code of IUi-based applications is not altered or translated.

Both the Bank of America and the Adelphi University are examples of success stories of using iUI.

There is not reported development environments specially designed for developing iUI-based applications. Moreover, there is a book entitled iPhone JavaScript Cookbook written by Arturo Fernández-Montoro, outlining the features of diverse frameworks for iPhone development such as iUI, PhoneGap and Sencha Touch.

Finally, the main capabilities as well as the platforms supported by this framework are presented in Tables 5 and 6, respectively; more detailed information can be found at iui-js.org website.

3.4. IBM WorkLight™

WorklLight™ is a mobile application framework for developing pure HTML5, hybrid and native applications. It is aimed at the development of enterprise applications. In detail, hybrid applications can be developed either as traditionally, i.e., by using Web technologies or by using a mixing of Web and native source code. In fact, the required development skills range from Web technologies to native programming languages

Table 5. Platforms for mobile applications supported by iUI™

iOS™	Android™	BlackBerry™	Palm WebOS™	Symbian™	Windows™ Mobile	Others
Yes	Yes	Limited models	Yes	Unknown	Yes	Tablet, desktop and Web environments

Table 6. Main capabilities of iUI™

Enterprise data synchronization	No
Multi-Threaded Applications	No
File uploading	Unknown
Image Library Browsing	Unknown
In Application Email	Unknown
Application distribution support	No
Self-contained, no web required	No
Web Services	Yes
Mobile APIs support	Unknown
Able to access the web for data	Yes
Geolocation support	Yes
Vibration support	Yes
Accelerometer support	Yes
Sound (play) support	Yes
Sound (record) support	Unknown
Camera support	Unknown
XMPP support	Unknown
File system IO support	Unknown
Gesture / Multi-touch support	Yes
Native date/time picker support	Unknown
SMS support	Yes
Telephone support	Yes
Maps support	Yes
Orientation change support	Yes
Contact support	Yes
SQLite support	Unknown
Native Language Application Development support	No
Graph Library Support	Unknown

Worklight™ is property of IBM™; in fact, it is part of the IBM™ Mobile Foundation, family of products that provides the essential elements needed for complete mobile development, deployment and management within a business. This framework has different products: 1) Worklight™ Studio: an Eclipse-based IDE, 2) Worklight™ Server: a Java-based server acting as a gateway between applications, external services and the enterprise back-end infrastructure, and 3) Worklight™ Device Runtime: client-side runtime code that embeds server functionality within the target-environment of deployed applications.

Worklight™ is not free, and it is available under two different paid editions; however, it is possible to obtain a free developer edition on its website, which consists of a single plugin for the Eclipse IDE packaging Worklight™ Studio and Worklight™ Server. Worklight™ is most notably used by TBC Corporation, a marketer of tires for the automotive replacement market and Lotte Card Co., Ltd., a Korean credit card company.

The main capabilities as well as the platforms supported by this framework are outlined in Tables 7 and 8, respectively. In addition, more information can be found in a more detailed way visiting the worklight.com website.

3.5. Rhodes™

It is a Ruby-based framework for rapidly developing mobile applications whose main purpose is to develop embedded applications. Unlike other frameworks for cross-platform development,

Table 7. Platforms for mobile applications supported by Worklight™

iOS™	Android™	BlackBerry™	Palm WebOS™	Symbian™	Windows™ Mobile	Others
Yes	Yes	Yes	For Web apps	For Web apps	Yes	

Table 8. Main capabilities of Worklight™

Enterprise data synchronization	Yes
Multi-Threaded Applications	Unknown
File uploading	Yes
Image Library Browsing	Yes
In Application Email	Yes
Application distribution support	Yes
Self-contained, no web required	Yes
Web Services	Yes
Mobile APIs support	Yes
Able to access the web for data	Yes
Geolocation support	Yes
Vibration support	Yes
Accelerometer support	Yes
Sound (play) support	Yes
Sound (record) support	Yes
Camera support	Yes
XMPP support	Yes
File system IO support	Yes
Gesture / Multi-touch support	Yes
Native date/time picker support	Yes
SMS support	Yes
Telephone support	Yes
Maps support	Yes
Orientation change support	Yes
Contact support	Yes
SQLite support	Yes
Native Language Application Development support	Yes
Graph Library Support	Yes

Rhodes™ only generates native applications, not Web-based (hybrid) applications, where views are written in HTML (including HTML5) whereas controls are written in Ruby.

Rhodes™ is property of Motorola™ Solutions, Inc., and it is free and open source under the MIT license; however, it is also available under a paid edition for organizations requiring high level of commercial grade support. HTML, JavaScript and Ruby are the programming languages needed to develop applications on top of this framework.

Rhodes™ is part of the so-called Rhomobile™ Suite, an HTML5 development platform comprised of RhoConnect: a back-end data connections manager, RhoStudio: an Eclipse plugin allowing the development, debugging and testing of RhoElements-based applications and RhoElements: an HTML5 development framework covering popular mobile operating systems. RhoStudio must be only installed with the aim of automatically obtaining all RhoMobile products.

Regarding technical documentation, a book entitled RhoMobile beginner's guide written by Abhishek Nalwaya about Rhodes can be found. There is also a book entitled Pro Smartphone Cross-platform Development written by Sarah Allen Vidal Graupera and Lee Lundrigan, covering diverse cross-platform toolkits such as Rhodes, PhoneGap and Appcelerator Titanium.

The main capabilities as well as the platforms supported by this framework are outlined in Tables 9 and 10, respectively; more information can be found at rhomobile.com website.

Table 9. Platforms for mobile applications supported by Rhodes™

iOS™	Android™	BlackBerry™	Palm WebOS™	Symbian™	Windows™ Mobile	Others
Yes	Yes	Yes	No	Yes	Yes	Tablet and desktop (Windows™)

Table 10. Main capabilities of Rhodes™

Enterprise data synchronization	Yes (via RhoConnect)
Multi-Threaded Applications	Yes (via Ruby)
File uploading	Yes
Image Library Browsing	Yes
In Application Email	Unknown
Application distribution support	Yes (via RhoGallery)
Self-contained, no web required	Yes
Web Services	Unknown
Mobile APIs support	Unknown
Able to access the web for data	Yes
Geolocation support	Yes
Vibration support	Yes
Accelerometer support	Yes
Sound (play) support	Yes
Sound (record) support	Unknown
Camera support	Yes
XMPP support	Unknown
File system IO support	Yes
Gesture / Multi-touch support	Yes
Native date/time picker support	Yes
SMS support	Yes
Telephone support	Yes
Maps support	Yes
Orientation change support	Yes
Contact support	Yes
SQLite support	Yes
Native Language Application Development support	Yes (via Rhodes extensions)
Graph Library Support	Yes (via HTML5 Canvas or SVG)

3.6. Appcelerator Titanium™

It is a cross-platform mobile development platform for building Android™ and Apple™ iOS native, hybrid and Web-based applications whose main purpose is to develop embedded applications.

Appcelerator Titanium™ has a wide range of products, including Titanium SDK which is a JavaScript-based SDK leveraging device and mobile operating system APIs, Titanium Studio which is an Eclipse-based IDE to develop, test and deploy mobile applications and Appcelerator Cloud Services which is a Mobile Back-end as a Service (MBaaS) providing public libraries of cloud application services like social integration or push notification as well as custom back-end services integration.

Appcelerator Titanium™ is available as part of the Appcelerator Titanium™ Mobile open source project under the Apache Public License v. 2; however, it is also released under three different paid editions covering enterprise extensions and under a limited free edition. All commercial editions include Titanium SDK and Titanium Studio products. Regarding development environments, the company recently acquired Aptana™ which built its own IDE called Titanium Studio. Appcelerator Titanium™ supports the following programming languages: HTML, Javascript, as well as PHP, Ruby and Python for the development of desktop applications.

Regarding Appcelerator Titanium™'s success stories, Blockbuster™, Inc., NBCUniversal Media™, LLC and Koninklijke Philips™ Electronics

Table 11. Platforms for mobile applications supported by Appcelerator Titanium™

iOS™	Android™	BlackBerry™	Palm WebOS™	Symbian™	Windows™ Mobile	Others
Yes	Yes	Beta versión	Unknown	Unknown	Unknown	Desktop (Windows™, Linux and Mac OS)

Table 12. Main capabilities of Appcelerator Titanium™

Enterprise data synchronization	No
Multi-Threaded Applications	Unknown
File uploading	Unknown
Image Library Browsing	Unknown
In Application Email	Unknown
Application distribution support	Yes (via Cloud services)
Self-contained, no web required	Yes
Web Services	Unknown
Mobile APIs support	Unknown
Able to access the web for data	Yes
Geolocation support	Yes
Vibration support	Yes
Accelerometer support	Yes
Sound (play) support	Yes
Sound (record) support	Yes
Camera support	Yes
XMPP support	Yes (Via JavaScript)
File system IO support	Yes
Gesture / Multi-touch support	Yes
Native date/time picker support	Yes
SMS support	Yes
Telephone support	Unknown
Maps support	Yes
Orientation change support	Yes
Contact support	Unknown
SQLite support	Yes
Native Language Application Development support	Yes
Graph Library Support	Unknown

N.V. are greater examples of companies using this framework.

Moreover, there are some books about Appcelerator Titanium. For instance, a book entitled Appcelerator Titanium Smartphone App Development Cookbook written by Boydlee Pollentine; Appcelerator Titanium: Patterns and best practices written by Boydlee Pollentine and Trevor Ward; and Appcelerator Up and Running written by John Anderson.

Finally, the main capabilities as well as the platforms supported by this framework are summarized in Tables 11 and 12, respectively. In addition, more detailed information can be found at appcelerator.com website.

3.7. iPFaces™

IPFaces™ is a mobile application framework for developing native form-oriented network applications by using PHP, ASP.NET and Java Web development skills. IPFaces™ works through function libraries, and it was created with the aim of screening the developer completely out from the mobile platforms itself. So far, no development environments are known about this framework.

This solution consists of two components: a device-specific client application and a set of language-specific server packages managing the entire application's logic. Client engines are distributed as freeware and also under a commercial license for supplying branded client applications whereas server packages are freely available as open source under the BSD license.

Table 13. Platforms for mobile applications supported by iPFaces™

iOS™	Android™	BlackBerry™	Palm WebOS™	Symbian™	Windows™ Mobile	Others
Yes	On roadmap	Beta versión	Unknown	Unknown	On roadmap	Java ME

Table 14. Main capabilities of iPFaces™

Enterprise data synchronization	On roadmap
Multi-Threaded Applications	Unknown
File uploading	Unknown
Image Library Browsing	Unknown
In Application Email	Unknown
Application distribution support	Yes (AppStore, Cloud services)
Self-contained, no web required	Yes
Web Services	Unknown
Mobile APIs support	Unknown
Able to access the web for data	Yes
Geolocation support	Yes
Vibration support	Unknown
Accelerometer support	Unknown
Sound (play) support	Unknown
Sound (record) support	Unknown
Camera support	Yes
XMPP support	Unknown
File system IO support	Unknown
Gesture / Multi-touch support	Unknown
Native date/time picker support	Unknown
SMS support	Unknown
Telephone support	Unknown
Maps support	Unknown
Orientation change support	Yes
Contact support	Unknown
SQLite support	No
Native Language Application Development support	No
Graph Library Support	Unknown

Regarding technical documentation, a book entitled IPFaces Mobile Framework written by Kn Tr Benoit can be found.

The main capabilities as well as the platforms supported by this framework are summarized in Tables 13 and 14, respectively; additional information can be found at ipfaces.org website.

3.8. Sencha Touch™

Sencha Touch™ is an HTML5 mobile application framework property of Sencha, Inc., and it is one of the most popular frameworks for cross-platform development. This framework works through function libraries, and it supports programming languages like HTML5, CSS3 and JavaScript,

Sencha Touch™ is part of the Sencha Complete software suite comprised of Sencha Architect: an HTML5 visual IDE enabling the design, development and deployment of both Web-based applications for desktop and mobile devices, Sencha ExtJS™: a JavaScript-based framework for developing cross-browser RIAs, Sencha GXT™: an application framework for Google Web Toolkit (GWT), among others solutions. Sencha Touch™ is licensed under a free commercial license, the open source GNU GPL v. 3 license and a paid commercial license for Original Equipment Manufacturer (OEM) uses.

Among the success stories of using Sencha Touch™, the DirecTV™, Vimeo™ and Intuit™ companies are clear examples.

Moreover, there are few books about Sencha Touch development, for instance, a book entitled Sencha Touch in Action written by Jesús García, Anthony De Moss and Mitchell Simoens; a book entitled Sencha Touch cookbook written by Ajit

Table 15. Platforms for mobile applications supported by Sencha Touch™

iOS™	Android™	BlackBerry™	Palm WebOS™	Symbian™	Windows™ Mobile	Others
Yes	Yes	Yes	No	No	No	Webkit-compliant desktop browsers (Google™ Chrome and Apple™ Safari)

Table 16. Main capabilities of Sencha Touch™

Enterprise data synchronization	Unknown
Multi-Threaded Applications	Unknown
File uploading	Unknown
Image Library Browsing	Unknown
In Application Email	Unknown
Application distribution support	Unknown
Self-contained, no web required	Yes (Offline support)
Web Services	Yes (JSONP, JSON, GWT RPC)
Mobile APIs support	Unknown
Able to access the web for data	Yes
Geolocation support	Unknown
Vibration support	Unknown
Accelerometer support	Unknown
Sound (play) support	Unknown
Sound (record) support	Unknown
Camera support	Unknown
XMPP support	Unknown
File system IO support	Unknown
Gesture / Multi-touch support	Yes
Native date/time picker support	Unknown
SMS support	No
Telephone support	No
Maps support	No (On roadmap)
Orientation change support	No
Contact support	Unknown
SQLite support	Unknown
Native Language Application Development support	Unknown
Graph Library Support	Unknown

Kumar. An eBook entitled Building a Sencha Touch Application is also available.

The main capabilities as well as the platforms supported by this framework are presented in Tables 15 and 16, respectively. In addition, more detailed information can be found at sencha.com website.

3.9. Corona SDK™

Corona SDK™ is a software development kit created by Walter Luh, co-founder of Ansca Mobile. It allows software programmers to build and deploy mobile applications for the iPhone, iPad, and Android™ devices. Corona lets developers use integrated Lua, layered on top of C++/OpenGL, to build graphically rich applications that are also lightweight in size and quick in development time. This approach is commonly appropriate for developing games for mobile devices. The SDK is the core of the Corona platform which includes support resources, development tools and cloud services, and it has a subscription-based purchase model that allows new features to be immediately rolled out to users (Corona SDK™, n.d.).

Regarding licensing, Corona SDK™ is available under a free and unlimited trial as well as under two different subscription editions which are also available at a discounted price for educators and students. Furthermore, there is an academic site license for institutions. This framework has been most notably used by companies such as Universal Pictures; Governance Employees Insurance Company (GEICO), an auto insurance

Table 17. Platforms for mobile applications supported by Corona SDK™

iOS™	Android™	BlackBerry™	Palm WebOS™	Symbian™	Windows™ Mobile	Others
Yes	Yes	No	No	No	No	-

Table 18. Main capabilities of Corona SDK™

Enterprise data synchronization	No
Multi-Threaded Applications	No
File uploading	Yes
Image Library Browsing	Yes
In Application Email	Yes
Application distribution support	Yes
Self-contained, no web required	Yes
Web Services	Yes
Mobile APIs support	Yes
Geolocation support	Yes
Vibration support	Yes
Accelerometer support	Yes
Sound (play) support	Yes
Sound (record) support	Yes
Camera support	Yes
XMPP support	No
File system IO support	Yes
Gesture / Multi-touch support	Yes
Native date/time picker support	Yes (General picker control)
SMS support	No
Telephone support	Yes
Maps support	Yes
Orientation change support	Yes
Contact support	No
SQLite support	Yes
Native Language Application Development support	Yes
Graph Library Support	Yes

company providing services in all U.S. states; and HIT Entertainment, a children's entertainment producer and rights owner based in London, to mention but a few.

Regarding technical documentation, there is a book entitled Corona SDK Mobile Game Development Beginner´s Guide written by Michelle M. Fernandez about the development of monetized games for iOS and Android-based devices.

Finally, the main capabilities as well as the platforms supported by this framework are presented in Tables 17 and 18, respectively. More detailed information can be found at coronalabs. com/products/corona-sdk/ website.

3.10. DragonRad™

DragonRad™ is a cross-platform mobile application development tool created by Seregon Solutions Inc. that allows developer to create, manage and deploy mobile applications. This tool has supports for the major mobile platforms such as iPhone, Android™, BlackBerry™ and Windows™ Mobile. The tool is focused on database driven mobile enterprise applications with easy and wide range of databases support. It provides the drag and drop environment which helps developers to save time. DragonRad™ facilitates the integration and synchronization of database system with native functions like contacts, calendar, payments, location-based services, maps, camera and native devices (Palmieri et al., 2012).

Actually, DragonRAD™ is composed of three components: 1) a visual drag & drop IDE with a WYSWYG editor called DragonRAD™ designer, 2) a server host managing the synchronization between the back-end databases and the mobile

Table 19. Platforms for mobile applications supported by DragonRad™

iOS™	Android™	BlackBerry™	Palm WebOS™	Symbian™	Windows™ Mobile	Others
Yes	Yes	Yes	No	No	Yes	-

Table 20. Main capabilities of DragonRad™

Enterprise data synchronization	Yes
Multi-Threaded Applications	No
File uploading	No
Image Library Browsing	No
In Application Email	No
Application distribution support	No
Self-contained, no web required	Yes
Web Services	Yes
Mobile APIs support	Yes
Geolocation support	Yes
Vibration support	Yes
Accelerometer support	No
Sound (play) support	Yes
Sound (record) support	Yes
Camera support	Yes
XMPP support	No
File system IO support	No
Gesture / Multi-touch support	No
Native date/time picker support	Yes
SMS support	No
Telephone support	Yes
Maps support	Yes
Orientation change support	No
Contact support	Yes
SQLite support	Yes
Native Language Application Development support	Yes
Graph Library Support	No

devices, and 3) a client engine that resides on the mobile device and executes applications developed using DragonRAD™ designer. DragonRAD™ designer is available under a full-featured 30-day trial as well as under a paid subscription edition including a single host license for free. Furthermore, standard mobile clients can be unlimitedly deployed at no extra cost; however, branded versions are available for an additional extra charge.

DragonRad™ is most notably used by Paradigm Housing Group, a housing and support services company based in London; ScotiaBank™ and Intergraph™ Corporation, a global provider of Spatial Information Management (SIM) software.

Moreover, there is a book entitled DragonRAD™ written by Evander Luther.

The main capabilities as well as the platforms supported by this framework are presented in Tables 19 and 20, respectively. More detailed information can be found at dragonrad.com website.

3.11. Mosync™

Mosync™ is an open source solution developed by Swedish company targeted to mobile market. It is licensed under the GNU General Public License (GPL) v. 2.0. Alternatively, it was released under two different paid subscription editions for commercial usage.

Mosync™ has fully fledged SDK which helps developer to build and package all type of applications. Simple, advanced and complex applications can share the same code base. Mosync™ SDK is proving to be very powerful tool with many components tightly coupled together like Libraries, Runtimes, Device Profile Database and Compilers and so on. It provides the full fledge

Table 21. Platforms for mobile applications supported by Mosync™

iOS™	Android™	BlackBerry™	Palm WebOS™	Symbian™	Windows™ Mobile	Others
Yes	Yes	Yes	No	Yes	Yes	-

Table 22. Main capabilities of Mosync™

Enterprise data synchronization	No
Multi-Threaded Applications	No
File uploading	Yes
Image Library Browsing	No
In Application Email	Yes
Application distribution support	No
Self-contained, no web required	Yes
Web Services	Yes
Mobile APIs support	Yes
Geolocation support	Yes
Vibration support	Yes
Accelerometer support	Yes
Sound (play) support	Yes
Sound (record) support	Yes
Camera support	Yes
XMPP support	No
File system IO support	Yes
Gesture / Multi-touch support	Yes
Native date/time picker support	Yes
SMS support	Yes
Telephone support	Yes
Maps support	Yes
Orientation change support	Yes
Contact support	Yes
SQLite support	Yes
Native Language Application Development support	Yes
Graph Library Support	Yes

Eclipse-based IDE and the use of standard C/C++, easy to use and well-documented APIs. The idea involved to support multiple mobile OS's is different from other tools and also in very isolated way from other mobile operating code. A Mosync-based application is built, targeting a device profile by using GNU Compiler Collection (gcc) and pipe-tool. Once the application has been written, pipe-tool is used to compile the resources involved in the application. Then GCC backend is called and path to target device profile passed to it. GCC uses it to produce Mosync™ intermediate language, which then fed in to pipe-tool. So, pipetool behaves as a bridge between Mosync™ applications to target device profile. The profile database helps the application in ensuring that it has correctly adapted to the device. The runtimes are libraries which are bound to provide support related to all like regarding graphics, audio, communications, input, uniform interface to low level system APIs and other device features (Palmieri et al, 2012).

Some success stories on the use of Mosync™ involve companies such as InMobi™, a mobile advertising company with offices in several countries around the world; GB Glace™, the largest ice cream company in Sweden; and Dalarns Tidningar, a local daily in the mid-west of Sweden.

So far, no books published about MoSync™ are known. Therefore, the main capabilities as well as the platforms supported by this framework are outlined in Tables 21 and 22, respectively. More detailed information can be found at mosync.com website.

Table 23. Platforms for mobile applications supported by Qt™

iOS™	Android™	BlackBerry™	Palm WebOS™	Symbian™	Windows™ Mobile	Others
No	No	No	No	Yes	No	Desktop (Microsoft™ Windows, Mac OS X and Linux)

Table 24. Main capabilities of Qt™

Enterprise data synchronization	No
Multi-Threaded Applications	Yes
File uploading	Yes
Image Library Browsing	No
In Application Email	Yes
Application distribution support	No
Self-contained, no web required	Yes
Web Services	Yes
Mobile APIs support	Yes
Geolocation support	Yes
Vibration support	Yes
Accelerometer support	Yes
Sound (play) support	Yes
Sound (record) support	Yes
Camera support	Yes
XMPP support	Yes
File system IO support	Yes
Gesture / Multi-touch support	Yes
Native date/time picker support	Yes
SMS support	Yes
Telephone support	Yes
Maps support	Yes
Orientation change support	Yes
Contact support	Yes
SQLite support	Yes
Native Language Application Development support	Yes
Graph Library Support	Yes

3.12. Qt™

Qt™ is a cross-platform application framework launched by an open source project called Qt project, which involves Nokia™ developers. In this sense, Qt was released under the GNU General Public License v. 3 and the GNU Lesser General Public License v. 2.1. Alternatively, it is available under a commercial license. This framework is widely used for developing application software with a graphical user interface (GUI), and it is also used for developing non-GUI programs such as command-line tools and consoles for servers.

Qt™, formally Qt™ SDK, mainly includes the framework, which is a set of APIs for C++ and JavaScript-like programming and the cross-platform Qt™ Creator IDE which is freely available. A GUI creation kit called Qt quick for the quick development of rich and touch-enabled GUIs for Symbian™ and MeeGo™-based mobile devices is contained within the Qt framework.

Qt™ is most notably used in Skype™, VLC™ media player, VirtualBox™, among others well-known software products. (Qt™ SDK, n.d.).

There are a lot of books about Qt programming. For instance, Foundations of Qt Development written by Johan Thelin, Beginning Nokia Apps Development written by Dan Zucker and Ray Rischapter and Programming with Qt written by Matthias Kalle Dalheimer.

The main capabilities as well as the platforms supported by this framework are outlined in Tables 23 and 24, respectively. Additional information can be found at developer.nokia.com/Develop/Qt/ website.

Table 25. Platforms for mobile applications supported by AppMobi™

iOS™	Android™	BlackBerry™	Palm WebOS™	Symbian™	Windows™ Mobile	Others
Yes	Yes	No	No	No	No	-

Table 26. Main capabilities of AppMobi™

Enterprise data synchronization	No
Multi-Threaded Applications	No
File uploading	Yes
Image Library Browsing	No
In Application Email	Yes
Application distribution support	Yes
Self-contained, no web required	Yes
Web Services	Yes
Mobile APIs support	Yes
Geolocation support	Yes
Vibration support	Yes
Accelerometer support	Yes
Sound (play) support	Yes
Sound (record) support	Yes
Camera support	Yes
XMPP support	No
File system IO support	No
Gesture / Multi-touch support	Yes
Native date/time picker support	No
SMS support	Yes
Telephone support	No
Maps support	No
Orientation change support	Yes
Contact support	Yes
SQLite support	No
Native Language Application Development support	No
Graph Library Support	No

3.13. AppMobi™

AppMobi™ XDK is an open source and cloud-based mobile development environment created by the AppMobi™ Company, which is a vendor of HTML5 mobile development and deployment tools and services. XDK stands for Cross Platform Development Kit and uses standard Web languages such as HTML5, CSS, and JavaScript to develop mobile applications for smartphones and tablets. Due to the cloud services infrastructure of the AppMobi™ XDK environment, it is possible to develop, debug and build applications in either Macintosh or PC architectures, using a free HTML5-powered IDE as a Web application for the Google Chrome Web browser or using an already available IDE, e.g. XCode and Eclipse. (AppMobi™ XDK, n.d.).

The products of the AppMobi™ platform has been most notably used by AOL™, Fox™ News Radio and Lancaster Day Care Center, a non-profit childcare and early education center based in Lancaster, Pennsylvania, USA.

Regarding bibliographical references, there is a book entitled Beginning Mobile Application Development in the Cloud written by Richard Rodger which covers the use of the cloud services provided by the AppMobi platform for developing cloud-based mobile applications.

The main capabilities as well as the platforms supported by this framework are outlined in Tables 25 and 26, respectively. Additionally, more detailed information can be found at appmobi. com website.

4. COMPARISON

The process of choosing a development approach for a native, Web or hybrid mobile application entails many parameters including budget, proj-ect time frame, target audience and application functionality.

In order to allow developers to choose the option that best fits the necessities and possibilities, the Table 27 summarizes the main features of the multiplatform development environments

Table 27. Comparison of cross-platform development frameworks

Feature/ Framework	Language	Access Native Code	IDE	Output App	Open Source	License	Development Platforms
PhoneGap™	HTML5, CSS3, JavaScript	Yes	Dreamweaver™ CS5, Xcode, Eclipse 3.4, Bada	Native	Yes	Apache License V. 2	Microsoft™ Windows™, Mac OS X, Linux
Application Craft™	HTML5, CSS3, JavaScript	Yes	Application Craft™ IDE (browser-based)	Native and Web	Yes (widgets)	Unknown	-
IUI™	HTML, CSS3, JavaScript	No	-	Web	Yes	MIT	-
IBM™ Worklight™	HTML5, CSS3, JavaScript	Yes	IBM™ WorkLight™ Studio	Native and hybrid	Yes	Unknown	Microsoft™ Windows™, Mac OS X, Linux
Rhodes™	HTML5, CSS3, JavaScript, Ruby	Yes	Rhostudio	Native and hybrid	Yes	MIT	Microsoft™ Windows™, Mac OS X, Linux
Appcelerator Titanium™	HTML5, CSS3, JavaScript	Yes	Titanium Studio	Native, Web and hybrid apps	No	Commercial	Microsoft™ Windows™, Mac OS X, Ubuntu
IPFaces™	ASP.Net, Java or PHP	-	Visual Studio (ASP. Net)	Web and Native	Yes	BSD (server packages)	-
Sencha Touch™	HTML5, CSS3, JavaScript,	No	Sencha Architect	Web and hybrid	Yes	GNU GPL V. 3	Microsoft™ Windows™, Mac OS X, Linux
Corona SDK™	Lua	Yes	Corona Project Manager	Native	No	Comercial	Microsoft™ Windows™, Mac OS X
DragonRAD™	Lua (Drag & drop)	No	DragonRAD™ Designer	Native	No	Comercial	Microsoft™ Windows™
MoSync™	HTML5, CSS3 JavaScript, C++	Yes	Based on Eclipse	Native, Web and hybrid apps	Yes (SDK)	GNU GPL V. 2 (SDK)	Microsoft™ Windows™, Mac OS X, Linux
Qt™	HTML5, CSS3, JavaScript, C++	Yes	Qt Creator	Native	Yes	GNU LGPL V. 2.1	Microsoft™ Windows™, Mac OS X, Linux/X11
AppMobi™ XDK	HTML5, CSS3, JavaScript	Yes	AppMobi™ XDK	Native, Web and hybrid apps	Yes	MIT X11	Microsoft Windows, Mac OS X

described in this chapter. This comparison considers features such as the underlying programming language, the possibility of writing source code in the device's native language, the type of outcome and the license used by the framework.

5. CONCLUSION

There are several frameworks for developing rich applications for diverse mobile devices. This kind of RIA is known as multi-device RIA. Nevertheless, this term can go beyond, covering the typical cross-browser rich Web applications as well as cross-platform desktop applications.

It is important to emphasize that the frameworks outlined in this chapter are not the only ones that exist. Currently, there is a great quantity of options for mobile development depending on what kind of application needs to be developed. The frameworks' creators know that there is a strong tendency towards the development of these types of applications; therefore, they endeavored to continue adding features to their respective developments in order to satisfy specific demands. For that reason, the information presented in this chapter is only a perspective on what the frameworks for mobile development are, considering that every day there is something new in this regard.

Moreover, although most of the mobile operating systems described at the beginning of this chapter belong to a larger platform which integrates: 1) libraries for native development based on languages such as C, C++ and Objective C, 2) IDEs and development tools such as emulators compilers and packagers 3) runtime environments such as the .NET Framework and the Adobe™ AIR™ and 4) (less frequently) frameworks for developing native applications starting from Web applications based on HTML, CSS and JavaScript such as the HP™'s Enyo and the RIM's WebWorks™ frameworks; there are a lot of cross-platform development frameworks which allows building native or hybrid applications for multiple mobile operating systems using: 1) the same code base written in HTML, CSS and JavaScript or 2) code written in non-native languages such as the scripting language Lua. These frameworks allows saving development time and effort since they address more than one mobile operating system at the same time and they leverage previous Web programing skills without requiring native code programing skills.

REFERENCES

AppMobi XDK. (n.d.). *AppMobi website*. Retrieved July 6, 2012, from http://www.appmobi.com/?q=node/27

Corona, S. D. K. (n.d.). *Corona Labs website*. Retrieved July 6, 2012, from http://www.coronalabs.com/products/corona-sdk/

Kappel, G., Proll, B., Retschitzegger, W., & Schwinger, W. (2003). Customisation for Ubiquitous Web Applications: a Comparison of Approaches. *Int. J. Web Eng. Technol.*, *1*(1), 79–111. doi:10.1504/IJWET.2003.003322

Palmieri, M., Singh, I., & Cicchetti, A. (2012). Comparison of cross-platform mobile development tools. In *Proceedings of 2012 16th International Conference on Intelligence in Next Generation Networks (ICIN)* (pp. 179–186). IEEE. doi:10.1109/ICIN.2012.6376023

Qt, S. D. K. (n.d.). *Nokia products*. Retrieved July 6, 2012, from http://qt.nokia.com/products

ADDITIONAL READING

Comparing Titanium and PhoneGap. (n.d.). *Kevin Whinnery*. Retrieved July 2, 2012, from http://kevinwhinnery.com/post/22764624253/comparing-titanium-and-phonegap

Comparison: App Inventor, DroidDraw, Rho-mobile, PhoneGap, Appcelerator, WebView, and AML. (n.d.). *Application Markup Language website*. Retrieved July 6, 2012 from http://www.amlcode.com/2010/07/16/comparison-appinventor-rhomobile-phonegap-appcelerator-webview-and-aml/

Mobile Frameworks Comparison Chart. (n.d.). *Markus Falk website*. Retrieved July 6, 2012, from http://www.markus-falk.com/mobile-frameworks-comparison-chart/

KEY TERMS AND DEFINITIONS

Hybrid Mobile Application: Applications built using Web technologies and wrapped in device-specific native application containers.

Mobile Device: A small, hand-held computing device. Cell phones, smartphones, tablet computers and PDAs are examples of mobile devices, which can differ in the quality and range of features.

Mobile Web Application: A mobile application written using Web standards and deployed as a mobile Web browser-based application.

Multi-Device Development Framework: A software platform designed to support the development of mobile applications either as embedded Web applications or as applications written in a cross-platform programming language such as Lua and Haxe.

Multi-Device Rich Internet Application: A kind of RIA that can run on a variety of devices starting from the same code base. This includes not only cross-browser Web applications but also out-of-browser applications, namely cross-platform desktop and mobile applications.

Native Mobile Applications: Applications written for a specific device's hardware and operating system.

Rich Internet Applications: Applications that are deployed over the Web; this type of applications combines features and functionality of Web applications and desktop applications.

Chapter 13
An Overview of RIAs Development Tools

ABSTRACT

Rich Internet Applications (RIAs) development has traditionally been addressed using framework-based development approaches (i.e., using application frameworks), which usually comprise tools such as Standard Development Kits (SDKs), class libraries, and Integrated Development Environments (IDEs). Nevertheless, another development approach that relies on Model-Driven Development (MDD) methodologies and tools has recently emerged as a result of the academic and commercial effort for alleviating the lack of development methodologies and support tools especially designed for the development of RIAs. In this chapter, a new classification of RIAs development approaches is proposed by introducing a third category: Rapid Application Development (RAD) approaches. Thereby, the chapter reviews not only IDEs for frameworks-based RIA development; it also addresses other support tools for MDD and RAD such as code generation tools. Additionally, the features, scope, and limitations of the analyzed tools are discussed by means of a series of usage scenarios addressing the RIAs implementation.

1. INTRODUCTION

RIAs engineering is an emerging area of the Software engineering which lacks of development approaches and software tools in comparison with Web engineering. Therefore, the development of RIAs is mainly driven by a set of programming languages such as ActionScript and JavaScript as well as application frameworks such as Adobe™ Flex™ and Microsoft™ Silverlight™.

However, some proposals based on the MDD (Model Driven Development) approach have recently emerged with the aim of solving the

aforementioned requirements. In fact, according to Toffeti, Comai, Preciado and Linaje (Toffeti et al., 2011), RIAs development is currently addressed 1) by using application frameworks which provide SDKs (Standard Development Kits), class libraries, IDEs (Integrated Development Environments), among other development tools, 2) by using MDD tools which generate executable code starting from high-level software models.

The use of software tools based on the RAD (Rapid Application Development) methodology is a current trend on RIAs development. Thus, the aforementioned classification has been extended

DOI: 10.4018/978-1-4666-6437-1.ch013

by adding a category for clustering approaches based on the RAD methodology. In this chapter, the most representative software tools in each category of the extended classification are described.

Additionally, the features, scope and limitations of the tools are discussed by means of a series of usage scenarios addressing the implementation of RIAs. In detail, these usage scenarios face some of the RIA development aspects identified by Toffetti (Toffetti et al., 2011). It is important to notice that, the usage scenarios are not achieved as use cases but as technical discussions summarizing the lessons learned in the development of sample RIAs by using the tools described in this chapter; therefore, technical details about implementation are not included. In most cases, these usage scenarios involve not only coding but also building activities, namely compiling and debugging, so that they are not completely accurate neither for the UI (User Interface) design tools nor for the RAD and MDD tools but for the IDEs described in this chapter. As far as possible, the execution of the resulting applications in debug mode is depicted by some screenshots throughout this chapter.

2. TOOLS FOR FRAMEWORK-BASED RIAS DEVELOPMENT

This section presents the most popular software tools available for developing RIAs based on the four major technologies for RIAs development. It is important to notice that most of the software tools considered in this section are Integrated Development Environments (IDEs). An IDE is a software application that provides comprehensive facilities to developers for software development and ideally integrates source code editing, visual designing, debugging and building capabilities. These features are considered for describing some IDEs in following subsections.

IDEs for RIAs development can be classified into the following two major groups accordingly

to its architecture: 1) standalone applications and 2) plug-in applications. Besides, a standalone application, a plug-in application is a set of software components that adds specific functionalities to a larger software application. From this perspective, it is important to notice that there are popular IDEs based on plug-in architectures such as Eclipse™, which can be extended for supporting many programming languages and frameworks through plug-ins. Therefore, there are many IDEs based on Eclipse™ available as both standalone and plug-in applications. For practical purposes, the aforementioned classification is used in this section. Furthermore, it is important to notice that besides the official development tools, i.e., the tools developed, supplied and maintained by technology owners, there are third-party development tools, i.e. tools developed, supplied and maintained by third-party open source communities or external software companies.

2.1. Adobe™ Flex™-Based RIAs Integrated Development Environments

Adobe™ Flex™ includes MXML (Macromedia FleX Markup Language) as well as Adobe™ Flash™ Player and Adobe™ AIR™ runtimes. MXML is an XML-based language for the design of application UIs whereas ActionScript is an object-oriented language for the definition of client-side application logic. MXML and ActionScript code are compiled together into a single SWF (Small Web Format) file. Depending on the application type, SWF files run either on Adobe™ Flash™ Player or on Adobe™ AIR™.

The official IDE for Adobe™ Flex™-based development is Adobe™ Flash Builder™, which is a commercial software application. Although Adobe™ launched Adobe™ Flash Builder™ also under an education free license; there are many open source options for Flex™ developers and they are described in this section.

Table 1. Overall features of Adobe™ Flash Builder™

General Features	
License type	Commercial
Developer	Adobe™ Systems Incorporated
Website	http://www.adobe.com/products/flash-builder-family.html
Latest stable release	4.7 (May, 2014)
Operating system	Microsoft™ Windows™, Mac OS™
Screenshot	

The scope and limitations of these tools are discussed by means of a usage scenario addressing the development of an Adobe™ Flex™-based mobile RIA. In detail, this scenario aims at developing a RIA able to capture and display video from Android™-based mobile devices cameras. The application is a single-view application that displays a 480x360 video at the top of the screen when the view is loaded. For that purpose, the Adobe™ Flex™ *Camera* and *Video* classes are used. The former allows applications to connect to client systems and mobile devices cameras and broadcast the video either locally or remotely whereas the latter is used to display the video captured from cameras. At the same time, this scenario is intended to complement the review of the support for multimedia content (namely video playback) on non-JavaScript-based frameworks for RIAs development that is provided in chapter 5.

According to the classification of RIA features by Toffetti et al. (Toffetti et al., 2011), this scenario considers the rich presentation aspect of RIAs development.

2.1.1. Adobe™ Flash Builder™

Adobe™ Flash Builder™ is an Eclipse™-based IDE for building cross-browser Web applications and cross-platform desktop and mobile applications with a common code base by using the ActionScript™ programming language and the Adobe™ Flex™ framework. Adobe™ Flash Builder™ is available under two paid editions as well as under an academic free edition. It is also available as a standalone application and as a plug-in for an already configured Eclipse™ environment. Besides the built-in code editors for both ActionScript and MXML, Adobe™ Flash

271

Table 2. Main capabilities of Adobe™ Flash Builder™

1. Source code editing	
Scripting language support (MXML)	Yes
Advanced code refactoring	No (only rename capability)
Syntax coloring	Yes
On-the-fly code analysis	Yes
Built in code-completion	Yes
Documentation comment tags	Yes (AsDoc)
Source code generation tools	Yes
2. Visual designing	
Drag and drop design	Yes
UML (Unified Modeling Language)-diagramming tools	No
Cascading Style Sheets (CSS)-editing tools	Yes
3. Debugging and compiling	
Compiler error/warning messages	Yes
Testing tools	Yes (FlexUnit)
Conditional breakpoints	Yes
On mobile device emulator emulating	Yes
On locally connected mobile device debugging/running	Yes (Android™ and BlackBerry™ Tablet OS-based mobile devices)
4. Building and publishing	
Building wizard	Yes
Signing wizard	Yes (integration with BlackBerry™ Tablet SDK for Adobe™ AIR™)
5. Extra tools	
Project file explorer	Yes
Web services integration wizard	Yes, SOAP (Simple Object Access Protocol) and REST (Representational State Transfer)
Advanced import/export capabilities	Yes
Application server integration wizard	Yes (Java, PHP, ColdFusion™, ASP.NET™)
Web framework integration	Yes (Zend™ Framework)
Update manager capability	Yes
Version control tools	Yes, CVS (Concurrent Versions System)

Builder™ provides a WYSWYG (What You See Is What You Get) editor for visually building UIs based on MXML. It also offers wizards for packaging and digitally signing mobile applications for Android™, Apple™ iOS and BlackBerry™ Tablet OS platforms.

The overall features of Adobe™ Flash Builder™ are described in Table 1.

The main capabilities of Adobe™ Flash Builder™ 4.5 are described in Table 2.

2.1.2. FlashDevelop

FlashDevelop is a free and open source IDE for Adobe™ Flash™, Adobe™ Flex™ and Haxe applications development. Haxe is an open source

Table 3. Overall features of FlashDevelop

General Features	
License type	Massachusetts Institute of Technology (MIT) license
Developer	FlashDevelop
Website	http://www.flashdevelop.org/
Latest stable release	4.6.1 (May, 2014)
Operating system	Microsoft™ Windows™
Screenshot	

high-level multi-platform programming language targeting different source code languages such as PHP, JavaScript and C#. FlashDevelop has text-editing capabilities for handling XML and HTML code; therefore, it can be used as a code editor for Web development. FlashDevelop supports both 2.0 and 3.0 versions of ActionScript. In this sense, it uses the free MTASC (Motion-Twin ActionScript 2 Compiler) compiler for building ActionScript 2.0 applications. It is a .NET™ framework-based application; therefore, it is only available for Microsoft™ Windows™ operating systems as a standalone application.

The overall features of FlashDevelop are described in Table 3.

The main capabilities of FlashDevelop 4.0.4 are described in Table 4.

2.1.3. Powerflasher FDT

Powerflasher FDT is a commercial IDE based on Eclipse™ for building Adobe™ Flash, Adobe™ Flex and Haxe applications. It is developed by PoweFlasher™ and it was released under a free and limited edition and under a complete edition. In addition, it is available as a standalone application and as a plug-in for an already configured Eclipse™ environment. Powerflasher FDT supports a complete mobile development workflow for Android™, Apple™ iOS and BlackBerry™ Tablet OS applications based on Adobe™ AIR™. It can be extended and customized by using a plug-in called SWFBridge™. SWFBridge™ is an open source platform that allows developers to use ActionScript and Adobe™ Flex™ to create new features such as views, plug-ins and tools for supporting custom workflows. Powerflasher

Table 4. Main capabilities of FlashDevelop

1. Source code editing	
Scripting language support (MXML)	Yes
Advanced code refactoring	Yes
Syntax coloring	Yes
On-the-fly code analysis	No
Built in code-completion	Yes
Documentation comment tags	Yes (JavaDoc)
Source code generation tools	Yes
2. Visual designing	
Drag and drop design	No
UML-diagramming tools	No (only through plug-ins)
CSS-editing tools	Yes
3. Debugging and compiling	
Compiler error/warning messages	Yes
Testing tools	No
Conditional breakpoints	No
On mobile device emulator emulating	Yes
On locally connected mobile device debugging/running	No
4. Building and publishing	
Mobile Applications Packaging wizard	No (it only has a standard building capability)
Mobile Applications Signing wizard	No
5. Extra tools	
Project file explorer	Yes
Web services integration wizard tool	No
Advanced import/export project capabilities	No (it has integration with Adobe™ Flash™ Creative Suite™)
Application server integration wizard	No (only manually)
Web framework integration	No
Update manager capability	Yes
Version control tools	No (only through plug-ins)

FDT exploits haxe capabilities in order to provide HTML5 and WebGL development support.

The overall features of Powerflasher FDT are described in Table 5.

The main capabilities of Powerflasher FDT 5.6.2 are described in Table 6.

2.1.4. CodeDrive™

CodeDrive™ is a commercial IDE for building ActionScript™ 3.0 applications using the Adobe™ Flex™ SDK. It is available as a Microsoft™ Visual Studio™™ 2010 extension and as a standalone application. CodeDrive™ allows developing Adobe™ Flash™-based front-ends for .NET™

Table 5. Overall features of Powerflasher FDT

General Features	
License type	Commercial
Developer	Powerflasher
Website	http://fdt.powerflasher.com/
Latest stable release	6 (May, 2014)
Operating system	Microsoft™ Windows™, Mac OS™, Linux™
Screenshot	

applications using the same IDE. CodeDrive™ is developed by iSpring Research and it was released under a paid edition; a fully-functional free trial version is also available. CodeDrive™ allows for joint debugging Adobe™ Flash™ and Microsoft™ Visual Studio™ projects as well as simultaneously debugging multiple Adobe™ Flash™ projects. The CodeDrive™ build engine is based on the RIO™ compiler and the Adobe™ Flex™ application compiler. RIO™ is an SDK supplied by iSpring Research for building RIAs such as players, games and e-learning courses based on Flash™ content.

The overall features of CodeDrive™ are described in Table 7.

The main capabilities of CodeDrive™ 1.5 are described in Table 8.

2.1.5. SapphireSteel Amethyst Plugin for Visual Studio™

SapphireSteel Amethyst is a commercial IDE based on Microsoft™ Visual Studio™ for developing Adobe™ Flash™ and Adobe™ Flex™-based Web and desktop applications. It is a product of SapphireSteel Software and it is released under a free limited edition and under a paid complete edition. SapphireSteel Amethyst 1.6 is supplied in separate versions for Microsoft™ Visual Studio™ 2008 and Microsoft™ Visual Studio™ 2010. It supports versions 3 and 4 of Adobe™ Flex™ as well as versions 9 and 10 of Adobe™ Flash™ Player. Like Adobe™ Flash Builder™, SapphireSteel Amethyst provides a drag and drop editor for visually building GUIs based on MXML. In addition, it enables developers to share code with Adobe™ Flash Creative Suite™ and Adobe™

Table 6. Main capabilities of Powerflasher FDT

1. Source code editing	
Scripting language support (MXML)	Yes
Advanced code refactoring	Yes
Syntax coloring	Yes
On-the-fly code analysis	Yes
Built in code-completion	Yes
Documentation comment tags	Yes (AsDoc)
Source code generation tools	Yes
2. Visual designing	
Drag and drop design	No
UML-diagramming tools	No
CSS-editing tools	No
3. Debugging and compiling	
Compiler error/warning messages	Yes
Testing tools	No
Conditional breakpoints	Yes
On mobile device emulator emulating	Yes
On locally connected mobile device emulating	Yes
4. Building and publishing	
Mobile Applications Packaging wizard	Yes
Mobile Applications Signing wizard	Yes (integration with BlackBerry™ Tablet SDK for Adobe™ AIR™)
5. Extra tools	
Project file explorer	Yes
Web services integration wizard	No
Advanced import/export project capabilities	Yes
Application server integration wizard	Yes, HTTP servers)
Web framework integration	No
Update manager capability	Yes
Version control tools	Yes (CVS)

Flash Builder™ to import and convert existing projects. Optionally, SapphireSteel Amethyst can be integrated with Midnight Coders' WebORB integration server, which allows creating Adobe™ Flex™ applications that communicate with ASP. NET™ servers.

The overall features of SapphireSteel Amethyst are described in Table 9.

The main capabilities of SapphireSteel 1.6 are described in Table 13.10.

2.1.6. Discussion

Besides Adobe™ Flash™ Builder, SapphireSteel Amethyst provides a visual UI editor for dragging and dropping MXML components. Nevertheless, unlike the other tools for Adobe™ Flex™-based

Table 7. Overall features of CodeDrive™

General Features	
License type	Commercial
Developer	iSpring Research
Website	http://www.codedrive.com/
Latest stable release	1.5 (May, 2014)
Operating system	Microsoft™ Windows™
Screenshot	

development described in this section, Amethyst 1.6 does not provide integration with the AIR Debugger Launcher (ADL) tool -the emulator for AIR™-based applications that is distributed in the Adobe™ Flex™ SDK. Thereby, the Android™ SDK emulator needs to be used to debug AIR™-based applications in Amethyst so that same configuration is required at both the Android emulator-side and the Amethyst-side. In fact, debugging in Amethyst requires applications to be actually installed in the Android™ emulator; therefore, they must be previously packaged and signed by using digital certificates. This process is covered by Amethyst; however, the configuration at the Android™ emulator-side, e.g., creation of Android Virtual Devices (AVDs) needs to be done by hand. Because the Android™ emulator is not the primary target of AIR™-based application debugging task, the hardware capabilities to be emulated need to be carefully considered. For instance, the camera is not emulated in the Android™ emulator before Android™ API level 14. API level is set during AVD creation. From this perspective, for the usage scenario stated at the beginning of this section, a lower level of the Android™ API was selected; thereby, camera was not emulated. Unlike the other tools for Adobe™ Flex™-based development that support ADL-based debugging, flashdevelop 4.0.4 does not provide a debug configuration wizard; therefore, the ADL parameters such as the model of the device to be emulated and the screen size need to be directly configured in the batch file executing the ADL tool.

Table 8. Main capabilities of CodeDrive™

1. Source code editing	
Scripting language support (MXML)	No
Advanced code refactoring	No (only rename capability)
Syntax and semantic coloring	Yes
On-the-fly code analysis	Yes
Built in code-completion	Yes
Documentation comment tags	Yes (AsDoc)
Source code generation tools	Yes (No setters/getters generation)
2. Visual designing	
Drag and drop design	No
UML-diagramming tools	No
CSS-editing tools	Yes
3. Debugging and compiling	
Compiler error/warning messages	Yes
Testing tools	No
Conditional breakpoints	Yes
On mobile device emulator emulating	No
On locally connected mobile device emulating	No
4. Building and publishing	
Mobile Applications Packaging wizard	No (it only has a standard building capability)
Mobile Applications Signing wizard	No
5. Extra tools	
Project file explorer	Yes
Web services integration wizard	No
Advanced import/export project capabilities	No
Application server integration wizard	No (it only has a database server integration wizard)
Web framework integration	No
Update manager capability	Yes
Version control tools	No

2.2. JavaFX™-Based RIAs Integrated Development Environments

JavaFX™ is a free and open source application framework for building Web browser-based and out-of-browser RIAs as well as desktop applications. JavaFX™ uses FXML, which is an XML-based user interface markup language. It also uses JVM -based programming languages such as Java and Groovy for defining business logic. FXML and Java source code are compiled into Java bytecode; therefore, JavaFX™ applications can run on any desktop and Web browser that runs the JRE (Java Runtime Environment).

NetBeans™ IDE is considered to be the official IDE for JavaFX-based development. In fact, it provides tight integration with the official JavaFX™ UI design tool: JavaFX™ Scene Builder.

Table 9. Overall features of SapphireSteel Amethyst

General Features	
License type	Commercial
Developer	SapphireSteel Software
Website	http://www.sapphiresteel.com/Adobe-Flex-IDE-Amethyst-Beta-2
Latest stable release	2 (May, 2014)
Operating system	Microsoft™ Windows™
Screenshot	

Nevertheless, virtually any Java IDE may be used to develop JavaFX™ applications by means of some configuration. These options are described in this section.

JavaFX™ does not currently support the development of mobile applications (JavaFX 2.0). In addition, due to the lack of support for Webcam access on JavaFX-based desktop applications, the usage scenario employed to discuss the features of the tools for JavaFX-based development is aimed at developing a Web browser-based RIA showing advanced client-server communication mechanisms. In fact, this scenario is intended to provide an overview of the client-server communication aspect of RIAs development (Toffetti et al., 2011), namely the ability of retrieving data from two or more simultaneous sources in asynchronous mode. The impact of this aspect on RIA UIs implementation is actually addressed in chapter 8. In detail, the application developed in the above described usage scenario is a single-page application that asynchronously loads four remote images, each one from a different source. The application is forced to load the images asynchronously by setting to true the *backgroundLoading* property of the JavaFX™ *Image* class. This causes the image-loading operation to occur in a separate execution thread to keep the UI responsiveness. As can be inferred, the JavaFX™ *Image* class is used for loading images from URLs (Uniform Resource Locators). The images need to be further displayed by using the *ImageView* class.

2.2.1. NetBeans™ IDE

NetBeans™ IDE is a free and open source IDE developed by Oracle™ Corporation. It is built on top of NetBeans™ Platform. NetBeans™ Platform is a Java-based framework for desktop applications development. NetBeans™ Platform-

Table 10. Main capabilities of SapphireSteel

1. Source code editing	
Scripting language support (MXML)	Yes
Advanced code refactoring	Unknown
Syntax and semantic coloring	Yes
On-the-fly code analysis	Yes
Built in code-completion	Yes
Documentation comment tags	Yes (AsDoc)
Source code generation tools	Yes
2. Visual designing	
Drag and drop design	Yes
UML-diagramming tools	Yes
CSS-editing tools	-
3. Debugging and compiling	
Compiler error/warning messages	Yes
Testing tools	No
Conditional breakpoints	Yes
On mobile device emulator emulating	No
On locally connected mobile device emulating	No
4. Building and publishing	
Applications Packaging wizard	No (it only has a standard building capability)
Applications Signing wizard	No
5. Extra tools	
Project file explorer	Yes
Web services integration wizard	No
Advanced import/export project capabilities	No (it only allows importing and converting Adobe™ Flash Builder™ projects)
Application server integration wizard	No (it only has a database server integration wizard)
Web framework integration	Yes (Midnight Coders' WebORM)
Update manager capability	Yes
Version control tools	Yes, TFSV (Team Foundation Server Version Control)

based applications such as NetBeans™ IDE can be extended by using software components called modules; here, modules are comparable to plug-ins. NetBeans™ IDE officially supports Java-based technology as well as Groovy, PHP, JavaScript and C/C++ programming languages; however, there are third-party modules for supporting other languages such as Python and Scala.

The overall features of NetBeans™ IDE are described in Table 11.

The main capabilities of NetBeans™ IDE 7.2 are described in Table 12.

Table 11. Overall features of NetBeans™ IDE

General Features	
License type	Dual: CDDL (Common Development and Distribution License) and GPL (GNU General Public License) v. 2.0
Developer	Oracle™ Corporation
Website	http://netbeans.org/
Latest stable release	8 (May, 2014)
Operating system	Microsoft™ Windows™, Mac OS™, Linux™ and Solaris™
Screenshot	

2.2.2. JavaFX™ Scene Builder™

JavaFX™ Scene Builder is a commercial free software tool for visually designing JavaFX™ applications' UIs in FXML. It is a component of the JavaFX™ platform. It was initially developed by Sun™ microsystems and it is actually maintained by Oracle™ Corporation. Although JavaFX™ Scene Builder can be used in combination with any Java IDE for writing JavaFX™ applications' business logic, it provides tight integration with NetBeans™ IDE. JavaFX™ Scene Builder offers a drag and drop WYSWYG UI editor; this editor supports CSS external files binding for look and feel customization.

The overall features of JavaFX™ Scene Builder are described in Table 13.

The main capabilities of JavaFX™ Scene Builder 1.0 are described in Table 14.

2.2.3. E(fx)clipse Plugin for Eclipse™

E(fx)clipse is a free and open source Eclipse™-based IDE for developing JavaFX™ 2.0 applications. It is developed by BestSolution.at and it is available only as a plug-in for an already configured Eclipse™ environment. E(fx)clipse is also a runtime platform that enables developers to develop JavaFX™ applications on top of Eclipse™ Equinox which is an implementation of the OSGi technology. OSGi is a set of specifications that define a service platform and a dynamic component model for Java. E(fx)eclipse provides a DSL (Domain-Specific Language) called fxgraph for the definition of a JSON (JavaScript Object

Table 12. Main capabilities of NetBeans IDE

1. Source code editing	
Scripting language support (FXML)	Si
Advanced code refactoring	Yes
Syntax and semantic coloring	Yes
On-the-fly code analysis	Yes
Built in code-completion	Yes
Documentation comment tags	Yes (JavaDoc)
Source code generation tools	Yes
2. Visual designing	
Drag and drop design	No (only Swing controls)
UML-diagramming tools	No (only through plug-ins)
CSS-editing tools	Yes
3. Debugging and compiling	
Compiler error/warning messages	Yes
Testing tools	Yes (JUnit)
Conditional breakpoints	Yes
On mobile device emulator emulating	-
On locally connected mobile device emulating	-
4. Building and publishing	
Applications Packaging wizard	Yes, JAR (Java ARchive) and JNLP (Java Network Launching Protocol) files
Applications Signing wizard	Yes (JAR files)
5. Extra tools	
Project file explorer	Yes
Web services integration wizard	Yes (SOAP and REST)
Advanced import/export project capabilities	No (it only allows importing Eclipse™ projects)
Application server integration wizard	Yes
Web framework integration	Yes (Java frameworks)
Update manager capability	Yes
Version control tools	Yes (Git™, Mercurial, Subversion™ and CVS)

Notation)-like object graph which is translated into FXML code. It also provides a CSS editor that recognizes the CSS properties used by JavaFX™ 2.0 besides the properties commonly supported by popular Web browsers.

The overall features of E(fx)clipse are described in Table 15.

The main capabilities of E(fx)clipse 0.1.0 are described in Table 16.

2.2.4. Discussion

NetBeans™ IDE 7.2 does not integrate a visual UI editor for dragging and dropping FXML components; thereby, an additional tool needs to be

Table 13. Overall features of JavaFX™ Scene Builder

General Features	
License type	Commercial
Developer	Oracle™ Corporation
Website	http://www.oracle.com/technetwork/java/javafx/tools/index.html
Latest stable release	1.1 (May, 2014)
Operating system	Microsoft™ Windows™ and Mac OS™
Screenshot	

used for visually designing JavaFX™-based UIs: JavaFX™ Scene Builder. This allows for a separation of developer and designer roles so that one specific tool can be provided to each role. In fact, JavaFX™-based UIs can be programmatically defined in NetBeans™ IDE (in "development mode") and further edited in JavaFX™ Scene Builder (in "design mode"). Therefore, NetBeans™ IDE provides tight integration with JavaFX™ Scene Builder. This ensures the integration of the developers and designers works. Similarly, e(fx)clipse 0.1.0 does not provide a visual FXML editor. In fact, this Eclipse™-based tool does not provide a perspective for JavaFX™-based development; thereby, JavaFX™-based applications are implemented, debugged and executed as pure Java-based applications. In Eclipse™, a perspective defines the initial set and layout of views in a workbench window. A workbench window is a collection of one or more perspectives ("Eclipse documentation - Previous Release," n.d.).

2.3. Microsoft™ Silverlight™-Based RIAs Integrated Development Environments

Microsoft™ Silverlight™ is a free application framework for building both Web browser-based and out-of-browser RIAs as well as applications for Windows™ Phone devices. On the one hand, Silverlight™ uses an XML-based user interface markup language called XAML (eXtensible Application Markup Language). On the other hand, it uses .NET™ Framework-supported program-

Table 14. Main capabilities of JavaFX™ Scene Builder 1.0

1. Source code editing	
Scripting language support (FXML)	Yes
Advanced code refactoring	-
Syntax and semantic coloring	-
On-the-fly code analysis	-
Built in code-completion	-
Documentation comment tags	-
Source code generation tools	Yes (FXML source code)
2. Visual designing	
Drag and drop design	Yes
UML-diagramming tools	No
CSS-editing tools	No (it only allows linking external CSS files)
3. Debugging and compiling	
Compiler error/warning messages	-
Testing tools	-
Conditional breakpoints	-
On mobile device emulator emulating	-
On locally connected mobile device emulating	-
4. Building and publishing	
Applications Packaging wizard	-
Applications Signing wizard	-
5. Extra tools	
Project file explorer	No
Web services integration wizard	-
Advanced import/export project capabilities	Yes
Application server integration wizard	-
Web framework integration	-
Update manager capability	No
Version control tools	No

ming languages, including dynamic languages such as IronPhyton and type-safe languages such as Visual C#™, for application business logic definition. The runtime for Silverlight™ applications is available as a plug-in for the most popular Web-browsers.

Microsoft™ Visual Studio™ is considered to be the official IDE for Microsoft™ Silverlight™. As in the case of JavaFX, there is a UI design tool for Microsoft™ Silverlight: Microsoft™ Expression Blend™. This tool provides tight integration with Visual Studio™. In addition to these official tools, there are other third-party tools based on popular extensible plug-in systems such as Eclipse™. These options are described in this section.

As in the case of the tools for Adobe™ Flex™-based development, the scope and limitations of

Table 15. Overall features of E(fx)clipse

General Features	
License type	EPL (Eclipse Public License)
Developer	BestSolution.at
Website	http://efxclipse.org/
Latest stable release	0.9.0 (May, 2014)
Operating system	Microsoft Windows™, Mac OS™ and Linux™
Screenshot	

the tools for Silverlight™-based development are discussed by means of a usage scenario addressing the development of a mobile application able to capture video from Windows™ Phone-based mobile devices' cameras. In detail, the application is a single-page application that displays a 640x480 video at the top of the screen (below the default title panel, which includes the application and page names) when the page is loaded. For that purpose, the Silverlight™ *CaptureDeviceConfiguration* and *CaptureSource* classes are used. The former is used to access to audio and video capture devices such as webcams and mobile devices' cameras whereas the latter allows applications to capture audio and video from these devices.

2.3.1. Microsoft™ Visual Studio™

Microsoft™ Visual Studio™ is a commercial IDE supplied by Microsoft™ Corporation for developing XML Web services, console applications, traditional Web applications, Windows™-based desktop applications, RIAs and Windows™ Phone applications. In fact, it supports .NET™ Framework and Microsoft™ Silverlight™ platforms. Visual Studio™ 2012 was released under three different paid editions as well as under separate free limited editions for Web development and Windows™-based applications development. It provides a set of visual designers, e.g. UML use case and class diagram designers and a drag and drop UI designer for the Windows™ Presentation Foundation API which uses the XAML language. The Visual Studio functionality can be extended

Table 16. Main capabilities of E(fx)clipse

1. Source code editing	
Scripting language support (FXML)	Yes
Advanced code refactoring	Unknown
Syntax and semantic coloring	Yes
On-the-fly code analysis	Yes (Only available in the Java code editor)
Built in code-completion	Yes
Documentation comment tags	Yes (JavaDoc)
Source code generation tools	Yes (Only available in the Java code editor)
2. Visual designing	
Drag and drop design	No
UML-diagramming tools	No
CSS-editing tools	Yes
3. Debugging and compiling	
Compiler error/warning messages	Yes
Testing tools	Yes (JUnit)
Conditional breakpoints	Yes
On mobile device emulator emulating	-
On locally connected mobile device emulating	-
4. Building and publishing	
Applications Packaging wizard	Yes (JAR and JNLP files)
Applications Signing wizard	Yes (JAR files)
5. Extra tools	
Project file explorer	Yes
Web services integration wizard	No
Advanced import/export project capabilities	Yes
Application server integration wizard	Unknown
Web framework integration	No
Update manager capability	Yes
Version control tools	Yes (CVS)

by using add-ins; add-ins are attached applications that can be integrated into the IDE. Add-ins can be implemented in any Component Object Model (COM)-consuming programming language. In this sense, the add-in called Microsoft™ Silverlight™ Tools for Visual Studio™ must be installed in Visual Studio™ to provide support for the Silverlight™ platform.

The overall features of Microsoft™ Visual Studio are described in Table 17.

The main capabilities of Microsoft™ Visual Studio™ 2012 are described in Table 18.

2.3.2. Microsoft™ Expression Blend™

Microsoft™ Expression Blend™ is a commercial software tool for designing Windows Presentation

Table 17. Overall features of Microsoft™ Visual Studio

General Features	
License type	Commercial
Developer	Microsoft™ Corporation
Website	http://www.microsoft.com/visualstudio/11/en-us
Latest stable release	12.0.30110.00 (Visual Studio™ 2013)
Operating system	Microsoft™ Windows™
Screenshot	

Foundation and Microsoft™ Silverlight™ application UIs using XAML. It supports multiple target platforms, including versions 3 and 4 of Microsoft™ Silverlight™ and versions 3 and 4 of Microsoft™ .NET™ Framework. Microsoft™ Expression Blend™ is developed by Microsoft™ Corporation and it was released as a version for Windows™ Phone applications development as well as part of Microsoft™ Expression Studio™, a complete suite of tools for designing Web browser-based RIAs and Windows™-based applications. Regarding to its main features, Microsoft™ Expression Blend™ includes both a WYSIWG editor and a code editor with XAML, Visual C#™ and Visual Basic .NET autocompletion. Furthermore, it enables visual designers to import existing Adobe™ Photoshop and Adobe™ Illustrator files as design assets.

The overall features of Microsoft™ Expression Blend™ are described in Table 19.

The main capabilities of Microsoft™ Expression Blend™ 4.0.20525.0 are described in Table 20.

2.3.3. Eclipse4SL Plugin for Eclipse™

Eclipse4SL is an Eclipse™-based free and open source IDE developed by Soyatec for the development of Microsoft™ Silverlight™ applications. It is available only as a plug-in for the Eclipse™ IDE. Unlike Microsoft™ Visual Studio™, Eclipse4SL is a multi-platform IDE because it can be used in both Microsoft™ Windows™ and Mac OS™ operating systems. The latest stable release of Eclipse4SL only supports version 2 of Microsoft™ Silverlight™ platform. The purpose of this open source project is to provide

Table 18. Main capabilities of Microsoft™ Visual Studio™

1. Source code editing	
Scripting language support (FXML)	Yes
Advanced code refactoring	Yes (Only available for Visual C#™ development)
Syntax and semantic coloring	Yes
On-the-fly code analysis	Yes
Built in code-completion	Yes
Documentation comment tags	Yes (XML Documentation Comments)
Source code generation tools	Yes
2. Visual Designing	
Drag and drop design	Yes
UML-diagramming tools	Yes
CSS-editing tools	Yes
3. Debuging and Compiling	
Compiler error/warning messages	Yes
Testing tools	Yes (Microsoft™ Unit Testing Framework)
Conditional breakpoints	Yes
On mobile device emulator emulating	No (Only available in Visual Studio 2010)
On locally connected mobile device emulating	No (Only available in Visual Studio 2010)
4. Building and Publishing	
Applications Packaging wizard	Yes (Only in Visual Studio™ for Windows™ Phone)
Applications Signing wizard	No (Signing is performed in the Windows™ Phone Dev Center)
5. Extra Tools	
Project file explorer	Yes
Web services integration wizard	Yes (Only XML Web Services)
Advanced import/export project capabilities	No (it only allows exporting project templates)
Application server integration wizard	Yes
Web framework integration	Unknown
Update manager capability	Yes
Version control tools	Yes, (TFSV)

interoperability between Silverlight™ and Java by involving Eclipse™ RCP (Rich Client Platform). RCP is a platform for building and deploying native rich UIs to a variety of desktop operating systems. Eclipse4SL offers a WYSIWYG editor and a XAML code editor as well as a Visual C#™ code editor for building the applications' business logic. Projects created by using Eclipse4SL are compatible with Microsoft™ Visual Studio™ and Expression Blend™ development tools.

The overall features of Eclipse4SL are described in Table 21.

The main capabilities of Eclipse4SL 1.0.0 are described in Table 22.

Table 19. Overall features of Microsoft™ Expression Blend™

General Features	
License type	Commercial
Developer	Microsoft™ Corporation
Website	http://www.microsoft.com/expression/products/Blend_Overview.aspx
Latest stable release	4.0.20525.0 (May, 2014)
Operating system	Microsoft™ Windows™
Screenshot	

2.3.4. Discussion

Unlike Visual Studio™, eclipse4SL does not support Windows™ Phone applications development. Likewise, eclipse4SL does not provide debugging facilities; therefore, applications cannot be debugged but only executed using eclipse4SL. In fact, Visual Studio™ provides a built-in Windows™ Phone emulator for both debugging and running (releasing) Windows™ Phone applications. However, this emulator is not a fully-featured emulator. For instance, the camera is not emulated before version 8 of Windows™ Phone. From this perspective, for the purposes of the usage scenario stated in this section, version 7.1 of Windows™ Phone was used; as a result, the camera was not emulated. Despite the aforementioned drawbacks, eclipse4SL seems to be a powerful tool for Silverlight™-based Web applica-

tion design and development because it integrates a visual XAML editor. In fact, this Eclipse™-based tool provides a perspective that integrates a Silverlight™ component palette, a Silverlight™ project explorer, a C# editor, a XAML editor and a WYSIWYG view. Finally, it is important to notice that, in Visual Studio™, Silverlight™-based Web applications are created as solutions containing two projects: one for the Silverlight™ application itself and one for an ASP.NET™-based Web application hosting the Silverlight™ code. Similarly, in eclipse4SL, applications consist of two separate projects. This can be confusing for non-experienced Silverlight™ developers.

Table 20. Main capabilities of Microsoft™ Expression Blend™

1. Source Code Editing	
Scripting language support (XAML)	Yes
Advanced code refactoring	No (Only rename capability)
Syntax and semantic coloring	Yes
On-the-fly code analysis	Yes
Built in code-completion	Yes
Documentation comment tags	No
Source code generation tools	Yes
2. Visual Designing	
Drag and drop design	Yes
UML-diagramming tools	No
CSS-editing tools	No (Only in the Expression Blend™ 5 Dev Preview)
3. Debuging and Compiling	
Compiler error/warning messages	Yes
Testing tools	No (Only in Visual Studio™)
Conditional breakpoints	No (Only in Visual Studio™)
On mobile device emulator emulating	Yes (Only in the Expression Blend™ for Windows™ Phone)
On locally connected mobile device emulating	Yes
4. Building and Publishing	
Applications Packaging wizard	No (Only in Visual Studio™)
Applications Signing wizard	No (Signing is performed in the Windows™ Phone Dev Center)
5. Extra Tools	
Project file explorer	Yes
Web services integration wizard	No
Advanced import/export project capabilities	Yes
Application server integration wizard	No
Web framework integration	No
Update manager capability	No
Version control tools	Yes, TFSV is integrated)

2.4. Multi-Target Integrated Development Environments

In this section a standalone IDE called IntelliJ IDEA™ is analyzed. This tool targets both JavaFX™ and Adobe™ Flex™-based RIAs development. It can be viewed as a third-party IDE for framework-based RIAs development in the sense that it is not officially provided as part of an application framework although it supports the underlying programming languages and development workflows. The usage scenario employed to discuss the scope and limitations of IntelliJ IDEA™ is the same usage scenario employed in the case of the tools for Adobe™ Flex™-based development. Therefore, the discussion is given in the context of the other tools for Adobe™ Flex™-based development.

Table 21. Overall features of Eclipse4SL

General Features	
License type	EPL v. 1.0
Developer	Soyatec
Website	http://www.eclipse4sl.org/
Latest stable release	1.0.0 (May, 2014)
Operating system	Microsoft™ Windows™ and Mac OS™
Screenshot	

2.4.1. IntelliJ IDEA™

IntelliJ IDEA™ is a commercial IDE built in top of the open source IntelliJ™ platform. IntelliJ™ is a Java-based platform for building language-aware IDEs that integrates components such as text editors, UI frameworks and version control tools. IntelliJ IDEA™ is developed by JetBrains Software Company and it is released under a free and open source limited edition as well as under a complete edition. IntelliJ IDEA™ functionality can be extended and customized trough plug-ins. New programing and XML-based languages support are an example of improvement added by plug-ins. IntelliJ IDEA™ brings support for polyglot development based on Java, Groovy, Python, Ruby, JavaScript, among other programming languages. IntelliJ IDEA™ also provides support for Web, mobile and enterprise frameworks, e.g.,

Spring, Adobe™ Flex™, Apache Struts™ and persistence frameworks like Hibernate™. In addition, like Oracle™ JDeveloper and Microsoft™ Visual Studio™, IntelliJ IDEA™ offers an UML diagramming tool for designing classes, packages and database diagrams. Because IntelliJ IDEA™ is primarily a Java-based IDE, it can be manually configured for developing JavaFX™ 2.0 applications. JavaFX™ 1.0 support is available via a third-party plug-in.

The overall features of IntelliJ IDEA™ are described in Table 23.

The main capabilities of IntelliJ IDEA™ 11.1.3 are described in Table 24.

2.4.2. Discussion

Unlike the other tools for Adobe™ Flex™-based development, IntelliJ IDEA™ 11.1.3 does not

Table 22. Main capabilities of Eclipse4SL

1. Source Code Editing	
Scripting language support (XAML)	Yes
Advanced code refactoring	No (Only rename capability)
Syntax and semantic coloring	Yes
On-the-fly code analysis	Yes
Built in code-completion	No (Not live code-completion)
Documentation comment tags	No
Source code generation tools	Yes
2. Visual Designing	
Drag and drop design	Yes (Only in XAML code view)
UML-diagramming tools	No
CSS-editing tools	No
3. Debuging and Compiling	
Compiler error/warning messages	Yes
Testing tools	No
Conditional breakpoints	No
On mobile device emulator emulating	No (It does not support Windows Phone™ development)
On locally connected mobile device emulating	No (It does not support Windows Phone™ development)
4. Building and Publishing	
Applications Packaging wizard	No (It only has a standard building capability)
Applications Signing wizard	No
5. Extra Tools	
Project file explorer	Yes
Web services integration wizard	No (Web services clients implementation is possible by using Windows Communication Foundation APIs)
Advanced import/export project capabilities	Yes
Application server integration wizard	Unknown
Web framework integration	Unknown
Update manager capability	Yes
Version control tools	Yes (CVS)

provide a means for editing AIR descriptor files. These configuration files are automatically generated by IntelliJ IDEA™ and they are not shown in the folder structures of the AIR-based application projects. In fact, neither the compiler output files are shown in theses folder structures. However, custom descriptor files can be created on demand as part of the build configurations of the applications. For this purpose, a wizard is provided.

Table 23. Overall features of IntelliJ IDEA™

General Features	
License type	Commercial
Developer	JetBrains
Website	http://www.jetbrains.com/idea/
Latest stable release	13.1
Operating system	Microsoft Windows™, Mac OS™ and Linux™
Screenshot	

3. MDD TOOLS FOR RIAS DEVELOPMENT

Another development approach for RIAs is based on MDD methodologies and software tools from both researchers and software vendors. MDD methods employ high-level software models for describing applications without specifying implementation issues. MDD tools ideally generate executable code starting from software models.

Due to the lack of RIAs systematic development approaches, some hypermedia, multimedia and Web existing methodologies have been recently extended adopting MDD as a development framework for addressing RIAs development (Toffetti et al., 2011). Thus, the type of development approach is used as a key attribute for describing MDD tools for RIAs development.

Although the typical phases in MDD are requirement analysis, design (at different abstraction levels), implementation, testing and maintenance, most of MDD approaches are focused on design, especially on presentation design and they are centered on user interactions. However, RIAs design addresses data, business logic and communication details besides presentation details. Thereby, these aspects are considered in this section for describing the main capabilities of MDD tools for RIAs development.

3.1. WebRatio™

WebRatio™ is a MDD environment developed by Homeria Open Solutions, which supports planning, production and maintenance of customized Web applications. It is available either as a standalone application or as a plug-in embeddable

Table 24. Main capabilities of IntelliJ IDEA™

1. Source Code Editing	
Scripting language support (XAML)	Yes
Advanced code refactoring	Yes
Syntax and semantic coloring	Yes
On-the-fly code analysis	Yes
Built in code-completion	Yes
Documentation comment tags	Unknown
Source code generation tools	Yes
2. Visual Designing	
Drag and drop design	Yes
UML-diagramming tools	Yes
CSS-editing tools	Yes
3. Debuging and Compiling	
Compiler error/warning messages	Yes
Testing tools	Yes (FlexUnit)
Conditional breakpoints	Yes
On mobile device emulator emulating	Yes
On locally connected mobile device emulating	Yes
4. Building and Publishing	
Applications Packaging wizard	Yes (Only Android™ and Apple™ iOS applications)
Applications Signing wizard	Yes (Only Android™ and Apple™ iOS applications)
5. Extra Tools	
Project file explorer	Yes
Web services integration wizard	Yes (SOAP and REST)
Advanced import/export project capabilities	No (Only import/export settings capability)
Application server integration wizard	Yes (HTTP servers)
Web framework integration	Yes (Spring, Apache Struts™, Hibernate™ among others)
Update manager capability	Yes
Version control tools	Yes (Git and SVN)

in an already configured Eclipse™ environment. WebRatio™ offers a business logic model which is expressed in the OMG's BPMN (Business Process Modeling Notation) as well as a technology-independent application model which relies on the WebML modeling language. The latter allows for specifying all the functional requirements of an application. Starting from both models WebRatio™ is able to automatically generate functional

and ready-to-deploy Web applications (Acerbis et al., 2007). Although WebRatio™ can be extended by adding business logic components and custom layout templates defined in a rendering language such as HTML, CSS, JavaScript and AJAX (Asynchronous JavaScript And XML), server-side of generated applications is based on Java J2EE technology. The Ajax support allows generating Web browser-based RIAs with functionalities

Table 25. Overall features of WebRatio™

Overall Features	
Research Field	Web Engineering - WebML extensions
Server-side Technology	Java J2EE
Client-side Technology	HTML + Ajax
Modeling Language	WebML (data, hypertext and presentation design), BPMN (business logic design).
Model Scope	Data computation, data storage and client-server communication aspects.
Application Type	Web 2.0 applications
Screenshot	

Table 26. Main capabilities of WebRatio™

1. Presentation	
Partial page refreshing	Yes
Client-side event-handling	Yes
Desktop-like GUI controls	No
Multimedia content	No
2. Data computation	
Client data validation	Yes
Client data sorting	Yes
Client data filtering	Yes
3. Data storage	
Client data storage	No
4. Client-server communication	
Asynchronous communication	Yes
Data synchronization	No

Table 27. Overall features of RUX-Tool

Overall Features	
Research Field	HCI (Human Computer Interaction) - RUX-Method
Server-side Technology	-
Client-side Technology	HTML + Ajax
Modeling Language	Visual DSL for abstract UI designing
Model Scope	Presentation aspects
Application type	RIAs
Screenshot	

Table 28. Main capabilities of RUX-Tool

1. Presentation	
Partial page refreshing	Yes
Client-side event-handling	Yes
Desktop-like GUI controls	Yes
Multimedia content	Yes
2. Data computation	
Client data validation	Yes
Client data sorting	Unknown
Client data filtering	Unknown
3. Data storage	
Client data storage	No
4. Client-server communication	
Asynchronous communication	Yes
Data synchronization	No

Table 29. Overall features of AlexandRIA

Overall Features	
Research Field	RIAs Engineering - PPMRD
Server-side Technology	PHP and JSP
Client-side Technology	Adobe™ Flex (MXML + ActionScript) and HTML + JavaScript.
High level Constructs	Reusable business logic components (Cloud APIs-based), application templates and configuration files templates.
Code Generation Scope	Executable (native) code automatic generation
Application Type	Cross-browser RIAs, cross-platform desktop and mobile applications (Android™, Apple™ iOS, BlackBerry™ Tablet OS).
Screenshot	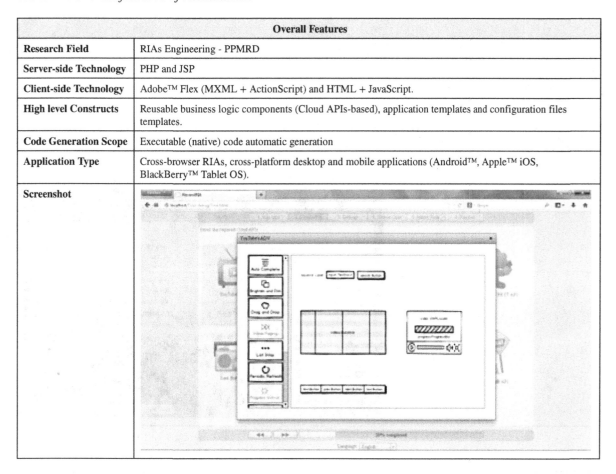

Table 30. Main capabilities of AlexandRIA

1. Presentation	
Partial page refreshing	Yes
Client-side event-handling	Yes
Desktop-like GUI controls	Yes
Multimedia content	Yes
2. Data computation	
Client data validation	Yes
Client data sorting	Yes
Client data filtering	Yes
3. Data storage	
Client data storage	No
4. Client-server communication	
Asynchronous communication	Yes (cloud services back-end)
Data synchronization	No

Table 31. Overall features of Adobe™ AIR™ Launchpad

Overall Features	
Research Field	-
Server-side Technology	-
Client-side Technology	Adobe™ Flex™ (MXML + ActionScript)
High level Constructs	Unknown
Code Generation Scope	Source code automatic generation
Application Type	Multi-platform desktop applications and native mobile applications (Android, Apple™ iOS and BlackBerry™ Tablet OS).
Screenshot	

Table 32. Main capabilities of Adobe™ AIR™ Launchpad

1. Presentation	
Partial page refreshing	Yes
Client-side event-handling	Yes
Desktop-like GUI controls	Yes
Multimedia content	Yes
2. Data computation	
Client data validation	No
Client data sorting	No
Client data filtering	No
3. Data storage	
Client data storage	Yes
4. Client-server communication	
Asynchronous communication	No
Data synchronization	No

such as drag and drop, selective page refresh and dynamic form events handling.

The overall features of WebRatio™ are described in Table 25.

The main capabilities of the MDD tool are described in Table 26.

3.2. RUX-Tool

RUX-Tool is an MDD tool developed by Homeria Open Solutions, which implements RUX-Method (Rich User eXperience Method). RUX-Method addresses the design of multi-device Web browser-based RIAs in three levels: 1) the abstract interface design, which represents a high-level specification, 2) the concrete interface design, which is specific to a device or group of devices but platform-independent and 3) the final interface design, which allows automatically obtaining the final UI code targeting both an implementation platform and a device or set of devices. RUX-Method defines a rich UI control library and the transformation rules between the aforementioned UI design levels (Linaje et al., 2007). RUX-Tool, which is a RIA itself, is available as a plug-in for WebRatio™. In fact, RUX-Tool works together with WebRatio™ to obtain the content structure and the business logic of legacy WebML-designed applications. Conceptually, RUX-Method can be integrated with any Web methodology for obtaining the data and business logic whereas the final UI code is automatically generated using RIA technologies such as Ajax, Adobe™ Flex™ or OpenLaszlo™.

The overall features of RUX-Tool are described in Table 27.

The main capabilities of the MDD tool are described in Table 28.

4. RAD TOOLS FOR RIAS DEVELOPMENT

RIAs development can be achieved by using RAD approaches. RAD is a software development methodology that suggests minimal software modeling and exploits software prototyping (Martin, 1991). Therefore, the use of automation tools is fundamental in RAD approaches. Prototyping tools, diagramming tools and code generators are three kinds of RAD tools that allow enabling higher productivity and saving development time, effort and budget (Linaje et al., 2007).

For practical purposes, in this section code generators are only considered. From this context, as a fundamental principle of RAD tools, code generators must generate source code from high-level constructs. In addition, code generators must generate executable code at least in a semi-automatic way. These aspects are considered for describing the overall features of code generators for RIAs development in following subsections. Furthermore, because RIAs design addresses data, business logic, presentation and communication issues, all these aspects for describing the main capabilities of code generators for RIAs development are considered. Main capabilities besides overall features can be used as criteria for performing evaluations and comparisons between different code generators for RIAs development.

4.1. AlexandRIA

AlexandRIA is an academic code generation tool that automates a UI pattern-based approach for multi-device RIAs code generation BY using Adobe™ Flex™ and PhoneGap™ as underlying cross-platform development frameworks (Colombo-Mendoza et al., 2013). AlexandRIA uses predefined GUI/business logic components as well as application and configuration file templates as high level constructs. In fact, the code generation approach implemented by AlexandRIA is a domain-specific approach focused on generating cloud services APIs-based multi-device RIAs. Here, the term "multi-device RIA" clusters Web browser-based RIAs, desktop RIAs as well as RIAs for mobile devices. AlexandRIA allows developers to generate source and native code of multi-device RIAs from a set of preferences selected throughout a wizard. The source code generated by AlexandRIA is ready-to-import in Adobe™ Flash Builder™ 4.5. Similarly, the application installers generated by AlexandRIA are ready-to-deploy on target devices, if applicable. AlexandRIA is a Web browser-based RIA itself and it is available via Internet.

The overall features of AlexandRIA are described in Table 29.

The main capabilities of the RAD tool are described in Table 30.

4.2. Adobe™ AIR™ Launchpad

Adobe™ AIR™ Launchpad is a commercial RAD tool developed by Adobe™ Labs, which allows generating ready-to-compile source code of Adobe™ AIR™-based applications, i.e., desktop applications and mobile applications for Android™, Apple™ iOS and BlackBerry™ Tablet OS operating systems, which are deployed on the Adobe™ AIR™ runtime. Basically, Adobe™ AIR™ Launchpad is a code generator. The outputted applications are not intended to be fully-functional applications but starting projects that can be imported in Adobe™ Flash Builder™. Adobe™ AIR™ Launchpad, which is available as a standalone application, offers a set of predefined capabilities that can be selected throughout a wizard. In this sense, with the aim of allowing developers to use the source code as starting point for developing fully-functional Adobe™ AIR™-based applications, the selected capabilities are implemented in a way that can be easily customized and extended.

The overall features of Adobe™ AIR™ Launchpad are described in Table 31.

The main capabilities of the RAD tool are described in the Table 32.

5. CONCLUSION

RIAs development is a complex and time-consuming task compared to traditional Web applications (Web 1.0) development. In fact, RIAs are a new generation of Web applications that have become a solution to the drawbacks of Web 1.0 applications such as the entire pages reloading, the slow response time and the lack of multimedia support. Nowadays, RIAs development is addressed in three different ways: 1) by using application frameworks, which provide SDKs, class libraries, IDEs, among other development tools, 2) by using MDD tools, which generate executable code starting from high-level software models and 3) by using code generators, which are based on RAD approaches and use underlying application frameworks. Therefore, RIA developers must face the challenge of selecting the option that best fits the needs of their development project, including calendar, budget and the problem domain. In this sense, this chapter can be used as a starting guide for selecting a RIAs development approach.

In the case of framework-based RIAs development, application frameworks usually provide official development tools together with the development kits. Nevertheless, in some cases it is possible to opt for other tools from third-party vendors, including open-source projects, in order to save projects' budget, avoid high learning curves, take advantage of current development skills, and take advantage of current development infrastructures, among other purposes. It is important to notice that, in some cases, these alternative development tools are non-fully-featured tools due to the proprietary nature of the underlying RIA technologies, e.g., Microsoft™ Silverlight™.

For selecting an MDD tool for RIAs development, the complexity of the underlying MDD approach needs to be evaluated. The accurateness of the MDD approach for the analysis and design phases of the development project needs to be also assessed. This is because MDD tools require a previous modeling effort in order to semi-automatically or automatically generate source code in a particular implementation technology. Moreover, this kind of development tools can be leveraged in technology migration projects because the XSL transformations underlying MDD tools can be adapted to virtually any XML-based implementation technology. This means that a single model can be used to generate code in different technologies.

Finally, the most critical factor in selecting a code generation tool for RIAs development is the scope of the functionality provided by these tools because in most cases the functionality is limited to specific domains or to finite sets of sample code that can be continuously extended in order to seem infinite. This may be more suitable for small projects or projects for educational purposes. Likewise, the degree of automation of the standard implementation tasks, namely coding, compiling, linking, debugging and testing is another crucial factor in selecting a code generation tool for RIAs development because in most cases it is desirable to obtain not only source code but also executable code.

REFERENCES

Acerbis, R., Bongio, A., Brambilla, M., & Butti, S. (2007). WebRatio 5: an eclipse-based CASE tool for engineering web applications. In *Proceedings of the 7th international conference on Web engineering* (pp. 501–505). Berlin: Springer-Verlag. Retrieved from http://dl.acm.org/citation. cfm?id=1770588.1770642

Colombo-Mendoza, L. O., Alor-Hernández, G., Rodríguez-González, A., & Colomo-Palacios, R. (2013). Alexandria: A Visual Tool for Generating Multi-device Rich Internet Applications. *Journal of Web Engineering*, *12*(3-4), 317–359.

Eclipse documentation - Previous Release. (n.d.). *Concepts*. Retrieved May 11, 2014, from http://help.eclipse.org/juno/index.jsp?topic=%2Forg.eclipse.platform.doc. user%2Fconcepts%2Fconcepts-4.htm

Linaje, M., Preciado, J. C., & Sánchez-Figueroa, F. (2007). Engineering Rich Internet Application User Interfaces over Legacy Web Models. *IEEE Internet Computing*, *11*(6), 53–59. doi:10.1109/MIC.2007.123

Martin, J. (1991). *Rapid Application Development. New York*: Macmillan USA.

Toffetti, G., Comai, S., Preciado, J. C., & Linaje, M. (2011). State-of-the Art and trends in the Systematic Development of Rich Internet Applications. *Journal of Web Engineering*, *10*(1), 70–86.

ADDITIONAL READING

Developing applications in MXML. (n.d.). *Adobe™ help*. Retrieved May 11, 2014, from http://help.adobe.com/en_US/flex/using/WS-2db454920e96a9e51e63e3d11c0bf69084-79b5. html

Introduction to FXML. (n.d.). *Oracle™ docs*. Retrieved May 11, 2014, from http://docs.oracle. com/javafx/2/api/javafx/fxml/doc-files/introduction_to_fxml.html4

Linaje, M., Preciado, J. C., Morales-Chaparro, R., Rodríguez-Echeverría, R., & Sánchez-Figueroa, F. (2009). Automatic Generation of RIAs Using RUX-Tool and Webratio. In *Proceedings of the 9th International Conference on Web Engineering* (pp. 501–504). Berlin: Springer-Verlag. doi:10.1007/978-3-642-02818-2_48

Overview, X. A. M. L. (n.d.). *Microsoft MSDN*. Retrieved May 11, 2014, from http://msdn.microsoft.com/en-us/library/ms752059.aspx

Stearn, B. (2007). XULRunner: A New Approach for Developing Rich Internet Applications. *IEEE Internet Computing*, *11*(3), 67–73. doi:10.1109/MIC.2007.75

KEY TERMS AND DEFINITIONS

Framework-Based Development Approach: The process of using application frameworks, i.e., Standard Development Kits, class libraries, Integrated Development Environments, among other development tools to develop software applications.

Integrated Development Environment (IDE): A software application that provides comprehensive facilities to developers for software development and ideally integrates source code editing, visual designing, debugging and building capabilities.

Model-Driven Development: Any software development methodology that uses domain models as the inputs to implementation generators so that the primary artifacts are not the implementations (algorithms), i.e., the outputs, but the models.

Plug-In Application: A set of software components that adds specific functionalities to a larger software application. From this perspective, there are popular IDEs based on plug-in architectures such as Eclipse™, which can be extended for supporting many programming languages and frameworks through plug-ins.

Rapid Application Development: A software development methodology that disregards traditional requirements gathering techniques in favor of software prototyping.

Rich Internet Application: Applications that are deployed over the Web; this type of applications combines features and functionality of Web applications and desktop applications.

Standalone Application: A software application that runs in its own system process as opposite to the application that runs as an add-on of an existing system process.

Chapter 14
AlexandRIA:
A Visual Tool for Generating Multi-Device RIAs

ABSTRACT

Model-Driven Development (MDD) tools for Rich Internet Applications (RIAs) development are focused on software modeling, and they leave automatic code generation in a second term. On the other hand, Rapid Application Development (RAD) tools for RIAs development enable developers to save development time and effort by leveraging reusable software components. AlexandRIA is a RAD tool that allows developers to automatically generate both source and native code of multi-device RIAs from a set of preferences selected throughout a wizard following the phases of a User Interface (UI) pattern-based code generation approach for multi-device RIAs. In this chapter, the use of the UI design process behind AlexandRIA is demonstrated by means of a sample development scenario addressing the development of a cloud services Application Programming Interfaces (APIs)-based cross-platform mobile RIA. This scenario is further revisited in a case study that addresses the automatic generation of an equivalent application using AlexandRIA.

1. INTRODUCTION

Nowadays, developers have the need of specifying the features and functionalities of RIAs (Rich Internet Applications) with legacy requirements to reduce development efforts and ensure less error-prone applications. Here, the automation tools for software development activities have become a major feature of RIAs development processes. From this perspective, most of the automation tools for software development are based on MDE (Model-driven Engineering) ap-

proaches such as RUX-Tool (Linaje et al., 2007), which is a software tool that automates the Rich User eXperience Method (RUX-Method) allowing engineering the adaptation of legacy model-based Web 1.0 applications to Web 2.0 GUIs. In a nutshell, RUX-Tool is focused on software modeling leaving the automatic code generation in a second term.

Moreover, there is another approach which is focused on automatic code generation through settings establishment: Adobe™ AIR™ Launchpad. It allows generating ready-to-compile source code

DOI: 10.4018/978-1-4666-6437-1.ch014

of AIR™-based applications i.e. desktop applications and applications for Android™, Apple™ iOS and BlackBerry™ Tablet OS platforms deployed on the Adobe™ AIR™ runtime. Nevertheless, Adobe™ AIR™ Launchpad is not based on a RIAs development process; besides, it does not entirely cover the generation of multi-device RIAs because it does not consider Web browser-based RIAs.

The aforementioned drawbacks are improved by AlexandRIA. AlexandRIA is a code generation software tool that allows developers to generate both source and native code of cloud services APIs-based multi-device RIAs from a set of preferences selected throughout a wizard following the phases of a UI pattern-based code generation approach for multi-device RIAs. This code generation approach is mainly focused on RIA's UI (User Interface) details; nevertheless, it incorporates high-level abstractions for distributing business logic operations between client and server as well as for defining advanced client-server communication mechanisms.

AlexandRIA agrees with the RAD (Rapid Applications Development) tools philosophy in the sense that it uses a set of reusable software components (Fraternali, 1999). These components encapsulate functionalities provided by several cloud services APIs (Application Programming Interfaces) such as Twitter™ REST, Flickr™ and Google™ Custom Search APIs, to mention but a few.

In addition, AlexandRIA is focused on generating multi-device RIAs. Here, the term multi-device refers to the ability of RIAs to deploy consistently on different Web browsers, desktop operating systems and mobile platforms as Web, desktop and mobile applications, respectively, starting from the same code base. It is important to notice that, this term is closely related to the plugin-based RIAs such as the Adobe™ Flex™ and Microsoft™ Silverlight™-based RIAs.

In this chapter, the use of the UI design process proposed as part of the code generation approach implemented by AlexandRIA is demonstrated within the constraints of AlexandRIA by means of a sample development scenario addressing the development of a cloud services APIs-based native mobile RIA for different mobile devices. This scenario is further revisited in a case study addressing the automatic generation of an equivalent application by using AlexandRIA.

2. ALEXANDRIA: A UI PATTERN-BASED APPROACH FOR GENERATING MULTI-DEVICE RIAS

AlexandRIA automates a UI pattern-based code generation approach for multi-device RIAs which is intended to address the following drawbacks of current proposals on RIAs engineering such as RUX-Method (Linaje et al., 2007), PPRD (Martínez-Nieves et al., 2010) and UWE-R (Machado et al., 2009): they do not entirely address multi-device RIAs; therefore, they do not cover the development of multi-device RIAs in an automatic or semi-automatic way.

As a proof of concept, Adobe™ Flex™ 4.5 and PhoneGap™ 1.0 were selected as the cross-platform development frameworks for implementing the aforementioned code generation approach. Thereby, AlexandRIA is currently based on both ActionScript and JavaScript technologies. Finally, it is important to notice that the code generation algorithm implemented by AlexandRIA is a domain-specific approach focused on generating cloud services APIs-based multi-device RIAs, i.e., the functionalities of the applications to be generated by AlexandRIA are implemented in terms of data and operations from cloud services APIs as is widely explained in section 14.3 of this chapter.

Although this code generation approach is mainly focused on RIA's UI details, it incorporates high-level abstractions for distributing business logic operations between client and server as well as for defining advanced client-server communication mechanisms. The cloud services APIs operations are out of the scope of the business logic distribution task, only the operations at AlexandRIA-side, i.e., domain-independent operations such as data validation and filtering are considered to this aim. It is important to notice that, the data storage distribution is out of the scope of this code generation approach because the data layer of the applications generated by AlexandRIA is entirely represented by means of cloud services APIs data.

In detail, the code generation approach implemented by AlexandRIA comprises the following phases:

1. Identify the type of multi-device RIA to be generated as well as the target platform
2. Define the data and domain-specific business logic operations by means of functionalities provided by cloud services APIs.
3. Design the UI as an abstract composition of interaction design patterns
4. Link UI events to business logic operations at AlexandRIA-level in order to determine the distribution of these business logic operations between client and server.
5. Refine the abstract UI in order to obtain a concrete UI
6. Establish the application configuration settings according to the type of multi-device RIA to be generated and the target platform.
7. Generate the source code starting from reusable UI/business logic components encapsulating cloud services APIs and UI components implementing interaction design patterns according to the concrete GUI. In this phase, the generation of a folder structure for locating the source code files to be generated is a prerequisite. The folder structure varies depending on the type of multi-device RIA to be generated.
8. Compile the source code and generating the executable code according to the target platform, if applicable.

3. CLOUD APIS

The cloud services APIs considered by AlexandRIA are: Twitter™ REST API, Flickr™ API, Google™ Custom JSON/Atom Search API, Google™ Maps JavaScript API, finding eBay™ API, last.fm™ API, YouTube™ Player API, YouTube™ Data API, Digg™ API, Yahoo! ™ Weather API and Delicious API. The main features of these services APIs are described in Table 1.

Most of the aforementioned APIs are REST-based APIs. However, there are a few APIs partially based on both, the SOAP protocol and the REST style. In all cases AlexandRIA uses the REST-based style for interacting with these APIs. For the APIs composed of only one method, the full URL is included. It is important to notice that, in some cases, there are not API methods but feeds so that, the words included are not additional parameters to be added to a base URL but part of the call URL.

In AlexandRIA, the functionalities provided by the above described cloud services APIs are encapsulated by a set of reusable MXML/ActionScript and HTML (HyperText Markup Language)/JavaScript-based UI/business logic components. Similarly, a set of reusable MXML/ActionScript and HTML/JavaScript-based UI/business logic components implementing some of the interaction patterns proposed by Scott & Neil (2009) are leveraged by AlexandRIA. These two kinds of software components are the high level constructs of the code generation engine. In fact, starting from these simple components, composed components implementing functionalities from cloud services APIs by means of interaction design patterns are built on-the-fly. Hereafter, these derived components are referred as composed UI/business logic components. For performance purposes, AlexandRIA has one pre-built composed UI/business logic component for each cloud services API. In any case, the applications generated by AlexandRIA use composed UI/business logic components as follows: if more than one cloud

Table 1. Cloud Services APIs used by AlexandRIA's source code generation engine

Cloud Services API	Description	Request Formats	Response Formats	Used Operations
Twitter™ REST API	The Twitter™ REST API methods lets developers access core Twitter™ data, this includes: tweets and timelines, user information, saved searches, trending topics, among other data.	REST	• REST • JSON • RSS • Atom	statuses/home_timeline.xml
Flickr™ API	It lets developers interact with Flickr™'s user accounts, manage stored photos and photo metadata, uploading new photos, manage photo galleries, manage Flick™ user groups, among other actions.	• REST • SOAP • XML-RPC	• REST • JSON • SOAP • XML-RPC • PHP	flckr.photos.search
Google™ JSON/ Atom Custom Search API	It enables developers to retrieve either Web search or image search results searching over a website or a collection of websites by using a customized search engine powered by Google™.	REST	• JSON • Atom	https://www.googleapis.com/customsearch/v1
Google™ Maps JavaScript API v. 2.0	It allows developers to embed Google™ maps in desktop applications as well as in applications for mobile devices. It allows manipulating maps just like on the Google™ Maps website and customizing them by adding specific content.	-	-	maps.google.com/maps
Finding eBay™ API	The finding eBay™ API allows developers to search for items listed on the eBay™ website. It offers both standard search and search refinement capabilities.	• REST • SOAP	• REST • JSON • SOAP	findItemsAdvanced
Last.fm™ API	It allows developers to interact with Last.fm™ core data i.e. artists, albums and tracks stored on the Last.fm™ website. Also, it allows managing user's Last.fm™ libraries and retrieving Last.fm™ user accounts and user groups data.	• REST • XML-RPC	• REST • XML-RPC	• artist.search • artist.gettopalbums
YouTube™ Data API v. 2.0	The YouTube™ Data API allows applications to carry out the actions that a user can carry out on the YouTube™ website.	REST	• JSON • JSON-IN. SCRIPT • JSONC • RSS • Atom	videos
YouTube™ JavaScript Player API	The YouTube™ JavaScript Player API lets developers control the chromeless and embedded YouTube™ players via JavaScript functions.	-	-	http://www.youtube.com/v/videoId
Digg™ API	It lets developers programmatically interact with Digg™ for retrieving information such as digg counts and comments related to the news stories and videos submitted to the Digg™ website. Also, it allows managing Digg™ user accounts.	REST	REST	story.getPopular
Yahoo!™ Weather API	It enables developers to get up-to-date weather information about wind, atmospheric pressure, humidity, visibility and astronomical conditions for specific locations.	REST	RSS	• http://where.yahooapis.com/v1/places • http://weather.yahooapis.com/forecastrss
Google™ Suggest API	Although this is not an official API, there is a public method exposed by Google™ that allows obtaining real-time feedback of search criteria similar to that a user enters during a search.	REST	REST	http://google.com/complete/search

continued on following page

Table 1. Continued

Cloud Services API	Description	Request Formats	Response Formats	Used Operations
Delicious™ Feeds API	It allows developers to retrieve data feeds for public and private bookmarks stored on the Delicious website. In this sense, the Delicious™ Feeds API exposes URLs (Uniform Resource Locator) for filtering bookmarks by tag and by user. It also allows for retrieving data feeds for Delicious™ user accounts.	REST	• JSON • RSS	tag/{tag}

services API is required, then a tabbed application or a view-based application in which each tab or view links just one composed UI/business logic component is generated. Otherwise, a single-view application is generated. In any case, the resulting applications are composed of either a set of full-screen application views or a single full-screen application view.

In detail, the UI design method proposed as part of the code generation approach automated by AlexandRIA, which hereafter is referred as AGUIDM, is based on the ADV (Abstract Data View) design model and it comprises two abstraction levels at two design levels as follows. It is important to notice that this design method follows a bottom-up approach.

1. **Abstract UI at view level:** Where the UI of each application's view is modeled as a composed ADV made up of interaction design patterns modeled in turn as simple ADVs; here, the ADV design model is extended in order to allow developers to specify if the business logic operations are at AlexandRIA-side, which are executed in response to certain UI events must be executed either as client-side or server-side operations.

2. **Abstract UI design at application level:** Where the application's UI is modeled as a composed ADV made up view GUIs modeled in turn as composed ADVs.

3. **Concrete UI design at view level:** Which is achieved by simply adding look and feel details to each abstract view GUI, i.e., to each ADV model representing the UI of an application's view. The resulting ADV models are called CDVs (Concrete Data Views).

Actually, there is another lower design level: the interaction pattern level. However, no design activity at this level is currently considered by AGUIDM.

4. **Concrete UI design at application level:** Which is achieved by simply adding look and feel details to the application's abstract GUI, i.e., to the ADV representing the application GUI. This also results in a CDV.

In the context of RIAs, the ADV design model has been already used as a means for specifying the structure and behavior of rich GUIs (Urbieta et al., 2007; Rossi et al., 2008; Martínez-Nieves et al., 2010). The AGUIDM proposal is explained below by means of a practical sample that addresses the generation by using AlexandRIA of a thin client application for Android™ and Apple™ iOS-based mobile devices. This application is intended to allows users to search for music albums on the eBay™ website. In this section, only the design of the UI at view level is addressed. Nevertheless, this sample is further revisited and refined in following sections of this chapter.

Figure 1. ADV of the pre-built composed UI/business logic component encapsulating the finding eBay™ API

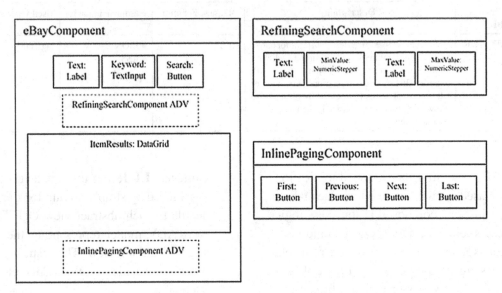

The simple UI/business logic component encapsulating the finding eBay™ API uses the method *findItemsAdvanced* to allow users to search for items listed on the eBay™ website and to refine the search results by entering both a minimum and a maximum item price. By default, this behavior is implemented by means of the refining search pattern. Additionally, this behavior is in part implemented by using the inline paging interaction pattern because of the amount of items that can be retrieved for a request. Thereby, a pre-built UI/business logic component encapsulating the finding eBay™ API and implementing the aforementioned interaction patterns is provided by AlexandRIA. The ADV of this pre-built component (which is further viewed as an application view) is an ADV composed of both an ADV implementing the refining search pattern by means of the Adobe™ Flex™ *NumericStepper* control or the HTML5 *input (type=numeric)* element and an ADV implementing the inline paging pattern by means of the Adobe™ Flex™ *Button* control or the HTML5 *button* element.

It is important to take into consideration that the patterns to be implemented by an AlexandRIA-based application can be varied during abstract UI design at view level as explained in following section of this chapter. Nevertheless, the predefined structure of the ADVs at interaction pattern level cannot be customized. In fact, the predefined structure of the ADVs cannot be customized neither at view level nor at application level.

The ADV of the pre-built composed UI/business logic component encapsulating the finding eBay™ API is depicted in Figure 1.

In general, the ADVs of the pre-built composed UI/business logic components represent the entry point of AGUIDM because they are the result of automating the abstract UI design phase (at view level) of AGUIDM in the context of some code generation use cases by using AlexandRIA. Thereby, it is considered that they represent the views of the applications to be generated.

AGUIDM extends the ADV design model in the sense that details about implementation are added to the UI model in order to identify the intended RIA technology in early stages of the code generation process. Namely, the elements composing the UI are matched with the equivalent UI controls in the intended RIA technology

Figure 2. Specifying business logic distribution preferences for the pre-built composed UI/business logic component encapsulating the finding eBay™ API

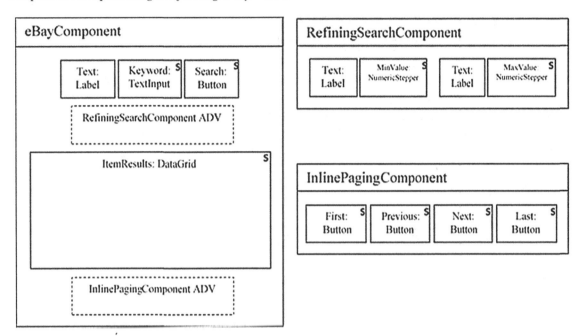

by specifying the names of these UI controls. Thereby, it can be inferred that the UI/business logic component represented by the ADV depicted in Figure 2 is not the HTML/JavaScript-based eBay™ component but the MXML/ActionScript-based eBay™ component.

Because the required application is a thin client application, it is necessary to define all the business logic operations of the composed UI/business logic components linked to its only view as server-side operations. For instance, the specification of the business logic distribution preferences for the pre-built composed UI/business logic component encapsulating the finding eBay™ API is addressed below. By default, the business logic operations at AlexandRIA-side are considered to be client-side operations so that the opposite must be explicitly specified. For this purpose, the UI elements that trigger domain-independent business logic operations must be marked with an "S" label as is depicted in Figure 3. The ADV depicted in Figure 3 is the result from carrying out the abstract UI design phase at view level.

AGUIDM distinguishes three kinds of domain-independent operations: input data validation, data retrieving and output data filtering. The first one is commonly related to text input controls such as text boxes and text areas, the second one is typically related to command controls such as buttons and links; finally, the third one is commonly related to data presentation controls such as data grids and tables. It is important to notice that, at a lower level of abstraction (implementation phase of the code generation approach automated by AlexandRIA), data retrieving operations encapsulate cloud services APIs operations (domain-specific operations), e.g., the *findItemsAdvanced* method in the case of the UI/business logic component encapsulating the finding eBay™ API.

Based on AGUIDM, the look and feel of each view of the application is specified as a result of carrying out the concrete UI design phase at view level. Although the structure of rich GUIs cannot

Figure 3. Specifying look and feel properties for the pre-built composed UI/business logic component encapsulating the finding eBay™ API

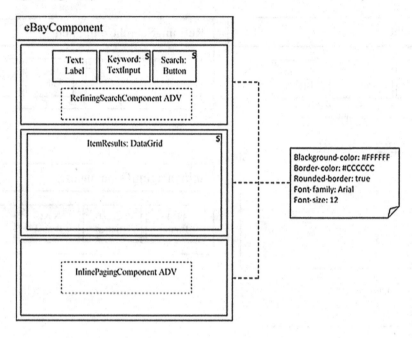

Figure 4. Adding the brighten and dim interaction pattern to the pre-built composed UI/business logic component encapsulating the eBay™ API

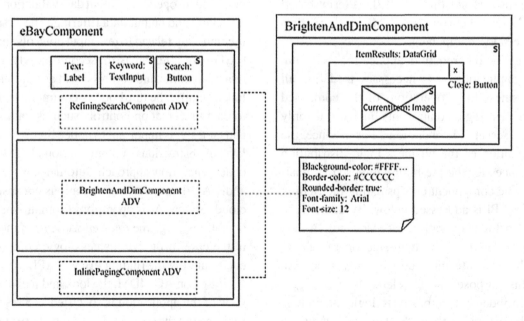

be specified by using AGUIDM, the modular nature of the AGUIDM-based GUIs is leveraged by AlexandRIA towards the specification of the look and feel properties so that GUIs are considered to be composed of the following regions: data input region, data presentation region and pagination region. Each of these regions is represented by a control container in the ADV model. Because AlexandRIA does not currently support the specification of the look and feel properties for each individual UI control, the look and feel of a view is specified for each of its regions independently. Similarly, only the following categories of look and feel properties are currently supported by AlexandRIA: background-related properties, font-related properties and border-related properties. As can be inferred, no layout-related preferences are currently supported by AlexandRIA. Therefore, only these kinds of look and feel properties are addressed in this chapter. Figure 4 depicts the specification of the look and feel properties for the pre-built composed UI/business logic component encapsulating the finding eBay™ API. As can be inferred, the notation used by AGUIDM is inspired by the UML (Unified Modeling Language) Note model element.

4. INTERACTION DESIGN PATERNS

Scott & Neil (2009) proposed a set of interaction design patterns in the context of six principles for designing rich user experiences; they also provided a set of best practices for each interaction pattern. These interaction patterns represent the building blocks of AGUIDM and AlexandRIA in the sense that the AGUIDM-based GUIs are considered to be made up of a set of views and each view is considered to be made up of a set of interaction patterns represented as simple ADVs. The interaction patterns currently implemented by AlexandRIA are briefly described in Table 2.

Table 2 depicts the matching of each above described interaction pattern with the Alexan-

dRIA's simple UI/business logic component implementing it by default, i.e., with a cloud services API representing the domain in which it is used. Nevertheless, thanks to the modular nature of AGUIDM and taking into account that design patterns can be reused irrespective of the domain of the problem to be solved (in this case in the context of designing rich user experiences), interaction patterns can be freely replaced in ADVs of these pre-built composed UI/business logic components, resulting in other composed UI/business logic components. It is important to notice that each pre-built composed UI/business logic component can encapsulate more than one cloud services API at a time as depicted in Table 2.

Revisiting the sample introduced in previous section of this chapter, let us suppose that the application requires showing a full-size image of the items retrieved from eBay™. At this point in the generation process, the easy way to do this is by adding the brighten and dim pattern to the ADV resulting from carrying out the abstract UI design phase (at view level) of AGUIDM and further replicate the change to the ADV resulting from carrying out the concrete UI design phase (at application level). With the aim of preserving the continuity of the sample, Figure 2 depicts the result of this change by means of the later ADV model. It is important to notice that, the support of this kind of requirements change is fully covered by AlexandRIA.

As can be inferred from Figure 5, the brighten and dim pattern is not applied to the input data region of the UI as in the case of the refining search component but to the data presentation region. In fact, the refining search pattern is not replaced by the brighten and dim pattern. This is because the kinds of design problem solved by these two patterns are different. In fact, the design principles behind these two patterns are the following: stay on the page and react immediately, respectively. Nevertheless, this does not mean that the patterns implemented by AlexandRIA are domain-specific patterns but that the patterns

Table 2. Interaction patterns implemented by AlexandRIA

Interaction Pattern	Description	External Use Cases	AlexandRIA Components
Inline Paging	It allows refreshing just the search results area (e.g. data grid control) while the rest of the UI controls remains stable. It is also known as pages refreshing.	Adobe™ website Alibaba.com website	Almost all
Live Suggest	It lets providing real-time search term suggestions for creating searches. It is also knows as winnowing.	IMDB website Pinterest website	Google™ JSON/ Atom Custom Search API and Google™ Suggest API
Scrolled Paging	It combines inline paging and virtual scrolling such that paging is performed as normal while the content is scrolled into view.	Disney™ website AOL™ Radio website	Flickr™ APÍ
Virtual Scrolling	It allows loading additional content on demand, i.e. as is required by the user. Instead of page refreshing, this approach gives the illusion of a boundless virtual space.	LinkedIn™ website DZone (dzone. com)	Twitter™ REST API
Refining Search	It provides a set of live filters that allow the search results to be tuned in real time. It is also known as faceted browse.	Bing™ omio (omio.com)	Finding eBay™ API
Virtual Panning	It creates a virtual canvas by allowing users the freedom to roam in two-dimensional (2D) spaces.	Foursquare™ website Yahoo! ™ Maps	Google™ Maps JavaScript API
Drag and Drop	It enables selecting objects itself, i.e. without extra controls (e.g. checkbox control) for dragging and dropping them into new locations over the GUI.	Outlook™ Academia.edu	Delicious API
Brighten and Dim	It enables dimming the entire application window and showing and overlay in the normal, non-dimmed state.	Facebook™ KAYAK (kayak. com)	Last.fm™ API
List Inlay	It allows showing a list of items organized in rows and columns. The details about the items are showed in place, i.e., within the list itself, as requested.	Amazon™'s mobile website	Yahoo! ™ Weather API
Periodic Refresh	It lets applications show fresh community content on a periodic basis without direct interaction of a particular user.	iTunes™ StackOverflow website	Digg™ API
Progress Indicator	It indicates the user that the application is currently busy with a time-consuming operation, showing how much progress was made on the task.	Internet Explorer™ Spotify™	YouTube™ Data API and YouTube™ JavaScript Player API

are used in a specific context: data input, data presentation and pagination. In fact, the domain of the application remains stable.

5. CASE STUDIES

AlexandRIA, which is a Web browser-based RIA itself, gives tool support to the UI pattern-based code generation approach for multi-device RIAs outlined in section 2 of this chapter. For that purpose, AlexandRIA adopts a RAD philosophy. Thereby, the fully-automatic generation of source and native code of multi-device RIAs is covered by AlexandRIA by means of a visual wizard that guides developers through the phases of the aforementioned code generation approach in a step-by-step way.

Figure 5. Selecting the required cloud services APIs

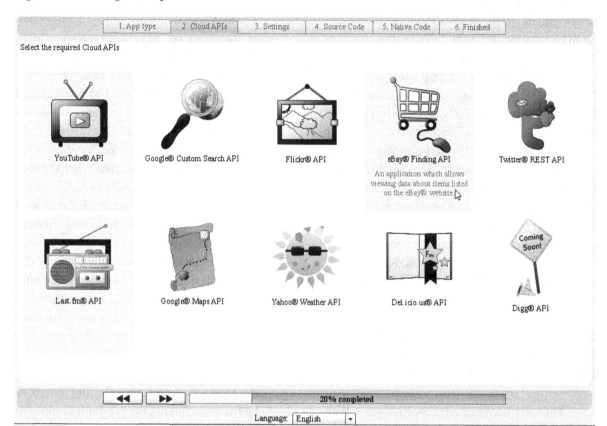

AlexandRIA allows developers to generate both source and native code of: 1) Web browser-based RIAs, 2) desktop RIAs and 3) mobile Web browser-based RIAs and 4) native mobile RIAs. Possible target platforms for native mobile RIAs are Android™, Apple™ iOS, BlackBerry™ Tablet OS and Windows™ Phone whereas desktop RIAs are multi-platform and Web browser-based RIAs are cross-browser, so that there are no options related to target platforms for these two kinds of multi-device RIAs.

In order to prove the suitability of AlexandRIA for the development of cloud services APIs-based multi-device RIAs, let us refined the sample application scenario addressed throughout the previous sections of this chapter into a case study on generating a thin client mobile RIA based on more than one cloud services API by using AlexandRIA. Taking into account the domain of the afore-mentioned application, i.e., music, the functionality to be provided to users may be extended by means of other cloud services APIs already supported by AlexandRIA that are related to the domain of music; namely, the Last.fm™ API and the YouTube™ APIs. They can complement the functionality provided by the finding eBay™ API as follows. The former is leveraged by AlexandRIA to allow searching for information about artists and their albums on Last.fm™ whereas the latter is leveraged by AlexandRIA to allow for searching and playing back videos on YouTube™. In a real case development scenario, this requirement change may have serious implications for the project's budget and calendar because requirements change management is an effort and time-consuming task. In fact, effort and time commonly impose constraints on software development. Here, automation tools like AlexandRIA becomes relevant. In this sense, AlexandRIA is a suitable solution for non-experienced cloud-services APIs-based application developers because it allows saving effort and time on analyzing cloud services APIs and determining the operations that must be implemented.

AlexandRIA provides the following valuable elements: 1) a set of reusable cloud services APIs-based and interaction patterns-based multi-device software components, 2) a set of device-specific application templates and 3) a code generation engine which allows generating source and native code of cloud services APIs-based RIAs for different platforms and devices following the steps described in the following case study.

5.1. Generating a Multi-Device RIA for Android™ and Apple™ iOS-Based Mobile Devices

1. The user accesses AlexandRIA via a Web browser by using a URL.
2. Once AlexandRIA has been completely rendered, the user can select the type of multi-device RIA to be generated; one or more target platforms can be selected, if applicable; this phase of the wizard corresponds to the first phase of the code generation approach outlined in section 2 of this chapter.
3. The next phase of the wizard is the specification of both the cloud services APIs to be used and the interaction design patterns to be implemented by means of an abstract GUI. Sections 3 and 4 of this chapter respectively provide a review of the cloud services APIs and interaction design patterns currently supported by AlexandRIA. Starting from these high-level constructs, AlexandRIA can build both a MXML/ActionScript-based UI/business logic component and a HTML/JavaScript-based UI/business logic component for each combination of cloud

services API and interaction design pattern. These components are reused irrespective of the types of multi-device RIA offered by AlexandRIA; i.e., they are multi-device components. For this case study, not only the finding eBay™ API is selected as is required in the sample application scenario introduced in section 3 of this chapter but also the Last. fm™ API and the YouTube™ APIs are selected. From this perspective, when the user selects a cloud services API, the ADV model of the corresponding pre-built composed UI/business logic component is displayed. Each ADV model represents the UI of an application's view to be implemented and it is composed of the ADV models representing the interaction patterns to be implemented by default. Here, the user can customize each ADV model by selecting other interaction design patterns from a palette including all the available options. For this case study, the interaction pattern to be implemented by the view linking the pre-built composed UI/business logic component encapsulating the finding eBay™ API is changed from the refining search pattern to the brighten and dim pattern as is stated in section 4 of this chapter. The distribution of the Business logic operations behind the UI components composing the resulting ADV model can be specified by hovering over the regions of the ADV model containing the intended UI components and selecting either the "server-side" or the "client-side" option from a slider that is consequently revealed. As can be inferred, AlexandRIA does not currently support the specification of business logic distribution preferences for each individual UI control so that, these preferences are specified for each UI region as in the case of the look and feel preferences. It is worth mentioning that the aforementioned behavior is inspired by an interaction pattern not addressed in this chapter: hover-reveal tools.

For this case study, all the business logic operations in all the application's views are marked as server-side operations because the application required is intended to be a thin client application. Finally, the abstract UI at application level is specified at the end of this phase of the wizard by selecting the application template to be used for implementing the application as a composition of application views; namely, a view-based application template or a tabbed application template can be used. As can be inferred, this phase of the wizard corresponds to the abstract UI design phase (at both view and application abstraction levels) of AGUIDM, i.e., it corresponds to the first, second and third phases of the code generation approach automated by AlexandRIA. Figure 6 depicts the set of cloud services APIs selected in this case study. Figure 5 depicts the ADV model for the pre-built composed UI/business logic component encapsulating the finding eBay™ API. Figure 7 depicts the resulting ADV model for the composed UI/business logic component encapsulating the finding eBay™ API.

4. Once the required cloud services APIs and interaction design patterns have been selected, different parameters need to be configured according to the type of RIA to be generated. There are parameters applicable to all RIA types, i.e., multi-device parameters such as 1) the application name, 2) the application title, 3) the DPI (Dots Per Inch) measure, which allows automatically scaling the application for different screen densities; this feature is a decisive factor in the development of density-independent applications for mobile devices, 4) the style of each of the views composing the application and 5) the style of the application as the composition of application views. Here, style is the conjunction of diverse look and feel properties such as background and fonts colors. The look and feel properties specified in section 4 of this chapter by means of a CDV for a composed UI/business logic component encapsulating the finding eBay™ API are considered in this case study for all the remaining application's views as well as for the application itself. In the case of code generation of native mobile RIAs, the parameters to be configured in this phase are: 1) parameters applicable to all offered mobile platforms, i.e., multi-platform parameters such as the "launching in a full-screen mode" and the "screen auto-orienting" features and 2) properties only applicable to the required target platforms such as the iPhone™/iPad™ support in the case of applications for Apple™ iOS-based devices, or the application install location in the case of applications for Android™-based devices. Finally, it is important to notice that, the only required parameters are the application name and title; the other parameters are optional and they can take default values. The settings established in this case study for the multi-device parameters are depicted in Figure 8. The resulting CDV model for the composed UI/business logic component that encapsulates the finding eBay™ API is depicted in Figure 9. As can be inferred, this phase of the wizard automates the concrete UI design phase (at both view and application abstraction levels) of AGUIDM, i.e., it corresponds to the fifth and sixth phases of the code generation approach automated by AlexandRIA.

5. Once the application configuration has been finished, AlexandRIA displays a summary of the requirements specified by the user throughout the previous phases of the wizard, and it allows generating the application source code either as simple source code files or Adobe™ Flash Builder 4.5 compatible project files in the case of Adobe™ Flex™-based applications code generation. Here the application's folder structure is generated

and the source code generation process is immediately triggered. This phase of the wizard corresponds to the seventh phase of the code generation approach implemented by AlexandRIA.

6. The next phase of the wizard is the generation of the corresponding native code. In the case of code generation of desktop RIAs and native mobile RIAs, AlexandRIA asks for the digital certificate files and corresponding passwords needed to sign an installation file for each required target platform. In the specific case of code generation of applications for Apple™ iOS-based devices also a provisioning profile must be provided. AlexandRIA performs real-time validations of digital certificates such as password validations and expiration date validations. Furthermore, AlexandRIA performs certification authority identity validations in the specific case of code generation of native mobile applications for Apple™ iOS-based devices. In any case, once all required re-

sources have been provided and validated, AlexandRIA displays the "generate native code" option. Once this option has been selected by the user, the native code generation process is triggered. A series of information messages is displayed while the native code is being generated. This phase of the wizard corresponds to the eighth phase of the code generation approach implemented by AlexandRIA.

7. The last phase of the wizard is the generation of a ZIP file that packages the previously generated source and native code files. Once the ZIP file is generated, a "download ZIP file" option is displayed. The user downloads the ZIP file by clicking this option. Here, the AlexandRIA wizard is finished. The user must unpack the ZIP file in order to obtain a folder structure. The folder structure of native mobile RIAs contains multi-device source code files as well as installation files depending on the selected target platforms; these installation files located in the root

Figure 6. ADV model of the pre-built composed UI/business logic component encapsulating the finding eBay™ API

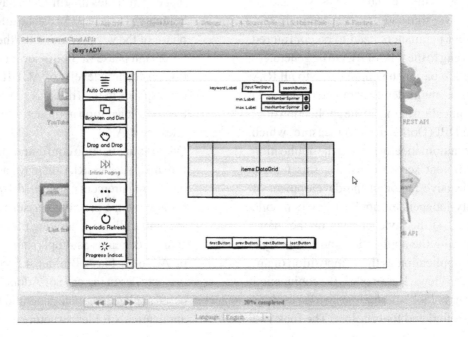

Figure 7. Resulting ADV model for the composed UI/business logic component encapsulating the finding eBay™ API

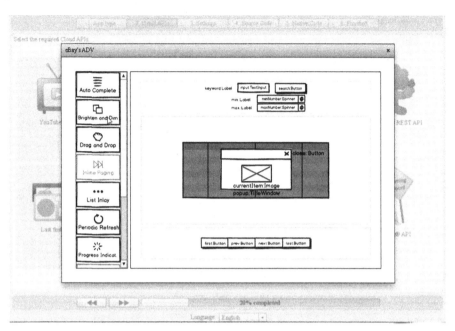

folder. In this case study, an ipa file and an apk file are provided because both Apple™ iOS and Android™ were selected as target platforms. Figure 10 depicts the native mobile RIA running on a Nexus 7™ tablet computer.

5.2. Generating a Web Browser-Based Multi-Device RIA

As a complementary case study aimed at proving the suitability of AlexandRIA for generating the same RIA for different platforms and devices, i.e., for generating multi-device RIAs, the generation of the Web browser-based version (desktop) of the native mobile RIA addressed in the previous section of this chapter is also addressed in this section. For that purpose, only the differences between these two cases for the phases of the wizard are emphasized here.

In the first phase of the wizard, no target platforms need to be selected because the type of RIA to be generated is a Web browser-based RIA.

In the third phase of the wizard, besides the parameters applicable to all RIA types, one additional parameter only applicable to Web browser-based RIAs either mobile or desktop version needs to be configured: the programming language to be used for generating the server-side Web page comprising the server-side business logic. In this sense, AlexandRIA currently supports PHP and JSP (Java Server Pages) server-side technologies. Figure 11 depicts the settings defined in this case study for the parameters only applicable to Web browser-based RIAs.

Once the source code files have been generated, in the case of Web browser-based RIAs code generation, an application wrapper (HTML-based Web page) is generated in the fourth phase of the wizard. This is because Web browser-based RIAs generated by AlexandRIA actually are Flash content. Flash content needs to be embedded as multimedia content into HTML-based Web pages.

Figure 8. Setting the configuration for the multi-device parameters

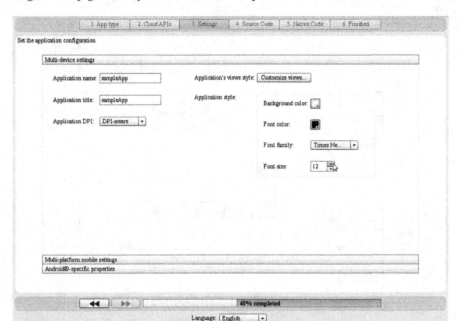

Figure 9. Resulting CDV model for the composed UI/business logic component encapsulating the finding eBay™ API

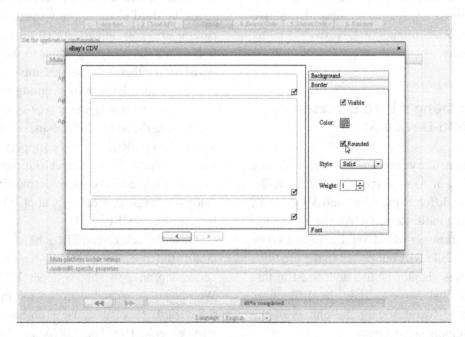

Figure 10. Screenshot of the native mobile RIA running on a Nexus 7™ tablet computer

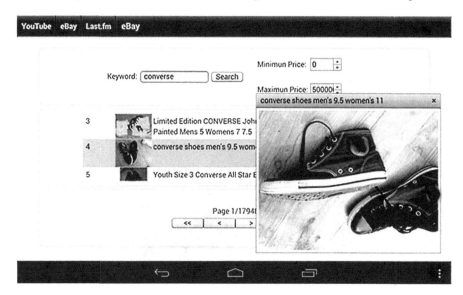

Figure 11. Setting the configuration for the parameters only applicable to Web browser-based RIAs

Finally, as explained in the previous case study, a ZIP file packaging a folder structure containing the previously generated source and native code files is generated in the last phase of the wizard. In the case of Web browser-based RIAs, the folder structure includes a deployable folder containing both the application wrapper and a server-side Web page implementing server-side business logic. The latter represents a back-end for the application. For this case study, a PHP-based Web page is provided by AlexandRIA. As can be inferred, Web-based RIAs generated by AlexandRIA must

Figure 12. Screenshot of the Web browser-based RIA running on the Firefox™ Web browser

be executed by using an HTTP server like Apache HTTP Server™ or a servlet container like Apache Tomcat™, in the case of PHP and JSP-based backends, respectively.

Figure 12 depicts the execution of the Web browser-based RIA generated in this case study by using the Firefox™ Web browser.

6. CONCLUSION

RIAs engineering is an emerging area of Software Engineering that everyday defines new boundaries. Nowadays, RIAs development involves Web, desktop and applications for mobile devices development. At this point, the UI pattern-based code generation approach for RIAs automated by AlexandRIA becomes relevant because it covers multi-device RIAs code generation from conception to deployment.

AlexandRIA automates the aforementioned code generation approach for RIAs under the RAD philosophy enabling developers save de-

velopment time and effort and, at the same time, ensuring less error-prone applications. As a proof of concept, AlexandRIA is implemented by using both the Adobe™ Flex 4.5 and PhoneGap™ frameworks; however, it can be easily adapted to other cross-platform development frameworks. Unlike other contributions that are mainly based on MDE approaches and focused on improving GUIs of legacy Web 1.0 applications, AlexandRIA is focused on multi-device RIAs code generation leaving the software modeling in a second term.

As a proof of concept, multi-device RIAs generated by AlexandRIA are based on cloud services APIs because the use of cloud services is increasingly common in the development of Web 2.0 applications. Furthermore, in order to provide rich user experiences, multi-device RIAs generated by AlexandRIA implement cloud services by means of interaction patterns already proposed in the Web Engineering literature. In fact, the interaction patterns constitute the building blocks of the UI design process proposed as part of the code generation approach automated by AlexandRIA.

REFERENCES

Fraternali, P. (1999). Tools and approaches for developing data-intensive Web applications: A survey. *ACM Computing Surveys, 31*(3), 227–263. doi:10.1145/331499.331502

Linaje, M., Preciado, J. C., & Sánchez-Figueroa, F. (2007). Engineering Rich Internet Application User Interfaces over Legacy Web Models. *IEEE Internet Computing, 11*(6), 53–59. doi:10.1109/MIC.2007.123

Machado, L., Filho, O., & Ribeiro, J. (2009). UWE-R: An extension to a web engineering methodology for rich internet applications. *WSEAS Trans. Info. Sci. and App., 6*(4), 601–610.

Martínez-Nieves, L. A., Hernández-Carrillo, V. M., & Alor-Hernández, G. (2010). An ADV-UWE Based Phases Process for Rich Internet Applications Development. In *Proceedings of Electronics, Robotics and Automotive Mechanics Conference (CERMA)*, (pp. 45–50). CERMA. doi:10.1109/CERMA.2010.16

Rossi, G., Urbieta, M., Ginzburg, J., Distante, D., & Garrido, A. (2008). Refactoring to Rich Internet Applications. A Model-Driven Approach. In *Proceedings of the 2008 Eighth International Conference on Web Engineering* (pp. 1–12). Washington, DC: IEEE Computer Society. doi:10.1109/ICWE.2008.41

Scott, B., & Neil, T. (2009). *Designing Web Interfaces: Principles and Patterns for Rich Interactions*. O'Reilly Media.

Urbieta, M., Rossi, G., Ginzburg, J., & Schwabe, D. (2007). Designing the Interface of Rich Internet Applications. In *Proceedings of Web Conference*, (pp. 144–153). doi:10.1109/LA-Web.2007.14

ADDITIONAL READING

Bozzon, A., Comai, S., Fraternali, P., & Carughi, G. T. (2006). Conceptual modeling and code generation for rich internet applications. In *Proceedings of the 6th international conference on Web engineering*, (pp. 353–360). New York: ACM. doi:10.1145/1145581.1145649

Busch, M., & Koch, N. (2009). *Rich Internet Applications. State-of-the-Art* (Tech. Rep. No. 0902). München, Germany: Ludwig-Maximilians-Universität München.

Finkelstein, A. C. W., Savigni, A., Kimmerstorfer, E., & Pröll, B. (2002). Ubiquitous Web Application Development - A Framework for Understanding. In *Proc. of SCI2002* (pp. 431–438). SCI.

Martinez-Ruiz, F. J., Arteaga, J. M., Vanderdonckt, J., Gonzalez-Calleros, J. M., & Mendoza, R. (2006). A first draft of a Model-driven Method for Designing Graphical User Interfaces of Rich Internet Applications. In *Proceedings of Web Congress*, (pp. 32–38). doi:10.1109/LA-WEB.2006.1

Melia, S., Gomez, J., Perez, S., & Diaz, O. (2008). A Model-Driven Development for GWT-Based Rich Internet Applications with OOH4RIA. In *Proceedings of Eighth International Conference on Web Engineering, 2008. ICWE '08* (pp. 13–23). doi:10.1109/ICWE.2008.36

Sorokin, L., Montero, F., & Märtin, C. (2007). Flex RIA development and usability evaluation. In *Proceedings of the 2007 international conference on Web information systems engineering*, (pp. 447–452). Berlin: Springer-Verlag. Retrieved from http://dl.acm.org/citation.cfm?id=1781503.1781552

Valverde, F., & Pastor, O. (2008). Applying Interaction Patterns: Towards a Model-Driven Approach for Rich Internet Applications Development. In *Proceedings of 7th International Workshop on Web-Oriented Software Technologies* (pp. 13–18). Vydavateľstvo STU.

Valverde, F., & Pastor, O. (2009). Facing the Technological Challenges of Web 2.0: A RIA Model-Driven Engineering Approach. In *Proceedings of the 10th International Conference on Web Information Systems Engineering*, (pp. 131–144). Berlin: Springer-Verlag. doi:10.1007/978-3-642-04409-0_18

KEY TERMS AND DEFINITIONS

Abstract Data View: A design model adopted by some Rich Internet Application development approaches as a means to design rich user interfaces starting from the specification of the objects composing the user interfaces and their relationships with other software components.

Business Logic Distribution: The dimension of the Rich Internet Applications development process which is related to the specification of the business logic operations either as client-side or server-side operations.

Cloud Service: A Web service from a Web 2.0 website such as social networking services and video sharing websites.

Concrete Data View: An extension of the Abstract Data View design model that allows adding concrete look and feel details to an abstract User Interface model.

Interaction Design Pattern: A kind of user interface patterns aimed at achieving effective user experiences, i.e., rich interactions.

Multi-Device Rich Internet Application: A kind of RIA that can run on a variety of devices starting from the same code base. This includes not only cross-browser Web applications but also out-of-browser applications, namely cross-platform desktop and mobile applications.

Rich Internet Application: Applications that are deployed over the Web; this type of applications combines features and functionality of Web applications and desktop applications.

Chapter 15
New Trends on RIAs Development

ABSTRACT

Rich Internet Applications (RIAs) are considered one kind of Web 2.0 application; however, they have demonstrated to have the potential to transcend throughout the steps in the Web evolution, from Web 2.0 to Web 4.0. In some cases, RIAs can be leveraged to overcome the challenges in developing other kinds of Web-based applications. In other cases, the challenges in the development of RIAs can be overcome by using additional technologies from the Web technology stack. From this perspective, the new trends in the development of RIAs can be identified by analyzing the steps in the Web evolution. This chapter presents these trends, including cloud-based RIAs development and mashups-rich User Interfaces (UIs) development as two easily visible trends related to Web 2.0. Similarly, semantic RIAs, RMAs (Rich Mobile Applications), and context-aware RIAs are some of the academic proposals related to Web 3.0 and Web 4.0 that are discussed in this chapter.

1. INTRODUCTION

This chapter aims to outline the new trends in the development of Rich Internet Applications (RIAs). According to an exhaustive state-of-the-art analysis and from the authors' point of view, these trends are defined in the context of the steps on the Web evolution as is depicted in Figure 1, from Web 2.0 to Web 4.0, passing through cloud computing as a trend on the Web 2.0 evolution.

Cloud computing could be the best example of where the RIAs development is going both in commercial and academic fields. In this context, RIAs enable cloud providers to mainly achieve the

SaaS (Software as a Service) cloud model thanks to the desktop-like features and functionalities of RIAs. Nevertheless, in the case of the PaaS (Platform as a Service) cloud model, RIAs can play a major role. In fact, a variant of the PaaS model in which applications are intended to be delivered as native-like mobile applications has recently arisen.

In the case of Web 3.0, a new kind of RIA known as semantic RIA has been recently proposed in the literature. Semantic RIAs try to solve the issues related to interoperability between systems by using Semantic Web and Linked Data principles. This is an example of how the RIA drawbacks can

DOI: 10.4018/978-1-4666-6437-1.ch015

Figure 1. The Web evolution

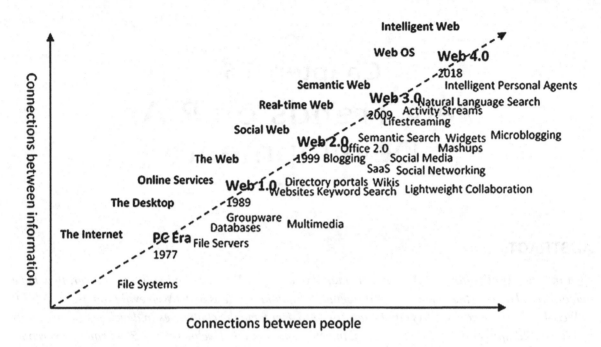

be achieved by using Web semantic technologies. At a lower level of abstraction, semantic Web technologies can be leveraged in the context of Web 2.0 applications development. In fact, an effort by the W3C (World Wide Web Consortium) aimed at encouraging developers to use knowledge representation languages common to Semantic Web in Systems and Software Engineering practices was active until 2006.

Finally, in the case of Web 4.0, the necessity of a ubiquitous Web has driven the emergence of mobile Web applications distributing data and business logic between mobile devices themselves and remote servers. These applications take advantage of RIA technologies not only to offer rich user experiences but also to enable data and business logic distribution. Here, the use of HTML5 (HyperText Markup Language 5) and JavaScript-based RIA frameworks at the client-side seems to be the most natural solution for technology heterogeneity purposes. At the same time, the availability of the mobile devices' hardware resources through JavaScript APIs (Ap-

plication Programming Interfaces) has enabled the context-awareness capability in mobile Web applications.

The aforementioned trends are widely described in the following subsections. It is important to notice that this chapter is not intended to technically explain the concepts related to each of the topics that converge on the current trends on RIAs development but outline the importance of these concepts for the development of RIAs.

2. RIAS AND CLOUD COMPUTING

Cloud computing is a style of computing in which dynamically scalable and often virtualized resources are provided as a service over the Internet. Users do not need having knowledge of, expertise in, or control over the underlying infrastructure in the cloud that supports the services rendered to them. Cloud computing refers to both the applications delivered as services over the Internet and, the hardware and systems software in the data centers that provide those services. The services themselves have been referred as SaaS whereas the underlying high-level systems software and the low-level hardware have been known as PaaS and IaaS (Infrastructure as a Service), respectively.

According to the NIST (National Institute of Standards and Technology) (Mell & Grance, 2011), Cloud computing is composed of five essential characteristics: 1) on-demand self-service which is the consumer ability to unilaterally provision computing capabilities as needed automatically without requiring human interaction with each service provider, 2) broad network access which is the availability of computing capabilities over the network through standards mechanisms that promote use by heterogeneous client platforms, 3) resource pooling which is the pooling of provider's computing resources to serve multiple consumers by using a multi-tenant model, 4) rapid elasticity which is the ability to elastically provision and release computing capabilities, in some cases automatically, in order to rapidly commensurate with demand and 5) measured service which is the system ability to control and optimize resource use by leveraging a metering capability at some level of abstraction appropriate to the type of service.

With the on-demand self-service characteristic a new pay-per-use or pay-as-you-go deployment mode have arisen besides the already existing modes: 1) the traditional client/server style based on in-house dedicated infrastructure, 2) the outsourced style which relies on Intranet-based clients and third-party operated and managed infrastructure and 3) the ASP (Application Service Provider) style relying on Web-based clients and cloud infrastructure.

From this perspective, RIA technology can be used by vendors to deliver Interned-hosted versions of their applications to be accessed by remote customers and paid for on a per-use subscription basis. Therefore, RIA technology enables vendors to achieve the first cloud model, i.e., SaaS. In terms of Deb, Bannur, & Bharti (2007), RIA technologies are a strong enabler for the SaaS model because of the rich functionality that otherwise could only be achieved by using desktop applications.

Nevertheless, RIA technologies can also play a role in the second cloud model, i.e., PaaS. In this context, a variation of the PaaS model in which RIAs can be deployed on the cloud and can then be accessed without worrying about deployment and scalability was identified by Punjabi (2012) based on the fact that moving offerings to the cloud is an increasingly frequent strategy from business intelligence vendors such as Oracle™¹ and IBM™ ("IBM Cloud Computing," 2014). It is important to notice that, in these platforms, RIAs are primarily leveraged to present final results to end users through rich user interfaces.

Furthermore, the boom of the mobile market, namely smartphones and tablet computers, has resulted in a new trend in the RIA-empowered cloud computing market: mobile PaaS. In general, mobile cloud computing is defined as the availability of cloud computing services in a mobile ecosystem (Cox, 2011). A mobile PaaS is expected to integrate services for building, deploying, integrating and managing mobile applications. For development purposes, cloud vendors have been taking advantage of the current skills and knowledge of the Web developers, bringing Web standards such as HTML, CSS (Cascading Style Sheets) and JavaScript to the mobile development. As a result, the so-called hybrid mobile applications have taken place; hybrid mobile applications are built by using Web technologies and they are then wrapped in device-specific native application containers. In this context, JavaScript-based mobile RIA frameworks such as jQuery Mobile and Sencha™ Touch have been traditionally integrated into the development tool stacks of the mobile PaaS as a means to enable hybrid mobile applications to adopt RIA-type features related not only to presentation concerns but also to other aspects of RIA development such as definition of client-side business logic and the use of client-side data storage mechanisms. However, the necessity of leveraging hardware capabilities such as accelerometers and cameras across mobile devices has caused cloud vendors to provide support for native mobile applications as well. Here, non-JavaScript-based RIA frameworks such as Adobe™ Flex™ and Microsoft™ Silverlight™ have been primarily used with presentation purposes.

According to the above, the applications can be accessed by remote clients via heterogeneous desktop and mobile devices of diverse "shapes and sizes". In addition, taking advantage of the RIA capability to distribute processing and storage between the client and server tiers, providers can improve the application responsiveness by distributing these aspects between the cloud and the client device.

In fact, unlike traditional Web applications, RIAs use client-side programming languages and user interface markup languages that typically require Web browser plug-ins (this is not truth in the case of JavaScript-based RIA frameworks) or desktop runtime environments to be installed on the client device in order to download and execute the application code. In the case of Web browser-free RIAs, this prerequisite can allows applications to take advantage of the client hardware to provide higher performance and device native capabilities, resembling traditional client-installed applications or even distributed applications that refer to the aforementioned traditional client/server delivering model (Dunlop, Ettl, & Abani, 2010).

Other advantage of delivering cloud services to remote devices by using RIA technologies are the possibility of reducing load on the network and on the cloud infrastructure because the applications are executed on the client-side. Furthermore, thanks to the storage distribution capabilities of some RIA technologies, providers can offer data replication facilities that allow consumers to work offline and in a synchronized way when they are connected.

As an example of a cloud provider leveraging RIA technologies, Salesforce.com™, Inc., which was pioneered the delivery of sales force

automation and CRM (Customer Relationship Management) software over Internet, uses the Adobe™ Flex™ framework for enabling developers to add dynamic, interactive user experiences to their force.com-based applications. In detail, force.com™, which is the Salesforce.com™'s PaaS, offers a non-general purpose programming language called Apex, an XML-based UI (User Interface) markup language called Visualforce™ and Web standards such as HTML5, CSS3 and JavaScript for developing Web applications. Force.com™ also offers a toolkit for "Adobe™ AIR™ and Flex™" aimed at the development of both offline desktop applications and Web applications wrapped using Visualforce™-based Web pages (Deb et al., 2007).

Recently, Antenna™ Software has offered the Antenna™ Mobility Platform AMPchroma™ which is an enterprise grade PaaS for native, hybrid and Web-based mobile applications. AMPchroma™ gives support to JavaScript-based frameworks such as jQuery Mobile, Sencha Touch and Dojo Mobile besides the Web standards like HTML5 and CSS3, enabling developers to build rich hybrid and Web-based mobile applications. Besides, it supports native SDKs (Standard Development Kits) for Apple™ iOS, Android™, BlackBerry™ and Windows™ Mobile platforms. AMPchroma™-based hybrid and native applications use a runtime environment called AMP client which provides real-time and offline facilities, and it exposes device capabilities such as GPS (Geo Positioning System) and camera (Antenna Inc., 2010).

In the case of academic proposals, March et al. from HP™ Laboratories Singapore (2011) proposed a framework that merges mobile and cloud computing concepts for the development of rich mobile applications viewed as a new generation of distributed mobile applications that provides rich functionalities. This framework called μCloud employs a software composition approach which allows creating the applications by mashing-up modular components. Indeed, the applications are modeled as directed graphs in which nodes represent cloud-side, device-side and hybrid components. μCloud addresses design challenges of cloud-enabled mobile applications, e.g., the reliability under diverse network conditions, including disconnection. It also addresses the typical constraints of stand-alone mobile applications such as the limitations of mobile devices resources and energy which are overcomed by offloading resource-intensive complex tasks to the Cloud. In addition, the application portability is achieved by implementing on the Cloud those tasks that do not require device-specific capabilities.

As can be inferred from the aforementioned case studies, the increase in cloud-based application development and consumption is driving up demand for RIA technologies, causing both software vendors and developers move to the RIA and cloud markets, specifically to PaaS and SaaS models.

3. RIAS AND MASHUPS

The repurposing of information from data sources such as Web Services and Atom/RSS (Really Simple Syndication) feeds, with the aim of solving the needs of an individual or interested community is part of Web 2.0 trends. Due to this, a new generation of Web 2.0 applications called mashups has emerged. A mashup is a Web application that integrates data from multiple sources to provide a unique service (Tuchinda, Szekely, & Knoblock, 2008).

Regarding the Web 2.0 trends, according to Tim O'Reilly (O'Reilly, 2007), the delivery of rich user experiences to traditional Web applications is considered a principle of Web 2.0 along with others such as the understanding of Web as a platform and the harnessing of collective intelligence. The delivery of rich user experiences was a challenge early achieved by Macromedia™ with the introduction of the term "Rich Internet Application" in 2002 (Allaire, 2002) to highlight the

capabilities of Flash™ in order to deliver not just multimedia content but also UI-style application experiences. The term "Rich Internet Application" was later expanded with the introduction of the term "AJAX" (Asynchronous JavaScript And XML) by Google™ Inc. to name the collection of technologies behind the Gmail™ and Google Maps™ websites. According to this, RIAs can also be considered a kind of Web 2.0 application.

Moreover, there are two main tasks in mashup application development: 1) accessing data sources which imply analyzing diverse APIs and consuming required Web services or RSS/Atom feeds and 2) building UIs, which implies presenting the information from all the required sources in one place.

Besides RSS/Atom feeds, Web services are a common data source for mashups. Whether they are WSDL (Web Services Description Language)-based Web services or RESTfull Web services, RIA technologies such as ActionScript as part of Adobe™ Flex™, or a JavaScript-based framework wrapping the XMLHttpRequest object like jQuery can be used to send asynchronous HTPP (Hyper-Text Transfer Protocol) requests to them. This kind of HTTP request allows updating parts of a Web page without reloading the whole Web page, which is one of the distinguishing characteristics of RIAs known as visual continuity.

Nevertheless, is at the second task where RIAs can play a major role, because it is not easy to merge heterogeneous information from different sources and adequately display the merged information through a unique UI (Deb, Bannur, & Bharti, 2007). In fact, mashups can take advantage of the single-page navigation model of RIAs which help preventing the disturbance of the user mental flow, providing containers such as tabs, accordions and view stacks, as well as controls like pop-up dialog boxes. In (Pietschmann, Voigt, Rümpel, & Meißner, 2009) an approach for service-oriented composition of Web application rich UIs was proposed. This approach called CRUISe (Composition of Rich User Interface Services) was indented to simplify the development and maintenance of Web UIs by enabling the encapsulation and reusing of rich UI components. As a result, UIs are dynamically adapted by selecting, customizing and exchanging UI parts at runtime. CRUISe-based applications are built as mashup applications made up of generic pure JavaScript-based components from SOA (Service Oriented Architecture)-based Web services. Because of the dynamics involved in the service integration activity leveraging CRUISe, UIs are initially designed as platform-independent visual models, and they are further refined into platform-specific mashup skeletons. Therefore, other client-side development technologies, including non-JavaScript-based RIA frameworks such as Adobe™ Flex™ and JavaFX™ can be used to empower the capabilities of the final applications allowing for a variety of target platforms.

Since its emergence, mashups have widely covered the Internet market with consumer-focused applications. In recent years, mashups have gained popularity in the enterprise market. Organizations are starting to realize that they can put their well-defined services together with other existing services, internal or external to the organization, to provide new and interesting views on the data. As examples of Internet-based mashups, the Housingmaps™ website combines property listings from the Craigslists™ classified advertisements website with map data from Google Maps™ in order to show the list of properties available at a location selected on a map. The usage of AJAX technologies enables Housingmaps™ to update the property listings without reloading the whole Web page, and therefore keeping the location loaded on the map. Another example of Internet-based mashup taking advantage of AJAX technologies is the Yelp™ website which provides a search engine for restaurants, home services, bars and other local services in conjunction with user reviews and recommendations. Yelp™ also integrates Google Maps™ data in order to show the location of each service.

Because data are the core element of mashups, this kind of Web 2.0 applications can be easily coupled to enterprises business process. In fact, traditional software vendors are increasingly offering mashup platforms targeting enterprises (Clarkin & Holmes, 2007). As an example, IBM™ offers the IBM™ Mashup Center which enables the rapid creation, sharing and discovery of reusable application building blocks such as widgets that can be easily assembled into new applications or leveraged within existing applications. In detail, the IBM™ Mashup Center provides many ready-to-use widgets for building mashup applications. Additional widgets can be developed using JavaScript-based frameworks such as Dojo, non-JavaScript-based frameworks like Adobe™ Flex™ and Lotus™ Widget Factory which is a UI tool for developing custom widgets without writing code (Leung, 2009). Likewise, IBM™ offers EGL Rich UI. EGL is a higher-level programming language for developing business applications and services. EGL code compiles into COBOL, Java and JavaScript. EGL Rich UI is a development tool for EGL that uses UI widgets as application building blocks; it is available in both IBM™ Rational™ EGL Communication Edition and IBM™ Rational™ Business Developer IDEs. EGL Rich UI is intended to ease the way RIAs and mashups are developed by simplifying the programming model, hidden the complexities of JavaScript and AJAX and enabling developers of all backgrounds to quickly build Web 2.0 applications. EGL Rich UI developers can write EGL applications using external JavaScript libraries such as Dojo and YUI. In addition, non-JavaScript-based RIA frameworks such as Mcrosoft™ Silvelight™ and Adobe™ Flex™ can also be used to extend the widget set of EGL Rich UI (Barosa, 2010).

As can be inferred from the academic and commercial proposals analyzed, mashup applications are increasingly taking advantage of RIA technologies not only to address the challenges related to UI designing but also to improve the way of how data sources are accessed.

4. RIAS AND WEB 3.0

The Web 3.0 also known as Semantic Web is a movement led by the W3C standards organization. According to the W3C, it provides a common framework that allows data to be shared and reused across application, enterprise, and community boundaries. The term was coined by Tim Berners Lee in 2001 (Berners-Lee, Hendler, & Lassila, 2001). Five years after that, the term was revisited; the semantic Web was defined as a Web of actionable information derived from data through a semantic theory for interpreting the symbols. In this sense, the semantic theory provides an account of meaning in which the logical connections of terms establishes interoperability between systems.

According to some proposals (Hermida, Meliá, Montoyo, & Gómez, 2011; Linaje et al., 2011), one of the RIA drawbacks is the complicated access to the data to some types of Web clients, which results in limited interoperability between systems. For instance, due to the lack of HTML code in RIAs, the search engines are not capable of correctly indexing the mentioned subset of RIAs. In addition, unlike the HTML elements, the RIA UI controls lack of tags and attributes that allow developers to add the necessary semantics for assistive technologies, enabling disabled users to perceive and interact with information. The aforementioned drawbacks have recently addressed by using semantic Web technologies as is explained below.

In fact, there was an effort by the W3C's Semantic Web activity called Semantic Web Best Practices & Deployment Working Group aimed at providing hands-on support for developers of Semantic Web applications. This W3C group was closed in 2006 after achieving its mission. Nevertheless, as part of the deliverables produced by this group, a draft was published outlining the benefits of applying knowledge representation languages common to Semantic Web, such as RDF (Resource Description Framework) and OWL (Web Ontology Language), in Systems and Software Engineering practices. Although this effort did not primarily target RIAs but traditional Web applications, some architectural elements common to both kinds of Web applications were identified in the characterization of the Semantic Web as a set of formalized corpora of interrelated, reusable contents, intended to be rigorously described, identified, discovered and shared among software systems and systems' design teams both during design and at runtime. For instance, in such characterization, functional components including JavaScript-based scripts are classified as active content in the sense that they are referenced as fragments within flat documents such as HTML-based files; here, these flat documents are known as passive content. Besides JavaScript, non-JavaScript-based RIA technologies like Adobe was published Flex was published can also be engaged in this characterization of the Semantic Web because Adobe was published Flex was published -based Web applications actually are SWF files embedded in HTML files (in its simplest form). From this prespective, SWF (Small Web Format) files do not represent media content but functional components.

As part of the work done by the W3C's Semantic Web Best Practices & Deployment Working Group, a list of RDF and OWL tools for semantic Web development called SemanticWebTools was compiled and maintained until January 2010 so that this list is currently conserved but it is no longer maintained; although, many of the tools included are currently available on Internet. The SemanticWebTools list comprises several categories of development tools including development environments; such category is refined by programming language. For instance, Table 1 summarizes the features of some of the tools for JavaScript-based development included in the SemanticWebTools list.

The WAI (Web Accessibility Initiative) is a W3C's initiative developing strategies, guidelines and resources to help make the Web accessible

Table 1. Tools for JavaScript-based development included in the SemanticWebTools

Tool	Description	Features
Hercules	It is a free open source JavaScript-based framework for building semantic Web applications. It was developed by Arielworks Hercules Team.	• RDF/XML parser • Turtle parser • JavaScipt-based SPARQL (SPARQL Protocol and RDF Query Language) query engine
AOT (OpenLink AJAX Toolkit)	It is a JavaScript-based toolkit for RIAs development. It was developed by OpenLink Software. It includes a collection of rich UI widgets, an event management system and a platform-independent data access layer called AJAX Database Connectivity. These elements are the basis of the ODE (OpenLink Data Explorer) Web browser extension. ODE is a RDF data browser; it allows interacting with RDF-based Linked Data via a Web browser-based UI.	• RDF graph visualizer widget • RDF/XML parser • Client-side RDF triple store mechanism • Fresnel Lens RDF Processor
Rdfstore-js	It is a pure JavaScript implementation of a RDF triple store mechanism supporting the SPARQL query and data manipulation language. It is an open source project licensed under the GNU (GNU's Not Unix) LGPL-3.0 (Lesser General Public License, Version 3.0) software license. Rdfstore-js can be directly executed in a Web browser or can be included as an external library in a node.js-based application.	• Turtle/N3 parser • RDF graph events API • W3C RDF Interfaces API • MongoDB™-based persistent storage

to people with disabilities. It provides a suite of technical documentation specifically addressing Rich Internet Applications. This suite called WAR-ARIA (Accessible Rich Internet Applications) defines a way to make dynamic content and advanced UI controls developed with AJAX, HTML and JavaScript more accessible to people with disabilities. The WAI-ARIA 1.0 working draft (W3C, 2014) provides an ontology of roles, states and properties defining the attributes that must contain the widgets introduced by RIA technologies in order to be interpreted by assistive technologies and accessibility APIs. With the aim of giving support to WAI-ARIA, a semantic approach based on an extension to the RUX-Method, a MDD (Model Driven Development) method for designing RIA UIs, was proposed in (Linaje et al., 2011). The cores of the proposal are two components: 1) an ontology called ontoRUX that extends the WAI-ARIA ontology by adding OWL

restrictions to this taxonomy to keep the semantic consistency of the accessibility properties and 2) an editor tool called editRUX which is aimed at enriching the components of the RUX-Tool Component Library with accessibility attributes, and it is integrated in RUX-Tool, the MDD tool that implements RUX-Method.

Hermida, Meliá, Montoyo, & Gómez (2011) proposed the concept of semantic RIA as an extension of traditional RIAs, which uses ontologies and linked data principles for overcoming the issues of RIAs related to interoperability between systems. In order to address the design and development of semantic RIAs, an MDD methodology designed as an extension of the OOH4RIA methodology (Melia, Gomez, Perez, & Diaz, 2008) was also proposed. OOH4RIA specifies an almost complete RIA through two server-side models and two RIA presentation models. The proposed process called Sm4RIA (Semantic Models for RIAs) extends the

OOH4RIA MOF (Meta Object Facility)-based metamodel by means of: 1) a set of meta classes which relates the RIA client and server concepts to semantics concepts and 2) a set of model-to-model transformations to automatically obtain domain, navigation and presentation ontologies from OOH4RIA models.

In (Balkić, Pešut, & Jović, 2007) a semantic approach for modeling, deploying and integrating RIAs was proposed. It is based on an ontology bringing diverse knowledge items and processes together to provide an integrated view of the knowledge domain to application clients as well as a platform for semantic data mining techniques. It consists of a repository for storage and retrieval of data and metadata, which is based on the JCR (Java Content Repository) API, OWL and the RDF model for data interchange on the Web. An application framework defining five modular components or domains of an ontology-based system was also proposed. It covers application data, document data, security constraints, business process definitions and configuration data.

Moreover, as an example of software vendors offering solutions integrating semantic Web and RIA technologies, the TopQuadrant™ company provides an application assembly toolkit for rapidly creating dynamic semantic Web applications starting from ontologies and optionally RDF data. This toolkit called TobBraid Ensemble™ includes pre-packaged applications that can be customized using an in-browser editor by adding, removing and reconfiguring RIA components based on Adobe™ Flex™. Custom components can be developed using the so-called SDK for Ensemble™. TobBraid Ensemble™ targets RIAs, from collaborative systems to mashup applications.

As can be inferred from the academic and commercial proposals analyzed, RIA developers can take advantage of Web semantic technologies to address some deficiencies of RIA and, at the same time, semantic Web applications can take advantage of RIA technologies, using rich UIs as front-ends.

5. RIAS AND WEB 4.0

We 4.0 is still an underground idea in progress and there is no exact definition of how it would be; however, according to the trends in the development of Web-based applications and the boom of smart devices, it is widely accepted that Ubiquitous Web is a next step in the evolution of Web. Web 4.0 is about connecting intelligences in a Ubiquitous Web where a new model of interaction between humans and machines is delivered (Aghaei et al., 2012; Davis, 2010).

In this sense, there is a W3C's initiative called Ubiquitous Web Domain which is a focusing on technologies to enable Web access for anyone, anywhere, anytime, using any device. This includes Web access from mobile phones as well as emerging environments such as consumer electronics, interactive television, and even automobiles. The Ubiquitous Web will provide people with access whenever and wherever they find themselves, with applications that dynamically adapt to the user's needs, device capabilities and environmental conditions.

Nowadays, Web applications are becoming ubiquitous applications, i.e., applications that are accessible for anyone, anywhere, anytime, using any device. In this area, ubiquity is based on the existing technologies, and it is not a new idea. Nevertheless, ubiquity offers new opportunities for Web applications in terms of: time-awareness, location-awareness, device-awareness, context-awareness and personalized services.

As can be inferred, a key element of Ubiquitous Web is mobile devices. In this context, mobile Web applications represent the next step in Web development. Here, the use of HTML5 and JavaScript-based RIA frameworks seems to be the most suitable solution because it eliminates the necessity of installing additional runtime environments on mobile devices so that compatibility issues with mobile operating systems are avoided resulting in a wider range of supported mobile devices. In fact, according to the results of testing on real devices that are summarized in the mobilehtml5 Website[2] by Maximilano Firtman, most of the features of HTML5 are currently available on the most popular mobile Web browsers in the first quarter of 2014 according to the netmarketshare Website, namely, Safari™, Android™ Browser, Chrome™ and Opera Mini™. HTML5 is the 5th major revision of the core language of the World Wide Web: HTML. It introduces new features to help Web developers; likewise, it defines new elements based on research into prevailing development practices; finally, it defines conformance criteria for user agents in an effort to improve interoperability. In detail, in the context of mobile Web development, it provides four useful elements: 1) the Canvas element; it provides scripts with a resolution-dependent bitmap canvas which can be used for rendering graphs, game graphics, art or other visual images on the fly without requiring any additional plug-in, 2) touch events API; it is a set of low-level events that represent one or more points of contact with a touch-sensitive surface; it allows for user experiences that seamless native mobile user experiences by revolutionizing traditional Web navigation models, 3) application cache API; it enables mobile Web applications to be used in offline mode; by means of this API, mobile Web applications can also improve responsiveness and reduce client-server communication by accessing locally cached resources rather than remote resources and 4) video and audio elements; the video element allows for playing movies and audio files with captions whereas the audio element allows for playing sounds and audio streams without requiring external plug-ins; in both cases, typical playback controls can easily be integrated.

In the context of academic proposals addressing ubiquitous mobile applications, Abolfazli, Sanaei, Gani, Xia, & Yang, (2014) formally define RMAs (Rich Mobile Applications) as online (Web-based) mobile applications that are characterized by several rich traits inherited from RIAs meant to deliver rich user experiences to mobile users. These applications rely on a multi-tier architecture in which

functionality and data is distributed between the mobile device and one or more remote servers, allowing for anywhere anytime usage. From this perspective, ubiquitously accessing functionality and data under heterogeneous connectivity and bandwidth conditions is identified as one of the current trends in the development of RMAs that demands for more technology and research efforts.

At a lower level of abstraction, in order to give support to the development of ubiquitous Web applications, several proposals have arisen. For instance, the UWA (Ubiquitous Web Applications) methodology defines four modeling activities: 1) requirements elicitation, 2) hypermedia design covering information, navigation and presentation models, 3) transaction design and 4) customization design. The latter allows developers to specify how the application adapts itself to the context, user, device, time, communication channels and location. UWA can be seen as a framework that integrates the metamodels defining the aforementioned activities and an IDE (Integrated Development Environment) based on the IBM™ Rational Rose™ product family (UWA Consortium, 2002).

Similarly, proposals aimed at giving support to the development of context-aware RIAs, or from another perspective, context-aware Web applications taking advantage of rich UIs have recently emerged. In this sense, Cirilo, Prado, Souza, & Zaina (2010) proposed an MDD process to develop rich UIs for context-sensitive ubiquitous applications. This process called RichUbi defines activities and artifacts that aid the modeling and the partial code generation of rich UIs for different platforms. The process is performed in two main steps: 1) domain engineering which comprises the specification, design and implementation of a rich UI domain metamodel aimed at modeling rich UIs, the construction of a set of model-to-model transformations for semi-automatic code generation, as well as the construction of a set of content adapters for performing the dynamic UI adaptation and 2) application engineering which focuses on building applications of a certain problem domain, and it comprises analysis, design, implementation and testing disciplines. In (Linaje-Trigueros, Preciado, & Sánchez-Figueroa, 2010) an MDD approach to obtain multi-device context-aware RIAs was proposed. This approach combines the WebML (Web Modeling Language) extension for context-awareness and RUX-Method. The WebML extension addresses context-aware features at data and hypertext levels whereas RUX-Method was extended according to its UI levels and transformations in order to achieve context-awareness at presentation level. In detail, device-aware presentation was solved by using the so-called RUX Device Repository (RUX-DR) which is a storage of device capabilities. Location-aware presentation was solved by exploiting the single-page navigation paradigm of RIAs. Time-aware presentation and user personalization were simply solved by using dynamic UI properties.

6. CONCLUSION

Although RIAs are considered one kind of Web 2.0 applications, they have shown the ability to transcend through the steps in the Web evolution, from Web 2.0 to Web 4.0, and even beyond the Web in the fields of desktop and mobile applications where smart devices play a major role towards a ubiquitous Web. From this perspective, it seems that Web development no longer refers to traditional Web applications but to Web 2.0 applications, especially RIAs. It seems that the potential of RIAs has not yet been fully exploited to design new client-server architectures promoting a ubiquitous Web.

In some cases, developers can take advantage of RIAs to overcome the challenges in developing other kinds of Web-based applications such as cloud-based applications, namely maintenance and deployment. In other cases, the challenges in the development of RIAs such as availability and data heterogeneity can be overcome by us-

ing further technologies such as ontologies and linked data. In fact, RIAs are not the solution to all the problems of Web development, and it is not the purpose of this chapter to state the opposite but to outline the main research directions for RIAs and guide forthcoming efforts on these directions. In this context, for further information about possible research directions related to the necessity of development approaches for RIAs, the work of Toffetti, Comai, Preciado, & Linaje (2011) can be reviewed.

The fact that business intelligence companies such as IBM™ and Oracle™ are moving their solutions to cloud taking advantage of RIA technologies is clear and it is the rudder that will guide the future of RIAs.

Finally, it is important to notice that, in the Web evolution, there are many ideas that are not exactly defined, and they are works in progress. However, current practices in the development of Web applications and the boom of smart devices, including interactive televisions and automobiles, are showing where it is going the Web.

REFERENCES

Abolfazli, S., Sanaei, Z., Gani, A., Xia, F., & Yang, L. T. (2014). Rich Mobile Applications: Genesis, taxonomy, and open issues. *Journal of Network and Computer Applications*, *40*, 345–362. doi:10.1016/j.jnca.2013.09.009

Aghaei, S., Nematbakhsh, M. A., & Farsani, H. K. (2012). Evolution of the World Wide Web : From Web 1.0 to Web 4.0. *International Journal of Web & Semantic Technology*, *3*(1), 1–10. doi:10.5121/ijwest.2012.3101

Allaire, J. (2002). *Macromedia Flash MX—A next-generation rich client*. San Francisco, CA: Macromedia, Inc. Retrieved from http://download.macromedia.com/pub/flash/whitepapers/richclient.pdf

Antenna Inc. (2010, January 11). *Harnessing the Power of the Mobile Cloud*. Jersey City, NJ: Antenna Inc. Retrieved from http://www.antennasoftware.com/pdf/whitepaper_Antenna_Mobile_Cloud.pdf

Balkić, Z., Pešut, M., & Jović, F. (2007). *Semantic Rich Internet Application (RIA) Modeling, Deployment and Integration*. Presented at the International Conference on Advances in the Internet, Processing, Systems and Interdisciplinary Research. Opatija, Croatia.

Barosa, R. (2010). *Build Web 2.0 applications using EGL*. IBM Boston. Retrieved from http://public.dhe.ibm.com/software/dw/rational/emz/Build_Web_2.0_application_using_EGL.pdf

Berners-Lee, T., Hendler, J., & Lassila, O. (2001). The Semantic Web. *Scientific American*, *284*(5), 34–43. doi:10.1038/scientificamerican0501-34 PMID:11396337

Cirilo, C. E., do Prado, A. F., de Souza, W. L., & Zaina, L. A. M. (2010). Model Driven RichUbi - A Model-Driven Process to Construct Rich Interfaces for Context-Sensitive Ubiquitous Applications. In *Proceedings of the 2010 26th Brazilian Symposium on Software Engineering* (pp. 100–109). Los Alamitos, CA: IEEE Computer Society. doi:10.1109/SBES.2010.20

Clarkin, L., & Holmes, J. (2007, October). Enterprise Mashups. *Microsoft Developer Network*. Retrieved December 20, 2012, from http://msdn.microsoft.com/en-us/library/bb906060.aspx

IBM Cloud Computing Platform as a Service (PaaS) - United States. (2014, May 9). Retrieved May 20, 2014, from http://www.ibm.com/cloud-computing/us/en/paas.html

Consortium, U. W. A. (2002). *Ubiquitous Web Applications*. Presented at the eBusiness and eWork Conference 2002. Prague, Czech Republic.

Cox, P. A. (2011, March 11). *Mobile cloud computing*. Retrieved October 22, 2012, from http://www.ibm.com/developerworks/cloud/library/cl-mobilecloudcomputing/

Davis, M. (2010, February 2). *Web 3.0 And The Next Internet: New Directions And Opportunities For...* Business & Mgmt. Retrieved from http://www.slideshare.net/ajmalik/web-30-and-the-next-internet-new-directions-and-opportunities-for-scientific-technical-and-medical-publishing

Deb, B., Bannur, S., & Bharti, S. (2007). *Rich Internet Applications (RIA): Opportunities and Challenges for Enterprises*. Bangalore, India: Infosys Technologies. Retrieved from http://www.infosys.com/IT-services/application-services/white-papers/Documents/rich-internet-applications.pdf

Dunlop, J., Ettl, R., & Abani, P. (2010). *Cloud computing: how client devices affect the user experience*. Intel. Retrieved from http://download.intel.com/it/pdf/Cloud-Computing-How-Client-Devices-Affect-User-Experience.pdf

Hermida, J. M., Meliá, S., Montoyo, A., & Gómez, J. (2011). Developing semantic rich internet applications using a model-driven approach. In *Proceedings of the 2010 international conference on Web information systems engineering* (pp. 198–211). Berlin: Springer-Verlag. doi:10.1007/978-3-642-24396-7_16

Leung, R. C. (2009, June 29). *Integrating Flex applications with IBM Mashup Center*. Retrieved December 22, 2012, from http://www.ibm.com/developerworks/lotus/library/mashups-flex/

Linaje, M., Lozano-Tello, A., Perez-Toledano, M. A., Preciado, J. C., Rodriguez-Echeverria, R., & Sanchez-Figueroa, F. (2011). Providing RIA user interfaces with accessibility properties. *Journal of Symbolic Computation*, *46*(2), 207–217. doi:10.1016/j.jsc.2010.08.008

Linaje-Trigueros, M., Preciado, J. C., & Sánchez-Figueroa, F. (2010). Multi-Device Context-Aware RIAs Using a Model-Driven Approach. *Journal of Universal Computer Science, 16*, 2038–2059.

March, V., Gu, Y., Leonardi, E., Goh, G., Kirchberg, M., & Lee, B. S. (2011). μCloud: Towards a New Paradigm of Rich Mobile Applications. *Procedia Computer Science, 5*, 618–624. doi:10.1016/j.procs.2011.07.080

Melia, S., Gomez, J., Perez, S., & Diaz, O. (2008). A Model-Driven Development for GWT-Based Rich Internet Applications with OOH4RIA. In *Proceedings of the 2008 Eighth International Conference on Web Engineering* (pp. 13 –23). Los Alamitos, CA: IEEE Computer Society. doi:10.1109/ICWE.2008.36

Mell, P., & Grance, T. (2011). *The NIST definition of Cloud Computing* (No. Tech. Rep. 800-145) (p. 7). Gaithersburg, MD: National Institute of Standards and Technology. Retrieved from http://csrc.nist.gov/publications/nistpubs/800-145/SP800-145.pdf

O'Reilly, T. (2007). What is Web 2.0: Design Patterns and Business Models for the Next Generation of Software. *Communications & Strategies, 1*(65), 17–38.

Pietschmann, S., Voigt, M., Rümpel, A., & Meißner, K. (2009). CRUISe: Composition of Rich User Interface Services. In *Proceedings of the 2009 Ninth International Conference on Web Engineering* (pp. 473–476). Berlin: Springer-Verlag. doi:10.1007/978-3-642-02818-2_41

Punjabi, M. (2012). *Evolutionary Trends in Rich Internet Applications* (No. 1). Infosys Labs Briefings. Retrieved from http://www.infosys.com/infosys-labs/publications/Documents/winning-it/evolutionary-trends.pdf

Toffetti, G., Comai, S., Preciado, J. C., & Linaje, M. (2011). State-of-the Art and trends in the Systematic Development of Rich Internet Applications. *Journal of Web Engineering, 10*(1), 70–86.

Tuchinda, R., Szekely, P., & Knoblock, C. A. (2008). Building Mashups by example. In *Proceedings of the 13th international conference on Intelligent user interfaces* (pp. 139–148). New York, NY: ACM. doi:10.1145/1378773.1378792

W3C. (2014). *Accessible Rich Internet Applications (WAI-ARIA) 1.0* (No. 1.0). Retrieved from http://www.w3.org/TR/wai-aria/complete

ADDITIONAL READING

The Antenna Mobility Platform. AMPchroma™. (n.d.). *Antenna Software website*. Retrieved December 22, 2012, from http://www.antennasoftware.com/products/overview

TopBraid Ensemble™. (n.d.). *TopQuadrant™ Website*. Retrieved December 22, 2012, from http://www.topquadrant.com/products/TB_Ensemble.html

Ubiquitous Web Domain. (n.d.). *W3C Website*. Retrieved December 22, 2012, from http://www.w3.org/UbiWeb/

W3C Data Activity. (n.d.). *W3C Website*. Retrieved March 25, 2014, from http://www.w3.org/2013/data/

Web Accessibility Initiative (WAI). (n.d.). *W3C Website*. Retrieved December 22, 2012, from http://www.w3.org/WAI/

What is force.com? (n.d.). *Force.com website*. Retrieved December 22, 2012, from http://www.salesforce.com/platform/what/

KEY TERMS AND DEFINITIONS

Cloud Computing: A style of computing in which dynamically scalable and often virtualized resources are provided as a service over the Internet. It refers to both the applications delivered as services over the Internet and, the hardware and systems software in the data centers that provide those services.

Context-Aware Rich Internet Application: A kind of RIA taking advantage of the information about the context in which it is delivered such as location and time in order to provide rich user experiences.

Mashup: A Web application that integrates data from multiple sources to provide a unique service.

Rich Internet Application: Applications that are deployed over the Web; this type of applications combines features and functionality of Web applications and desktop applications.

Rich Mobile Application: An online (Web-based) mobile application that is characterized by several rich traits inherited from Rich Internet Applications meant to deliver rich user experiences to mobile users. It relies on a multi-tier architecture in which functionality and data is distributed between the mobile device and one or more remote servers, allowing for anywhere anytime usage.

Semantic Rich Internet Application: A kind of Rich Internet Application that tries to solve the issues related to interoperability between systems by using Semantic Web and Linked Data principles.

Web 2.0: A collection of several principles such as the delivery of rich user experiences to traditional Web applications, the understanding of the Web as a platform and the harnessing of collective intelligence.

Web 3.0: A movement, also known as the Semantic Web, that is led by the W3C standards organization. According to the W3C, it provides a common framework that allows data to be shared and reused across application, enterprise, and community boundaries.

Web 4.0: The Ubiquitous Web, in which intelligences are connected delivering a new model of interaction between humans and machines.

ENDNOTES

[1]   https://www.oracle.com/cloud/paas.html
[2]   http://mobilehtml5.org/

Compilation of References

Abolfazli, S., Sanaei, Z., Gani, A., Xia, F., & Yang, L. T. (2014). Rich Mobile Applications: Genesis, taxonomy, and open issues. *Journal of Network and Computer Applications*, *40*, 345–362. doi:10.1016/j.jnca.2013.09.009

Acerbis, R., Bongio, A., Brambilla, M., & Butti, S. (2007). WebRatio 5: an eclipse-based CASE tool for engineering web applications. In *Proceedings of the 7th international conference on Web engineering* (pp. 501–505). Berlin: Springer-Verlag. Retrieved from http://dl.acm.org/citation.cfm?id=1770588.1770642

Adobe AIR. (2011). *Adobe AIR*. Retrieved January 30, 2011, from http://www.adobe.com/products/air/

Adobe. (2011). *Flex overview*. Retrieved January 29, 2011, from http://www.adobe.com/products/flex/overview

Aghaei, S., Nematbakhsh, M. A., & Farsani, H. K. (2012). Evolution of the World Wide Web : From Web 1.0 to Web 4.0. *International Journal of Web & Semantic Technology*, *3*(1), 1–10. doi:10.5121/ijwest.2012.3101

Alexander, C., Ishikawa, S., & Silverstein, M. (1977). *A Pattern Language: Towns, Buildings, Construction*. Oxford University Press.

Allaire, J. (2002). *Macromedia Flash MX—A next-generation rich client*. San Francisco, CA: Macromedia, Inc. Retrieved from http://download.macromedia.com/pub/flash/whitepapers/richclient.pdf

Alor-Hernandez, G., Hernandez-Carrillo, V. M., Ambros-Antemate, J. F., & Martinez-Nieves, L. A. (2012). Improving the Shopping Experience in B2C E-Commerce Systems using Rich Internet Applications. In K. Rezaul (Ed.), Strategic and Pragmatic E-Business: Implications for Future Business Practices (pp. 72–99). Academic Press. doi:10.4018/978-1-4666-1619-6.ch004

Amazon Web Services. (2013). *Amazon Web Services*. Retrieved March, 2013, from http://aws.amazon.com/es/

Antenna Inc. (2010, January 11). *Harnessing the Power of the Mobile Cloud*. Jersey City, NJ: Antenna Inc. Retrieved from http://www.antennasoftware.com/pdf/whitepaper_Antenna_Mobile_Cloud.pdf

Apache Tika. (2013). *A content analysis toolkit*. Retrieved March, 2013, from http://tika.apache.org/

AppMobi XDK. (n.d.). *AppMobi website*. Retrieved July 6, 2012, from http://www.appmobi.com/?q=node/27

Architecture, S. (n.d.). *MSDN*. Retrieved May 10, 2013, from http://msdn.microsoft.com/en-us/library/bb404713(v=vs.95).aspx

Balkić, Z., Pešut, M., & Jović, F. (2007). *Semantic Rich Internet Application (RIA) Modeling, Deployment and Integration*. Presented at the International Conference on Advances in the Internet, Processing, Systems and Interdisciplinary Research. Opatija, Croatia.

Barbosa, D. A., Honório, L. M., Leite da Silva, A. M., & Lopes, C. (2009). Concepts of Aspect-Oriented Modeling Applied to Optimal Power Flow Problems. In *Proceedings of Intelligent System Applications to Power Systems*, (pp. 1-6). IEEE. doi:10.1109/ISAP.2009.5352929

Baresi, L., Garzotto, F., & Paolini, P. (2001). Extending UML for Modeling Web Applications. In *Proceedings of the 34th Annual Hawaii International Conference on System Sciences*. IEEE Comput. Soc. Retrieved from http://ieeexplore.ieee.org/lpdocs/epic03/wrapper.htm?arnumber=926350

Barosa, R. (2010). *Build Web 2.0 applications using EGL*. IBM Boston. Retrieved from http://public.dhe.ibm. com/software/dw/rational/emz/Build_Web_2.0_application_using_EGL.pdf

BCS. *(2011). Windows 7 market share excedes 20% mark.* Retrieved February 6, 2011, from http://www.bcs.org/ content/conWebDoc/38577

Bebjak, M., Vranic, V., & Dolog, P. (2007). Evolution of Web Applications with Aspect-Oriented Design Patterns. In *Proceedings of AEWSE*. AEWSE.

Berners-Lee, T., Hendler, J., & Lassila, O. (2001). The Semantic Web. *Scientific American, 284*(5), 34–43. doi:10.1038/scientificamerican0501-34 PMID:11396337

Bibeault, B., & Katz, Y. (2008). jQuery in Action. Greenwich, CT: Manning Publications Co.

Bieber, M., Galnares, R., & Lu, Q. (1998). Web Engineering and Flexible Hypermedia. In P. Brusilovksy & P. De Bra (Eds.), *Proceedings of the 2nd Workshop on Adaptive Hypertext and Hypermedia Hypertext 98*. Retrieved from http://wwwis.win.tue.nl/ah98/Bieber.html

Booch, G., Rumbaugh, J., & Jacobson, I. (1999). *The Unified Modeling Language User Guide*. Addison-Wesley.

Bozzon, A., Comai, S., Fraternali, P., & Carugui, G. T. (2006). Capturing RIA concepts in a web modeling language. In *Proceedings of the 15th international Conference on World Wide Web WWW 06*, (pp. 907-908). ACM. Retrieved from http://discovery.ucl.ac.uk/1320284/

Brambilla, M., Preciado, J. C., Linaje, M., & Sanchez Figueroa, F. (2008). Business Process-based Conceptual Design of Rich Internet Applications. In *Proceedings of Eighth International Conference on Web Engineering*, (pp. 155-156). IEEE. Retrieved from http://ieeexplore. ieee.org/lpdocs/epic03/wrapper.htm?arnumber=4577879

Brisaboa, N. R., Penabad, M. R., Places, A. S., & Rodriguez, F. J. (2002). A documental database query language. *Advances in Databases, 2405*, 242–245.

Buchanan, M. (2013). *A Guide to Understanding Video Containers & Codecs*. Retrieved January, 2013, from http://library.rice.edu/services/dmc/guides/video/VideoFormatsGuide.pdf

Busch, M., & Koch, M. (2009). *State of the art. Rich Internet Applications* (Technical Report 0902). Academic Press.

Castillo, C. (n.d.). 1 Introduction to JavaFX Media. *JavaFX Documentation*. Retrieved May 9, 2013, from http://docs. oracle.com/javafx/2/media/overview.htm#CJAHFAHJ

Ceri, S., Fraternali, P., Bongio, A., Brambilla, M., Comai, S., & Matera, M. (2002). *Designing Data-Intensive Web Applications. Database.* Morgan Kaufmann Publishers Inc. Retrieved from http://www.amazon.com/ dp/1558608435

Chen, H. Y., Lin, Y. H., & Cheng, C. M. (2012). COCA: Computation Offload to Clouds Using AOP. In *Proceedings of the 12th IEEE/ACM International Symposium on Cluster, Cloud and Grid Computing (CCGrid 2012)* (pp. 466-473). Washington, DC: IEEE Computer Society. doi:10.1109/CCGrid.2012.98

Christiansson, B., Forss, M., Hagen, I., Hansson, K., Jonasson, J., & Jonasson, M. et al. (2008). *GoF Design Patterns - with examples using Java and UML2. Logica Java Architects Training Crew.* Authors.

Cirilo, C. E., do Prado, A. F., de Souza, W. L., & Zaina, L. A. M. (2010). Model Driven RichUbi - A Model-Driven Process to Construct Rich Interfaces for Context-Sensitive Ubiquitous Applications. In *Proceedings of the 2010 26th Brazilian Symposium on Software Engineering* (pp. 100–109). Los Alamitos, CA: IEEE Computer Society. doi:10.1109/SBES.2010.20

Clarke, S., & Baniassad, E. (2005). *Aspect-Oriented Analysis and Design - The Theme Approach*. Addison-Wesley Professional.

Clarkin, L., & Holmes, J. (2007, October). Enterprise Mashups. *Microsoft Developer Network*. Retrieved December 20, 2012, from http://msdn.microsoft.com/en-us/ library/bb906060.aspx

Colombo-Mendoza, L. O., Alor-Hernandez, G., & Rodríguez-González, A. (2011). *An Extension to PPRD for Source Code Generation of Multi-device RIAs*. Paper presented at the International Conference on Computers and Advanced Technology in Education. New York, NY.

Colombo-Mendoza, L. O., Alor-Hernández, G., Rodríguez-González, A., & Colomo-Palacios, R. (2013). Alexandria: A Visual Tool for Generating Multi-device Rich Internet Applications. *Journal of Web Engineering*, *12*(3-4), 317–359.

Consortium, U. W. A. (2002). *Ubiquitous Web Applications*. Presented at the eBusiness and eWork Conference 2002. Prague, Czech Republic.

Corona, S. D. K. (n.d.). *Corona Labs website*. Retrieved July 6, 2012, from http://www.coronalabs.com/products/corona-sdk/

Country Info Service. (2013). *Country Info Service*. Retrieved March, 2013, from http://webservices.oorsprong.org/websamples.countryinfo/CountryInfoService.wso

Cox, P. A. (2011, March 11). *Mobile cloud computing*. Retrieved October 22, 2012, from http://www.ibm.com/developerworks/cloud/library/cl-mobilecloudcomputing/

Crane, D., Bibeault, B., & Locke, T. (2007). *Prototype and Scriptaculous in Action*. Greenwich, CT: Manning Publications Co.

Cross-Browser. (2014). *X-library*. Retrieved January, 2014, from http://www.cross-browser.com/

Czarnecki, K. (1999). *Generative Programming: Principles and Techniques of Software Engineering Based on Automated Configuration and Fragment-Based Component Models*. (PhD thesis). German: Technische Universitat Ilmenau.

Davis, M. (2010, February 2). *Web 3.0 And The Next Internet: New Directions And Opportunities For...* Business & Mgmt. Retrieved from http://www.slideshare.net/ajmalik/web-30-and-the-next-internet-new-directions-and-opportunities-for-scientific-technical-and-medical-publishing

Deb, B., Bannur, S., & Bharti, S. (2007). *Rich Internet Applications (RIA): Opportunities and Challenges for Enterprises*. Bangalore, India: Infosys Technologies. Retrieved from http://www.infosys.com/IT-services/application-services/white-papers/Documents/rich-internet-applications.pdf

Debnath, M. (2012, May 3). *JavaFX 2.0: A Platform for Rich Enterprise Client Apps*. Retrieved November 26, 2012, http://www.devx.com/Java/Article/48067

Detroyer, O., & Leune, C. (1998). WSDM: A user centered design method for Web sites. *Computer Networks and ISDN Systems, 30*(1-7), 85-94. Retrieved from http://linkinghub.elsevier.com/retrieve/pii/S0169755298000427

Dojotoolkit. (2014). *Dojotoolkit*. Retrieved February, 2014, from http://www.dojotoolkit.org/

Dolog, P., & Stage, J. (2007). Designing Interaction Spaces for Rich Internet Applications with UML. *Techniques, 4607*, 358-363. Retrieved from http://www.springerlink.com/index/10.1007/978-3-540-73597-7

Dolog, P., Vrani'c, V., & Bielikov'a, M. (2001). Representing change by aspect. *ACM SIGPLAN Notices, 36*(12), 77–83. doi:10.1145/583960.583970

Duhl, J. (2003). *Rich Internet Applications*. Framingham, MA: IDC, Inc.

Dunlop, J., Ettl, R., & Abani, P. (2010). *Cloud computing: how client devices affect the user experience*. Intel. Retrieved from http://download.intel.com/it/pdf/Cloud-Computing-How-Client-Devices-Affect-User-Experience.pdf

Ebay Developers Program. (2013). *Ebay API*. Retrieved March, 2013, from http://developer.ebay.com/common/api/

Eclipse documentation - Previous Release. (n.d.). *Concepts*. Retrieved May 11, 2014, from http://help.eclipse.org/juno/index.jsp?topic=%2Forg.eclipse.platform.doc.user%2Fconcepts%2Fconcepts-4.htm

Eguíluz Pérez. J. (2008). *Introducción a AJAX*. Librosweb. Retrieved February, 2014, from http://librosweb.es/ajax/

Ekabua, O. (2012). Using Aspect Oriented Techniques to Build-in Software Quality. *International Journal of Computer Science Issues, 9*(4), 250–255.

Elrad, T., Filman, R. E., & Bader, A. (2001). Aspect oriented programming: Introduction. *Communications of the ACM, 44*(10), 28–32. doi:10.1145/383845.383853

Escalona, M., & Koch, N. (2004). Requirements Engineering for Web Applications – A Comparative Study. *Journal of Web Engineering, 2*(3), 193-212. Citeseer. Retrieved from http://citeseerx.ist.psu.edu/viewdoc/download?doi=10.1.1.153.5974&rep=rep1&type=pdf

Escalona, M. J., Torres, J., & Mejías, M. (2002). Requirements Capture Workflow in Global Information Systems. In *Proceedings of OOIS*. Springer-Verlag. doi:10.1007/3-540-46102-7_31

Fain, Y., Rasputnis, V., & Tartakovsky, A. (2010). *Enterprise Development with Flex* (p. 688). O'Reilly Media.

Fayad, M. E., & Adam, A. (2001). Thinking objectively: An Introduction to Software Stability. *Communications of the ACM, 44*(9), 95–98. doi:10.1145/383694.383713

Fielding, R. T. (2000). *Architectural styles and the design of network-based software architectures*. (PhD dissertation). University of California, Irvine, CA.

Flash Player. (2012). *Statistics*. Retrieved December 18, 2012, from: http://www.adobe.com/mx/products/flashruntimes/statistics.html

Fraternali, P. (1999). Tools and approaches for developing data-intensive Web applications: A survey. *ACM Computing Surveys, 31*(3), 227–263. doi:10.1145/331499.331502

Freedman, A. (1999). *Diccionario bilingüe de computación*. Mc Graw Hill.

Gamma, E., Helm, R., Johnson, R., & Vlissides, J. (1994). *Design Patterns: Elements of reusable Object-Oriented Software*. Boston, MA: Addison-Wesley Longman Publishing Co., Inc.

Garzotto, F., Paolini, P., & Schwabe, D. (1993). HDM - A model-based approach to hypermedia applications design. *ACM Transactions on Information Systems, 11*(1), 1–23. doi:10.1145/151480.151483

Google Developers – GoogleMaps. (2013). *API Google Maps*. Retrieved March, 2013, from https://developers.google.com/maps/?hl=es

Google Developers – Youtube. (2013). *Youtube API Resources*. Retrieved March, 2013, from https://developers.google.com/youtube/

Harmon, J. E. (2008). Dojo: Using the Dojo JavaScript Library to Build Ajax Applications. Addison-Wesley Professional.

Hennicker, R., & Koch, N. (2000). A UML-based methodology for hypermedia design. In *Proceedings of the 3rd international conference on The unified modeling language advancing the standard* (Vol. 1939, pp. 410-424). Springer-Verlag. Retrieved from http://portal.acm.org/citation.cfm?id=1765218&dl=GUIDE&coll=GUIDE

Heo, S. H., & Choi, E. M. (2006). Representation of Variability in Software Product Line Using Aspect-Oriented Programming. In *Proceedings of the Fourth International Conference on Software Engineering Research, Management and Applications (SERA '06)* (pp. 66-73). Washington, DC: IEEE Computer Society.

Hermida, J. M., Meliá, S., Montoyo, A., & Gómez, J. (2011). Developing semantic rich internet applications using a model-driven approach. In *Proceedings of the 2010 international conference on Web information systems engineering* (pp. 198–211). Berlin: Springer-Verlag. doi:10.1007/978-3-642-24396-7_16

Hmida, M. M. B., Tomaz, R. F., & Monfort, V. (2005). Applying AOP concepts to increase Web services flexibility. In *Proceedings of Next Generation Web Services Practices*. IEEE.

Holmes, J. (2012). *Taking Abstraction a step further*. Retrieved April, 2014, from https://weblogs.java.net/blog/2004/09/29/taking-abstraction-one-step-further

Holmes, J. (2013). Enterprise Mashups. MSDN Architecture Journal. *MSDN Architecture Center*. Retrieved March 2013, from http://msdn.microsoft.com/en-us/architecture/bb906060.aspx

Holzinger, A., Brugger, M., & Slany, W. (2011). Applying aspect oriented programming in usability engineering processes: On the example of tracking usage information for remote usability testing, In *Proceedings of the International Conference on e-Business (ICE-B 2011)* (pp. 1-4). Seville, Spain: IEEE.

Holzinger, A. (2005). Usability engineering methods for software developers. *Communications of the ACM, 48*(1), 71–74. doi:10.1145/1039539.1039541

IBM Cloud Computing Platform as a Service (PaaS) - United States. (2014, May 9). Retrieved May 20, 2014, from http://www.ibm.com/cloud-computing/us/en/paas. html

Indiana University. (2009).*Google Picasa 3: The Basics.* Retrieved from http://ittraining.iu.edu/free/picba.pdf

Ivory, M. Y., & Hearst, M. A. (2001). The state of the art in automating usability evaluation of user interfaces. *ACM Computing Surveys, 33*(4), 470–516. doi:10.1145/503112.503114

Jacobson, I., Booch, G., & Rumbaugh, J. (1999). *The Unified Software Development Process.* Addison-Wesley.

Jacobson, I., & Ng, P. W. (2005). *Aspect-Oriented Software Development with Use Cases.* Addison Wesley Professional.

Javahery, H., Sinnig, D., Seffah, A., Forbrig, P., & Radhakrishnan, T. (2007). Pattern-based UI design: adding rigor with user and context variables. In *Proceedings of the 5th international conference on Task models and diagrams for users interface design (TAMODIA'06)* (pp. 97-108). Berlin: Springer-Verlag. doi:10.1007/978-3-540-70816-2_8

Jboss. (2013). *Aspect Oriented Programming (AOP) Support.* Retrieved January, 2013, from http://docs.jboss.org/jbossas/jboss4guide/r2/html/aop.chapt.html

JQUERY. (2012). *Documentation.* Retrieved September, 2012, from http://docs.jquery.com/

jquery-aop. (2014). *API Reference.* Retrieved April, 2014, from http://code.google.com/p/jquery-aop/wiki/Reference

Juárez Martínez, U. (2008). *Énfasis: Programación Orientada a Aspectos de Grano Fino.* (PhD thesis). Centro de Investigación y de Estudios Avanzados del Instituto Politécnico Nacional.

Kappel, G., Proll, B., Retschitzegger, W., & Schwinger, W. (2003). Customisation for Ubiquitous Web Applications: a Comparison of Approaches. *Int. J. Web Eng. Technol., 1*(1), 79–111. doi:10.1504/IJWET.2003.003322

Kiczales, G., Lamping, J., Mendhekar, A., Maeda, C., Lopes, C., Loingtier, J. M., & Irwin, J. (1997). Aspect-oriented programming. In M. Aksit, & S. Matsuoka (Eds.), *Ecoop'97: Object-Oriented Programming* (pp. 220–242). Berlin: Springer-Verlag.

Koch, N., & Wirsing, M. (2001). Software engineering for adaptive hypermedia applications. *Ph Thesis FAST Reihe Softwaretechnik, 12.* Retrieved from http://citeseerx.ist.psu.edu/viewdoc/download?doi=10.1.1.24.4017&rep=rep1&type=pdf

Korozi, M., Leonidis, S., Margetis, G., & Stephanidis, C. (2009). MAID: a Multi-platform Accessible Interface Design Framework. In *Proceedings of the 5th International Conference on Universal Access in Human-Computer Interaction. Part III: Applications and Services (UAHCI '09)* (pp. 725-734). Berlin: Springer-Verlag. doi:10.1007/978-3-642-02713-0_77

Kulesza, U., Sant'Anna, C., Garcia, A., Coelho, R., Von Staa, A., & Lucena, C. (2006). Quantifying the Effects of Aspect-Oriented Programming: A Maintenance Study. In *Proceedings of Software Maintenance,* (pp. 223-233). IEEE.

Kwanwoo, L., Botterweck, G., & Thiel, S. (2009). Feature-Modeling and Aspect-Oriented Programming: Integration and Automation. In *Proceedings of the 2009 10th ACIS International Conference on Software Engineering, Artificial Intelligences, Networking and Parallel/Distributed Computing (SNPD '09)* (pp. 186-191). Washington, DC: IEEE Computer Society.

Laddad, R. (2003). *AspectJ in Action: Practical Aspect-Oriented Programming.* Greenwich, CT: Manning Publications Co.

Laszlo Systems, Inc. (2013a). *Architecture.* Retrieved January 29, 2013, from: http://www.openlaszlo.org/architecture

Laszlo Systems, Inc. (2013b). *OpenLaszlo Architecture.* Retrieved February 6, 2011, from: http://www.openlaszlo.org/lps4.9/docs/developers/architecture.html

Laszlo Systems, Inc. (2013c). *OpenLaszlo Showcase.* Retrieved February 6, 2011, from: http://www.openlaszlo.org/showcase

Lee, H., Lee, C., & Yoo, C. (1998). A scenario-based object-oriented methodology for developing hypermedia information systems. In *Proceedings of the Thirty First Hawaii International Conference on System Sciences,* (pp. 47-56). IEEE Comput. Soc. Retrieved from http://ieeexplore.ieee.org/lpdocs/epic03/wrapper.htm?arnumber=651682

Leung, R. C. (2009, June 29). *Integrating Flex applications with IBM Mashup Center.* Retrieved December 22, 2012, from http://www.ibm.com/developerworks/lotus/library/mashups-flex/

Li, H., Zhang, J., & Wang, L. (2010). The research and application of web-based system with Aspect-Oriented features. In *Proceedings of Computer Engineering and Technology (ICCET),* (pp. V4-480). IEEE.

Linaje, M., Preciado, J.C., Morales-Chaparro, R., & Sanchez-Figueroa, F. (2008). On the Implementation of Multiplatform RIA User Interface Components. In *Proceedings of ICWE 2008 Workshops, 7th Int. Workshop on Web-Oriented Software Technologies,* (pp. 44-49). ICWE. Retrieved from http://icwe2008.webengineering.org/Program/Workshops/ISBN978-80-227-2899-7/icwe2008ws-CD/individual-files/02icwe2008ws-iwwost08-linaje.pdf

Linaje, M., Lozano-Tello, A., Perez-Toledano, M. A., Preciado, J. C., Rodriguez-Echeverria, R., & Sanchez-Figueroa, F. (2011). Providing RIA user interfaces with accessibility properties. *Journal of Symbolic Computation,* *46*(2), 207–217. doi:10.1016/j.jsc.2010.08.008

Linaje-Trigueros, M., Preciado, J. C., & Sánchez-Figueroa, F. (2010). Multi-Device Context-Aware RIAs Using a Model-Driven Approach. *Journal of Universal Computer Science,* *16*, 2038–2059.

Lippert, M., & Lopes, C. V. (2000). A study on exception detection and handling using aspect-oriented programming. In *Proceedings of the 2000 International Conference on Software Engineering* (pp. 418-427). IEEE.

Lowe, D., & Eklund, J. (2002). *Client Needs and the Design Process in Web Projects.* Paper presented at the Web Engineering Track of the WWW2002 Conference. New York, NY.

Lucene (2013). *Apache Lucene Core.* Retrieved March, 2013, from http://lucene.apache.org/core/

Machado, L., Filho, O., & Ribeiro, J. (2009). UWE-R: An extension to a web engineering methodology for rich internet applications. *WSEAS Trans. Info. Sci. and App.,* *6*(4), 601–610.

Mahemoff, M. (2006). *Ajax Design Patterns.* O'Reilly.

March, V., Gu, Y., Leonardi, E., Goh, G., Kirchberg, M., & Lee, B. S. (2011). μCloud: Towards a New Paradigm of Rich Mobile Applications. *Procedia Computer Science,* *5*, 618–624. doi:10.1016/j.procs.2011.07.080

Martínez-Nieves, L. A., Hernández-Carrillo, V. M., & Alor-Hernández, G. (2010). An ADV-UWE Based Phases Process for Rich Internet Applications Development. In *Proceedings of Electronics,Robotics and Automotive Mechanics Conference (CERMA),* (pp. 45–50). CERMA. doi:10.1109/CERMA.2010.16

Martinez-ruiz, F., Arteaga, J., Vanderdonckt, J., Gonzalez-calleros, J., & Mendoza, R. (2006). A first draft of a Model-driven Method for Designing Graphical User Interfaces of Rich Internet Applications. In *Proceedings of 2006 Fourth Latin American Web Congress,* (pp. 32-38). IEEE. Retrieved from http://ieeexplore.ieee.org/lpdocs/epic03/wrapper.htm?arnumber=4022089

Martin, J. (1991). *Rapid Application Development.* New York: Macmillan USA.

McCune, D., & Subramaniam, D. (2008). Getting to Know Flex. In *Adobe Flex 3.0 for Dummies* (pp. 9–16). Indianapolis, IN: Wiley Publishing, Inc.

Medicare Supplier. (2013). *MediCareSupplier.* Retrieved March, 2013, from http://www.webservicex.net/medicareSupplier.asmx

Meliá, S., Gómez, J., Pérez, S., & Díaz, O. (2008). A Model-Driven Development for GWT-Based Rich Internet Applications with OOH4RIA. In *Proceedings of 2008 Eighth International Conference on Web Engineering,* (pp. 13-23). IEEE. Retrieved from http://ieeexplore.ieee.org/lpdocs/epic03/wrapper.htm?arnumber=4577865

Melia, S., Gomez, J., Perez, S., & Diaz, O. (2008). A Model-Driven Development for GWT-Based Rich Internet Applications with OOH4RIA. In *Proceedings of the 2008 Eighth International Conference on Web Engineering* (pp. 13 –23). Los Alamitos, CA: IEEE Computer Society. doi:10.1109/ICWE.2008.36

Mell, P., & Grance, T. (2011). *The NIST definition of Cloud Computing* (No. Tech. Rep. 800-145) (p. 7). Gaithersburg, MD: National Institute of Standards and Technology. Retrieved from http://csrc.nist.gov/publications/nistpubs/800-145/SP800-145.pdf

Miano, J. (1999). *Compressed Image File Formats: Jpeg, Png, Gif, Xbm, Bmp.* New York, NY: ACM Press/ Addison-Wesley Publ. Co.

Microsoft. (2011a). *Arquitectura de Silverlight.* Retrieved January 30, 2011, from: http://msdn.microsoft.com/es-es/library/bb404713(v=VS.95).aspx

Microsoft. (2011b). *Información general sobre Silverlight.* Retrieved January 30, 2011, from: http://msdn.microsoft.com/es-es/library/bb404700(v=VS.95).aspx

Moonlight. (2011). *Moonlight.* Retrieved January 30, 2011, from: http://www.mono-project.com/Moonlight

Mootools. (2012). *Mootools.* Retrieved August, 2012, from: http://mootools.net/

Mootools.net. (2013). *API Documentation.* Retrieved January, 2013, from http://mootools.net/docs/core

Namscimbene, C. (2005). *Adobe & Macromedia Sales Engineer en el distribuidor ALAB S.A.* Retrieved 6 July 2011 from http://www.canal-ar.com.ar/noticias/noticiamuestra.asp?Id=2639

Neil, T. (2009). *Designing Rich Applications.* Slideshare Website. Retrieved May 28, 2012, from http://www.slideshare.net/theresaneil/designing-rich-applications

Newton, A. (2008). *MooTools Essentials: The Official MooTools Reference for JavaScript and Ajax Development.* Berkely, CA: Apress.

Nilsson, E. G. (2009). Design patterns for user interface for mobile applications. *Advances in Engineering Software,* 40(12), 1318–1328. doi:10.1016/j.advengsoft.2009.01.017

O'Reilly, T. (2005). What is Web 2.0. Design Patterns and Bussiness Models for the Next Generation of Software. *Design,* 65(65), 17-37. Retrieved from http://papers.ssrn.com/sol3/papers.cfm?abstract_id=1008839

O'Reilly, T. (2007). What is Web 2.0: Design Patterns and Business Models for the Next Generation of Software. *Communications & Strategies,* 1(65), 17–38.

Olsina, L. (1998). *Building a Web-based Information System applying the Hypermedia Flexible ProcessModeling Strategy.* Paper presented at the 1st International Workshop on Hypermedia Development, Hypertext´98. Pittsburgh, PA.

Openrico. (2014). *Openrico.* Retrieved August, 2014, from: http://openrico.org/

Oracle Corporation. (2011). *Develop Expressive Content with the JavaFX Platform.* Retrieved January 29, 2011, from: http://javafx.com/about/overview/index.jsp

Ortiz, G., Bordbar, B., & Hernandez, J. (2008). Evaluating the Use of AOP and MDA in Web Service Development. In *Proceedings of Internet and Web Applications and Services,* (pp. 78-83). IEEE. doi:10.1109/ICIW.2008.24

Osmani, A. (2010). *Essential JavaScript & jQuery Design Patterns For Beginners.* Addy Osmani.

Package javafx.scene.media. (n.d.). *JavaFX 2.2.* Retrieved May 9, 2013, from http://docs.oracle.com/javafx/2/api/javafx/scene/media/package-summary.html

Palmieri, M., Singh, I., & Cicchetti, A. (2012). Comparison of cross-platform mobile development tools. In *Proceedings of 2012 16th International Conference on Intelligence in Next Generation Networks (ICIN)* (pp. 179–186). IEEE. doi:10.1109/ICIN.2012.6376023

Patel, S. V., & Pandey, K. (2009). SOA Using AOP for Sensor Web Architecture. In *Proceedings of Computer Engineering and Technology,* (vol. 2, pp. 503-507). IEEE. doi:10.1109/ICCET.2009.152

Pietschmann, S., Voigt, M., Rümpel, A., & Meißner, K. (2009). CRUISe: Composition of Rich User Interface Services. In *Proceedings of the 2009 Ninth International Conference on Web Engineering* (pp. 473–476). Berlin: Springer-Verlag. doi:10.1007/978-3-642-02818-2_41

Ponnalagu, K., Narendra, N. C., Krishnamurthy, J., & Ramkumar, R. (2007). Aspect-oriented Approach for Non-functional Adaptation of Composite Web Services. In *Proceedings of Services,* (pp. 284-291). IEEE. doi:10.1109/SERVICES.2007.18

Preciado, J. C., Linaje, M., Comai, S., & Sanchez-Figueroa, F. (2007). Designing Rich Internet Applications with Web Engineering Methodologies. In *Proceedings of 2007 9th IEEE International Workshop on Web Site Evolution*, (pp. 23-30). IEEE. Retrieved from http://ieeexplore.ieee.org/lpdocs/epic03/wrapper.htm?arnumber=4380240

Preciado, J. C., Linaje, M., Morales-Chaparro, R., Sanchez-Figueroa, F., Zhang, G., Kroiß, C., & Koch, N. (2008). Designing Rich Internet Applications Combining UWE and RUX-Method. In *Proceedings of 2008 Eighth International Conference on Web Engineering*, (pp. 148-154). IEEE. Retrieved from http://ieeexplore.ieee.org/lpdocs/epic03/wrapper.htm?arnumber=4577878

Preciado, J. C., Linaje, M., Sanchez, F., & Comai, S. (2005). Necessity of methodologies to model Rich Internet Applications. In *Proceedings of Seventh IEEE International Symposium on Web Site Evolution*, (pp. 7-13). IEEE. Retrieved from http://ieeexplore.ieee.org/lpdocs/epic03/wrapper.htm?arnumber=1517975

Preciado, J. C., Linaje, M., Sanchez, F., & Comai, S. (2005). Necessity of methodologies to model Rich Internet Applications. In *Proceedings of the Seventh IEEE International Symposium on Web Site Evolution* (pp. 7–13). Washington, DC: IEEE Computer Society. doi:10.1109/WSE.2005.10

Prototypejs. (2014). *Prototypejs*. Retrieved January, 2014, from: http://www.prototypejs.org/

prototypejs.org. (2013). *API Documentation*. Retrieved January, 2013, from http://prototypejs.org/learn

Punjabi, M. (2012). *Evolutionary Trends in Rich Internet Applications* (No. 1). Infosys Labs Briefings. Retrieved from http://www.infosys.com/infosys-labs/publications/Documents/winning-it/evolutionary-trends.pdf

Qooxdoo. (2014). *Qooxdoo*. Retrieved April, 2014, from: http://qooxdoo.org/

Qt, S. D. K. (n.d.). *Nokia products*. Retrieved July 6, 2012, from http://qt.nokia.com/products

Raj, A., & Komaragiri, V. (2009). RUCID: Rapid Usable Consistent Interaction Design Patterns-Based Mobile Phone UI Design Library. In *Proceedings of the 13th International Conference on Human-Computer Interaction. Part I: New Trends* (pp. 677-686). Berlin: Springer-Verlag. doi:10.1007/978-3-642-02574-7_76

Rambadt, M. (2009). *Monitoring of Web Services Using UNICORE 6 as an Example*. (MS thesis). Aachen University of Applied Sciences, Aachen, Germany. Retrieved November 30, 2012, from http://www.ibm.com/developerworks/aix/library/au-aem_rest/

Raymond, S., & Pereira, S. (2006). *Prototype Quick Reference*. O'Reilly Media, Inc.

Resendiz, M. P., & Aguirre, J. O. O. (2005). Dynamic invocation of Web services by using aspect-oriented programming. In *Proceedings of Electrical and Electronics Engineering*, (pp. 48-51). IEEE.

RibosoMatic. (2013). *Listado de librerías, frameworks y herramientas para AJAX, DHTML y JavaScript*. Retrieved August, 2013, from: http://www.ribosomatic.com/articulos/top-librerias-ajax-dhtml-y-javascript/

Richard, J., Robert, J.-M., Malo, S., & Migneault, J. (2011). Giving UI Developers the Power of UI Design Patterns. In *Proceedings of the 2011 international conference on Human interface and the management of information - Volume Part I (HI'11)* (pp. 40-47). Berlin: Springer-Verlag. doi:10.1007/978-3-642-21793-7_5

Rivero, J. M., & Buzzo, M. H. (2007). *Definición de Rich Internet Applications a través de Modelos de Dominio Específico*. Retrieved from: http://revista.info.unlp.edu.ar/tesinas/tesis51.pdf

Rosales-Morales, V. Y., Alor-Hernández, G., & Juárez-Martínez, U. (2011). An overview of multimedia support into JavaScript-based Frameworks for developing RIAs. In *Proceedings of 2011 21st International Conference on Electrical Communications and Computers (CONIELECOMP)* (pp. 66–70). doi:10.1109/CONIELECOMP.2011.5749341

Rossi, G., Urbieta, M., Ginzburg, J., Distante, D., & Garrido, A. (2008). Refactoring to Rich Internet Applications. A Model-Driven Approach. In *Proceedings of 2008 Eighth International Conference on Web Engineering*, (pp. 1-12). IEEE. Retrieved from http://ieeexplore.ieee.org/lpdocs/epic03/wrapper.htm?arnumber=4577864

Rossi, G., Urbieta, M., Ginzburg, J., Distante, D., & Garrido, A. (2008). Refactoring to Rich Internet Applications. A Model-Driven Approach. In *Proceedings of the 2008 Eighth International Conference on Web Engineering* (pp. 1–12). Washington, DC: IEEE Computer Society. doi:10.1109/ICWE.2008.41

Ruengmee, W., Silva, R. S., Bajracharya, S. K., Redmiles, D. F., & Lopes, C. V. (2008). XE (eXtreme editor) -bridging the aspect-oriented programming usability gap. In *Proceedings of the 2008 23rd IEEE/ACM International Conference on Automated Software Engineering* (pp. 435-438). IEEE Computer Society. doi:10.1109/ASE.2008.67

Sandvine. (2012). *Global Internet Phenomena Report: 2H 2012*. Retrieved January, 2013, from www.sandvine.com/news/global_broadband_trends.asp

Schwabe, D., & Rossi, G. (1998). Developing Hypermedia Applications using OOHDM. *Methodology, 98*, 1-20. Retrieved from http://citeseerx.ist.psu.edu/viewdoc/summary?doi=10.1.1.40.4780

Scott, B. (2009). *RIA Patterns. Best Practices for Common Patterns of Rich Interaction*. Retrieved from http://www.uxmatters.com/mt/archives/2007/03/

Scott, B., & Neil, T. (2009). *Designing Web Interfaces: Principles and Patterns for Rich Interactions* (1st ed.). O'Reilly Media, Inc.

Search Engine Mashup. (2007, July 6). *EurekAlert.org*. Retrieved November 16, 2012, from http://www.eurekalert.org/pub_releases/2007-07/ip-sem070407.php

Seffah, A., Forbrig, P., & Javahery, H. (2004). Multidevices "Multiple" user interfaces: Development models and research opportunities. *Journal of Systems and Software, 73*(2), 287–300. doi:10.1016/j.jss.2003.09.017

Seffah, A., & Taleb, M. (2012). Tracing the evolution of HCI patterns as an interaction design tool. *Innovations in Systems and Software Engineering, 8*(2), 93–109. doi:10.1007/s11334-011-0178-8

Sencha. (2014). *Sencha ExtJS*. Retrieved April, 2014, from: http://www.sencha.com/products/extjs/

sencha.com. (2013). *API Documentation*. Retrieved January, 2013, from http://docs.sencha.com/extjs/4.1.3/

Simmons, A. (2007). *Enhancing eCommerce ROI through Rich Internet Applications (RIAs)*. Montreal, Canada: Integration New Media, Inc.

Smeets, B., Boness, U., & Bankras, R. (2008). Introducing Rich Internet Applications (RIAs). In *Beginning Google Web Toolkit: From Novice to Professional* (pp. 1–19). New York: Apress.

sohodox.com. (2013). *Document Indexing: The Key to Finding Documents Quickly*. Retrieved May, 2013, from http://www.sohodox.com/articles/document-indexing-the-key-to-finding-documents-quickly#sthash.CdBN-Beue.dpuf

Springsource.org. (2014). *Spring Framework Reference Documentation*. Retrieved April, 2014, from http://static.springsource.org/spring/docs/3.2.x/spring-framework-reference/pdf/spring-framework-reference.pdf

Subramaniam, D. (2010, March 8). *A brief overview of the Spark architecture and component set*. Retrieved May 9, 2013, from http://www.adobe.com/devnet/flex/articles/flex4_sparkintro.html

Support, M. (n.d.). *OpenLaszlo wiki*. Retrieved May 22, 2013, from http://wiki.openlaszlo.org/MediaSupport

Supported Media Formats, P., & Fields, L. (n.d.). *MSDN*. Retrieved May 9, 2013, from http://msdn.microsoft.com/en-us/library/cc189080(v=vs.95).aspx

Swiz Framework. (2014). *Getting Started with Swiz AOP*. Retrieved April, 2014, from http://swizframework.org/post.cfm/getting-started-with-swiz-aop

Tahir, A., & Ahmad, R. (2010). An AOP-Based Approach for Collecting Software Maintainability Dynamic Metrics. In *Proceedings of the 2010 Second International Conference on Computer Research and Development (ICCRD '10)* (pp.168-172). Washington, DC: IEEE Computer Society. doi:10.1109/ICCRD.2010.26

Tarta, A. M., & Moldovan, G. S. (2006). Automatic Usability Evaluation Using AOP. In *IEEE International Conference on Automation, Quality and Testing. IEEE Robotics, 2*, 84–89.

Theserverlabs. (2011). *Rich Internet Applications, Frameworks evaluation*. Retrieved February 6, 2011, from: http://www.theserverlabs.com/brochures/RIA_Frameworks-TSL-evaluation.pdf

Tidwell, J. (2011). *Designing Interfaces* (2nd ed.). Sebastopol, CA: O'Reilly Media, Inc.

Toffetti, G., Comai, S., Preciado, J. C., & Linaje, M. (2011). State-of-the Art and trends in the Systematic Development of Rich Internet Applications. *Journal of Web Engineering, 10*(1), 70–86.

Tuchinda, R., Szekely, P., & Knoblock, C. A. (2008). Building Mashups by example. In *Proceedings of the 13th international conference on Intelligent user interfaces* (pp. 139–148). New York, NY: ACM. doi:10.1145/1378773.1378792

Understanding Video Formats. (n.d.). *Adobe Flash Platform*. Retrieved May 9, 2013, from http://help.adobe.com/en_US/as3/dev/WS5b3ccc516d4fbf351e63e3d-118a9b90204-7d46.html

Urbieta, M., Rossi, G., Ginzburg, J., & Schwabe, D. (2007). Designing the Interface of Rich Internet Applications. In *Proceedings of 2007 Latin American Web Conference LAWEB 2007*, (pp. 144-153). IEEE. Retrieved from http://ieeexplore.ieee.org/lpdocs/epic03/wrapper.htm?arnumber=4383169

USF College of Education. (n.d.). *Online Photo Sharing with Flickr*. Retrieved from http://fcit.usf.edu/laptop

Valverde, F., & Pastor, O. (2008). Applying Interaction Patterns: Towards a Model-Driven Approach for Rich Internet Applications Development Francisco Valverde, Oscar Pastor. In *Proceedings of IWWOST* (pp. 13-18). Retrieved from http://icwe2008.webengineering.org/program/workshops/isbn978-80-227-2899-7/icwe2008ws-cd/individual-files/02icwe2008ws-iwwost02-valverde.pdf

Veit, F. (2008). *Introducción a Tecnologías Enriquecidas para Internet*. (Unpublished thesis). Facultad de Ingeniería, Universidad ORT Uruguay, Uruguay.

Verheecke, B., Vanderperren, W., & Jonckers, V. (2006). Unraveiliny crossoutting concerns in Web services middleware. *Software, IEEE, 23*(1), 42–50. doi:10.1109/MS.2006.31

Vilain, P., Schwabe, D., & Souza, C. S. D. (2000). A Diagrammatic Tool for Representing User Interaction in UML. *Lecture*, 133-147. Retrieved from http://citeseerx.ist.psu.edu/viewdoc/summary?doi=10.1.1.32.4062

Viveros García, M. C., & García Godoy, D. (2009). *Elaboración de una guía para el desarrollo de aplicaciones en extjs. (Unpublished thesis)*. Instituto Tecnológico de Orizaba.

W3C. (2014). *Accessible Rich Internet Applications (WAI-ARIA) 1.0* (No. 1.0). Retrieved from http://www.w3.org/TR/wai-aria/complete

Wikipedia. (2011). *Rich Internet Application*. Retrieved 02 Feb 2011, from http://en.wikipedia.org/wiki/Rich_Internet_application

Xu, Y., & Huang, H. (2009). A Petri Net-Based Model for Aspect-Oriented Web Service Composition. In *Proceedings of Management and Service Science*, (pp. 1-4). IEEE. doi:10.1109/ICMSS.2009.5305764

Xu, Y., Tang, S., Tang, Z., Xu, Y., & Xiao, R. (2007). Constructing Web Service Flows with Reusable Aspects. In *Proceedings of Internet and Web Applications and Services*, (pp. 21-21). IEEE. doi:10.1109/ICIW.2007.27

Yourdon, E. (1989). *Modern Structured Analysis*. Prentice-Hall.

Zhang, J., Meng, F., & Liu, G. (2009). Research on Multi-tier Distributed Systems Based on AOP and Web Services. In *Proceedings of Education Technology and Computer Science*, (Vol. 2, pp. 203-207). IEEE. doi:10.1109/ETCS.2009.307

Zhou, J., Ji, Y., Zhao, D., & Liu, J. (2010). Using AOP to ensure component interactions in component-based software. In *Computer and Automation Engineering (IC-CAE), 2010 the 2nd International Conference on* (Vol. 3, pp. 518-523). Singapore: IEEE Computer Society.

About the Authors

Giner Alor-Hernández is a full-time researcher of the Division of Research and Postgraduate Studies of the Instituto Tecnológico de Orizaba. He received a MSc and a PhD in Computer Science of the Center for Research and Advanced Studies of the National Polytechnic Institute (CINVESTAV), Mexico. He has headed 10 Mexican research projects granted by CONACYT, DGEST, and PROMEP. He has been committee program member of around 30 international conferences sponsored by IEEE, ACM, and Springer Verlag. He is editorial board member of 5 indexed journals. He has been guest editor of 3 JCR-indexed journals. He is author/co-author around 100 papers in computer science published in refereed journals and conferences. His research interests include Web services, e-commerce, Semantic Web, Web 2.0, service-oriented and event-driven architectures, and enterprise application integration. He is an IEEE and ACM Member. He is National Researcher recognized by the National Council of Science and Technology of Mexico (CONACYT).

Viviana Yarel Rosales-Morales is a PhD student of the Division of Research and Postgraduate Studies at Instituto Tecnológico de Orizaba, México. She received a MSc degree in Computer Systems in 2011 at Instituto Tecnológico de Orizaba, México. She obtained a scholarship sponsored by the National Council of Science and Technology (CONACYT) for PhD studies. She has been involved in some Mexican research projects granted by CONACYT, DGEST, and PROMEP. Her research interests include Web services, e-commerce, Web 2.0, rich Internet applications, JavaScript-based frameworks, Aspect-Oriented Programming, Design Patterns, UI Patterns, user experience, and enterprise application integration.

Luis Omar Colombo-Mendoza is a PhD student in the Informatics program at University of Murcia, Spain. He received an MSc degree in Computer Systems in 2012 at Instituto Tecnológico de Orizaba, México. He obtained a scholarship sponsored by the National Council of Science and Technology (CONACYT) for PhD studies. He has been involved in some Mexican research projects granted by CONACYT, DGEST, and PROMEP. His research interests include Web 2.0 and rich Internet applications, user experience, mobile computing, Semantic Web, recommender systems, context-aware systems, and cloud computing.

Index